John Hope Mason was a Scholar in History at Corpus Christi College, Cambridge, where he took a First in the Anglo-Saxon and Old Norse Tripos. He has since worked mainly in the theatre and opera, both as a writer and a director.

The Indispensable Rousseau

Compiled and presented by
JOHN HOPE MASON `

QUARTET BOOKS
LONDON   MELBOURNE   NEW YORK

First published by Quartet Books Limited 1979
A member of the Namara Group
27 Goodge Street, London W1P 1FD

Copyright © 1979 by John Hope Mason

ISBN hardcover   0 7043 2190 4
        paperback   0 7043 3220 5

Distribution in the U.S.A. by
Horizon Press, 156 Fifth Avenue
New York, N.Y.10010

Printed in Great Britain by
Billing & Sons Limited,
Guildford, London and Worcester

CONTENTS

PREFACE

The problems that obsessed Rousseau are our problems. The insights he brought to them, the way he handled them, and the solutions he put forward to them, should be of interest to us.

This book sets out to make available in English some of the most important of Rousseau's writings, to convey his range, perception and compelling vitality. Given the scope and complexity of his work this can obviously be no more than an introduction; there are several areas that I have had to neglect or only treat in a summary fashion. The works that have suffered most are those which are least suited to short extracts, in particular *The New Heloïse* and the autobiographical works. While I have made extensive use of these writings in the course of the book, I have not been able to give them the detailed individual attention which they merit. Apart from this I believe the selection I have made is representative.

I hope that some of the lesser-known texts may help to make his best-known work — *The Social Contract* — more accessible, and may help to correct the imbalance and distortion often given to Rousseau's views as a result of considering *The Social Contract* in isolation. It should not be the first of his works to be read, but the last.

The difficulty of some of his writings is of course compounded in translation. I have therefore included a short chapter (Chapter 3) that draws attention to some of his important concepts and the way he uses certain words.

My treatment of the works has been for the most part chronological, from the *Discourse on the Arts and Sciences* (Chapter 4) to the *Reveries of the Solitary Walker* (Chapter 22). In this way I have tried to indicate the connections between the moral, aesthetic, political and religious aspects of Rousseau's thought — they are all interrelated — as well as providing an outline of how his thought developed. In addition, I have given a brief account of the place of each work in his life.

I have also included, at the end, some of Rousseau's epigrams. They can be used to decorate the walls of our decaying cities, to enliven the minds of our tired politicians, or to comfort, in the meanwhile, the downhearted.

In writing this book I have incurred an obvious debt to many Rousseau scholars; I hope they will consider it as useful to the general reader as their own works have been to me. I am especially grateful to Professor Samuel S. B. Taylor and Dr Robert Wokler, who both found time to read and discuss aspects of the book with me, and gave much useful advice.

J. M. Dent & Sons (for the United Kingdom and Commonwealth) and E. P. Dutton & Co. (for the United States of America) very kindly gave permission to quote from G. D. H. Cole's translations revised by J. H. Brumfitt of the *Discourses* (Chapters 4, 5 and 6) and *The Social Contract* (Chapter 12), and from Barbara Foxley's translation of *Emile* (Chapters 13 and 14), both published in the Everyman's Library Series (I have made minor modifications to both for the sake of clarity and consistency). Thomas Nelson & Sons kindly gave permission to quote from the Frederick Watkins translation of the *Constitutional Project for Corsica* (Chapter 18) and the *Considerations on the Government of Poland* (Chapter 21). Other translations are my own.

Finally, I would like to express my thanks to Cecil Rowling for his sensitive help with the translation; my particular thanks to Christopher May, who gave up a great deal of his own time to help in innumerable ways, and gave much invaluable advice; and my fond thanks to Anthea Masey, who shared some of the pleasures, and helped overcome many of the problems, in this attempt to make a wider world aware of the indispensable Jean-Jacques.

Note: Any words between brackets [ ] have been inserted by the translator for the sake of clarity. Author's comments are also enclosed in square brackets.

Alongside all extracts reference is given to the page numbers of the French original. These are the numbers printed without brackets in the margin. The relevant edition, to which these page numbers refer, is cited under the appropriate chapter heading in the Notes. (Except for Chapters 7, 10 and 19, the references are to the Pléiade edition of the *Œuvres Complètes*.)

Rousseau, prenant toujours la nature pour maître,
Fut, de l'humanité, l'apôtre and le martyr;
Les mortels, qu'il voulut forcer à se connaître,
S'étaient trop avilis pour ne pas l'en punir:
Pauvre, errant, fugitif, et proscrit sur la terre,
Sa vie à ses écrits servit de commentaire:
La fière vérité, dans ses hardis tableaux,
Sut, en dépit des grands, montrer ce que nous sommes.
Il devait de nos jours trouver des échafauds,
Il aura des autels, quand il naîtra des hommes.

Anon. c.1767

Rousseau, always taking nature as his master,
Was humanity's apostle and martyr;
The creatures to whom he wished to bring self-knowledge
Were too corrupted not to punish him for it:
Poor, vagrant, refugee, rejected on this earth,
His life was a commentary on what he wrote:
In the bold portrait of humanity which he made,
The proud truth of what we are is displayed.
In our time he was destined for nothing but torture;
When we become human we will build him an altar.

1 INTRODUCTION

I

Rousseau stood on the edge of the modern world. He looked within him, and saw what human nature was. He looked around him and saw what men had done to themselves. He looked ahead of him, and saw what we could become.

Human nature is essentially good, said Rousseau. There is no original sin, men are not naturally aggressive or competitive. Our first feeling is a sense of our own well-being, and our next impulse is pity, a sense of fellow-feeling with anyone who suffers. He distinguished the essential from the acquired. Much has happened to alter or obscure our true nature, but the original good feeling is still accessible to us all. We will only be happy if we realize that feeling, if we have a sense of ourselves and are true to it.

Evil arises with society. It stems from the inequalities which set us apart and in opposition to one another; it stems from our acceptance of conventional values, seeing ourselves through other people's eyes rather than our own; and it stems from the bad social forms which reinforce those inequalities and values. But these social forms are not God-given, they are human constructions; they can therefore be changed. Since they come between us and our true nature, they must be changed. To create a just society will be to realize ourselves most completely.

Rousseau regarded freedom as being as fundamental to man as his natural pleasure in living. A just society must therefore be one in which everyone is free. For that freedom to be effective none must stand in dependence on another; in other words, all must be equal; there must be equal rights and no large disparity between rich and poor. But freedom and equality can often be in conflict; how can that conflict be overcome? It will be overcome if our political and social decisions are based on a shared sense of the common good, based in turn on fraternity. It was Rousseau's political theory that first brought together in one inseparable whole the great ideals of liberty, equality and fraternity. It is to him that we still need to turn for the principles of true (as opposed to apparent) democracy.

To Rousseau these were not mere ideals, imaginative models to inspire us or guide us. They were emotional needs. We will only find happiness in being true to ourselves, but we live in society and a crucial part of ourselves is what we share with our fellow-men. The personal and the political are essentially interrelated. We can only remake ourselves in society and through society. At the same time, social change must be accompanied by personal change. Political freedom will be meaningless without an inner freedom. We must free ourselves individually from greed, restlessness, and the need for power. We must learn to be happy within the limits of what we have, rather than in the perpetual increase of desires, and to live in the present, rather than in continual anticipation of the future.

Rousseau made people feel differently about themselves and their society. But that was not all. Because he also made people aware of the way both these aspects of our lives must be related to the context from which they cannot escape, though it is often ignored — the natural world we all inhabit. We must recognize what we owe to nature, not only in ourselves but in the world around us. We must live in harmony with the world, instead of just using it.

Personal fulfilment is therefore inseparable both from the movement towards a true democracy and the concern for nature, what we would now call ecological responsibility. Given present-day conditions these objectives are almost as hard to realize now as they were two hundred years ago. But they are no less imperative for that; and the satisfactions are no less certain. For to find fulfilment of this kind is to experience with exhilarating certainty the feeling that is often elusive, and has often been denied, the feeling that Rousseau insisted on and spent his life asserting — the sense that life is good, and that happiness is possible.

II

No one is indifferent to Rousseau. In his own lifetime he was either admired or reviled and it has been the same ever since. Voltaire ended up calling him a charlatan, a hypocrite and a criminal. Dr Johnson thought him 'one of the worst of men: a rascal, who ought to be hunted out of society, as he has been'. For Kant,* on the other hand, he was 'the Newton of the moral order', a man who had discovered principles of such importance that he had altered our whole conception of the world. 'There was a time', Kant wrote, 'when I thought all [my work] would be the glory of humanity, and I despised the rabble who knew nothing. Rousseau has corrected me . . . I have learnt to honour men.'

In his own lifetime Rousseau was famous; with the French Revolution he became notorious. His name was invoked on all sides, his words quoted on all occasions. Robespierre and Saint-Just made his arguments their own, in justification of their policies. The Girondins had brought the ashes of Voltaire to a place of honour in the Pantheon; the Jacobins brought in the ashes of Rousseau. There were those who protested, correctly, that their later actions were not consistent with *The Social Contract*, and that far from fulfilling Rousseau's ideas they were betraying them. But these protests went unheeded, and a lasting connection was made between his ideas and the worst excesses of the Terror.

For Coleridge Rousseau's work was 'a speculative cobweb'. For Shelley, in his last major poem *The Triumph of Life*, he was the Virgil to his own Dante: as the Chariot of Life goes by destroying all who dance around it, Rousseau appears and explains to the poet that all men and women up to now have been crushed by Life because 'their philosophy/Taught them not this — to know themselves; their might/Could not repress the mutiny within'. For Tolstoi he was an enduring influence, comparable only to the Gospels; for Durkheim he was a forerunner of sociology. But to Proudhon he was hateful; *The Social Contract* was 'a code of capitalist and mercantilist tyranny'.

It has been the same in this century. 'In our time', wrote Bertrand Russell, 'Hitler is an outcome of Rousseau.' But to Lévi-Strauss Rousseau is the 'founder of the sciences of man', and has been a lifelong inspiration. The remarkable thing about these reactions is not just their variety but their intensity. It is impossible to disagree with Rousseau without feeling a need to push him away from you; it is unusual to agree with him without wanting to thank him.

---

* Kant was a very methodical man, so precise in his habits that people set their clocks by his afternoon walk. One afternoon he did not appear. People looked up in alarm: had time stood still? No. The philosopher had been sent a copy of *Emile* and had been unable to put it down.

The fact that there has been such controversy is not surprising if you turn from the criticism and look at the works themselves. They present a strange sight: diffuse, concise, lucid, cryptic, littered with rhetorical flourishes and didactic ramblings; at times facing one way, at other times another, referring now to the present, now to the future, with no clear line drawn between them; confusion and order, obscurity and logic.

In his *Confessions* Rousseau provided an explanation for this:

> Two almost irreconcilable elements are united in me, without my being able to see how. A passionate temperament, with lively impetuous feelings, and confused ideas, slow to be born, which never appear till too late. You could say that my heart and my mind do not belong to the same individual. Feeling comes quicker than lightning to fill my soul, but instead of illuminating me it burns me and dazzles me. I feel everything and see nothing. I am carried away but stupid.
>
> In order to think I must be calm . . . My ideas sort themselves out in my head with the most incredible difficulty. They ferment there until they excite me, warm me, give me palpitations, and in the middle of all that emotion I see nothing clearly. I cannot write a single word, I must wait. Imperceptibly this great movement calms down, the chaos clears away; each element begins to take its place, but slowly and after long and confused agitation.
>
> Have you ever seen the opera in Italy? In the scene-changes at those great theatres an appalling disorder reigns, which goes on and on and on. All the scenery is mixed up; everywhere you see a frightful pandemonium; you think it is all going to collapse. Nevertheless, bit by bit, everything takes shape, nothing is missing, and you are amazed to see emerging from this prolonged tumult a ravishing spectacle. This procedure is virtually what takes place in my brain when I want to write . . .
>
> That is the reason for the extreme difficulty I find in writing. My crossed-out, scribbled down, jumbled up, indecipherable manuscripts bear witness to the pain they have cost me. There is not one of them that I have not had to transcribe four or five times before giving it to the printer. I have never been able to do anything with a pen in hand, a table and paper in front of me. It is walking among rocks and woods, it is at night in bed when I cannot sleep, that I write in my brain; you can judge how slowly, especially for a man who is completely lacking in verbal

memory . . . There are some of my sentences I have turned round
and round in my head five or six nights before they were in a
state to put on paper.[1]

So it is that Rousseau's thought is bound up with his personality in a
particularly intricate way. To read his works is to meet the man.
This is not in itself unusual, perhaps; but Rousseau himself was very
unusual. 'A proteus [and] a chameleon . . . are less changeable
creatures than I am',[2] he wrote when he was in his thirties. He
described himself as alternately misanthropic, sociable, indulgent
and austere, with two main moods predominating, in one of which
he was 'wisely mad' and in the other 'madly wise'. 'Nothing is so
unlike me as myself'.* Moreover, 'it is this very irregularity which
forms the basis of my constitution'.[4] This instability, which was
accompanied by an extraordinary susceptibility to external influences,
was central to his character; it remained with him all his life. In
his *Confessions* and *Dialogues* he wrote of the 'opposition' and
'contradiction' in himself,[5] and Hume, who knew Rousseau well,
described him as 'one of the most singular of all human beings, . . .
his extreme sensibility of temper is his torment'; 'he is like a man
who were stripped not only of his clothes but of his skin'; 'he writes
and speaks and acts from the impulse of his genius more than from
the use of his ordinary faculties'.[6]

These features of Rousseau's personality are reflected in his
writing and help to account for some of its peculiarities. This is not
to suggest that Rousseau's personality in some way explains his
work, or to imagine that an analysis of his character will take care
of the problems that his work presents. Rather is it to call attention
to the way in which tendencies that seem to be in contradiction to
one another — backward-looking/forward-looking, solitary/sociable,
sensual/moral, aesthetic/utilitarian — are in fact essentially interrelated.

In an important sense these opposing tendencies were defined by
one another. Each element in Rousseau tended to be exaggerated —
he himself spoke of how his imagination could 'carry everything
to the extreme'[7] — but that did not make it separate or exclusive.
His sense of solitude was to some extent so strong *because* of the
significance he gave to being in society; the desire for virtue was so

* These words occur in the draft of the periodical Rousseau and Diderot were
going to write alternately. Some years later Diderot used almost exactly the
same words to describe that prototypical modern man, Rameau's Nephew.[3]

strong *because* of his sensuality.* Rousseau himself was aware of this interconnection between apparently irreconcilable elements: 'You want man always to be consistent; I doubt that is possible. But it is possible for him to be always true.'[9]

Nevertheless, there were obvious incompatibilities. These he wanted to overcome. Being pulled in different directions he felt an acute need to achieve some kind of unity in himself. The desire to be one, without contradiction, complete and whole, was among the vital impulses behind his writing. This search for an emotional stability and coherence underlies all his work.

Rousseau was not only dealing with difficult and complex issues; he *felt* those issues, they related to his personal experience, in an essential and inextricable way. This is not a weakness or handicap. On the contrary, it is something that gives his work much of its compelling quality. Issues for him could never be resolved solely on rational grounds; they had to relate to the whole of his experience. They had to have a psychological validity, to provide an emotional satisfaction.

As a result Rousseau did not build a self-contained system of abstract ideas. His thought is not detachable from the feelings it relates to. To reduce his ideas to a system would be to empty them of the emotional content which in part brought them into being and in part provides them with body. It is true that Rousseau referred to his work as a 'system'; but what he meant by that was 'the true system of the human heart',[10] 'the true system of nature'.[11]

Despite its opposing tendencies Rousseau's thought is coherent; it makes sense. The tensions that are unresolved are as much evidence of its coherence as the elements that are in obvious harmony; because the very tensions themselves arise out of that emotional desire for wholeness which animates all his work. It is this quality that gives his writing both its comprehensive range and its essential unity. It is also something that gives it an extraordinary modernity.

III

People have often failed to grasp this coherence. Aspects of his work have been dealt with in isolation and been taken to support dia-

---

* D'Alembert, a fair-minded man, wrote: 'Of all the *philosophes* he was the most lustful.'[8]

metrically opposed views. The most common of these have been, firstly, the idea that Rousseau praised the Noble Savage, in preference to man in society, and secondly, that his political writing is a blueprint for totalitarianism.

The Noble Savage theory has two main aspects — 'back to nature' and the 'rejection of reason'. Misunderstanding about the former began early in Rousseau's career. Attacking the society of his day he contrasted the savage favourably with the European. Then, in his *Discourse on Inequality*, he put forward the theory that man in a state of nature was free from the destructive habits and gross injustices that were evident in developed society. It was assumed that he was suggesting that we would do better to go back to the wilds. 'Thank you for your new book against the human race', wrote Voltaire. 'You make one want to walk on all fours';[12] in a satirical play, *The Philosophes*, Rousseau was portrayed as wandering around on his hands and knees chewing a lettuce.

In the same *Discourse* he asserted that the first characteristic that distinguished human beings from animals was not their reason but their freedom. Elsewhere, in the same work, he wrote: 'the man who meditates is a depraved animal.'[13] These assertions, together with his continual stress on the need for right feeling, for developing our feelings before we develop our reason, and the emotional force of the works themselves, made him seem an apostle of the irrational.

Neither of these views is correct. Rousseau never suggested we could go back to nature: 'Human nature does not turn back. Man can never return to the time of innocence and equality once he has left it.'[14] Moreover, unlike Diderot in his *Supplement to the Voyage of Bourgainville*, he did not idealize primitive man. His picture of man in a state of nature was not an Arcadian dream but a theory of what we were before the development of society, the characteristics we had (and have) apart from society.

The principal feature of this theory was that man is naturally good. 'Let us lay it down as an incontrovertible rule that the first impulses of nature are always right; there is no original perversity in the human heart.'[15] The state of nature is the seed from which our personality should grow. When it does grow it will, of course, grow up in society. We are in society now and we cannot opt out of it. The task is therefore not to escape or go back, but to remake society, and to remake ourselves according to our good natural impulses rather than according to society's imposed, conventional values.

We can only do this with the aid of our reason. Rousseau may demote reason from its Platonic eminence but he does not discard it.* In a state of nature we do not think rationally; the faculty of reason develops in society. When we come together in society we have to make choices, and to make responsible choices we need to reason. Only in society do we develop a moral sense; only with the aid of reason can we exercise that moral sense. 'Isolated man remains always the same; he only makes progress in society.'[16] Reason alone is no more than an instrument — Rousseau always had a keen sense of the limitations of reason — but it is an essential instrument. Without it we will have neither virtue in our lives nor justice in our society.

Rousseau maintained that we are naturally good; that before our lives became organized into those forms which led to present-day society, we were good. He does not suggest that we were consciously good, but that we lived in peace rather than in a state of war. It was only when we became trapped in certain social forms that our good qualities were stifled or distorted. It follows from this analysis that if we can change the social forms that have had such a harmful effect, then we could regain an inner sense of goodness, and achieve a social sense of co-operation. Faced with the grotesque injustices of his own society Rousseau was inevitably led to consider what those changes might be.

He approached the problem from two different angles. He not only asked: what form of society would allow men to live in peace and justice? But he also asked: what sort of men could produce such a society? He did not take the determinist view that men were no more than the product of their society or environment. On the contrary, men were distinguished by their capacity for freedom. He could not therefore imagine that by merely changing the social structures he could, *ipso facto*, change the people who lived within those structures. There could be no social renewal without a corresponding personal and moral renewal.

His political writing, and particularly *The Social Contract*, must therefore be considered in conjunction with *Emile*, his great work on education. They essentially complement one another: 'the two together form a complete whole', wrote Rousseau.[17] It is the failure to make this connection that has caused the misunderstanding of

---

* His sentence about the man who meditates being a depraved animal is about man in a state of nature, pre-rational man. In particular he is talking about health; he is following Plutarch, Cicero and Montaigne in suggesting that unlike animals human beings can actually make themselves ill. It is also true, however, that Rousseau sometimes regarded the capacity for reflection as a mixed blessing.

Rousseau's political philosophy and the violent disagreement as to what that philosophy is. Is he an individualist or a collectivist? Does he favour democracy or does he lead to totalitarianism? Did he begin as a liberal and end up a communist; or did he set out as a revolutionary and end up as a conservative? His own protestations that his work was all of a piece have been regarded as just another paradox from a virtuoso of paradox.

If you set *The Social Contract* alongside *Emile* it is possible to see why they should be regarded as works apart; they are so different. The first is tautly written, strictly reasoned, and highly abstract; the second is a long, rambling rumination, in a vaguely fictional framework. Students of political theory examine the first, educationalists discuss the second, and rarely do their worlds overlap.

But even considered apart *The Social Contract* does not justify the most frequent accusation that is levelled against Rousseau; namely, that in it he has written a blueprint for totalitarianism. The purpose of the book is to set out 'the principles of political right', to discover how political bodies can be legitimate, and reconcile the needs of the individual with those of society.

A legitimate state is created by people acting together to form themselves into an association for their common good. That they shall be acting freely none must be dependent on one another, in other words, all must be equal. Once the state is formed, the people then make the laws which determine the conditions they will live under. As our lives in a state of nature are free only within the laws of nature itself, so in society we can only be free under laws we ourselves make. But for those laws to have an authority in society comparable to the authority natural laws have in nature, we must all participate in making them. Furthermore, to decide on just laws we must be motivated by the desire for the common good. These are the essential arguments of *The Social Contract*.

In developing these arguments Rousseau raises many of the difficulties they produce. Sometimes he meets these difficulties satisfactorily, at other times not; there are obvious areas of disagreement here. It is also true that some of his statements are not only forcefully expressed but are definitely and deliberately severe. But neither these statements nor the areas of disagreement should call in doubt the general character of the arguments themselves, or their clear intention. Which is not to restrict freedom or subject people to systematic or tyrannical control, but rather to lay down conditions for a general and equal freedom, and ensure opportunities for the people themselves to remain in control. Being so abstract in character *The Social Contract* does not display how passionately Rousseau believed in the need for that freedom and opportunity. But read the *Discourse on Inequality* (Chapter 5) or the *Letters from the Mountain* (Chapter 16) and you will not be left in any doubt.

Furthermore, Rousseau had a strong sense of history and of each country's individual character. He thought different governments were suitable to different conditions. The ideal civil state of *The Social Contract* is, in one sense, outside history, a projection into the future, as the state of nature is a projection into the past. In another sense it had a very specific historical meaning for Rousseau, in that it was based on the true (as opposed to the abused) constitution of Geneva, as he saw it. This constitution itself had severe limits; there was no universal franchise, even among the adult males, and Rousseau himself was not in favour of extending the suffrage. Similarly, when he came to draw up constitutions for Corsica and Poland a vital aspect of his task, in his view, was to relate his proposals to the actual conditions of the time. There was never any question of a blanket imposition of an ideal state. 'Let us not seek the chimera of perfection but the best possible according to the nature of man and the constitution of society.'[18]

This respect for historical conditions was a vital element in Rousseau's thought. It relates to his awareness of the differences between people, societies, languages and religions, the recognition of which is the basis of all tolerance. It also relates to his belief that what a people are, their customs, habits and way of life, is infinitely more important than what anyone might want to impose on them. He had no illusions about the strength of laws; laws are as strong as people want them to be. 'The law only works externally and rules actions; customs alone reach within and direct the will.'[19] That is why everyone's participation and a desire for the common good is the only way to achieve good laws and, with them, a just society.

For all these reasons any form of despotism, however well intentioned, benevolent or enlightened it might be, was utterly unthinkable to Rousseau. His whole philosophy was developed in opposition to the actual despotism of his day, the potential despotisms he could see emerging, and the general tendency towards despotism that exists wherever men have access to power.

IV

Rousseau saw the need for change and wanted it. There is a constant tension in his work between the actual and the possible, between things as they are and things as they might be. At the same time he feared change. He was aware that upheavals were imminent but he was afraid of what they might bring. Several times in his writing he speaks of a revolution 'almost as much to be feared as the evil it could cure'.[20]

This was partly because violence in any form horrified him. But it was also because he saw little improvement in the new intellectual and economic orthodoxies that would take the place of the old order. In intellectual matters this is evident from his quarrel with the *philosophes*; in economic matters it can be seen in his remarks on luxury* and on his fellow-citizens, the bourgeoisie of Geneva. The *philosophes* put forward a narrow materialistic view of men, motivated only by self-interest; the Genevan bourgeoisie were narrow materialistic men, animated only by self-interest. What hope did any of them give for a free society of the kind he proposed? Obsessed with their work they had no time for the common good, obsessed with their own interest they had no awareness of it. Their concept of freedom was only that 'of acquiring [things] without obstacle and possessing [them] in security'.[21]

Rousseau's concern for equality is one that many people today share, in theory at least. But his concept of freedom, 'the noblest faculty of man',[22] is one that we have neglected and continued to neglect. Because his analysis of man in society is, historically speaking, a pre-economic analysis, it has been regarded as insubstantial, well meaning perhaps, but lacking an essential dimension. This view is seriously mistaken. Although he did not examine his society explicitly in terms of economic laws or forces, Rousseau attacked with great clarity and precision its economic thinking and its economic behaviour.

I should like to draw attention to three central themes in Rousseau's thought which are, I believe, of particular importance today.

The first of these is that Rousseau did not separate people's behaviour from their responsibility for the prevailing economy. We are not the victims of circumstances, we have freedom to choose. This is the meaning of moral freedom. To be subject to appetites or

---

* For the economic significance of 'luxury' in the eighteenth century, see p. 44.

impulses over which you have no control, or to pressures from society which you cannot resist, is not to be free. We are subject to these pressures, of course; but the individual should learn to overcome those desires which do not correspond to real needs. To be swayed hither and thither by every fashion or momentary impulse is not freedom but a kind of slavery, an inner slavery. There is no reason why we should not achieve freedom of this kind: 'the limits of the possible in moral matters are less narrow than we think.'[23]

We must see our world for what it is. We must see 'the way to true happiness by learning to distinguish the reality from the appearance; [by distinguishing] natural man from the fantastic and artificial person that our institutions and our prejudices have substituted for him'.[24] We must become aware of how social and economic conditions affect us, and then we must exercise the freedom we have to escape those conditions and alter them.

We must alter them because we cannot detach ourselves from our society; our lives are inextricably involved with our fellow-men. This is the second central theme, and Rousseau himself predicted the consequences of neglecting it. Present society is unjust enough — 'this supposed social order which in fact conceals the most cruel disorders'[25] — but what if its current tendencies are developed further? The overriding characteristic of our behaviour in society at the moment is that we always give priority to our self-interest. Now the more our private interests and desires increase the greater must be the conflict between them and the common good. 'The less individual wishes relate to the general will [that is, the desire for the common good] . . . the more the repressive force [of the state] must increase.'[26] The reckless pursuit of our purely personal desires will inevitably lead to restricted freedom for us all.

Moreover, the greater the proliferation of private interests, the more elaborate the lives we lead, the more laws will be called into being. The greater the number of laws the less respect there is for any of them.[27] So not only will our freedom be restricted, but the social order itself will begin to collapse. 'When the citizens are greedy, mean-spirited and faint-hearted, preferring rest to freedom, they do not hold out for long against the redoubled efforts of the government. It is thus that [the government] continually increasing, the sovereign authority finally disappears, and most republics fall and perish before their time.'[28]

As we live now we want the best of both worlds; we want to be left alone to do whatever we like, and we want a free but caring society.

Rousseau tells us that we cannot have both, that these desires are in direct opposition. To achieve social freedom we have to participate in our society, and 'the public good [must be] a real motive'.[29] Social freedom is not being free to do whatever you want but being free from laws or restraints that you have had no part in making. To take part in determining the conditions under which we live is an essential condition of freedom. That is why he writes: 'rest and liberty seem to me incompatible. You must choose.'[30]

With this concept of freedom Rousseau parts company with liberalism. For the liberal freedom is essentially the liberty to do as you want in undisturbed privacy, with the least interference from the state or any outside interest. The private nature of this freedom is what makes artistic activity so important to the liberal. The arts to him are perhaps the most important area of freedom, because in their imaginary world he can extend himself to his utmost without coming into conflict with anyone else. It is no accident that the combination in the nineteenth century of this liberal ethic with the force of capitalism — 'Expansion is everything'[31] — produced so much 'great' art. In this view the amount of artistic activity that takes place, or that is allowed to take place, becomes the most significant measure of the amount of freedom that exists; and the artist, being the person who enjoys the maximum amount of this freedom, becomes the most highly-regarded individual.

For Rousseau, however, freedom is itself creative in the sense that it is only by acting freely together that we can create a just and happy society. It is not the artist who counts most but the citizen; it is not a sense of art that matters most but the sense of community, fraternity, and the common good. Society is not *them*, it is *us*, and we can only realize our freedom in creating a just society. This may not be a comfortable thought, in that it demands more of us than we have usually been brought up to give, but 'what makes mankind really flourish is less [a comfortable] peace than [an active] freedom'.[32]

A just society will only be created by people who share this view of freedom, who do not crowd their lives with exclusively personal interests, or the pursuit of ever-increasing private desires, but who realize their potential through society, in society, in the pursuit of the common good. It will come into being, in other words, not by a mere change of structure but a change of heart, mind and intention among those who compose it: 'by transforming each individual, who is by himself entirely self-contained and solitary, into part of a greater whole . . .; by altering the constitution of man in order to strengthen it; by substituting for the physical and independent existence, which we have all received from nature, a moral and communal existence'[33] which we will all share in society.

This is the meaning of social freedom. One of Rousseau's most important legacies is not merely to have asserted this, as a desirable goal, but to have indicated how this transformation could be effected. It is impossible to understand Rousseau, in fact, without realizing the central significance he gave to the sense of feeling part of a greater whole. 'Man's proper study is that of his relationships.'[34] 'Our sweetest existence is relative and collective, and our true ego is not completely inside us.'[35]

Every aspect of his thought reflects this sense of realizing what we are in what we share. A word that continually occurs in his writing is *concours*, which means literally concourse* but which has usually been translated here as co-existence or co-operation. It describes the mutual interaction of individual units, the living together of separate elements. There need be no fundamental opposition between the different parts. There are tensions, certainly, but those tensions are only aggravated and become destructive if people live by a morality, or an economy, of self-interest, and try to possess everything for themselves instead of sharing with others.

When we come together with other people we form a new entity. Rousseau uses a legal phrase, *personne morale*, to describe this entity, both in a domestic context, with the union of a man and a woman (see p. 204), and in the larger scale, with the creation of a just society (see p. 163). In this new entity we discover elements in ourselves which we are otherwise unaware of. In the company of others we realize most fully what we can be in ourselves.

> When you consider with the eye of a philosopher the play of all the parts of this vast universe, you soon see that the greatest beauty of each of the pieces which compose it does not consist in each one itself. Each part has not been formed to dwell alone and independent but rather to co-operate with all the others, for the perfection of the whole machine. It is the same in the moral order. The vices and virtues of each man do not relate only to him. Their greatest relationship is with society, and it is what they are in respect of the general order that constitutes their essence and their character.[36]

* Or concurrence. (Not to be confused with concurrence, which means competition.)

The comparison Rousseau makes here, between our experience of the world and our experience of society, brings me to the third central theme in his work. In his writing about nature he gave the most vivid descriptions of the sense of an extended personality, of a person being not only defined but also enriched by his *concours* with what surrounds him. This is not accidental. Because not only are the personal and the social realms interlinked but they both operate in, and essentially depend on, the natural realm. We will therefore find no lasting happiness unless we are in harmony with that. Human nature is part of the natural order; human happiness will only be achieved by understanding that. It was on this issue that Rousseau came to differ most from the *philosophes*.

In the seventeenth century Bacon and Descartes and the leading figures of the scientific revolution had developed a view of man that owed nothing to either God or nature. Man was independent and separate. He was the centre of his world and all that lay around him was an instrument he could use to achieve whatever he wanted. This view was extended and elaborated in the Enlightenment. Bacon was the acknowledged mentor of the *Encyclopedia*. Here were the intellectual tools that would make possible the actual transformation of the world in the industrial revolution. In this sense the nineteenth century was the triumph of the Enlightenment.

Rousseau was not against science or scientific development or the benefits which technical advances had brought.[37] What he opposed was the 'mad pride and conceited self-admiration'[38] that accompanied these advances.

> What is the first lesson of wisdom? Humility . . . Let us be humble as humankind, so that we can be proud of ourselves individually. Let us not say in our imbecile vanity that man is king of the world and that the sun, the stars, the firmament, the air and the seas were made for him; that plants grow to feed him or that animals exist so that he can devour them. With this kind of reasoning why should not everyone think that the rest of the human race was created to serve him?[39]

To take an instrumental attitude to nature is no different from taking an instrumental attitude to our fellow-men. The passion to dominate is common to both.

Rousseau felt himself to be part of nature and he brought this feeling alive for many of his contemporaries and the next generation. But this aspect of his work was then hived off into some religious or literary form, in the romantic movement. The sense of wholeness was itself made separate and apart. It became no more than a tiny isolated revolt beside the immense, relentless achievements of the next century. There is an awful poignancy in Rousseau's protest against the self-assurance of the *philosophes*. It is as if he had seen into the future.

We have seen that future. We are emerging at last from the long shadow of the nineteenth century. Now we can begin to repair the damage it inflicted and to dismantle the apparatus that it needed. We have seen that all human activities have their limits, that the life of this world we inhabit is carefully balanced, and we are only part of a greater whole. We have become aware that no economy can be considered apart from the world's economy; we can see that a system that continually increases the gulf between the rich of the world and the poor must eventually destroy us all. We have learnt that continual growth and increasing consumption do not make us happier, that they create as many problems as they may solve, and that a way of life that puts most value on material possession, and concerns itself most with still further acquisition, has a terrible emptiness at the centre. An emptiness that is literally terrible, breeding violence and terror.

All this we have heard, all this we know.

What we need now is a sense of value that can replace our obsessive self-interest, which can give us a sense of potential that is not based on the need for power or the lust for domination. We need a sense of value that not only brings us all together, but brings us together in ourselves; one that will give us the resources we need individually, to enable us to take the action that is needed in the world. We will only find that value in a sense of wholeness, in ourselves and in our common humanity. People have looked for this sense in the young Marx. I believe the results do not take us far. Marx was saturated with the nineteenth century; his energy came more from a sense of power than a sense of wholeness, as his ambition and his later work made manifest. We must look elsewhere if we want illumination. The time has come to read Rousseau.

2 LIFE

Jean-Jacques Rousseau was born in Geneva in 1712. His father, Isaac, a watchmaker, was a citizen of Geneva and therefore had political rights which his son was later able to inherit. Isaac was a man of erratic character; after his first son, François, had been born, in 1705, he had left his wife and child to go and work in Constantinople for six years. He returned only when he heard that his mother-in-law had died. Jean-Jacques' mother, Suzanne, died a week after giving birth to him; his brother ran away to Germany, and when he was ten his father became involved in a quarrel which forced him to leave the city. Despite these events he remembered his childhood as a happy time. He developed early a passion for reading and with his father read the books his mother had left; first novels, then histories and biographies, most notably Plutarch's *Lives*.

When his father left the city the boy was boarded for two years with a pastor, M. Lambercier, in a village outside Geneva; this was his first experience of country life. 'The countryside was so new to me that I could never stop enjoying it', he wrote later in his *Confessions*. 'I developed a feeling for it that was so strong that nothing has ever been able to eradicate it.'[1] Then he was apprenticed to an engraver in the city, and his life suffered a drastic alteration.

> The tyranny of my master ended by making the work I would have liked insufferable, and by giving me faults I would have hated, namely, lying, deception, and theft. Nothing has taught me better the difference there is between filial dependence and abject slavery than the memory of the changes which this period effected in me. Timid and shy by nature, no fault could have been further from me than impudence. I had enjoyed an honest freedom which had only been restrained bit by bit; now it vanished completely.[2]

Three years of his apprenticeship were as much as Rousseau did. One Sunday he went into the country with some friends; they arrived back in the evening too late, the city gates were shut. Rather than face the inevitable punishment from his master he decided to run away. The border with Savoy was close; next morning he crossed it. He was not yet sixteen.

Apart from a stay of three months in 1754, and a few short visits before he went to Paris, Rousseau spent the rest of his life away from Geneva. Yet his native city had a lasting influence on him. It is important to realize that this was not a Calvinist influence. The laws of Geneva were strict; ostentatious spending on clothes or entertainment was forbidden, and all theatrical activities were banned. (The ban on theatre was first made in 1617, fifty years after Calvin's death; Calvin himself had used the theatre for propaganda purposes, staging such plays as *The Triumph of Jesus Christ* and the *Comedy of a Sick Pope*.) But these laws were not peculiar to Geneva. Zurich had stricter regulations about personal behaviour, affecting smoking, drinking and eating, and Berne had the most rigid censorship in Europe. Compared with them Geneva was enlightened; the work of Newton was known there before Voltaire's translations made it widely available in French, the work of Locke also, the sceptical and iconoclastic Pierre Bayle had been a student there, and at the end of the century Thomas Jefferson put the Academy of Geneva on a par with the University of Edinburgh. The severities of Calvin's theology and government had been softened; dogma was considered secondary to a morally upright life and the practical side of religious life. In his article on 'Geneva' for the *Encyclopedia* in 1757 D'Alembert wrote: 'The respect for Jesus Christ and the Scriptures is perhaps the only thing which distinguishes the Christianity of Geneva from pure deism.' This was a deliberate exaggeration, but that he could even make such a statement indicates how far the city had moved out of its Calvinist straitjacket.

The strongest influence Geneva had over Rousseau was its example — the unsophisticated simplicity of its citizens' lives and its history of independence and freedom. In the middle ages the town had been an episcopal seat, where the bishop had temporal power but where the Dukes of Savoy had become the real masters. The citizens had gradually won some rights from the bishops, and then, in 1526, they threw off the domination of both bishop and duke and set up their own civic republic. Ten years later they renounced the Roman Church and established compulsory education, with free education for the poor. It was these events, and not the theocratic state that Calvin set up some years later, that most impressed Rousseau.

The eighteenth century saw a revival of this independent spirit. Although the constitution of the city was in theory democratic, in effect the rule had passed to a few patrician families who lived together in the upper town, most of whom were involved in the banking for which Geneva had become famous. The citizens occupied in watch-making and jewellery were also becoming prosperous, but they found their political rights blocked. A self-consciously democratic opposition grew up, demanding regular assemblies and voting rights. The first manifestation of this came in 1707; thirty years later it led to riots and bloodshed, and Zurich, Berne and France had to intervene to mediate. The third time it erupted was in 1763, and the focus of it then was Rousseau himself.

On leaving the city and its territory the fifteen-year-old boy was taken in by a Catholic priest and then handed on to Madame de Warens at Annecy. She was an attractive woman of twenty-eight who had left her husband and the Protestant faith to become an agent for the King of Sardinia; the Catholic Kingdom of Sardinia then included Savoy and Piedmont, in northern Italy. Mme de Warens was employed to find converts to Catholicism, and also on certain secret projects of foreign policy. In addition, she speculated in business schemes of her own. For the next fourteen years Rousseau's life revolved around her. She was at various stages his protectress, friend, sister, mother and mistress. For the first few years he remained on the move, first in Turin, the capital of the Kingdom, where he became a Catholic, then back to Savoy, then wandering about in a variety of unlikely occupations, but always coming back to 'Maman'.

In 1732 he settled down with her, and he later regarded the years that followed as the happiest in his life. With only his childhood reading, occasional lessons, and a short spell in a seminary, training unsuccessfully to be a priest, his education had been fitful and sparse. He now set about equipping himself for whatever life he might lead. What that was he did not yet know; he had a passionate interest in music and worked for a short while as a music-teacher; but he also had literary ambitions. He read widely — Plato and the classics, Descartes, Locke, Leibniz, Montaigne, Malebranche, Voltaire, Jansenist theologians, anatomy, physiology, geometry, history. 'At the end of several years spent in not thinking except exactly like another person, without reflecting, that is to say, and almost without reasoning, I found I had gathered a large enough fund of ideas to be

self-sufficient and to be able to think without anyone else's help.'[3]
The two summers spent in this way at Les Charmettes, a house in the
country outside Chambery, remained in his memory like an idyll.

> I got up with the sun and I was happy; I went for a walk and I
> was happy. I saw Maman and I was happy; I left her and I was
> happy. I wandered through woods, among hills, along valleys.
> I read, I was lazy; I worked in the garden, I picked the fruit,
> I helped in the house, and happiness followed me everywhere.
> It was not in any specific thing, it was completely within me. It
> could not leave me for a single moment.[4]

In 1740 he went to Lyons to work as a tutor to the two sons of
M. de Mably. He wrote a paper on the education of the elder, the
Project for the Education of M. de Sainte-Marie. It is not notable
for its originality, though it does contain elements of his mature
thought: 'The goal one should have in front of one in the education
of a young man is to form in him the heart, the judgement, the mind,
in that order'; 'if he has allowed his heart to be corrupted, science
in his hands will be like weapons in the hands of a madman'; 'good
sense depends much more on the feelings of the heart than the bright-
ness of the mind, and it is common experience that the most learned
and enlightened people are not always those who conduct themselves
best in the affairs of life.'[5]

Rousseau was not a success as a teacher; he was impatient and
awkward and after a year he returned to Mme de Warens. But he
was now twenty-nine and he was no longer her favourite. The time
had come to move on. He had developed a new method of notating
music; the more he examined it the better it seemed to be. He decided
to take it to Paris. 'From that moment I believed my fortune was
made . . . and I only dreamt of leaving for Paris, not doubting that
in presenting my project to the Academy I would make a revolution.
I had brought back some money from Lyons; I sold my books. In a
fortnight my decision was made and put into effect.'[6]

He had some letters of introduction to help him, and soon after he
had arrived in the capital he presented his method to the Academy.
It was not well received. In his disappointment he wrote a *Dissertation
on Modern Music*. This brought him to the attention of Mme
Dupin, the rich and beautiful wife of the Receiver-General of Finance;
she invited him to act as tutor to her son. Then, through another
introduction, he was offered the post of secretary to the French
Ambassador in Venice. He accepted eagerly. His literary and musical

projects had come to nothing and he was ill at ease in Parisian society. Perhaps he would succeed elsewhere.

The year he spent in Venice left an indelible mark on Rousseau. The Venetian Republic was always an extraordinary phenomenon. In the eighteenth century it was at its most bizarre. Though most of the trade routes that had been the key to its power had by now lost their importance, the splendours and formalities survived, while the cunning and energy that had once made the city's wealth now went to make its pleasure. The contrast between the city republic of Venice, with its autocratic and convoluted government, its months of Carnival and its famous courtesans, and the city republic of Geneva, with its simple democratic government and its modest puritanical ways, could not fail to make an impression. His work gave him insight into the working of the former, which he called in *The Social Contract* (Bk III, Ch. 5) 'a state dissolved'; its government was a hereditary aristocracy, 'the worst of all governments'.

In addition to this, his personal experience in the embassy was frustrating and humiliating. The ambassador turned out to be tactless, incompetent and tyrannical. To Rousseau, always sensitive and now becoming aware of his abilities, the quarrels between them revealed more than a mere personal incompatibility. 'The justice and futility of my complaints left in my soul a seed of indignation against our mad civil institutions, where real public good and true justice are always sacrificed to I don't know what apparent order, which in effect destroys all order, and only adds the sanction of public authority to the oppression of the weak and the iniquity of the strong.'[7] It was in Venice that Rousseau learnt that 'everything depended radically upon politics'.[8]

A further result of his year there was an enduring love of Italian music. 'I had never heard singing till then.'[9] Like almost all Italian cities at this period Venice had a brilliant musical culture. Italian opera did not suffer from any social restrictions; it was accessible to the whole population and was infectiously enjoyed by them. This fact, together with the directness of the music, the flexibility of the form, and the invention of the composers, swept Rousseau into enthusiastic delight. It was a love that did not fade. When Boswell on his Grand Tour visited him twenty years later, he asked him if he would like anything brought back from Italy. 'A few pretty tunes from the Opera', was Rousseau's reply.[10]

The Paris to which Rousseau returned, and where he now settled, was the intellectual capital of Europe. France was no longer the rich and dominant kingdom it had been in the seventeenth century, but as its power had declined abroad a restless critical spirit had developed within, attacking the outworn institutions of an entrenched monarchy and a declining church. Only the nobility had some political rights and only in the *Parlements*, the appeal courts in the larger towns, was there any effective check on the monarchy. As a result the intellectual challenge was also a political challenge; censorship existed and books were often published anonymously or in the safety of republican Holland. To the vast majority of the population — eighty per cent were peasantry — this activity was obviously remote or unknown. But in Paris itself there was a definite sense of advance and change. It was *le siècle des lumières*, the Enlightenment.

This advance had gained momentum as the century progressed. Montesquieu's *Persian Letters* had appeared in 1721, Voltaire's popularizations of Locke and Newton in the 1730s. Now in the 1740s a large number of wide-ranging and thought-provoking books appeared — Montesquieu's *Spirit of the Laws*, Condillac's *Essay on the Origin of Human Knowledge*, Diderot's *Philosophical Letters* and *Letters on the Blind*, La Mettrie's *Man the Machine*, the first volume of Buffon's *Natural History*. Most important of all, Diderot and D'Alembert began work on the *Encyclopedia*, originally intended only as a translation of Ephraim Chambers' *Cyclopedia* but becoming in their hands an immense compendium of information and propaganda, technological facts and many-sided speculation. The first volume appeared in 1751, the last in 1772. Its publication was frequently threatened and twice interrupted, but Diderot's tireless efforts brought it to eventual completion.

Rousseau became involved in this intellectual atmosphere and shared its sense of potential. 'Every subject will be within my competence . . . I will open eyes. I will write what I see.'[11] He wrote for the opera and the stage, not very successfully, and compiled an extensive, unfinished work on chemistry. He had known Condillac before he came to Paris — the latter was the uncle of the boys he had tutored in Lyons — now he became a close friend of Diderot. 'The three of us used to meet once a week at the Palais-Royal and used to go and eat together . . . there I formed the project for a periodical which Diderot and I were going to produce alternately. I made a draft for the first number and that led to me getting to know D'Alembert; Diderot had spoken to him about it.'[12] He was asked to write articles on music for the *Encyclopedia*.

It was also at this period that Rousseau began living with Thérèse

Levasseur, a girl from Orléans who was a chambermaid at the Hôtel Saint-Quentin where he lodged. When they first met, in 1745, she was twenty-three and he thirty-three. A year later she gave birth to a child; Jean-Jacques took the child to the Foundlings' Hospital. Four more children were born, and all four were put in the Foundlings' Hospital. This episode, which was later to cause Rousseau himself almost as much pain as it must have caused Thérèse, has always remained something of a mystery. For almost twenty years it remained a secret, known to almost no one but the couple and Thérèse's mother; when it was made public, by Voltaire, it had terrible consequences. Why did he do it?

He himself gave several explanations. He had no money and did not want the children to grow up in poverty. He was afraid of Thérèse's relations, who were unreliable and a bad influence. He was ill and thought he did not have long to live. This fact of his illness should not be underestimated. He suffered most of his adult life from a constriction of the urethra which was as physically painful as it was socially awkward. At times the inability to urinate caused the uraemia to infect his kidneys and poison his whole system; several times he believed he was going to die and thought of suicide to ease the agony. But while this may account for the abandoning of perhaps one or two of the children it is hard to accept it as an explanation for all five. The only fact that can be brought in mitigation is that the practice was not uncommon. In some years at this period as many as a third of the children born in Paris were treated in this way. But once again, this does not account for all the children being abandoned. Even now, when we may understand and accept the strangeness of Rousseau's character, this event remains hard to explain and impossible to excuse. The abandoning of the children took place between 1746 and 1754. Its consequences for Rousseau lasted until his death.

In 1749 Diderot was imprisoned at Vincennes for his *Letters on the Blind*, which attacked one of the arguments for the existence of God, that drawn from the beauty and harmony of the visible world. One afternoon in October Rousseau went to visit him. He described what followed in his *Second Letter to Malesherbes*. 'I had in my pocket a copy of the *Mercure de France* which I started leafing through as I walked. My eye fell on the question of the Academy of Dijon which gave rise to my first writing.' (This was a competition which anyone could enter by writing an essay on the subject: Has the re-establishment of the Sciences and the Arts contributed to purify morals?)

If anything was like a sudden inspiration it was the impulse that took hold of me as I read that. Suddenly I felt my mind dazzled by a thousand lights; a crowd of vivid ideas suddenly appeared in front of me with a force and confusion that threw me into an indescribable disturbance; I felt my head go giddy as if I was drunk. A violent palpitation shook me and surged up in my chest; not being able to breathe while walking, I sank down under one of the trees by the road, and I spent half an hour there in such agitation that when I got up I saw the whole front of my shirt was wet with tears that I had shed unawares. Oh! if I had ever been able to write a quarter of what I saw and felt under that tree, with what clarity I could have made visible all the contradictions of the social system, with what force I would have exposed the abuse of our institutions, with what simplicity I would have shown that man is naturally good and that it is only through these institutions alone that men become wicked. All that I have been able to retain of that mass of great truths which illuminated me in a quarter of an hour under that tree has been weakly scattered in my three main writings, that is, the *First Discourse*, that on *Inequality*, and my *Treatise on Education;* these three works are inseparable and together form a complete whole. All the rest has been lost . . . That is how, when I least thought of it, I became a writer, almost in spite of myself.[13]

Arriving at Vincennes in a state of great excitement he told Diderot of his 'illumination'. Diderot encouraged him to enter the prize competition. In July 1750 his *Discourse on the Arts and Sciences* won the Dijon prize.

This news reawoke in me all the ideas that it had suggested, animated them with new force and ended by reinvigorating in my heart that first taste of heroism and virtue that my father and my *patrie* and Plutarch had put there in my childhood. I no longer found anything great and beautiful except in being free and virtuous, above fortune and opinion, and in being sufficient in myself.[14]

In other words, he wanted to bring his life into line with his principles. He had condemned luxury, social conventions and intellectual fashions. At the same time he had been working as secretary and cashier to the rich Dupin family, sharing their life in Paris or in their château at Chenonceaux. Now he gave up this job and took to earning his living by copying music. He had been apprenticed as an artisan; now he would be one. He gave up gold lace and white stockings with incredible joy; 'I put down my sword, and sold my watch, saying to myself: "Heaven be praised, I will no longer need to know the time".'[15] 'Better than that, I uprooted from my heart the greediness and envy which gave a price to all I was leaving.'[16] He wrote later: 'To have the right to despise the rich you must be economical and prudent yourself, so as never to need wealth.'[17] It was this determination to make his life a witness to his belief that gave his work its moral authority, and was later to cause him such suffering.

His 'reform' was not completed all at once. He continued to live in Paris and reworked an early play, *Narcissus*, which was staged at the Comédie Française. He wrote an opera, *The Village Sorcerer*, which was so successful when it was performed before Louis XV at Fontainebleau that he was offered a royal pension. Rousseau declined it, but that did not prevent his success from seeming strikingly inappropriate for a man who had condemned the arts and culture so bitterly. Furthermore, he was still associated with the Encyclopedists. He was asked to write an article on Political Economy, and he became the champion of progressive opinion in the musical quarrel — the War of the Bouffons — between French classical opera and Italian comic opera.

However, he soon had an opportunity to reassert his initial criticism and develop his ideas. 'In 1753 the Academy of Dijon set as a subject for an essay the Origin of Inequality among Men . . . To meditate at my ease on this great subject I made a trip of seven or eight days to Saint-Germain with Thérèse, our landlady and a friend of hers. The weather was fine.' Apart from mealtimes he spent the days alone.

> Plunged in the depths of the forest I searched out and found the image of the first times, the history of which I proudly traced. I laid hands on the petty lies of men, I dared to strip bare their nature, to follow the progress of time and things which have disfigured it, and, comparing the man of men with the man of nature, to show men in their supposed perfection the true source of their miseries. Exalted by this sublime contemplation my soul rose up towards the divinity, and there, seeing my fellows following the blind path of their prejudices, errors, misfortunes and crimes, I cried out to them in a weak voice

which they could not hear: 'Madmen, you who complain endlessly about nature, learn that all your evils come from yourselves'.[18]

The *Discourse on Inequality* depicted man in a state of nature living peacefully and happily, and traced the stages by which this happiness had been lost. Although it ended with a grim picture of men living under despotism Rousseau did not regard this conclusion as inevitable. There were free countries, as well as despotic countries. Foremost among the former, in his view, was Geneva, and he wrote a long dedication to the Republic of Geneva as a foreword to this *Discourse*. In the summer of 1754, when he had completed the work, he paid a long visit to his native city with Thérèse. He was received back into the Protestant Church and took up his rights as a citizen. The visit was so enjoyable that 'I thought only of returning to Paris to dispose of my things, put my few affairs in order . . . and return with Thérèse to settle in Geneva for the rest of my days.'[19] He planned to come back in the spring of the new year; but he did not do so, and he was never to enter the city again.

In the *Confessions* he gives a number of reasons for this. He felt that the dedication he had written was poorly received; he thought he would be unable to find sufficient work copying music. Then Voltaire bought a property, Les Délices, outside the city, and although relations between the two men were at this time still courteous, Rousseau must have been aware of the fundamental differences between them. His friendship with Diderot was much more important to him, and was probably a further factor in his not going to Switzerland.

Then he was offered the use of the Hermitage, a small cottage on the estate of Madame d'Epinay, near the forest of Montmorency. That decided him. 'Ever since I had been thrown into the world [of affairs] . . . I had not ceased to regret my dear Charmettes and the sweet life I had led there. I felt I was made for a quiet life and the countryside; it was impossible for me to live happily anywhere else.'[20]

The move to the Hermitage, in April 1756, completed Rousseau's 'reform', and the six years that followed were the most creative and fruitful of his life. He had plans for a book on political institutions, out of which came *The Social Contract*, for a treatise on education, which became *Emile*, for a *Dictionary of Music*, for a selection from the writings of the Abbé de St-Pierre, and for a work called *The Sensitive Morality* (see Chapter 18). During this period he developed the implications of the ideas he had first glimpsed in his 'illumination' and then set out in the first two *Discourses*.

> I was led by a new route into another intellectual world with a simple and proud economy which I could not think of without enthusiasm. The more I examined it the more I saw only error and madness in the doctrine of our wise men, only oppression and misery in our social order . . . Until then I had been good; now I became virtuous, or at least intoxicated with virtue . . . I did not play a rôle: I really became what I appeared [to be]. For the four years at least that this excitement lasted in all its force, there was nothing great and beautiful that can enter the heart of man, between heaven and earth, of which I was not capable . . . I was truly transformed.[21]

Among the works he undertook in his first year at the Hermitage was one that was not initially related to any of his previous ideas: it was a novel, a love-story, which eventually became *The New Heloïse*. While he was writing it he fell in love himelf, with the Comtesse d'Houdetot. His love was not returned, unlike Saint-Preux's love for Julie in the novel, but the book owed something of its intensity to the affair. It was this book which brought Rousseau a European-wide reputation.

His move from Paris led to an irrevocable breach between Diderot and himself. The two men were each developing in different directions and the end of their friendship was not only painful, it left wounds which never healed. The final break came with Rousseau's *Letter to D'Alembert* in which he attacked at length and in detail the suggestion made by D'Alembert, in his article for the *Encyclopedia* on Geneva, that a theatre should be built in the city.

At the end of 1757 Rousseau quarrelled with Madame d'Epinay and left the Hermitage. He moved with Thérèse to Montlouis, also near the Forest of Montmorency, on the estate of the Duke of Luxembourg. Here he completed *The New Heloïse*, which was published in 1761, and *The Social Contract* and *Emile*, both of which were published in 1762, the former in Amsterdam, the latter in Paris. He included in *Emile* a long statement of his religious belief, the *Profession of Faith of a Savoyard Priest*, which openly attacked Christianity. The *Parlement* of Paris, wanting to show that it was not entirely godless, despite its expulsion of the Jesuits, condemned *Emile* for its desire 'to re-establish natural religion . . . that criminal system'. It also attacked the idea of an education based on nature, 'that kind of knowledge which instinct alone' suggests, and the way the author did 'misrepresent sovereign authority [and did] destroy the principles of that obedience which is due to kings'.[22] The book was publicly burnt and an order issued for Rousseau's arrest.

Rousseau was warned about the order and left France. He did not go to Geneva because he was uncertain of the reception he might get: *The New Heloïse* had not been well received by the city authorities. He went to Berne but was refused permission to remain there. So he took refuge in Môtiers, a village in the Jura mountains in the province of Neuchâtel, which was then under the political jurisdiction of Frederick the Great. Through the good offices of the governor of the province, a Scotsman who was himself a refugee — he had had to leave Scotland after the failure of the Jacobite rebellion in 1715 — Rousseau was allowed to settle there.

His doubts about Geneva were soon confirmed. The executive Small Council condemned both *Emile* and *The Social Contract* for having 'confused anarchy and liberty, [for having] brought the chaos of the state of nature into the system of civil societies, [for having] put an axe to the root of all governments, and in turn exalted and insulted Christianity'.[23] They ordered the books to be burnt and Rousseau to be arrested if he entered the city or its territory.

That the *Parlement* of Paris should condemn his work and order his arrest without trial or hearing surprised Rousseau. That the same should happen in the city he had held up to the world as a model of a just and free state horrified him. Not only on his own account, but because he expected a violent reaction. 'I trembled with fear that such an evident and obvious breach of every law, beginning with that of common sense, would throw Geneva upside down.' But nothing happened. 'All remained quiet.'[24]

In a way this quiet was even worse. If no one stood up against injustice what legality could there be for anyone? Rousseau was aware that the Small Council had abused its powers in the past, but he had had faith in the independence of the citizens. He had spoken up for them in his *Letter to D'Alembert*. Why were they silent now when they should have spoken up for him?

It soon became apparent that while his political views delighted the bourgeoisie his religious views shocked them. It was partly because of this that Rousseau wrote his *Letter to Christophe de Beaumont*, a long reply to the condemnation of *Emile* that had been made by the Archbishop of Paris. This *Letter* was published in Holland in March 1763. In Geneva its success was immediate; five hundred copies were sold the day it arrived there. Rousseau's supporters were delighted and his opponents alarmed. They took action against the book and prohibited its reprinting. Once again Rousseau expected his friends to protest. Nothing happened. His fellow-citizens were not the people he thought them to be. On all his published works he had proudly called himself 'Citizen of Geneva'. Now he renounced his citizenship, calmly and with dignity, but also with bitter disappointment.

This act galvanized the bourgeoisie into protest. They took up Rousseau's cause and asserted their case for the rights that had been denied them. In spite of the dangerous tensions that arose, (particularly dangerous for the ruling oligarchy in Geneva, since there was no standing army to enforce their authority), the Small Council stood firm. A brilliant exposition of their case for doing so, entitled *Letters from the Country*, silenced the opposition.

The bourgeoisie turned to Rousseau as the only person who could provide an effective reply. He was reluctant to become directly involved and would not agree to their request. He had been in Geneva during the troubles of 1737 and what he had seen then had frightened him. 'I swore that I would never get involved in any civil war, nor ever uphold liberty by force of arms.'[25] Nevertheless, the situation was not one he could accept, and he asked to see the relevant documents, as well as several histories of the city. In Môtiers he worked on a reply and in December 1764 it appeared, under the title *Letters from the Mountain*.

This work re-animated the democratic opposition. The short-term result in Geneva was a deadlock; the short-term result for Rousseau was drastic. In the Fifth Letter of the work he had referred to Voltaire as the author of a blasphemous pamphlet that had been published anonymously and which had not been banned by the Small Council. He did this not only as an example of the injustice of his own treatment but because he associated Voltaire, correctly, with the patrician oligarchy. His remarks infuriated Voltaire and the latter reacted with a ferocious counter-attack. He wrote an anonymous pamphlet, the *Sentiment of the Citizens:*

> If a man is mad we are sorry for him. But when his madness becomes savage we tie him up . . . (Who is this man, lecturing our citizens?) Is he a man of good, misled by false enthusiasm? . . . With shame and grief we must tell you; he is a man disfigured by the scars of his own debauchery . . . who drags with him, from village to village, and from mountain to mountain, a poor

creature . . . whose children he abandoned on the door-step of a
Poor House, renouncing all the feelings of nature as he discards
those of honour and religion.[26]

Rousseau had made his own life an example of the principles he
upheld. His motto had become a phrase by Juvenal that he had
first quoted in the *Letter to D'Alembert* and now used as an epigraph
for the *Letters from the Mountain*: '*Vitam impendere vero*', 'To
dedicate life to truth'.[27] He called himself 'a friend of truth' rather
than a philosopher. But now a secret and terrible truth of his own life
was revealed to the world.

The pastor at Môtiers had previously been friendly to Rousseau,
but under pressure from Geneva and Neuchâtel he now turned against
him. Hostility in the village grew. In September 1765 the pastor
preached a sermon that was aimed at him and that evening his
house was stoned. Rousseau was an outcast once more. He and
Thérèse fled from Môtiers and took refuge on the island of St-Pierre
in the Lake of Bienne, in the province of Berne. There he experienced
a remarkable happiness, but it was short lived. He was refused permission to stay. So, at the invitation of Hume, he and Thérèse came
to England.

'I think I could live with him all my life in mutual friendship and
esteem', wrote Hume.[28] Unfortunately this was not to be the case.
Having been driven out of France, Geneva, Môtiers and Berne
Rousseau had become obsessed with the fear of persecution. Ill and
isolated in England he imagined that Hume had become part of a
conspiracy against him; the two men quarrelled bitterly. After
fifteen months, during which he worked on his *Confessions*, he
returned to France under an assumed name.

For the next three years he wandered from place to place, from
Normandy, to Lyons, to Grenoble and in the Dauphiné. In 1770
he was allowed to settle again in Paris with Thérèse, whom he
had now married. He took up music-copying once more and finished
the *Confessions*. The revelation of the abandoning of his children
and his quarrel with Hume had destroyed the reputation he had
gained, with *The New Heloïse* and *Emile*, of being 'an apostle of
virtue', 'the Socrates of the century'. His *Confessions* were, in part,
an attempt at self-justification. When they were completed he began
some readings from them, but then these readings were prohibited,
at the request of Diderot and Madame d'Epinay.

This prohibition confirmed Rousseau's despair of making his case heard and he wrote another work in self-defence, the *Dialogues*. But he was not limited in these years only to justifying his previous writing or conduct. On the Island of St-Pierre he had worked on his *Constitutional Project for Corsica*, in Paris he wrote on botany and his *Considerations on the Government of Poland*, and with his last work, the unfinished *Reveries of the Solitary Walker*, he passed beyond autobiography into a realm of meditation and self-exploration that was as original as anything else he ever wrote.

Despite all the uncertainties and suffering that followed the publication of *Emile* and *The Social Contract* in 1762, Rousseau seems in the final years of his life to have attained a kind of happiness and peace of mind. The novelist Bernardin de St-Pierre, who came to know him in this period, has left a picture of a man living in great simplicity, in a fourth-floor apartment of just two rooms — a little kitchen and a room with two beds, a table and a few chairs, some plants on the windowsill and a spinet in the corner. 'Music is as necessary to me as bread', Rousseau told him. His only luxuries were coffee and ice-cream, and his greatest love was the green of the countryside. 'I have told my wife: when you see me very ill, beyond hope of recovery, have me carried out into the middle of a meadow. The sight of that will restore me.' In the afternoons he liked to botanize; in the mornings he copied music: 'One must have an occupation. This is both work and pleasure for me . . . Besides, I am the son of an artisan and I am an artisan myself. I am doing what I have done since I was fourteen.' 'One must be oneself', he insisted, 'I do not fear death'; 'I will die happy.'[29]

Rousseau died at Ermenonville, outside Paris, on 2 July 1778. He was sixty-six. Thérèse survived him by many years and after the French Revolution was given a state pension.

3 WORDS

Rousseau had an acute sense of language. He was aware of its limits — 'there is no language rich enough to provide enough nuances, terms and phrases for all the modifications our ideas can have'[1] — and of the way it continually changes — 'nothing is more common than words changing their meaning in the course of time'.[2] His ability to give verbal form to new areas of feeling made him a very influential writer, and his musical ear made him a master of French prose. At the same time he used certain words and phrases in an idiosyncratic way — 'my terms rarely have the ordinary meaning'.[3]

It is important to be aware of these factors and be familiar with his terminology when reading Rousseau. The purpose of this chapter is to draw attention to some of his terms.

The first important distinction to note is that between **self-love** (*amour de soi*) and **self-interest** (*amour-propre*, which can also be translated as vanity, pride or selfishness). Rousseau first made this distinction in the *Discourse on Inequality* (see p. 57), and it is crucial to all his subsequent work. In one sense his whole philosophy was an attempt to displace the cold emphasis given to self-interest by Hobbes, Locke and contemporary materialists, and replace it with the warmer quality of self-love. Self-love is our first feeling; self-interest only arises when we compare ourselves with others. Self-love is loving in ourself what makes us what we are, experiencing 'the sweet feeling of existence', the sense of well-being and being fulfilled in ourself; it is related to our 'original feelings, which all tend directly to our happiness . . . and are essentially loving and pleasant'.[4] Self-interest on the other hand is being outside yourself, not being satisfied with what you are but being envious of others and competitive; it is the result of seeing yourself in terms of other people's criteria — what Rousseau calls opinion or prejudice — rather than in terms of how you feel in yourself.

He made another distinction between **goodness** (*bonté*), which is natural to us, and **virtue** (*vertu*), which we achieve. When he says that man is naturally good he does not mean that whatever a man does will be good, or that every impulse is right or true; he means that our first and original impulses are good. In other words, goodness is an inherent characteristic, which can become an actual and experienced state if allowed to develop rightly. In the state of nature man was good, but not consciously so. Moral awareness only develops in society. To be good in society means making choices and by making the right choices we achieve virtue. Virtue, in other words, is active; it is the effort that overcomes a bad influence, a harmful appetite, or an inner weakness. By our reason we are able to make the right choice, by our virtue we are able to act on that choice. For Rousseau virtue in moral terms is an exact equivalent of justice in social terms.

He derived this sense of virtue to some extent from Montesquieu and other writers earlier in the century. Virtue to them was the quality manifest in the republics of ancient Greece and Rome, particularly Sparta and early Rome, both of which were admired by Rousseau and such contemporaries as Helvétius. It was the quality that made those republics such striking and damning contrasts to the French monarchy. Citizens with virtue had a sense of dedication, independence and simplicity; they put the public good before their private welfare. In Montesquieu's *Spirit of the Laws* virtue is the principal characteristic of a republic, as honour is in a monarchy and fear in a despotism. Virtue took a military form in wartime, because the citizens had to provide their own defence, but it was equally important in peacetime, because the citizens had political rights and used them.

These historical associations with the words **republic** and **citizen** run throughout Rousseau's work. He gave them a contemporary association when he related them to the city-republic of Geneva. Not every inhabitant of Geneva was a citizen (see Chapter 16); citizens were those who had the fullest political rights and civic responsibility. Not every state without a monarch was a republic (see p. 156); a republic was a state that was legitimately set up and justly administered. (Rousseau is not consistent in using these two words in this sense, but he often does so.)

Another word for a just state is **patrie** (literally, fatherland); as we

have no English equivalent I have left this word in French. To have
a *patrie* is to live under a lawful government, with proper political
rights. A *patrie* 'is not the walls nor the men who make up the *patrie*;
it is the laws, the morals [*mœurs*], the customs, the government, the
constitution, the manner of being which results from all that. [It] is
in the relations of the state to its members. When these relations
change or are destroyed the *patrie* vanishes.'5 The morals (see below)
and customs that Rousseau talks of in this passage are not just ways
of life but ways of feeling. To have a *patrie* is not only to have
opportunities to participate, but to have a sense of belonging and
community, a sense of pride and responsibility. (It is nothing to do
with the aggressive or expansionist type of nationalism that developed
in the following century.) Rousseau writes at length about love of the
patrie in his *Discourse on Political Economy* (see Chapter 6).

The words **state** and **government** in the above passage are not
synonymous. In Rousseau's political theory they are quite distinct,
and they must be distinguished, in turn, from the **sovereign.** The state
(*état*) is composed of all the inhabitants of a country; all the people
together form the state. At times Rousseau compares it to a body,
made up of all the people. It is only a passive body, however. To
become active it must have a will, and this will he calls the sovereign
(*souverain*). The sovereign is the source of supreme authority. But for
Rousseau, unlike his predecessors, this authority cannot belong to
a single person or a particular group; it must belong to all the people
acting together. They lay down the fundamental laws of the state and
set up a government (*gouvernement*) to administer the state as their
agents.

The sovereign has legislative power, the government has executive
power, but they are not equal, because the latter is only the instrument of the sovereign; it can be replaced whenever the sovereign
wishes. Moreover, when some citizens are appointed to the government they do not cease to be members of the sovereign. They continue to take part in the activity of the sovereign since they are equally
affected by the laws and must be able to help to decide on them.

The sovereign expresses itself through the **general will** (*volonté
générale*), which is the shared sense of the common good. This
concept is central to Rousseau's political theory. It first appeared in
the *Discourse on Political Economy* but was only developed fully in
The Social Contract (see Chapter 12). It gives rise to many difficulties.
The important thing to bear in mind as far as the literal meaning of
the phrase is concerned is that *volonté* does not only mean will, in

the sense of intention or decision, but also wish, in the sense of desire or want, i.e. it means not only will as in will-power, but also will as in willingness. As with *patrie*, there is an essential emotional dimension to the word.

Two words not used distinctively by Rousseau but which have changed their meaning since the eighteenth century are **magistrate** and **philosophe**. A magistrate at that time was not necessarily a judicial official confined to legal matters but could be any minister or administrator carrying out government business. A *philosophe* was a man of learning concerned not only with philosophy but a whole range of subjects — science, mathematics, law, politics, literature, economics, and history — as well as philosophy. The *philosophes* collectively were the men of learning in France, and particularly Paris, who were associated with the Enlightenment. The word could also be used specifically to mean a philosopher and I have also sometimes translated it as 'intellectual', since that has the pejorative overtone that Rousseau sometimes gave it.

A word that has no exact equivalent in English is *mœurs*, which refers to the customs, habits and whole way of life — behaviour, attitudes and feelings — of a person or a people. It has sometimes been translated as **morals** (not in the narrow sense we commonly use it, but in the broadest possible sense, as in 'his whole moral outlook'), at other times as **customs.**

Finally, **foresight** (*prévoyance*) is a word Rousseau used to denote the habit of not living in the present moment but of thinking ahead, i.e. not reading this sentence for itself but wondering how many more pages there are before the end of the book.

4 MORALS

I

'I saw another universe and I became another man . . . All my trivial passions were stifled by an enthusiasm for truth, liberty and virtue, and, what was more astonishing, this great excitement lasted in my heart for more than four or five years.'[1] With his prize-winning *Discourse on the Arts and Sciences*, also known as the *First Discourse*, Rousseau's important work began.

The question set by the Academy of Dijon was asking, in effect, whether the great developments in learning and culture that had taken place since the Renaissance had improved the way people lived. In his introduction Rousseau altered the question slightly so that it read: 'Has the restoration of the sciences and the arts tended to purify or corrupt morals?' For him it was not a question of how much improvement, but of how much degeneration. He later described his answer as 'absolutely lacking in logic and order; of all that has come from my pen the most weakly argued',[2] and the work is certainly notable more for its rhetoric than its logic. It is curiously unimpressive to read today.

Nevertheless, its importance is not in question. Because here Rousseau was, as he said himself, 'confronting head-on everything which is currently admired'.[3] When he attacked social privilege and wealth he was only adding his voice to that of several other critics of the time; though it is true that the openness of his criticism was unusual. But when he attacked the arts and sciences, the pursuit of learning and culture, and then went even further by connecting these activities to his social criticism — saying, as he did, that social corruption and the development of culture were integrally related — he set himself apart from his most progressive contemporaries. He was attacking the whole idea of civilization as it was generally understood, and the whole idea of progress as it was then advocated by his fellow-contributors to the *Encyclopedia*.

At the same time, Rousseau's attack was not indiscriminate. He did not condemn science or intellectual advance as such; he made individual exceptions in the case of 'great teachers' like Bacon, Descartes and Newton. What he was saying was that to be good is more important than to be cultured or knowledgeable. Our intellectual faculties must not be divorced from our moral sense. Nor should the pursuit of learning or culture depend on injustice, as was frequently the case at the time; many intellectuals were dependent on the aristocracy, if they were not actually aristocrats themselves, like Montesquieu, Buffon or Holbach, or effectively became aristocrats, like Voltaire.

It was an uncompromising position to adopt, and even though Rousseau subsequently demonstrated his seriousness of purpose by reforming his own way of life, it is perhaps not surprising that it was some time before other people appreciated how far-reaching his criticism was. The fact that the 'great teachers' he mentioned were the acknowledged mentors of the *Encyclopedia* also obscured the implications of what he was saying. Furthermore, Rousseau remained a close friend of Diderot. When he heard he had won the prize Diderot helped him to get the *Discourse* printed, as Rousseau was ill at the time. It was published in January 1751, with a frontispiece showing Prometheus and the Satyr. The epigraph was a line from Ovid, written during his exile in Scythia: 'Here I am a barbarian because men do not understand me.'[4]

Discourse on the Arts and Sciences

PART ONE

The mind, as well as the body, has its needs: those of the body are the basis of society, those of the mind are its ornaments.

So long as government and law provide for the security and well-being of men in their common life, the arts, literature, and sciences, less despotic though perhaps more powerful, fling garlands of flowers over the chains which weigh them down. They stifle in men's breasts that sense of original liberty, for which they seem to have been born, cause them to love their own slavery, and so make of them what is called a civilized people.

Necessity raised up thrones; the arts and sciences have made them strong. Powers of the earth, cherish all talents and protect those who cultivate them.* Civilized peoples, cultivate such pursuits: to them, happy slaves, you owe that delicacy and refinement of taste, which is so much your boast, that sweetness of disposition and urbanity of manners which make intercourse so easy and agreeable among you — in a word, the appearance of all the virtues, without the possession of any . . .   6–7

What happiness would it be for those who live among us, if our external appearance were always a true mirror of our hearts; if decorum were but virtue; if the maxims we professed were the rulers of our conduct; and if real philosophy were inseparable from the title of a philosopher! But so many good qualities seldom go together; virtue rarely appears in so much pomp and state.

Richness of apparel may proclaim the man of fortune, and elegance the man of taste; but the healthy man is known by different signs. It is under the homespun of the labourer, and not beneath the gilt and tinsel of the courtier, that we should look for strength and vigour of body . . .   7–8

Before art had moulded our behaviour, and taught our passions to speak an artificial language, our morals were rustic but natural; and the different ways in which we behaved proclaimed at first glance the difference of our dispositions. Human nature was not at bottom better then than now; but men found their security in the ease with which they could see through one another, and this advantage, of which we no longer feel the value, prevented their having many vices.

In our day, now that more subtle study and a more refined taste have reduced the art of pleasing to rules, there prevails in our morals a servile and deceptive conformity; so that one would think every mind had been cast in the same mould. Politeness requires this thing, decorum that; ceremony has its forms, and fashion its laws, and these we must always follow, never the promptings of our own nature.

We no longer dare seem what we really are, but lie under a perpetual restraint. In the meantime the herd of men, which we call society, all act under the same circumstances exactly alike, unless very particular and powerful motives prevent them. Thus we never know with whom we have to deal . . .

---

* Sovereigns always see with pleasure the increase among their subjects of the taste for pleasing arts and for superfluities which do not result in the export of money. They know very well that, besides nourishing that littleness of mind which is suitable for slavery, all the needs that the people give themselves are so many more chains upon them. (Note by Rousseau.)

What a train of vices must attend this uncertainty! Sincere friendship, real esteem, and perfect confidence are banished from among men. Jealousy, suspicion, fear, coldness, reserve, hate and fraud lie constantly concealed under that uniform and deceitful veil of politeness, that boasted candour and urbanity, for which we are indebted to the enlightened spirit of this age . . . Ignorance is held in contempt;

8–9   but a dangerous scepticism has succeeded it . . .

Where there is no effect, it is idle to look for a cause: but here the effect is certain and the depravity actual; our minds have been corrupted in proportion as the arts and sciences have improved. Will it be said that this is a misfortune peculiar to the present age? No, gentlemen, the evils resulting from our vain curiosity are as old as the world. The daily ebb and flow of the tides are not more regularly influenced by the phases of the moon than the morals of a people by the progress of the arts and sciences. As their light has risen above our horizon, virtue has taken flight, and the same

9–10   phenomenon has been constantly observed in all times and places . . .

[Rousseau then gives some examples from ancient history. His concluding example is that between Athens and Sparta. This contrast, a favourite of Rousseau's, was common at the time; it had formerly been made by Plutarch and Montaigne, two of Rousseau's favourite writers, more recently by Bossuet and Montesquieu, and was soon after to be used by Helvétius.]

Can it be forgotten that, in the very heart of Greece, there arose a city as famous for the happy ignorance of its inhabitants, as for the wisdom of its laws? A republic of demi-gods rather than of men, so greatly superior their virtues seemed to those of mere humanity . . . While the vices, accompanied by the fine arts, were being introduced into Athens, while its tyrant was carefully collecting together the works of the prince of poets,* Sparta was driving from her walls artists and the arts, the learned and their learning!

The difference was seen in the outcome. Athens became the seat of politeness and taste, the country of orators and philosophers. The elegance of its buildings equalled that of its language; on every side might be seen marble and canvas, animated by the hands of the most skilful artists. From Athens we derive those astonishing performances, which will serve as models to every corrupt age. The picture of [Sparta] is not so highly coloured. There, the neighbouring

---

* A reference to the first transcription of the poetry of Homer by the Athenian tyrant Pisistratus.

nations used to say, 'men are born virtuous, the very air of the country seems to inspire them with virtue'. But its inhabitants have left us nothing except the memory of their heroic actions. Should such monuments count for less in our eyes than the most curious relics of Athenian marble? . . .   12–13

[Rousseau then quotes, in criticism of Athens, a speech by Socrates taken from Plato's *Apology* and *Crito*, and he imagines what Fabricius, one of the founders of the Roman Republic, might have said if he had returned to see the corruption of Imperial Rome. He continues:]

Thus it is that luxury, profligacy, and slavery have been, in all ages, the scourge of our proud efforts to emerge from that happy ignorance, in which eternal wisdom had placed us. The thick veil with which she has covered all her operations seems to be a sufficient warning that she never designed us for fruitless researches. But is there, indeed, one lesson from which we could have profited, or which we have neglected with impunity? People, learn for once that nature would have preserved you from science, as a mother snatches a dangerous weapon from the hands of her child. Know that all the secrets she hides are so many evils from which she protects you, and that the very difficulty you find in acquiring knowledge is not the least of her benefits. Men are perverse; but they would have been far worse, if they had had the misfortune to be born learned.   15

PART TWO

There was an ancient tradition that passed from Egypt to Greece, which said that some god who was an enemy of the peace of mankind was the inventor of the sciences.* . . .   17

* It is easy to see the allegory in the fable of Prometheus; and it does not seem that the Greeks, who chained him to the Caucasus, had a better opinion of him than the Egyptians had of their god Teuthus. 'The satyr', says an ancient fable, 'wanted to kiss and embrace the fire, the first time he saw it; but Prometheus cried out to him: "Satyr, you will weep for the beard on your chin, because it burns when you touch it".' This is the subject of the frontispiece. (Note by Rousseau.)   17

[This explanation of his frontispiece did not satisfy some of his readers, and later in his *Letter to Lecat*, he explained further:]
The torch of Prometheus is that of the sciences made to animate the great geniuses . . . The Satyr who, seeing the fire for the first time, runs to it and wants to embrace it, represents the vulgar men who, seduced by the glitter of letters, indiscriminately give themselves up to study . . . The Prometheus who cries out and warns them of the danger is the citizen of Geneva. This allegory is beautiful, just; I believe it sublime.   102

To live without doing some good is a great evil, as much in the political as in the moral world; and hence every useless citizen should be regarded as a pernicious person . . . Would we have been less numerous, worse governed, less formidable, less flourishing, or more perverse, supposing [illustrious intellectuals] had taught us none 18–19 of all things [which they have taught us?] . . .

[Among the] evils [which] accompany literature and the arts . . . is luxury, produced by indolence and the vanity of man. Luxury is seldom unattended by the arts and sciences, and they never develop without it. I know that our philosophy, always fertile in remarkable ideas, pretends, in contradiction to the experience of all ages, that luxury contributes to the splendour of states. But . . . can it be denied that good morals are essential to make empires last, and that luxury is diametrically opposed to good morals? Let it be admitted that luxury is a certain indication of wealth: that it even serves, if you will, to increase such wealth; what conclusion is to be drawn from this paradox, so worthy of our time? And what will become of virtue if riches are to be acquired at any cost? The politicians of the ancient world were always talking of morals and virtue; ours speak of nothing but commerce and money. One of them will tell you that in such a country a man is worth just as much as he will sell for in Algiers: another, pursuing the same mode of calculation, finds that in some countries a man is worth nothing, and in others less than nothing; they value men as they do droves of oxen. According to them, a man is worth no more to the state than the amount he 19–20 consumes . . .

We cannot reflect on morals without recalling with pleasure the picture of the simplicity of the first times. It is [like] a beautiful coast, adorned only by the hands of nature, towards which our eyes constantly turn, and which we see receding with regret. While men were innocent and virtuous, and loved to have gods to witness their actions, they dwelt together in the same huts. But when they became vicious, they grew tired of such inconvenient onlookers, and banished them to magnificent temples. Finally, they expelled their deities even from these, in order to dwell there themselves; or at least the temples of the gods were no longer any more magnificent than the houses of the citizens. This was the height of degeneracy; nor could vice ever be carried to greater lengths than when it was seen, supported, as it were, on columns of marble and engraved on Corinthian capitals, at the entry to great men's palaces.

As the conveniences of life increase, as the arts are brought to

perfection and luxury spreads, true courage flags, military virtues
disappear . . .   22

If the cultivation of the sciences is prejudicial to military qualities,
it is still more so to moral qualities. Even from our infancy an absurd
system of education serves to adorn our wit and corrupt our judgement. We see, on every side, huge institutions, where our youth are
educated at great expense, and instructed in everything but their duty.
Your children will be ignorant of their own language, but they can
talk others which are not spoken anywhere . . . Magnanimity, equity,
temperance, humanity, and courage will be words they do not
understand. The dear name of *patrie* will never strike their ears; and
if they ever hear speak of God, it will be less to fear than to be
frightened of Him . . .   24

Whence arise all these abuses, unless it be from that fatal inequality
introduced among men by the distinction of talents and the cheapen-
ing of virtue? This is the most evident effect of all our studies, and
the most dangerous of all their consequences. The question is no
longer whether a man is honest, but whether he is clever. We do not
ask whether a book is useful, but whether it is well written. Rewards
are lavished on wit and ingenuity, while virtue is left unhonoured.
There are a thousand prizes for fine discourses, and none for good
actions . . .   25

A wise man does not go in chase of fortune; but he is by no means
insensible to glory, and when he sees it so ill distributed, his virtue,
which might have been animated by a little emulation, and turned to
the advantage of society, droops and dies away in obscurity and
indigence. Preferring pleasing talents to the useful ones must, in the
long run, inevitably result in this; and this truth has been only too
well confirmed since the revival of the arts and sciences. We have
physicists, geometricians, chemists, astronomers, poets, musicians,
and painters in plenty; but we have no longer a citizen among us;
or if there still remain a few, scattered over our abandoned countryside, they are left to perish there poor and despised. To this condition
are reduced those who give us our daily bread, and our children
milk; and such are our feelings towards them . . .   26

Those whom nature intended for her disciples have not needed
masters. Bacon, Descartes, and Newton, those teachers of mankind,
had themselves no teachers. What guide indeed could have taken
them so far as their sublime genius directed them? Ordinary masters
would only have cramped their intelligence, by confining it within
the narrow limits of their own capacity. It was from the obstacles

they met with at first that they learned to exert themselves . . . [and then] to traverse the vast field which they covered. If some men must be allowed to apply themselves to the study of the arts and sciences, it is only those who feel able to walk alone in their footsteps and to outstrip them. It is for these few to raise monuments to the glory of the human understanding. But if we are desirous that nothing should be above their genius, nothing should be beyond their hopes. This is the only encouragement they require. The soul gradually adapts itself to the objects on which it is employed, and thus it is that great
29   occasions produce great men . . .

As for us ordinary men, on whom Heaven has not been pleased to bestow such great talents; as we are not destined to reap such glory, let us remain in our obscurity. Let us not covet a reputation we should never attain, and which, in the present state of things, would never make up to us for the trouble it would have cost us, even if we were fully qualified to obtain it. Why should we build our happiness on the opinions of others, when we can find it in our own hearts? Let us leave to others the task of instructing mankind in their duty, and confine ourselves to the discharge of our own. We do not need to know more than this.

Oh Virtue! sublime science of simple souls, are such trouble and preparation needed to know you? Are not your principles engraved on every heart? Need we do more, to learn your laws, than re-enter into ourselves, and listen to the voice of conscience in the silence of the passions?

This is the true philosophy, with which we must learn to be content. Without envying the fame of those celebrated men, whose names are immortal in the republic of letters, let us endeavour to make, between them and us, that honourable distinction which was formerly seen to exist between two great peoples,* that the one knew how to speak,
30   and the other how to act, aright.

II

The publication of the *First Discourse*, according to the German-born *philosophe* Grimm, 'made a sort of revolution in Paris'. It was 'written with an intensity and passion that had not been seen in an academic essay'.[5] Another contemporary, the Marquis d'Argenson, described it as 'remarkable above all for the nobility and loftiness of its principles. The author is a good politician.'[6]

* Rousseau refers to Athens and Sparta.

The criticism of the arts and sciences, however, provoked many outraged replies. Over the next two years Rousseau answered several of these replies and in so doing explained himself more fully. In the *Discourse* he had praised military prowess: 'robust' and 'vigorous' were to remain favourite adjectives, but were they the only virtues he believed in? In his *Observations* he put forward another model, the example of Jesus Christ. He also made it clear that it was the abuse of the sciences that he was attacking. As for the arts, given the present state of affairs it would be dangerous to do away with them; they acted as palliatives to sick men.

Some alteration of his attitude to the arts was forced on Rousseau, because in the autumn of 1752 his opera *The Village Sorcerer* was performed at Fontainebleau and his early play *Narcissus* at the Comédie Française. The first was very successful; the second, written when he was living with Mme de Warens but since improved (with the help, among others, of Marivaux), was a failure. The text was published, however, and Rousseau wrote a long Preface to it.

While he modified his position with regard to the sciences and the arts, he strengthened it against luxury. When he wrote of 'luxury' in this context he was not only making a social or moral objection: that some live in opulence while others starve. He was making a direct challenge to the prevailing economic orthodoxy. Following the success of Mandeville's *The Fable of the Bees* and Melon's *Political Essay on Commerce*, luxury had come to be regarded as the most desirable and efficient agent of wealth, the most beneficial to society. Private vices brought public benefits, envy and vanity encouraged industry. Through luxury came progress; Voltaire, among many others, had sung its praises. In focusing his attention here Rousseau moved from being a moralist in the classical tradition to become a bitter and specific critic of his own society.

Observations in reply to the King of Poland

In establishing the new law it was not to scholars that Jesus Christ wanted to entrust his doctrine and his ministry. He followed in his choice the preference he always showed for the simple and childlike. And in the instructions he gave to his disciples one does not see a word about study or science . . . After his death a dozen poor fishermen and artisans undertook to instruct and convert the whole world. Their method was simple; they preached without art but with a full heart, and of all the miracles with which God honoured their faith

the most striking was the holiness of their lives. Their disciples [in
45　turn] followed their example and the success was prodigious . . .

[Then the church was attacked.] It was necessary to take up the
pen in self-defence. The Christians attacked the pagans in turn; to
attack them was to conquer them; the first successes encouraged
other writers. Under the pretext of exposing the depravity of paganism
people threw themselves into mythology and scholarship. They
wanted to display wit and learning, crowds of books appeared, and
morals began to grow slack. Soon no one was content any more with
the simplicity of the Gospel and the faith of the apostles; it was
always necessary to be cleverer than your predecessors. Subtleties
were extracted from every dogma; everyone wanted to maintain his
own opinion, no one wanted to agree . . .

[Then Christians themselves] became furious persecutors, worse
47　than the heathen . . .

[Today] science spreads and faith vanishes. Everyone wants to
teach good behaviour, no one wants to learn it. We have all become
48　doctors, and we have ceased to be Christians.

It was not with so much art and apparatus that the Gospel was
spread across the world and its overwhelming beauty filled the
hearts of men. This sacred book, the only one necessary for a
Christian . . . needs only to be meditated to convey to the soul the
love of its author, and the desire to fulfil his commands. Never has
virtue spoken such a gentle language; never has the most profound
wisdom been expressed with so much energy and simplicity. You
cannot leave off reading it without feeling better than you were
49　before . . .

However: let us not conclude that it is necessary today to burn
all the libraries and destroy the universities and academies. We
will only plunge Europe once again into barbarism, and our morals
will gain nothing from that. It is with grief that I am going to pronounce a great and fatal truth. There is only one step from knowledge
to ignorance; and the change from one to the other is common
among nations. But a people once corrupted has never been seen
to return to virtue. In vain do you suppose you destroy the sources
of evil; in vain do you do away with whatever feeds vanity, idleness
and luxury; in vain would you lead men back to that first equality,
preserver of innocence and source of all virtue. Once spoiled their
hearts will always be so. There is no remedy now, other than some
great revolution almost as much to be feared as the evil it could cure,
and which it is wrong to desire and impossible to foresee.

So let us leave the sciences and the arts to sweeten in some way the ferocity of the men whom they have corrupted. Let us try to make a wise distraction and work to alter their passions. Let us offer some sustenance to these tigers, so that they do not devour our children. When the evil is incurable the doctor applies palliatives, and matches the cure less to the needs than to the character of the disease.   55–6

Last Reply to M. Bordes

The sciences are the masterpieces of genius and reason . . . We are beholden to the mechanical arts for a great number of useful inventions which have added to the charms and conveniences of life. But let us consider how this knowledge relates to morals.

If heavenly intelligences cultivate the sciences only good will result; I have said as much about great men who are made to guide the others . . . But the faults of ordinary men poison the most elevated knowledge and make it harmful to nations. Wicked men draw many harmful things from it: the good draw little advantage . . .   72

[It is maintained that] luxury can be necessary to give bread to the poor. But if there was no luxury there would be no poor. Luxury feeds a hundred poor in our towns, and makes a hundred thousand starve in our countryside. The money which circulates in the hands of the rich and the artists, to provide for their superfluities, is lost for the subsistence of the labourer. The waste of provisions that goes to feed men is alone enough to make luxury hateful to humanity . . . There must be sauce in our kitchens; that is why so many sick have no soup. There must be liqueurs on our table; that is why the peasant only drinks water. There must be powder on our wigs; that is why so many poor have no bread . . . Luxury serves to support states as caryatids serve to support the palaces that they decorate; or rather, as beams with which one often props up rotten buildings, and which often end by bringing them down . . .   79 & n

It is put forward that the first men were wicked; from which it follows that man is naturally wicked . . . The annals of all the peoples that anyone dares to cite in proof are very much more favourable to the opposite belief . . . Before these horrible words of 'yours' and 'mine' were invented, before there was that cruel and brutal kind of men called masters, and that other kind of men, rascals and liars, called slaves; before there were men abominable enough to dare to have an excess while other men were dying of hunger; before a

mutual dependence had forced them all to become deceitful, jealous and treacherous, I would very much like someone to explain what
80 these vices and crimes could have consisted of . . .

It is put forward that ignorant nations who have had 'ideas of glory and virtue are particular exceptions which do not support any prejudice against the sciences . . . Look at Africa [it is said] where no mortal has yet been bold enough to penetrate or lucky enough to have tried to do so with impunity.' In other words, from somewhere we have not been able to venture, in the continent of Africa, where we are ignorant of what happens, we are asked to conclude that the people are full of vices.

Only if we were to have found the means of taking our own faults there must that conclusion necessarily follow. If I were the leader of one of the peoples of Nigritia,* I declare that I would set up on the frontier of the country a gallows where I would hang without appeal the first European who dared to venture in, and the first citizen who
90-1 would dare to venture out.

Preface to Narcissus

The Hobbeses and the Mandevilles and a thousand others have affected to distinguish themselves, and their dangerous doctrine has so borne fruit that . . . one is terrified to see how far our reasoning century has pushed the duties of man and citizen in its maxims.

The taste for letters, philosophy and the fine arts destroys the love of our first duties and of true glory. When talent has once laid claim to the honours due to virtue, everyone wants to be a charming person and none is concerned to be a good man. From this is born another inconsistency, that men are only rewarded for qualities that do not depend on themselves. Because our talents are born with us, our
966 virtues alone depend on us.

The taste for philosophy weakens all the bonds of respect and goodwill which attach men to society, and this is perhaps the most dangerous of the evils which it produces. The charm of study soon makes all other attachments insipid. Moreover, as a result of reflecting on humanity and observing men, the philosopher learns to judge them according to their worth, and it is difficult to have much affection for what one despises. Soon he retains in his own person all the interest that virtuous men share with their fellows. His

* Sudan.

contempt for others builds up his pride; his love of himself increases in proportion to his indifference to the rest of the universe. Family, *patrie*, become for him words empty of meaning; he is neither parent, citizen, nor man. He is a philosopher . . .   967

There is more; and of all the truths that I have put forward in considering wise men here is the most astonishing and cruel. All our writers regard as the masterpiece of politics in this century those sciences, arts, luxury, commerce, laws and other things which tighten the bonds of society among men [only] by personal interest; which put them all in mutual dependence, with reciprocal needs and common interests, so that everyone is obliged to compete with the goodness of others in order to be able to promote his own . . . It is a very remarkable thing to have put men in the impossibility of living among one another without standing in one another's way, usurping one another, deceiving one another, betraying one another, and mutually destroying one another! From now on we must take care not to allow ourselves ever to be seen as we are; because, for every two men whose interests agree, a hundred thousand perhaps are opposed to them, and there is no way of succeeding but to deceive or lose all those other people.

Here is the fatal source of the violence, betrayals, treacheries and all the horrors which are necessarily entailed in a state of things where each, pretending to work for the fortune and reputation of others, is only looking [for an opportunity] to raise his own above them and at their expense . . . Strange and fatal system, where accumulated wealth always facilitates the means of acquiring greater wealth, and where it is impossible for him who has nothing to acquire anything; where the honest man has no means of escaping misery, where the most unscrupulous are the most honoured, and where it is necesssary to renounce virtue to become an honest man! I know that orators have said all this a thousand times; but they spoke rhetorically and I give reasons. They have seen the evil, I reveal the causes of that evil; and, above all, I lay bare something very consoling and very useful by showing that all the vices belong not so much to man, as to man badly governed.   968-9

In Europe the government, laws, customs, and [personal] interest all put individuals in the necessity of mutually and continually deceiving one another. Everything makes duty a vice to them. They must be wicked to be wise, for there is no greater stupidity than doing good for rascals at one's own expense.

Among the savages personal interest speaks as strongly as among us, but it does not say the same things. The love of society and the care for common protection are the only bonds which unite them. This word property, which causes so many crimes to our honest people, has almost no meaning among them. They do not have any discussion of interests which divide them. Nothing leads them to deceive one another. Public esteem is the only good to which they aspire and which they value. It is very possible that a savage does a bad deed, but it is not possible that he does wrong habitually, for that would do nothing for him . . . I say with regret: the good man is he who has no need of deceiving anyone, and the savage is that

969 n. man.*

[The last of these pieces, written after the *First Discourse*, is an unfinished fragment, full of sombre promise.]

Preface to a Second Letter to Bordes

103 I believe I have discovered great things . . .

I am going to take up the thread of my ideas and continue to write as I have always done, as an isolated being who neither wants nor fears anyone, who speaks to others for their sake and not for his; a man who holds his brothers too dear not to hate their vices, and who would like them to learn for once to see themselves as wicked as they are, to desire at least to make themselves as good as they could be.

I know very well that the trouble I am taking is useless, and in my efforts I do not have the fanciful pleasure of reforming men . . . I know that they will be no less greedy for glory and money when I have convinced them that these two passions are the source of all their evils, and that they are wicked because of the one and unhappy because of the other . . . But I prefer to brave their abuse than to

104 share their failings.

This sad and great system, product of a sincere examination of the nature of man, his faculties and his future, is dear to me, although it humiliates me. For I am aware how important it is that our pride should not mislead us about what should be our true nobility, and how much there is to be feared that, in wishing to raise ourselves

105 above our nature, we only fall below it . . .

* 'The great rule of morality', Rousseau wrote later in his *Confessions*, 'perhaps the only one that is useful in practice, [is] to avoid those situations which put our duties in opposition to our interests, and which show us our [own] good in another person's evil.'[7] One of his concerns in *The Social Contract* was 'to reconcile what right permits with what interest prescribes, so that justice and utility are not divided'.[8]

5 INEQUALITY

The subject set by the Academy of Dijon for a prize essay in 1753 was: 'What is the origin of the inequality among men and has it been authorized by natural law?' In his answer Rousseau concentrated on the first part of the question. He was concerned less with natural law than with natural man, man as he was before human society. This was an essential preliminary to any discussion of natural law. Hobbes had asserted that in a state of nature men, being motivated only by an aggressive self-interest, ambition and greed, must have lived in a state of perpetual war. This conception was what Rousseau set out to replace.

His essay was part-hypothetical, part-historical. It owed something to classical writers, to recent travel literature, and to natural history, particularly the work of Buffon, which he held in high regard. But it was also, to some extent, imaginative; an evocation and an appeal. Against the view of man as grasping and selfish Rousseau put forward the image of man as free and innocent.

'Let us begin by setting aside all the facts', he wrote. This remark, which has caused much comment, can be taken several ways. It can be seen as a rejection of the Biblical account of the origins of man, without overtly saying so. It can be seen as an admission of the imperfect state of our knowledge about primitive man — 'the whole earth is covered with nations of whom we know nothing except their names'[1] — and the resulting inadequacy of what facts we have. Or it can be seen as an affirmation of the conjectural quality of the work, alongside the remark that the state of nature 'no longer exists, [and] perhaps never did exist'. In this sense Rousseau was talking about the essential character of human nature, man as he is outside (as well as before) society, now and at all times. This hypothetical element goes hand-in-hand with the historical account.

The First Part of the *Discourse* portrays man in a state of nature. In the Second Part Rousseau showed how man's original qualities had been lost through subsequent developments. He suggested four main stages: first, natural man, before language or society; second, men settling in families and villages, early society; third, the development of agriculture and metallurgy, and the institution of property, society became a state of war; fourth, the start of government and political order, which reinforced the unequal conditions that arose in the third stage.

The *Discourse* is not only a work of great breadth and rich suggestion. It is also of major historical significance. If Rousseau had written nothing but this he would still be remembered today. What he had put forward was a secular version of the fall of man, in which the institution of property and the division of labour took the place of eating the forbidden fruit, and in which the perpetuation of inequalities replaced original sin. Man was not naturally bad, he had become so; and the cause of this lay less in him than in the social forms in which he had become trapped. The *Discourse* takes human affairs out of all religious frameworks; it transforms what had previously been the central religious questions into social and political questions. What we are is the result of our own development. Furthermore, treated in this way, the questions were given an evolutionary dimension. A sense of change is essential to the theory. The implications of all this were truly revolutionary.

They remained, at this stage, no more than implications. There was nothing hopeful in this picture. Of the two qualities Rousseau picked out as distinguishing men from animals, one was freedom and the other was the faculty of improving himself. (He called this second faculty 'perfectibility', a word he seems to have been the first to use.) The first has become stifled and the second developed out of all proportion, with disastrous consequences. All our progress had taken us further away from our natural condition, which had not been evil or miserable, but good and peaceful. Inside the theory of social evolution there was a theory of personal alienation. This aspect of the *Discourse* was also to be of great significance.

Despite its ending, however, there is a clear indication that this work is not conclusive. It is, rather, an essential first step. 'People begin by looking for the rules which it would be expedient for men to agree on for their common utility; and then give the name of natural law to this collection of rules, with no further proof than the good which they suppose would result from the universal practice of them.'[2] 'Under the pompous name of the study of man everyone does scarcely anything except study the men of his own country.'[3] The first task should be rather to discover what man is, naturally, and that means making no compromises with the *status quo*.

It is true that at this stage Rousseau accepts the version of the social contract put forward by Locke and the theorists of the Natural Law school, the contract of submission, as opposed to the contract of association which he will develop later. But his remarks on the theory are inconclusive; he says that 'the investigations into the nature of the pact fundamental to all government still remain to be made' (see p. 63). In this work therefore he is laying the foundations on which his mature work will be based.

The *Discourse* moves from a remote and happy past to a grim and forbidding future, where the only value is a cash-value and the only government is despotism. But while he was not hopeful Rousseau did not accept this development as inevitable. He had an alternative, by way of contrast. This was Geneva. The more comprehensive his criticism of Paris and French society grew, the more he needed an image to set against it. He had always been proud of his native city, its history of freedom and its ideal of responsible citizenship. He now identified himself with the city publicly by writing a long dedication to the Republic of Geneva, which he put at the front of his *Discourse*. The dedication spells out the conditions for a good state: it should be limited in size, with a democratic constitution, not interested in foreign conquest, with general assemblies deciding on the most important matters; a free people, used to and able to use their freedom, with no one above the law, and 'no other masters than the wise laws you have made, administered by honest magistrates you have chosen'.[4]

In the summer of 1754, when he had completed the *Discourse* and this dedication, Rousseau went to Geneva for a stay of several months. He was received back into the Protestant Church and claimed his rights as a citizen. In the autumn he returned to Paris. His essay did not win the prize but the following year it was published in Amsterdam. The epigraph was from Aristotle: 'Not in corrupt things but in those which are well ordered according to nature should one consider what is natural.'[5]

Discourse on the Origin and Foundations of Inequality among Men

PREFACE

Like the statue of Glaucus, which was so disfigured by time, the sea and storms that it looked less like a god than a wild beast, the human soul [has been] altered in society by a thousand perpetually recurring causes, by the acquisition of a multitude of truths and errors, by the changes happening to the constitution of the body, and by the continual conflict of the passions... [It has] so changed in appearance as to be hardly recognizable. Instead of a creature acting constantly from fixed and invariable principles, instead of that celestial and majestic simplicity impressed on it by its divine author, we find only the frightful contrast of passion mistaking itself for reason, and of understanding grown delirious . . .

122

Let not my readers imagine that I flatter myself with having seen what appears to me so difficult to discover. I have entered here upon certain arguments, and risked some conjectures, less in the hope of solving the difficulty than with a view to throwing some light upon it, and reducing the question to its proper form. Others may easily proceed farther on the same road, and yet no one find it easy to get to the end. For it is by no means a light undertaking to distinguish properly between what is original and what is artificial in the actual nature of man, or to form a true idea of a state which no longer exists, perhaps never did exist, and probably never will exist; and of which it is, nevertheless, necessary to have true ideas in order to form a proper judgement of our present state . . .

123

As long as we are ignorant of the natural man, it is in vain for us to attempt to determine either the law originally prescribed to him, or that which is best adapted to his constitution . . .

Throwing aside therefore all those scientific books which teach us only to see men such as they have made themselves, and contemplating the first and most simple operations of the human soul, I think I can see in it two principles prior to reason: one of them interests us deeply in our own welfare and preservation, and the other inspires us with a natural repugnance at seeing any other feeling creature, and particularly any of our own species, suffer pain or death. It is from the agreement and combination which the understanding is in a position to establish between these two principles, without its being necessary to introduce that of sociability, that all the rules of natural right appear to me to be derived — rules which our reason is afterwards obliged to establish on other foundations, when by its successive developments it has been led to suppress nature itself.

In proceeding thus, we shall not be obliged to make man a philosopher before he is a man. His duties towards others are not dictated to him only by the later lessons of wisdom; and, so long as he does not resist the internal impulses of compassion, he will never hurt any other man, nor even any feeling creature, except on those lawful occasions on which his own preservation is concerned and he is obliged to give himself the preference . . .   125–6

INTRODUCTION

The subject of the present discourse is this: To mark, in the progress of things, the moment at which right took the place of violence and nature became subject to law, and to explain by what sequence of miracles the strong came to submit to serve the weak, and the people to purchase imaginary peace at the expense of real happiness . . .   132

Let us begin by setting aside all the facts, for they do not affect the question . . .

Oh man, of whatever country you are, and whatever your opinions may be, listen: here is your history, such as I have thought to read it, not in books written by your fellow-creatures, who are liars, but in nature, which never lies . . . All that comes from her will be true . . .

The times of which I am going to speak are very remote; how much are you changed from what you once were! It is, so to speak, the life of your species which I am going to write, after the qualities which you have received, which your education and habits may have depraved, but cannot have destroyed entirely . . .

Discontented with your present state, for reasons which threaten your unfortunate descendants with still greater discontent, you will perhaps wish it were in your power to go back; and this feeling should be a panegyric on your first ancestors, a criticism of your contemporaries, and a terror to those who have the misfortune to come after you.   133

PART ONE

If we consider man just as he must have come from the hands of nature, we behold in him an animal weaker than some, and less agile than others; but taking him all round, the most advantageously equipped of any. I see him satisfying his hunger at the first oak, and slaking his thirst at the first brook; finding his bed at the foot of the tree which afforded him a meal; and with that, all his wants supplied.

134–5

While the earth was left to its natural fertility and covered with immense forests, whose trees were never mutilated by the axe, it would present on every side both sustenance and shelter for every species of animal. Men, dispersed up and down among the rest, would observe and imitate their industry, and thus attain even to the instinct of the beast . . .

135

With regard to those animals that do have more strength than man has skill, he is in the same position as all weaker animals, which notwithstanding are still able to subsist . . .

Add to this that it does not appear that any animal naturally makes war on man, except in the case of self-defence or excessive hunger . . . This is doubtless why negroes and savages are so little afraid of the wild beasts they may meet in the woods . . .

136–7

We should beware of confusing the savage man with the man we have daily in front of our eyes. Nature treats all the animals left to her care with a predilection that seems to show how jealous she is of that right. The horse, the cat, the bull, and even the ass are generally of greater stature and always more robust, and have more vigour, strength and courage when they run wild in the forests than when bred in the stall. By becoming domesticated they lose half these advantages; and it seems as if all our care to feed and treat them well serves only to deprave them. It is thus with man also; as he becomes sociable and a slave he grows weak, timid and servile . . .

139

Every animal has ideas, since it has senses; it even combines those ideas in a certain degree; and it is only in degree than man differs, in this respect, from the beast . . . It is not therefore so much the understanding that constitutes the specific difference between man and the beast, as the human quality of free agency. Nature lays her command on every animal and the beast obeys her. Man receives the same impulsion, but at the same time knows himself at liberty to acquiesce or resist; and it is particularly in his consciousness of this liberty that the spirituality of his soul is displayed. For physics may explain, to some measure, the mechanism of the senses and the formation of ideas; but in the power of willing, or rather of choosing, and in the feeling of this power, nothing is to be found but acts which are purely spiritual and wholly inexplicable by the laws of mechanism.

Another specific quality which distinguishes [the man from the animal] is the faculty of improving himself which, by the help of circumstances, gradually develops all the rest of his faculties, and

is inherent in the species as in the individual . . . [Rousseau calls
this faculty 'perfectibility'.] It would be sad were we forced to admit
that this distinctive and almost unlimited faculty is the source of all
human misfortune; that it is this which, in time, draws man out of
his original state, in which he would have spent his days in peace
and innocence; that it is this faculty which, successively producing in
different ages his discoveries and his errors, his vices and his virtues,
makes him at length a tyrant both over himself and over nature.   141–2

The passions originate in our wants, and their progress depends
on that of our knowledge; for we cannot desire or fear anything
except from the idea we have of it, or from the simple impulse of
nature. Now savage man, being destitute of every kind of enlightenment, can have no passions save those of the latter kind; his desires
never go beyond his physical wants. The only goods he recognizes
in the universe are food, a female and sleep; the only evils he fears
are pain and hunger . . .   143

His imagination paints no pictures; his heart makes no demands
on him. His few wants are so readily supplied and he is so far from
having the knowledge which is needful to make him want more
that he can have neither foresight nor curiosity . . . His soul, which
nothing disturbs, is wholly wrapped up in the feeling of its present
existence, without any idea of the future, however near at hand; while
his projects, as limited as his views, hardly extend to the close of the
day . . . The more we reflect on this subject, the greater appears the
distance between pure sensation and the most simple knowledge.   144

[Rousseau then discusses how only with the development of
language was man able to reflect, and develop his knowledge, and
how language only developed with society. His views were developed
at greater length in his *Essay on the Origin of Languages*.]

I know it is incessantly repeated that man in such a state would
have been the most miserable of creatures . . . but if I understand the
word 'miserable' it either has no meaning at all, or else signifies
only a painful deprivation of something, or a state of suffering
either in body or soul. I should be glad to have explained to me what
kind of misery a free being, whose heart is at ease and whose body
is in health, can possibly suffer . . . I ask if it was ever known that
a savage took it into his head, when at liberty, to complain of life or
to do away with himself.   151–2

It appears . . . that men in a state of nature, having no moral relations or known duties, could not be either good or bad, virtuous
or vicious . . . [But] let us not conclude with Hobbes, that because

man has no idea of goodness, he must be naturally wicked; that he is vicious because he does not know virtue; that he always refuses to do his fellow-creatures services which he does not think they have a right to demand; or that by virtue of the right he justly claims to all he needs, he foolishly imagines himself the sole proprietor of the whole universe. Hobbes had seen clearly the defects of all modern definitions of natural right; but the consequences which he deduces from his own show that he understands it in an equally false sense. In reasoning on the principles he lays down, he ought to have said that the state of nature, being that in which the care for our own preservation is the least prejudicial to that of others, was consequently the best calculated to promote peace, and the most suitable for mankind. He says the exact opposite, in consequence of having improperly admitted, as a part of savage man's care for self-preservation, the gratification of a multitude of passions which are the 152–3 work of society, and have made laws necessary . . .

That man in the state of nature is both strong and dependent involves two contrary suppositions. Man is weak when he is dependent, and is his own master before he comes to be strong. Hobbes did not reflect that the same cause, which prevents a savage from making use of his reason, as our jurists hold, prevents him also from abusing his faculties, as Hobbes himself allows. So it may justly be said that savages are not bad precisely because they do not know what it is to be good; because it is neither the development of the understanding nor the restraint of the law that hinders them from doing ill, but 153–4 [rather] the peacefulness of their passions, and their ignorance of vice.

There is another principle which has escaped Hobbes — an innate repugnance at seeing a fellow-creature suffer. This has been bestowed on mankind to moderate, on certain occasions, the ferocity of self-interest — or the desire for self-preservation, before the birth of self-interest* — and tempers the ardour with which he pursues his own

* Self-interest must not be confused with self-love; for they differ both in themselves and their effects. Self-love is a natural feeling which leads every animal to look after its own preservation, and which, guided in man by reason and modified by compassion, creates humanity and virtue. Self-interest is purely a relative and factitious feeling, which arises in the state of society, leads each individual to make more of himself than of any other, [and] causes all the mutual damage men inflict on one another. This being understood, I maintain that, in our primitive condition in the true state of nature, self-interest did not exist; for as each man regarded himself as the only true observer of his actions, the only being in the universe who took any interest in him, and the sole judge of his own merit, no feeling could take root in his soul that arose from com-
219 parisons which he was not led to make . . . (Note by Rousseau.)

welfare. I think I need not fear contradiction in holding man to be possessed of the only natural virtue, which could not be denied him by the most violent detractor* of human virtues. I am speaking of compassion, which is a disposition suitable to creatures so weak and subject to so many evils as we certainly are. It is so much the more useful and universal to mankind as it comes before any kind of reflection, and at the same time [it is] so natural that the very beasts themselves sometimes give evident proofs of it. Not to mention the tenderness of mothers for their offspring and the perils they encounter to save them from danger, it is well known that horses show a reluctance to trample on living bodies. One animal never passes by the dead body of another of its species without disquiet; some even give their fellows a sort of burial; while the mournful lowings of the cattle when they enter the slaughter-house show the impression made on them by the horrible spectacle which meets them.   154

We find, with pleasure, the author of *The Fable of the Bees* obliged to own that man is a compassionate and feeling creature . . . Mandeville well knew that with all their morality men would never have been more than monsters, if nature had not given them pity to support reason. But he did not see that from that quality alone flow all the social virtues, of which he denied man the possession.

Indeed, what is generosity, clemency or humanity but compassion applied to the weak, to the guilty, or to mankind in general? Even benevolence and friendship are, if we judge rightly, only the effects of compassion, constantly fixed upon a particular object . . . Even if it were true that pity is no more than a feeling, which puts us in the place of the sufferer, a feeling obscure but lively in the savage, developed yet feeble in civilized man, this truth would have no other consequence than to confirm my argument. Compassion must in fact be the stronger the more the animal beholding any kind of distress identifies himself with the animal that suffers. Now, it is plain that such identification must have been much more perfect in a state of nature than it is in a state of reason.   155

It is reason that engenders self-interest, and reflection that confirms it; it is reason that turns man's mind back upon itself, and divides him from everything that could disturb or afflict him. It is philosophy that isolates him and bids him say, at sight of the misfortunes of others 'Perish if you will, I am secure.' Nothing but such general evils as threaten the whole community can disturb the tran-

* A reference to Mandeville.

quil sleep of the philosopher or tear him from his bed. A murder may be committed with impunity under his window; he has only to put his hands to his ears and argue a little with himself, to prevent nature, which is shocked within him, from identifying itself with the unfortunate sufferer. Savage man does not have this admirable talent, and for want of reason and wisdom, he is always foolishly ready to obey the first promptings of humanity . . .

It is then certain that compassion is a natural feeling which, by moderating the activity of self-love in each individual, contributes to the preservation of the whole species . . . It is this compassion which in a state of nature supplies the place of laws, morals and virtues . . . Although Socrates and people with minds like his might be able to acquire virtue by reason, the human race would long since have ceased to be, had its preservation depended only on the
156 reasonings of the individuals composing it . . .

Let us conclude then that man in a state of nature, wandering up and down the forest without industry, without speech and without home, an equal stranger to war and to all ties, neither standing in need of his fellow-men nor having any desire to hurt them and perhaps not even distinguishing them one from another, must have been self-sufficient and subject to few passions. He could have had no feelings or knowledge but such as befitted his situation; that he felt only his actual necessities, and disregarded everything he did not think himself immediately concerned to notice, and his understanding made no greater progress than his vanity . . . Centuries passed in all the roughness of the first ages; already the species was
159–60 old, and man remained always a child . . .

PART TWO

The first man who, having enclosed a piece of ground, took it into his head to say 'This is mine', and found people simple enough to believe him, was the real founder of civil society. From how many crimes, wars, and murders, from how many horrors and misfortunes might not any one have saved mankind, by pulling up the stakes, or filling up the ditch, and crying to his fellows: 'Beware of listening to this imposter; you are undone if you once forget that the fruits of
164 the earth belong to us all, and the earth itself to nobody.'*

* These words would have had particular force for some of Rousseau's readers, as enclosures were at this time being introduced in many parts of France.

[Rousseau marks out the stages which led to this point. First, men discover the possibility of occasionally grouping together for a common task. Then, men learn how to build shelters and family life begins: villages grow up, men live by hunting and fishing; this is the 'real youth of the world'.]

This period of the development of human faculties, keeping a just mean between the indolence of the primitive state and the petulant activity of our self-interest, must have been the happiest and most stable of epochs. The more we reflect on it, the more we shall find that this state was the least subject to revolutions, and altogether the very best man could experience. So that he can have departed from it only through some fatal accident which, for the public good, should never have happened. The example of savages, most of whom have been found in this state, seems to prove that men were meant to remain in it, that it is the real youth of the world, and that all subsequent advances have been in appearance so many steps towards the perfection of the individual, but in reality towards the decrepitude of the species . . .

So long as men undertook only what a single person could accomplish, and confined themselves to such arts as did not require the joint labour of several hands, they lived free, healthy, honest and happy lives, in so far as their nature allowed, and they continued to enjoy the pleasures of mutual and independent intercourse. But from the moment one man began to stand in need of the help of another; from the moment it appeared advantageous to any one man to have enough provisions for two, equality disappeared, property was introduced, work became necessary, and vast forests became smiling fields, which man had to water with the sweat of his brow, and where slavery and misery were soon to germinate and grow up with the crops. Metallurgy and agriculture were the two arts which produced this great revolution. The poets tell us it was gold and silver, but for the philosophers, it was iron and corn, which first civilized men and ruined humanity . . .   171

The cultivation of the earth necessarily brought about its distribution; and property, once recognized, gave rise to the first rules of justice; for, to secure each man his own, it had to be possible for each to have something. Besides, as men began to look forward to the future, and all had something to lose, every one had reason to apprehend that reprisals would follow any injury he might do another . . .   173

In this state of affairs, equality might have been sustained, had the talents of individuals been equal, and had, for example, the use of iron and the consumption of commodities always exactly balanced each other; but as there was nothing to preserve this balance it was soon disturbed. The strongest did most work; the most skilful turned his labour to best account; the most ingenious devised methods of diminishing his labour. The husbandman wanted more iron or the smith more corn, and while both laboured equally, the one gained a great deal by his work, while the other could hardly support himself. Thus natural inequality develops imperceptibly with that of combination, and the differences between men, developed by their different circumstances, become more acute and permanent in their effects, and begins to have an influence, in the same proportion, over the lot of

174   individuals.

It now became the interest of men to appear what they really were not. To be and to seem became two totally different things; and from this distinction sprang insolent pomp and cheating trickery with all the numerous vices that go in their train . . . In consequence of a multiplicity of new wants men were now brought into subjection, as it were, to all nature, and particularly to one another; and each became in some degree a slave even in becoming the master of other men. If rich, they stood in need of services of others; if poor, of their assistance; and even a middle condition did not enable them to do without one another. So each man must now have been perpetually employed in getting others to interest themselves in his lot, and in making them, apparently at least, if not really, find their advantage in his own . . . There arose rivalry and competition on the one hand, and conflicting interest on the other, together with a secret desire on both of profiting at the expense of others. All these evils were the first effects of property and the inseparable attendants of

174–5   growing inequality . . .

Usurpations by the rich, robbery by the poor, and the unbridled passions of both, suppressed the cries of natural compassion and the still feeble voice of justice, and filled men with avarice, ambition and vice. Between the title of the strongest and that of the first occupier there arose perpetual conflicts, which never ended but in battles and bloodshed. The new-born state of society thus gave rise to the horrible state of war.

It is impossible that men should not at length have reflected on so wretched a situation, and on the calamities that overwhelmed them. The rich, in particular, must have felt how much they suffered by a constant state of war, of which they bore all the expense; and in which, though all risked their lives, they alone risked their property.

Besides, however speciously they might disguise their usurpations, they knew that they were founded on precarious and false titles; so that if others took from them by force what they themselves had gained by force, they would have no reason to complain . . .   176

The rich having feelings, so to speak, in every part of their possessions, it was much easier to harm them and therefore most necessary for them to take precautions against it . . .   179–80

Thus urged by necessity, the rich conceived at length the profoundest plan that ever entered the mind of man: this was to employ in his favour the forces of those who attacked him, to make allies of his adversaries, to inspire them with different maxims, and to give them other institutions as favourable to himself as natural right was unfavourable . . .   177

All ran headlong to their chains, in hopes of securing their liberty; for they had wit enough to perceive the advantages of political institutions without experience enough to enable them to foresee the dangers . . . Such was, or may well have been, the origin of society and law, which bound new fetters on the poor, and gave new powers to the rich; which irretrievably destroyed natural liberty, eternally fixed the law of property and inequality, converted clever usurpation into unalterable right and, for the advantage of a few ambitious individuals, subjected all mankind to perpetual labour, slavery and wretchedness.

Societies soon multiplied and spread over the face of the earth till hardly a corner of the world was left in which a man could escape the yoke . . .

Natural fellow-feeling lost, when applied to societies, almost all the influence it had over individuals, and survived no longer except in some great cosmopolitan spirits.   178

[Rousseau now deals with the development of government. He rejects the view that anyone gave up his freedom willingly.]

Politicians indulge in the same sophistry about the love of liberty as philosophers have about the state of nature. They judge by what they see of very different things, which they have not seen; they attribute to man a natural propensity to servitude because the slaves within their observation are seen to bear the yoke with patience; they fail to reflect that it is with liberty as with innocence and virtue: the value is known only to those who possess them, and the taste for them is lost as soon as they are lost . . . An unbroken horse shakes his mane, paws the ground and starts back impetuously at the sight of the bridle, while one which is properly trained suffers patiently even whip and spur; so savage man will not bend his neck to the yoke to which civilized man submits without a murmur, but prefers the most turbulent state of liberty to the most peaceful slavery. We cannot therefore, from the servility of nations already enslaved, judge of the natural dispositions of mankind for or against slavery; we should go by the prodigious efforts of every free people to save itself from oppression . . . When I behold numbers of naked savages, that despise European pleasures, braving hunger, fire, the sword and death, to preserve nothing but their independence, I feel that it is not for slaves to argue about liberty . . .

181–2

I regard it as certain then, that government did not begin with arbitrary power, but that this is the depravity, the extreme term of government . . .

Without entering at present on the investigations which still remain to be made into the nature of the pact fundamental to all government, I limit myself to following the common opinion in considering the institution of the body politic as a real contract between the people and the leaders they choose for themselves: a contract by which the two parties obligate themselves to observe the laws therein expressed, which form the bonds of their union.

184

[In this version of the social contract the people agree to be governed: Rousseau has not yet developed his own distinctive version which keeps the government under the will of the people, though he says: 'If the magistrate, who has all the power in his own hands, and appropriates to himself all the advantages of the contract, has none the less a right to renounce his authority, the people, who suffer for all the faults of their leader, must have a much better right to renounce their dependence' (185–6). But he regards this as 'a dangerous power'. He then depicts how governments came to abuse their authority.]

Intrigues set in, factions were formed, parties grew bitter, civil wars broke out; the lives of individuals were sacrificed to the supposed happiness of the state . . .

Ambitious leaders profited from these circumstances to perpetuate their offices in their own families; at the same time the people, already used to dependence, ease, and the conveniences of life, and already incapable of breaking its chains, agreed to an increase in its slavery, in order to secure its tranquillity . . .

If we follow the progress of inequality . . . we shall find that the establishment of laws and of the right of property was its first stage, the institution of magistracy the second, and the conversion of legitimate into arbitrary power the third and last . . . at which stage all the rest remain, when they have got so far, till the government is either entirely dissolved by new revolutions, or brought back again to legitimacy.   187

To understand this progress as necessary we must consider not so much the motives for the establishment of the body politic, as the forms it assumes in actuality, and the faults that necessarily attend it; for the flaws which make social institutions necessary are the same as make the abuse of them unavoidable . . . It would be easy to prove that every government which scrupulously complied with the ends for which it was instituted, and guarded carefully against change and corruption, was set up unnecessarily. For a country in which no one either evaded the laws or made a bad use of magisterial power could require neither laws nor magistrates . . .   187–8

Individuals only allow themselves to be oppressed so far as they are hurried on by blind ambition; by looking below rather than above them, they come to love domination more than independence, and submit to slavery so that they may enslave others. It is no easy matter to reduce to obedience a man who has no ambition to command; nor would the most skilful politician find it possible to enslave a people whose only desire was to be independent.

If this were the place to go into details, I could readily explain how, even without the intervention of government, inequality of credit and authority became unavoidable among private persons, as soon as their union in a single society made them compare themselves with one another, and take into account the difference which they found from the continual intercourse every man had to have with his neighbours. These differences are of several kinds; but riches, nobility or rank, power and personal merit being the principal distinctions by which men form an estimate of each other in society, I could prove that the harmony or conflict of these different forces is the surest indication of the good or bad constitution of a state.

I could show that among these four kinds of inequality, personal qualities being the origin of all the others, wealth is the one to which they are all reduced in the end; for as riches tend most immediately to the prosperity of individuals, and are easiest to communicate, they are used to purchase every other distinction. By this observation we are enabled to judge pretty exactly how far a people has departed from its primitive constitution and of its progress towards the extreme term of corruption. [From a survey] of all the different aspects under   188–9
which inequality has up to the present appeared, or may yet appear

. . . we should see oppression continually gain ground without its being possible for the oppressed to know where it would stop, or what legitimate means was left them of checking its progress. We should see the rights of citizens and the freedom of nations slowly extinguished, and the complaints, protests, and appeals of the weak treated as seditious murmurings . . .

From great inequality of fortunes and conditions, from the vast variety of passions and of talents, of useless and pernicious arts, of vain sciences, would arise a multitude of prejudices equally contrary to reason, happiness and virtue. We should see the magistrates fomenting everything that might weaken men united in society, by promoting dissension among them; everything that might sow in it the seeds of actual division, while it gave society the air of harmony; everything that might inspire the different ranks of people with mutual hatred and distrust, by setting the rights and interests of one against those of another, and so strengthen the power which com-

190 prehended them all.

It is in the midst of this disorder and these revolutions that despotism, gradually raising up its hideous head and devouring everything it saw that was sound and good in any part of the state, would at length trample on both the laws and the people, and establish itself on the ruins of the republic. The times which immediately preceded this last change would be times of trouble and calamity; but at length the monster would swallow up everything, and the people would no longer have either leaders or laws, but only tyrants. From this moment there would be no question of virtue or morality; for despotism wherever it prevails admits no other master; as soon as it speaks there is no honesty or duty to consult; the blindest obedience is the only virtue which is left to the slaves.

This is the last term of inequality, the extreme point that closes the circle, and meets that from which we set out. Here all private persons return to the law of the strongest, and so to a new state of nature, differing from that we set out from; for the one was a state of nature in its first purity, while this is the consequence of excessive corruption. There is so little difference between the two states in other respects, and the contract of government is so completely dissolved by despotism, that the despot is master only so long as he remains the strongest; as soon as he can be expelled, he has no right to complain of violence. The popular insurrection that ends in the death or deposition of a Sultan is as lawful an act as those by which he disposed, the day before, of the fortunes and lives of his subjects.

As he was maintained by force alone, it is force alone that overthrows
him . . .   191

If the reader thus discovers and retraces the lost and forgotten
road, by which man must have passed from the state of nature to
the state of society; if he carefully restores . . . those which want of
time has compelled me to suppress, or my imagination has failed
to suggest, he cannot fail to be struck by the vast distance which
separates the two states. It is in tracing this slow succession that he
will find the solution to a number of problems of politics and morals,
which philosophers cannot settle . . . He will explain how the soul
and the passions of men alter unawares, changing as it were their
nature; why our wants and pleasure in the end seek new objects; and
why, the original man having vanished by degrees, society offers to
us only an assembly of artificial men and factitious passions, which
are the work of all these new relations, and without any real foundation in nature. We are taught nothing on this subject by reflection
that is not entirely confirmed by observation. The savage and the
civilized man differ so much in the bottom of their hearts and their
inclinations that what constitutes the supreme happiness of one
would reduce the other to despair. The former breathes only peace
and liberty; he desires only to live and be free from labour . . .
Civilized man, on the other hand, is always moving, sweating,
worrying, and tormenting himself to find still more laborious
occupations; he works himself to death, and even hurries on towards
it, to put himself in a position to live, or he renounces life to acquire
immortality . . .   191–2

In reality, the source of all these differences is that the savage
lives within himself, while the social man lives constantly outside
himself; he only knows how to live in the opinion of others, so that
he seems to receive the consciousness of his own existence merely
from the judgement of others concerning him . . . Always asking
others what we are, and never daring to ask ourselves . . . we have
nothing to show for ourselves but a frivolous and deceitful appearance,
honour without virtue, reason without wisdom, and pleasure without
happiness . . .   193

It follows from this survey that, as there is hardly any inequality
in the state of nature, all the inequality which now prevails owes its
strength and growth to the development of our faculties and the
advance of the human mind, and becomes at last permanent and
legitimate by the establishment of property and laws. Secondly, it
follows that moral inequality, authorized by positive right alone,

clashes with natural right, whenever it is not proportionate to physical inequality — a distinction which sufficiently determines what we ought to think of that species of inequality which prevails in all civilized countries; since it is plainly contrary to the law of nature, however defined, that children should command old men, fools wise men, and that the privileged few should gorge themselves with superfluities, while the starving multitude are in want of the bare 193–4 necessities.

[Rousseau attached several long notes to this *Discourse* when he published it. In one of them, Note XV, he had made the distinction between self-love and self-interest, quoted above. In another, Note IX, he continued his attack on the economic arguments of Mandeville and those who favoured luxury.]

What can one think of a commerce where the reason of each individual dictates to him rules that are directly contrary to those which public reason preaches to society as a whole, and where each 202 finds his profit in the misfortune of another? . . .

Let us reflect what must be the state of things where all men are forced mutually to caress and destroy one another, and where they 203 are born enemies by duty and swindlers by interest . . .

Man in society . . . first needs the necessary, then the superfluous; then come delicacies, and then immense wealth, and then subjects, and then slaves. He does not have a moment's relaxation, and, what is more remarkable, the less natural and pressing his needs, the more his passions increase and, worse still, the power of gratifying them. So that after a long course of prosperity, having swallowed up quantities of treasure and ruined innumerable men, our hero will end up slaughtering everyone until he is sole master of the universe . . .

Consider the troubles of the mind which consume us, the violent passions which exhaust and ruin us, the excessive labours which overwhelm the poor, the still more dangerous indolence which occupies the rich, and which make the former die of want and the latter of excess . . . [Then] you will see how dearly nature makes us 203–4 pay for the scorn with which we have treated her lessons.

Luxury is a remedy a great deal worse than the evil it is supposed to cure; or rather, it is itself the worst of all evils in any state, however large or small. To feed the crowds of servants and paupers that it has made, it brings oppression and ruin on the labourer and the citizen. It is like those scorching winds of the *Midi* which, covering the grass and the fields with devouring insects, deprive useful animals of their 206 food and bring poverty and death wherever they occur.

[In another note, Note X, Rousseau made some speculations about early man and the possibility that some apes may have been our ancestors.]⁶

[I wonder whether] various animals [who are] similar to men, who have been taken by travellers without much examination to be animals — either because of some differences they noticed in their external structure, or only because these animals did not talk — may not in fact have really been primitive men . . .   208

[He quotes the descriptions of orang-utangs, as examples.]

   Hasty judgements, which are not the product of enlightened reason, are apt to be extreme. Under the names of Pongos, Mandrills, Orang-Utang, our travellers take . . . for animals the same creatures that the people of the ancient world, under the names of Satyrs, Fauns, Sylvans, took for divinities. Perhaps after more exact research they will be found to be men . . .   211

When Voltaire read this *Discourse* he wrote to Rousseau: 'I have received your new book against the human race . . . Never has so much talent been used to want to make us into animals; you make one want to walk on all fours . . . However, as it is more than sixty years since I lost the habit, I feel unfortunately that it will be impossible for me to regain it . . .'

He continued: 'I agree with you that literature and the sciences have sometimes caused a lot of evil', and then instanced the persecution and trouble that Galileo, or the Encyclopedists or he himself had suffered. 'Admit, Sir', he went on, 'the thorns attached to literature and a bit to reputation are only flowers compared to the other ills which at all times have overwhelmed the earth. Admit that Petrarch and Boccaccio did not produce the troubles of Italy . . .

   'Great crimes have mostly been committed by famous fools. What makes and will always make this world a vale of tears is the insatiable greed and unconquerable pride of men . . . literature nourishes the soul, corrects it, consoles it; it even makes you famous while you are writing against it . . .'⁷

In his reply Rousseau made some important comments on the arts as he now saw them.

Letter to Voltaire, 10 September 1755

226   I do not aspire to re-establish us in our animality, although I greatly regret, for my part, the little that I have lost . . .

In the progress of things there are hidden connections which the uninstructed do not see, but which will not escape the eyes of the wise man if he cares to think about it. It was not Terence, or Cicero, or Virgil, or Seneca, or Tacitus; it was not the scholars or poets who produced the misfortunes of Rome and the crimes of the Romans. But without the slow and secret poison which was corrupting little by little the most vigorous government history has known, neither Cicero nor Lucretius could either have existed or written at all . . .

The taste for literature and the arts is born in a people from an inner fault which it [in turn] increases; and if it is true that all human progress is harmful to the species, that of the mind and learning, which increases our pride and multiplies our mistakes, soon accelerates our misfortunes. But there comes a time when the evil is such that the very causes which have produced it are necessary to prevent it increasing; it is the knife that must be left in the wound, for fear that the wounded man would die if it were taken out.

As for me, if I had followed my original vocation* and if I had neither read nor written, I would undoubtedly have been more happy. Nevertheless, if literature was now abolished I would be deprived of the only pleasure that remains to me. It is in its company that I console myself for all my ills; it is among those who cultivate it that I taste the pleasures of friendship and learn to enjoy life without

227   fearing death. I owe to it the little that I am . . .

[He again makes the distinction he had made between 'great geniuses' and 'ordinary people' (see p. 43), saying that the latter should not take on the tasks suitable only to the former, and concluded:]

Let us look for the first sources of the disorders of society; we will find that all the evils of men come to them more from error than ignorance, and that what we don't know harms us a lot less than what we think we know. What surer way can there be of running

228   from mistake to mistake, than the craze for knowing everything?

Another criticism of the *Discourse on Inequality* came from Charles Bonnet, a distinguished naturalist and citizen of Geneva, who wrote

* As an engraver.

under the name of M. Philopolis. He maintained that the state of
society reflected the faculties of man, which in turn reflected the
work of God; we are the products of perfect wisdom. 'In the name
of good sense and reason let us take man as he is . . . let us let the
world turn as it will, and let us be sure that it will go on as well as
it can go.'[8] He also expressed astonishment that Rousseau might
prefer to go and live in the woods.

The extended simile which Rousseau used, in answering these
criticisms, is revealing. He had written, in his *Observations* to the
King of Poland, that 'a people once corrupted has never been seen
to return to virtue' (see p. 45). He held this belief throughout his
life; it is set out clearly in *The Social Contract* (Bk III, Ch. 10).
From the evidence of history he concluded that the way society had
evolved had never yet been an improvement. While the faculty of
perfecting himself was the source of man's distinctive achievement it
had also been the cause of his deterioration. Rousseau admired some
of the republics of the classical world not only because of the recorded
historical facts, but also because the people of the ancient world,
'being the first, were [therefore] closest to nature'.[9] As men grow old,
so also does human society.

Nevertheless, the purpose of his simile is to clarify the essential
distinction and difference between the nature of man and that of
society. The form which the latter takes is not an inevitable consequence of human nature. It can be altered or changed. Rousseau
refuses to accept that the way things are in society is the way they
have to be.

Letter to M. Philopolis

[Rousseau takes up the initial point made against him; that to criticize the state of society was, in effect, to attack the work of God.]

Let us suppose that some scholars found one day the secret of
hastening old age and the knack of encouraging men to make use
of this rare discovery. A matter of persuasion which would not
perhaps be as difficult to accomplish as it may at first sight appear.
For reason, that great medium of all our madnesses, would not
prevent us from missing out on this one. Intellectuals in particular
and intelligent people, to shake off the yoke of the passions and to
taste the precious calm of the soul, would rapidly achieve the age of
Nestor and willingly renounce the desires that one can satisfy, in
order to guarantee those that must be stifled. There would only be a

few thoughtless people who, blushing at their weakness, would insanely wish to stay young and happy instead of growing old to be 230–1 wise.

Let us suppose that an unusual, eccentric mind, a man of paradoxes, took it into his head to reproach the others for the absurdity of their advice, to show them that they were running towards death in seeking tranquillity, that they were only talking drivel by dint of being reasonable, and that if they had to be old one day, they should try to make that day as late as possible.

It is not necessary to ask if our sophists, fearing the outburst of their Arcanus, would quickly interrupt this troublesome chatterer. 'Wise old men', they would say to their followers, 'thank Heaven for the grace He gives you and be eternally glad that you have followed His wishes. You are decrepit, it is true, tired and feeble; that is the inevitable fate of men. But your understanding is sound. You are impotent in all your limbs, but your head is all the more free. You cannot do anything, but you speak like oracles, and if your griefs increase daily, your philosophy increases with them. Ignore this impetuous young man whose coarse good health deprives him of the benefits you get from your weakness — the happy disabilities which collect around you so many skilled chemists equipped with so many drugs that you are no longer ill, so many wise doctors, attuned to every beat of your pulse, knowing the Greek names for every kind of rheumatism, and so many eager comforters and faithful heirs who lead you happily to your last hour. What comfort you would have been without, if you had not been able to give yourselves the ills which have made them necessary.'

Can you not imagine them addressing our troublesome chatterbox . . . more or less like this: 'You idiot tub-thumper. Stop these impious statements. Do you dare to blame the will of Him who made the human race? Does not old age arise from the way man is made? Isn't it natural for man to grow old? What are you doing then in your seditious speech but attack a law of nature and thereby the will of the Creator? Since man grows old, God wants him to grow old. What are the facts but the expression of His will? Learn that God did not want to make men young and that to be keen to obey his orders you must hurry up and grow old.'

[Imagining that, says Rousseau, the 'man of paradox' would surely reply as follows:]

Since you suppose you attack me by my own system I beg you not to forget that according to me society is natural to the human race as old age to the individual, and people need arts, laws, governments as old men need crutches. But the whole difference is that the state of old age arises from the nature of man alone, while that of society arises from the nature of mankind, not immediately as you say, but only, as I have shown, with the aid of certain external circumstances which can be or cannot be, or at least can happen sooner or later, and therefore can hasten or slow down the progress . . . It is not therefore useless to show men the danger of going so fast and the miseries of a condition which they take to be the perfection of the species . . .   231–2

[Rousseau takes issue with Philopolis for employing the argument of Leibniz and Pope that 'All is good'.]

[You suppose] that it is enough that a thing exists for us not to be allowed to wish that it existed otherwise. But, Sir, if all is good as it is, all *was* good before there were any governments or laws; it was then unnecessary to establish them . . . If all is good as it is, in the way you suppose, what is the good of correcting our faults, healing our ills, correcting our mistakes? . . . Why do we get in the doctor when we have a fever? . . . If everything is the best it can be you ought to criticize any action; for every action must produce some change in the state of things, the moment it is done. You could not touch anything without doing harm, and the most perfect inaction is the only virtue left to man . . .   233–4

[He rejects any idea that he wants to go 'back to nature'.]

How do you know that I would go and live in the woods? . . . Far from seeing anything like that in my work, you should have seen very strong reasons for not choosing that kind of life. . . . The wise man today, if he is wise, will not go and look for happiness in the middle of a desert. Whenever possible you should make your home in your *patrie*, to love it and serve it.   235

This is my reply, sir. Notice how in this matter as in that of the *First Discourse*, I am always the monster who maintains that man is naturally good, and my opponents are always honest people, who, for the public edification, are compelled to prove that nature has only made criminals.   236

6 GOVERNMENT

In November 1755 Volume V of the *Encyclopedia* appeared. It included a long article by Rousseau on Political Economy. (The article was published separately in 1758 as the *Discourse on Political Economy*.) What Rousseau means by this is government, and it is here for the first time that he makes his crucial distinction between the government and the sovereign (see p. 34).

To illustrate the distinction he compares the body politic to a human body. This body has a will and this will is 'the general will'. It is in this article that the general will, 'this great and luminous principle'[1] as Rousseau called it, makes its entry in his political theory. It appeared simultaneously in an article by Diderot on Natural Right, in the same volume of the *Encyclopedia*, and Rousseau described Diderot's article as 'the source' of the idea. The exact extent of his debt to Diderot is unclear,[2] but the idea had not yet taken the specific and detailed form it was to have in *The Social Contract*. Neither the general will nor the sovereign is discussed at length here, because the subject of the article is not the state as a whole but government.

More particularly, Rousseau's subject is administration, the functions of government. In a passage which he later omitted he wrote: 'If I want to determine what the public economy consists of, I will find that its functions are reducible to three main ones: administering the laws, maintaining civil liberty, and providing for the needs of the state.'[3] It is with these three topics, therefore, that this article mainly deals.

The last of these topics should not be overlooked. Rousseau's political writing is often regarded as exclusively abstract and impractical. In fact it is remarkable for its realism. How the state raises money is obviously a matter of central importance and

Rousseau recognizes it as such. His concern is to keep the government's revenue as low as possible. He shows a similar concern in his *Letter to D'Alembert* and his proposals for Corsica and Poland.

There is a comparable realism behind the eloquent passage in this *Discourse* on the law and the *patrie*. Rousseau was of course not alone in his determination to see law replace the arbitrary rule of monarchs or the powerful interests of privileged groups. But he did feel in a particularly acute way the tension between the restrictions of law and the demands for freedom. It is in this context that his concept of the *patrie* should be understood. Because it is only if we have a a sense of belonging to a community that we will be able to associate ourselves with the public will which creates the law. In obeying a man, he wrote elsewhere, 'I obey the will of another; but in obeying the law I only obey the public will, which is as much my will as that of anyone else.'[4]

It is sometimes thought that Rousseau wrote this article before the *Discourse on Inequality*. The main reason for this lies in what he says about property. In the *Discourse on Inequality* the institution of property is seen as the first fatal step towards lasting inequality. When he then comes to discuss man in civil society he distinguishes between the rights that are inseparable and inalienable from man, life and liberty, from the right of property which is only a right 'of convention and of human institution'.[5] The meaning of this is made clear in *The Social Contract* (Bk I, Ch. 8): before men come together in a legitimate society there is only 'possession, which is only the result of force or the right of the first occupier'; when a legitimate society is formed, by the social contract, men then have 'property, which can only be based on a positive title'.[6] In other words, only the social contract makes property lawful; only the free consent of all members of the society, through the social contract, confers on each of its members the right to his property.

In the *Discourse on Political Economy*, however, Rousseau talks of property in virtually the same terms as Locke — 'the most sacred of all the rights of the citizens, and more important in certain respects even than liberty'.[7] 'It must be remembered that the foundation of the social pact is property, and its first condition [is] that everyone is maintained in the peaceful enjoyment of what belongs to him.'[8] Even though many of his proposals clearly distinguish his attitude to government from that of Locke these remarks on property do suggest that Rousseau has not yet developed his own mature view. They are therefore not included here, apart from a single reference to 'the right of property . . . the true foundation of political society' in the last extract.

Rousseau did see the right of property as an important right in society, since it was a guarantee of independence. But when he speaks of property, and this independence, he is not thinking of large properties or large estates; on the contrary, he is opposed to them, since they create only dependants, and the freedom of the owner is obtained at the expense of others. He is thinking rather of small properties that allow their owners a degree of self-sufficiency. This is made clear in *The Social Contract* (Bk I, Ch. 9) and also in his proposals for Corsica. It is not impossible that he is thinking in these terms in this *Discourse*, despite the above remarks.

Whether or not that is the case, his sense of the injustices of his society is as acute here as in the *Discourse on Inequality*. In addition, with his analysis of the functions of government, and the relation of the government to the people, he now moves from the criticism of what is wrong to the advocacy of what is right.

Discourse on Political Economy

I must ask my readers to distinguish well between public economy, which is my subject and which I call government, and the supreme authority, which I call sovereignty; a distinction which consists in the fact that the latter has the right of legislation and in certain cases binds the body of the nation itself, while the former has only the right of execution and is binding only on individuals . . .

I shall take the liberty of making use of a very common, and in some respects inaccurate, comparison, which will serve to illustrate my meaning.

The body politic, taken individually, may be considered as an organized, living body, resembling that of man. The sovereign power represents the head; the laws and customs are the brain, source of the nerves and seat of the understanding, will, and senses, of which the judges and magistrates are the organs; commerce, industry and agriculture are the mouth and stomach, which prepare the common subsistence; the public income is the blood, which a prudent economy, in performing the functions of the heart, causes to distribute through the whole body nutriment and life; the citizens are the body and its members, which make the machine live, move and work; and no part of this machine can be damaged without the painful impression being at once conveyed to the brain, if the animal is in a state of health.

244

The life of the one and the other is the ego common to the whole, the reciprocal sensibility and internal correspondence of all the parts. Where the communication ceases, where the formal unity disappears, and the adjoining parts belong to one another only by juxtaposition, the man is dead, or the state is dissolved.

The body politic, therefore, is also a moral being which has a will; and this general will, which tends always to the preservation and welfare of the whole and of each part, and is the source of the laws, constitutes for all the members of the state, in relation to one another and to it, the rule of what is just or unjust . . .   245

Every political society is composed of other smaller societies of different kinds, each of which has its interests and its rules of conduct . . . The influence of all these tacit or formal associations causes, by the influence of their will, as many different modifications of the public will. The will of these particular societies always has two relations: for the members of the association it is a general will; for the great society it is a particular will; and it is often right with regard to the first and wrong as to the second. An individual may be a devout priest, a brave soldier, or a zealous senator, and yet a bad citizen. A particular resolution may be advantageous to the smaller community, but pernicious to the greater. It is true that, particular societies always being subordinate to those that contain them, the latter should be obeyed rather than the former; the duties of the citizen should take precedence over those of the senator, and those of man over that of the citizen; but unhappily personal interest is always found in inverse ratio to duty, and increases in proportion as the association grows narrower and the engagement less sacred; invincible proof that the most general will is also always the most just, and that the voice of the people is in effect the voice of God.   246

It does not follow that the public decisions are always equitable . . . Nor is it less possible for the council of a democracy to pass unjust decrees, and condemn the innocent; but this never happens unless the people is seduced by private interests, which the credit or eloquence of some clever persons substitutes for those of the state; in which case the general will be one thing, and the result of the public deliberation another. This is not contradicted by the case of the Athenian democracy; for Athens was in fact not a democracy, but a very tyrannical aristocracy, governed by philosophers and orators. Carefully determine what happens in every public deliberation, and it will be seen that the general will is always for the common good; but very often there is a secret division, a tacit confederacy, which, for particular ends, causes the natural disposition of the assembly to be set at naught. In such a case the body of society is really divided into other bodies, the members of which acquire a general will, which is good and just with respect to these new bodies, but unjust and bad with regard to the whole, from which each is thus dismembered . . .

246–7

In establishing the general will as the first principle of the public economy, and the fundamental rule of government, I have not thought it necessary to inquire seriously whether the magistrates belong to the people, or the people to the magistrates; or whether in public affairs the good of the state should be taken into account, or only that of its rulers. That question has indeed long been decided one way in theory and another in practice; and in general it would be ridiculous to expect that those who are in fact masters will prefer any other interest to their own. It would not be improper therefore to call public economy either popular or tyrannical. The former is that of every state in which there reigns between the people and the rulers unity of interest and will; the latter necessarily exists whenever the government and the people have different interests and, consequently, opposing wills. The rules of the latter are written at length in the archives of history, and in the satires of Machiavelli. The rules of the former are found only in the writings of those philosophers who venture to proclaim the rights of humanity.

247

I. The first and most important rule of legitimate or popular government, that is to say, of government whose object is the good of the people, is therefore as I have observed, to follow in everything the general will. But to follow this will it is necessary to know it, and above all to distinguish it well from the particular will, beginning with oneself; this distinction is always very difficult to make, and only the most sublime virtue can provide sufficient enlightenment. Since in order to will it is necessary to be free, another difficulty which is almost as great arises — that of preserving at the same time public liberty and the authority of government. Look into the motives which have induced men, once united by their common needs in a general society, to unite themselves still more intimately by means of civil societies; you will find no other motive than that of assuring the property, life, and liberty of each member by the protection of all. But can men be forced to defend the liberty of any one among them without trespassing on that of others? And how can they provide for the public needs, without disturbing the individual property of those who are forced to contribute to them? With whatever sophistry all this may be covered over, it is certain that if any constraint can be laid on my will I am no longer free, and that I am no longer master of my own property, if anyone else can lay a hand on it. This difficulty, which would have seemed insurmountable, has been removed, like the first, by the most sublime of all human institutions, or rather by a divine inspiration, which teaches mankind to imitate here below the unchangeable decrees of the divinity. By what conceivable art has a means been found of making men free by making them subject? . . . How can it be that all should obey, yet nobody take upon him to command, and that all should serve, and yet have no masters, but be the more free, as, in apparent subjection, each loses no part of his liberty but what might be hurtful to that of another? These wonders are the work of law. It is to law alone that men owe justice and liberty. It is this salutary organ of the will of all which establishes, in civil right, the natural equality between men. It is this celestial voice which dictates to each citizen the precepts of public reason, and teaches him to act according to the rules of his own judgement, and not to be in contradiction with himself . . .   247–8

The most pressing interest of the ruler, and even his most indispensable duty, therefore, is to watch over the observation of the laws of which he is the minister, and on which his authority is founded. [At the same time] if he exacts the observance of them from others, he is the more strongly bound to observe them himself, since he enjoys all their favour . . . At bottom, as all social engagements are mutual in nature, it is impossible for any one to set himself above the law, without renouncing its advantages; for nobody is bound by any obligation to one who claims that he is under no obligation to others. For this reason no exemption from the law will ever be granted, on any ground whatsoever, in a well-regulated government . . .

The power of the laws depends much more on their own wisdom than on the severity of their administrators, and the public will derives its greatest weight from the reason which has dictated it . . . In fact, the first of all laws is to respect the laws; the severity of penalties is only a vain resource, invented by little minds in order to substitute terror for that respect which they have no means of obtaining . . .   249

Though the government be not master of the law, it is much to be its guarantor, and to possess a thousand means of inspiring the love of it. In this alone the talent of reigning consists. With force in one's hands, there is no art required to make the whole world tremble, nor indeed much to gain men's hearts; for experience has long since taught the people to give its rulers great credit for all the evil they abstain from doing it, and to adore them if they do not absolutely hate it. A fool, if he be obeyed, may punish crimes as well as another: but the true statesman is he who knows how to prevent them. It is over the wills, even more than the actions, of his subjects that his honourable rule is extended. If he could secure that every one should act aright, he would no longer have anything to do; and the master-

250 piece of his labours would be to be able to remain unemployed . . .

It is a great thing to preserve the rule of peace and order through all parts of the republic; it is a great thing that the state should be tranquil, and the law respected. But if nothing more is done, there will be in all this more appearance than reality; for that government which confines itself to mere obedience will find difficulty in getting itself obeyed. If it is good to know how to deal with men as they are, it is much better to make them become what they need to be. The most absolute authority is that which penetrates into a man's inmost being, and concerns itself no less with his will than with his actions. It is certain that all peoples become in the long run what the government makes them: warriors, citizens, and men, when it so pleases; or merely populace and rabble, when it so chooses. Hence every prince who despises his subjects dishonours himself, in showing that he does not know how to make them worthy of respect. Make men, therefore, if you would command men; if you would have them obedient to the laws, make them love the laws, and then they will only need to know their duty in order to do it. This was the great art of ancient governments, in those distant times when philosophers gave laws to men, and made use of their authority only to render them wise and happy . . . Our modern governments, which imagine that they have done everything when they have raised money, conceive

251–2 that it is unnecessary and even impossible to go a stage farther.

II.   The second essential rule of public economy is no less important than the first. If you would have the general will accomplished, bring all the particular wills into conformity with it; in other words, as virtue is nothing more than this conformity of the particular wills with the general will, establish the reign of virtue . . .

If our politicians were less blinded by their ambition, they would see how impossible it is for any establishment whatever to act in the spirit of its institution, unless it is guided in accordance with the law of duty; they would feel that the greatest support of public authority lies in the hearts of the citizens, and that nothing can take the place of morality in the maintenance of government . . . It is not only

upright men who know how to administer the laws; but at bottom
only good men who know how to obey them.   252

Public vices have a greater effect in enervating the laws, than have
the laws for repressing those vices . . .

The worst of all abuses is to pay an apparent obedience to the laws,
only in order actually to break them with security. For in this case
the best laws soon become the most pernicious; it would be a hundred
times better that they should not exist . . . In such a situation it is vain
to add edicts on edicts and regulations on regulations. Everything
serves only to introduce new abuses, without correcting the old. The
more laws are multiplied the more they are despised, and all the new
officials appointed to supervise them are only so many more people
to break them, and either share the plunder of their predecessors, or
to plunder apart on their own . . . And, the people, not seeing that its
vices are the first cause of its misfortunes, murmurs and cries out in
grief: 'All my ills come solely from those whom I pay to protect
me from such things' . . .   253

But when the citizens love their duty, and the guardians of the
public authority apply themselves sincerely to nourishing that love
by their own examples and concern, every difficulty vanishes; administration becomes so easy that it needs none of that art of darkness,
whose blackness is its only mystery. Those enterprising spirits, so
dangerous and so much admired, all those great ministers, whose
glory is inseparable from the miseries of the people, are no longer
regretted; public morality supplies what is wanting in the genius
of the rulers; and the more virtue reigns, the less need there is for
talent . . .   253-4

It is not enough to say to the citizens, be good; they must be taught
to be so; and even example, which is in this respect the first lesson, is
not the sole means to be employed; love of the *patrie** is the most
effective; for, as I have already said, every man is virtuous when his
particular will is in complete conformity to the general will, and we
voluntarily will what is willed by those whom we love.

It appears that the feeling of humanity evaporates and grows
feeble in embracing all mankind . . . It is necessary in some degree
to confine and limit our interest and compassion in order to make it
active. Now, as this inclination in us can be useful only to those with
whom we have to live, it is proper that our humanity should be
concentrated among our fellow-citizens, obtaining a new force from

* Translated as 'country' throughout the rest of this passage.

the habit of seeing them, and by reason of the common interest which unites them. It is certain that the greatest miracles of virtue have been produced by the love of country . . . Contrast Socrates with Cato; the one was the greater philosopher, the other more of the citizen. Athens was already ruined in the time of Socrates, and he had no other country than the world at large. Cato had the cause of his country always at heart; he lived for it alone, and could not bear to outlive it . . . A worthy pupil of Socrates would be the most virtuous of his contemporaries; but a worthy follower of Cato would be one of the greatest. The virtue of the former would be his happiness; the latter would seek his happiness in that of all. We should be taught by one, and led by the other; and this alone is enough to determine which to prefer; for no people has ever been made into a nation of

254–5 philosophers, but it is not impossible to make a people happy.

Do we wish men to be virtuous? Then let us begin by making them love their country. But how can they love it if their country be nothing more to them than to strangers, and grants them only what it allows anyone? It would be still worse, if they did not enjoy even the privilege of civil security, and if their lives, liberties, and property lay at the mercy of persons in power, without their being permitted, or its being possible for them, to make an appeal to the laws. For in that case, being subjected to the duties of the state of civil society, without enjoying even the rights of the state of nature, and without being able to use their strength in their own defence, they would be in the worst condition in which freemen could possibly find themselves, and the word 'country' would mean for them something merely odious and ridiculous. It must not be imagined that a man can lose or break an arm, without pain being conveyed to his head; nor is it any more credible that the general will should consent that any one member of the state, whoever he might be, should wound or destroy another, than it is that the fingers of a man in his senses should wilfully scratch his eyes out. The security of individuals is so intimately connected with the public confederation that, apart from the regard that must be paid to human weakness, that convention would in point of right be dissolved, if in the state a single citizen who might have been helped were allowed to perish, or if one were wrongfully confined in prison, or if in one case an obviously unjust sentence were given. For the fundamental conventions being broken it is impossible to conceive of any right or interest that could retain the people in the social union, unless they were held in by force alone, which causes the

255–6 dissolution of the civil state . . .

Is the welfare of a single citizen any less the common cause than that of the whole state?* It may be said that it is good that one should perish for all. I am ready to admire such a saying when it comes from the lips of a virtuous and worthy patriot voluntarily and dutifully sacrificing himself for the good of his country; but if we are to understand by it that it is lawful for the government to sacrifice an innocent man for the good of the multitude, I look upon it as one of the most execrable rules tyranny ever invented, the greatest falsehood that can be advanced, the most dangerous admission that can be made, and a direct contradiction of the fundamental laws of society. So little is it the case that any one person ought to perish for all, that all have pledged their lives and properties for the defence of each, in order that the weakness of individuals may always be protected by the strength of the public, and each member by the whole state. Suppose we take from the whole people one individual after another, and then press the advocates of this rule to explain more exactly what they mean by the body of the state; we shall see that it will at length be reduced to a small number of persons, who are not the people, but the officers of the people, and who, having bound themselves by personal oath to perish for the welfare of the people, would thence infer that the people is to perish for their welfare.

Need we look for examples of the protection which the state owes to its members, and the respect it owes to their persons? It is only among the most illustrious and courageous nations that they are to be found; it is only among free peoples that the dignity of man is realized . . .   256-7

Let our country then show itself the common mother of her citizens; let the advantages they enjoy in their country endear it to them; let the government leave them enough share in the public administration to make them feel that they are at home; and let the laws be in their eyes only the guarantees of the common liberty. These rights, great as they are, belong to all men; but without seeming to attack them directly, the ill-will of rulers may in fact easily reduce their effect to nothing. The law, which they thus abuse, serves the powerful at once as a weapon of offence, and as a shield against the weak; and the pretext of the public good is always the most dangerous scourge of the people. What is most necessary, and perhaps most difficult in government, is rigid integrity in doing strict justice to all,

---

* This question was later to have particular significance for Rousseau himself (see Chapter 16).

and above all in protecting the poor against the tyranny of the rich . . .

It is therefore one of the most important functions of government to prevent extreme inequality of fortunes; not by taking away wealth from its possessors, but by depriving all men of means to accumulate it; not by building hospitals for the poor, but by securing the citizens 258 from becoming poor . . .

There can be no *patrie* without liberty, no liberty without virtue, no virtue without citizens; create citizens, and you have everything you need. Without them you will have nothing but debased slaves, from the rulers of the state downwards. To form citizens is not the work of a day; and in order to have men it is necessary to educate them when they are children. It will be said, perhaps, that whoever has men to govern, ought not to seek, beyond their nature, a perfection of which they are incapable; that he ought not to desire to destroy their passions; and that the execution of such an attempt is no more desirable than it is possible. I will agree, further, that a man without passions would certainly be a bad citizen; but it must also be agreed that, if men are not taught to love something, it is impossible to teach them to love one object more than another — to prefer that which is truly beautiful to that which is deformed.

If, for example, they were early accustomed to regard their individuality only in its relation to the body of the state, and to be aware, so to speak, of their own existence merely as a part of that of the state, they might at length come to identify themselves in some degree with this greater whole, to feel themselves members of their country, and to love it with that exquisite feeling which no isolated person has for himself; to lift up their spirits perpetually to this great object, and thus to transform into a sublime virtue that dangerous disposition which gives rise to all our vices . . . It is too late to change our natural inclinations when they have taken their course, and self-interest is confirmed by habit; and it is too late to lead us out of ourselves when once the human ego, concentrated in our hearts, has acquired that contemptible activity which absorbs all virtue and constitutes the life and being of little minds. How can the love of country germinate in the midst of so many other passions which smother it? And what can remain for fellow-citizens from a heart already divided between avarice, a mistress, and vanity? From the first moment of life, men ought to begin learning to deserve to live; and, as at the instant of birth we partake of the rights of citizenship, that instant ought to be 259–60 the beginning of the exercise of our duty . . .

Public education, therefore, under regulations prescribed by the

government, and under magistrates established by the sovereign, is one of the fundamental rules of popular or legitimate government. If children are brought up in common in the bosom of equality; if they are imbued with the laws of the state and the precepts of the general will; if they are taught to respect these above all things; if they are surrounded by examples and objects which constantly remind them of the tender mother who nourishes them, of the love she bears them, of the inestimable benefits they receive from her, and of the return they owe her, we cannot doubt that they will learn to cherish one another mutually as brothers, to will nothing contrary to the will of society, to substitute the actions of men and citizens for the futile and vain babbling of sophists, and to become in time defenders and fathers of the country of which they will have been so long the   260–1
children . . .

III.   It is not enough to have citizens and to protect them, it is also necessary to consider their subsistence. Provision for the public wants is an obvious inference from the general will, the third essential duty of government . . .   262
   [Rousseau discusses private property. He then continues:]
The first step which the founder of a republic ought to take after the establishment of laws is to settle a sufficient fund for the maintenance of the magistrates and other officials, and for other public expenses . . .
   Before any use is made of this fund, it should be assigned or accepted by an assembly of the people, or of the estates of the country, which should determine its future use. After this solemnity which makes such funds inalienable, their very nature is, in a manner, changed, and the revenues become so sacred that it is not only the most infamous theft, but actual treason to misapply them or pervert them from the purpose for which they were destined . . .   264–5
   When public funds are once established, the rulers of the state become of right the administrators of them; for this administration constitutes a part of government which is always essential, though not equally so. Its influence increases in proportion as that of other resources is diminished; and it may justly be said that a government has reached the last stage of corruption when it has ceased to have sinews other than money. Now as every government constantly tends to become lax, this is enough to show why no state can subsist unless its revenues constantly increase. The first sense of the necessity of this increase is also the first sign of the internal disorder of the state . . .
   From this rule is deduced the most important rule in the adminis-

tration of finance, which is, to take more pains to guard against needs than to increase revenue. For whatever diligence be employed, the relief which only comes after the evil, and more slowly, always leaves the state in suffering. While a remedy is being found for one evil, another is beginning to make itself felt, and even the remedies themselves produce new difficulties; so that at length the nation is involved in debt and the people oppressed, while the government

266 loses its influence and can do very little with a great deal of money . . .

Apart from the public demesne . . . anyone sufficiently acquainted with the whole force of the general administration . . . would be astonished at the resources rulers can make use of for safeguarding all public needs, without trespassing on the goods of individuals. As they are masters of the whole commerce of the state, nothing is easier for them than to direct it into such channels as to provide for every need, without appearing to interfere. The distribution of provisions, money and merchandise in just proportions according to times and places, is the true secret of finance and the source of

266–7 wealth . . .

If we ask how the needs of a state grow, we shall find they often arise, rather like the wants of individuals, less from any real necessity than from the increase of useless desires, and that expenses are often augmented only to give a pretext for raising receipts; so that the state would sometimes gain by not being rich, and apparent wealth is in reality more burdensome than poverty itself would be. Rulers may indeed hope to keep the peoples in stricter dependence, by thus giving them with one hand what they take from them with the other; and this was in fact the policy of Joseph towards the Egyptians; but this political sophistry is the more fatal to the state, as the money never returns into the hands it went out of. Such principles only enrich the idle at the expense of the industrious.

A desire for conquest is one of the most evident and dangerous causes of this increase. This desire, occasioned often by a different species of ambition from that which it seems to proclaim, is not always what it appears to be, and has not so much, for its real motive, the apparent desire to aggrandize the nation as a secret desire to increase the authority of the rulers at home, by increasing the number of troops, and by the diversion which the objects of war occasion

267–8 in the minds of the citizens . . .

[Taxes.] In the first place, we have to consider the relationship of quantities, according to which, all things being equal, the person who has ten times the property of another man ought to pay ten times as much to the state. Secondly, the relationship of the use made, that is to say, the distinction between the necessary and the super-fluous. He who possesses only the common necessaries of life should pay nothing at all, while the tax on him who is in possession of super-fluities may justly be extended to everything he has over and above mere necessaries. To this he will possibly object that when his rank is taken into account, what may be superfluous to a man of inferior station is necessary for him. But this is a lie; for an aristocrat has two legs just like a cowherd, and like him again, but one belly . . .

A third relationship, which is never taken into account, though it ought to be the chief consideration, is the advantage that every person derives from the social confederacy; for this provides a power-ful protection for the immense possessions of the rich, and hardly leaves the poor man in quiet possession of the cottage he builds with his own hands. Are not all the advantages of society for the rich and powerful? Are not all lucrative posts in their hands? Are not all privileges and exemptions reserved for them alone? Is not the public authority always on their side? If a man of eminence robs his creditors, or is guilty of other misdeeds, is he not always assured of impunity? Are not the assaults, acts of violence, assassinations and even murders committed by the great, matters that are hushed up in a few months, and of which nothing more is thought? But if a great man himself is robbed or insulted, the whole police force is immediately in motion, and woe to the innocent whom they suspect . . . Yet all this respect costs him not a farthing; it is the rich man's right, and not what he buys with his wealth. How different is the case of the poor man! The more humanity owes him, the more society denies him. Every door is shut against him even when he has a right to its being opened; and if ever he obtains justice it is with much greater difficulty than others obtain favours . . .

271

Another no less important fact is that the losses of the poor are much harder to repair than those of the rich, and that the difficulty of acquisition is always greater in proportion as there is more need for it. 'Nothing comes out of nothing' is as true of life as in physics; money is the seed of money, and the first guinea is sometimes more difficult to acquire than the second million . . . The terms of the social pact between these two estates of men may be summed up in a few words: 'You have need of me, because I am rich and you are poor. We will therefore come to an agreement. I will permit you to have the honour of serving me, on condition that you bestow on me the little you have left, for the trouble I shall take to command you.'

Putting all these considerations carefully together, we shall find that, in order to levy taxes in a truly equitable and proportionate manner, the imposition ought not to be in simple ratio to the property of the contributors, but in compound ratio to the difference of their conditions and of the superfluity of their possessions . . .

272–3

Only the real statesman can rise, in imposing taxes, above the mere financial object: he alone can transform heavy burdens into useful regulations, and make the people wonder whether such establishments were not calculated rather for the good of the nation in general, than merely for the raising of money . . .

Duties on the importation of foreign commodities, of which the natives are fond, without the country standing in need of them; on the exportation of those of the produce of the country which are not too plentiful, and which foreigners cannot do without; on the productions of frivolous and all too lucrative arts; on the importations of all pure luxuries; and in general on all objects of luxury, will answer the end in view. It is by such taxes, indeed, by which the poor are eased and the burdens thrown on the rich, that it is possible to prevent the continual increase of inequality of fortune, the subjection of such a multitude of artisans and useless servants of the rich, the multiplication of idle persons in our cities, and the depopulation of

275–6 the countryside . . .

We may add to all this a very important distinction in matters of political right, to which governments, constantly tenacious of doing everything for themselves, ought to pay great attention. It has been observed that personal taxes and duties on the necessaries of life, as they directly trespass on the right of property, and consequently on the true foundation of political society, are always liable to have dangerous results, if they are not established with the express consent of the people or its representatives. It is not the same with articles the use of which we can deny ourselves; for as the individual is under no absolute necessity to pay, his contribution may count as voluntary. The particular consent of each contributor then takes the place of the general consent of the whole people: for why should a people oppose the imposition of a tax which falls only on those who desire to pay it? It appears to me certain that everything, which is not proscribed by law, or contrary to morality, and yet may be prohibited by the government, may also be permitted on payment of a certain duty. Thus, for example, if the government may prohibit the use of coaches, it may certainly impose a tax on them; and this is a prudent and useful method of censuring their use without absolutely forbidding it. In this case, the tax may be regarded as a sort of fine, the product of which compensates for the abuse it punishes . . .   277–8

7 MUSIC

I

'Jean-Jacques was born for music',[1] wrote Rousseau about himself. 'I began to love it in my childhood and it is the only art I have loved constantly throughout my life.'[2] He played the flute and cello when he was young, and keyboard instruments throughout his life. He taught music, wrote music and came to Paris with a new system of musical notation. In Venice he was captivated with Italian music and back in Paris he wrote articles on music for the *Encyclopedia*.

In the spring of 1752 he made a short trip to Passy, outside Paris, with a cellist friend, Mussard. The two men shared an enthusiasm for Italian opera and talked about it at length. Their conversation inspired Rousseau to write a light comic opera himself, *The Village Sorcerer*. In October that year it was performed before the king at Fontainbleau and was an immediate success: Rousseau was even offered a royal pension because of it. The following spring it was performed both at the Opera in Paris and again at the court, at Versailles, with Madame de Pompadour in one of the rôles. It was revived many times before the end of the century and won the admiration of both Gluck[3] and Dr Burney.*

This success would probably not have been so considerable if it had not coincided with an event of wider musical significance — the War (or Quarrel) of the Bouffons. An Italian *opera buffa* company came to Paris in August 1752 and performed Pergolesi's *La Serva Padrona* and some other comic operas. The style and content of *opera buffa* was the antithesis of French *tragédie lyrique*. The former was light in both subject matter and musical treatment; it dealt with

---

* The opera, wrote Burney, was 'composed in a familiar pleasing ballad style, neither entirely French or Italian', it was 'indisputable proof that popular strains may be produced by the writer of a dramatic poem'.[4]

contemporary subjects, usually involving middle- or lower-class characters on a domestic scale. *La Serva Padrona* was an early masterpiece of *opera buffa*: the comic operas of Mozart and Rossini were later masterpieces.

The French *tragédie lyrique*, on the other hand, developed by Lully in the seventeenth century, was grand and elaborate. It incorporated ballet and spectacular scenes, used mythological subjects, frequently in praise of the monarchy, and was always on a heroic scale. In *opera buffa* the vocal line was all-important and the orchestral numbers were linked by *recitativo secco*, half-sung, half-spoken passages with only a slight harpsichord accompaniment. In *tragédie lyrique* the emphasis was on the orchestral texture, the instrumental writing was rich and complex and the recitative was no less elaborate. Rameau was the acknowledged master of this grand opera.

The contrast between these two forms was highlighted by the fact that only one theatre in Paris was licensed to give opera, and the first performance of *La Serva Padrona* in 1752 was given as an intermezzo between the acts of Lully's *Acis and Galatea*. It provoked a bitter quarrel between the rival supporters.

> All Paris was divided into two parties more heatedly than if it had been a question of politics or religion. One group — the more powerful and numerous, made up of the great, the rich and the women — supported French music; the other — the more lively, proud, enthusiastic, made up of the connoisseurs, talented people and men of genius — [supported Italian music].[5]

The quarrel, in other words, was as much intellectual and social as it was musical. The *philosophes* all supported Italian music, and Grimm, Holbach and Diderot wrote pamphlets in its defence. Then Rousseau wrote one as well, his *Letter on French Music*.

> The description of the incredible effect of this pamphlet would be worthy of the pen of Tacitus. It was the time of the great quarrel between the *Parlement* and the clergy. The *Parlement* had just been dissolved; the excitement was at its height; there was every threat of an approaching revolt. The pamphlet appeared. In a moment all other quarrels were forgotten; people only thought of the danger to French music and the only revolt was against me . . . When you read that this pamphlet perhaps prevented a revolution in France you will think you are dreaming. But it is certainly true . . .[6]

Rousseau's account here is not as exaggerated as it may seem. Not only was he hanged in effigy outside the Opera but he was also in fear of being arrested. The quarrel had become a focus of social tensions and his *Letter* went further than any of the other pamphlets in attacking the *status quo*. It provoked at least thirty replies and the terms in which they were written indicate the truth of what Rousseau wrote later in his *Letter to Christophe de Beaumont*. 'One might have thought that the fate of the French monarchy depended on the glory of the Opera.'*

Letter on French Music

I think our language scarcely suitable for poetry, and not at all for music. On this point I am not afraid to appeal to the poets themselves. As for the musicians, everyone knows it is quite unnecessary to consult them on any point of reasoning. To make up for that, however, the French language seems to me good for philosophers and wise men; it seems made to be the organ of truth and reason . . .

522–3

All music can only be composed of three things: melody or song, harmony or accompaniment, and movement or measure . . .

Harmony, having its principle in nature, is the same for all nations; or, if there are any differences they are introduced by those of melody. It is therefore from the melody alone that national music should be derived, and the greatest influence on the character of song is given by the language. It is surely possible that some languages are more suitable for music than others. It is also possible that some are not suitable at all.

[One such language, says Rousseau, is French, with its 'lack of force in the sounds of the vowels' and 'the hardness and frequency of its consonants'.]

[In such a language] the music would be devoid of all agreeable melody, and the composer would try to supplement it by factitious and unnatural beauties. It would be filled with frequent and regular modulations; but cold, without grace or expression . . . Music with all that peevish ornament would remain stagnant . . . and its images, lacking force and energy, would depict few objects with lots of

* See page 232. What is more astonishing is the way Rousseau's pamphlet, and the Quarrel of the Bouffons generally, has remained a sensitive political matter. As recently as 1945 a book devoted to the subject was dedicated by its author 'To Thierry Maulnier, for Rameau — our musical Racine — and French Order against Rousseau and barbarian anarchy'.[7]

notes . . . The impossibility of inventing agreeable songs would oblige the composers to turn all their thoughts to harmony, and for want of real beauties they would introduce conventional beauties . . . Instead of a good music they would invent a learned music . . . To get rid of the dullness they would increase the confusion, and believe they were making music when they were only making a noise.   524–5

If it be asked what language must have the best grammar, I would reply: That of the people who reason best. If it be asked what nation should have the best music, I should answer: That whose language is best suited to music. [In Europe, such a language is Italian] for that language is soft, sonorous, harmonious and more accented than any other, and these four qualities are precisely the most suitable for song . . . It is not necessary to understand the language to judge this, you only need a pair of ears and good faith . . .   527

Every voice is good for Italian. . . .   529

For a piece of music to become interesting and convey to the soul the feelings that one wishes to excite there, it is necessary that all the parts co-operate to strengthen the expression of the subject; that the harmony only serves to make it more vigorous; that the accompaniment embellishes, without covering or disfiguring it; and that the bass, by a simple and uniform progress, in some way acts as a guide to both the singer and the listener, without either being aware of it. In a word, the whole ensemble should convey only a single melody to the ear, and one idea to the mind. This unity of melody appears to me a rule as indispensable to music, and no less important, as unity of action in a tragedy. It is founded on the same principle and directed to the same end . . . It is from this that the music [of the good Italian composers] draws its main effect . . .   531

The more our music makes an apparent improvement the worse it actually becomes . . .

In Italian operas [unlike the French] all the airs relate to the [dramatic] situation and belong to the scene.   536

[Rousseau examines a celebrated soliloquy in Lully's *Armida* — 'Enfin il est en ma puissance' — which had been praised by Rameau. He concludes:]

If we envisage it as singing we find it has neither movement, character nor melody. If we wish it to be only recitative we find it has nothing natural or expressive. Whatever name we wish to give it, it is full of drawn-out sounds, trills and other ornaments even more ridiculous in that situation than they usually are in French music . . . [It is] pedantic, without energy, and with no perceptible feeling . . . a tedious succession of sounds, modulated at random and only to make it last longer . . .

[So] I believe I have made it clear that there is neither movement nor melody in French music; because the language is not susceptible to it; because French song is only a continual barking, intolerable to any unprejudiced ear; that its harmony is gross, inexpressive and puerile; that French airs are no airs, and that their recitative is no recitative. From which I conclude that Frenchmen have no music, and cannot have any. Or if they do have, it will be so much the worse for them.

542

II

Burney thought 'there was too much good sense, taste and reason in this *Letter* for it to be read with indifference; it was abused, but never answered.'[8] Together with the success of *The Village Sorcerer* it contributed to the rebirth of the French *opéra comique* that occurred in the latter part of the century.

The preferences Rousseau asserted in his *Letter* — for melody rather than harmony, for an expressive music rather than 'a learned music', for a simple 'unity of melody' rather than a complex polyphony — were more than musical reflections of his own emotional temperament. They were also a direct attack on the principles that Rameau had developed at great length in his *Treatise on Harmony* and other writings.* This is the intellectual aspect of the Quarrel of the Bouffons.

Rameau wrote at great length about musical theory. Burney, in fact, believed that he would only be remembered as a theorist.[11] Many of his suggestions on technique were admired by Diderot, D'Alembert and Rousseau himself. But the assumptions and foundations of his theory were unacceptable to them. He believed that music expressed a universal order, through music we come into contact with a universal harmony. Rameau wrote: 'It is in music that nature seems to assign to us the physical principle of those first purely mathematical notions on which all the sciences are based: I mean, harmonic, arithmetic and geometric proportions.'[12] A study of harmony was the basis of music, and melody was only derived from

* Rameau — 'Harmony . . . can reach into the soul . . . Melody . . . can only amuse the ear'.[9] Rousseau — 'The pleasure [of Italian melody] did not stop at the ear, it reached into the soul.'[10]

harmony; from the science of harmony came knowledge of the nature of the world and vice versa. 'I owe my discoveries in music to the laws of nature alone.'[13]*

For Rousseau, on the other hand, music related not to the laws of nature, or abstract rules derived from them, but to human emotion; it was its expressive ability that he valued most. 'The art of the musician does not consist in depicting objects in their immediacy, but in putting the soul into a state similar to that in which their presence would put it [the soul].'[15] 'The best music is that which unites physical pleasure and moral pleasure, that is to say, the pleasure of the ear and the interest of the feeling.'[16] He made a distinction between mere *sensation*, which harmony produces, and human *sentiment* (feeling), which melody could produce. Vocal music, performed by the human voice, therefore had a value to him which instrumental music lacked; and since people communicate mostly in words the musical possibilities of a nation were essentially connected with their language. Discussion of music inevitably led to a discussion of language.

In the *Discourse on Inequality* Rousseau suggested that in the state of nature man did not originally have language. 'Although the organ of speech is natural to man, speech itself is nevertheless not natural to him.'[17] There was 'an immense distance . . . between the pure state of nature and the need for languages'.[18] In his *Essay on the Origin of Languages* he developed this idea. He seems to have begun the *Essay* because of his incomplete treatment of the problem in the *Discourse*, and then to have developed it in connection with the controversy over music.

It is a remarkable work, almost as rich in suggestion as the *Discourse on Inequality*, and it has recently received considerable attention. It deals not only with language and music but also aesthetics, anthropology, history and politics; an example in miniature of the way all these subjects are interrelated for Rousseau. He differed from his contemporaries, notably Condillac, in both extending the area of human development before language, and in relating the origin of language to feeling, rather than to physical need or to thought.

---

* D'Alembert later parodied this belief: 'Rameau ended by wishing to find the whole of geometry in musical proportions, the two sexes of animals in the major and minor modes, and finally the Trinity in the threefold resonance of the sounding body.'[14]

Essay on the Origin of Languages, in which Melody and Musical Imitation are discussed

II. THAT THE INVENTION OF SPEECH DOES NOT COME FROM NEEDS BUT FROM PASSIONS

It seems then that needs dictated the first gestures, and passions drew out the first voices . . .

The speech of the first men is portrayed to us as the language of geometricians, [but] we see that it was the language of poets.

41   That must be. One does not begin by reasoning but by feeling. It is supposed that men invented speech to express their needs . . . [But] the natural effect of the first needs was to separate men, and not to bring them together.

[It was because our needs spread us out over the earth that the whole earth became populated.]

From where then can the origin [of language] come? From moral needs, passions. All the passions bring people together, while the necessity of seeking a living forces them to flee from one another. It is neither hunger nor thirst but love, hatred, pity, anger which

43   drew from them the first voices . . .

III. THAT THE FIRST LANGUAGE MUST HAVE BEEN FIGURATIVE

As the first motives which made men speak were the passions, their first expressions were tropes. Figurative language was the first to be

45   born . . . At first only poetry was spoken . . .

[Rousseau then summarizes the development of language, from its expressive beginnings to its exact and inexpressive present, a development for the worse which is compounded by that of writing. He then puts forward a theory as to how, as men spread over the earth, different climates produced different languages. In Southern countries 'the first tongues [were] the daughters of pleasure' (127); in northern countries 'the languages [were] the sad daughters of necessity' (129), and 'it was not a question of energy but clarity' (131). These remarks have an obvious connection with his earlier comments on French and Italian, as languages suitable for music, and they lead him on to discuss melody and musical imitation.]

XIII. ON MELODY

No one doubts that man is modified by his senses. But instead of distinguishing the modifications, we confuse them with their causes. We give too much and too little of the power to sensations. We do not see that often they do not affect us only as sensations, but as signs or images, and that their moral effects also have moral causes. Just as the feelings that paintings excite in us do not come from the colours, the power that music has over our souls is not the work of sounds. Beautiful and delicate colours are pleasing to the sight; but this pleasure is purely of sensation. It is the line, the imitation, which gives life and soul to these colours. It is the passions it expresses that moves us. It is the objects it represents that affect us . . . Melody in music does precisely what line does in painting . . .   147–9

XV. THAT OUR MOST LIVELY SENSATIONS ARE FREQUENTLY PRODUCED BY MORAL IMPRESSIONS

The sounds in a melody do not act on us only as sounds but as signs of our affections, of our feelings. It is thus that they excite in us the emotions which they express and the image of which we recognize in [the melody] . . .

He who wants to philosophize about the force of sensations should begin by distinguishing pure sensual impressions from the intellectual and moral impressions which we receive by way of the senses, but of which the senses are only the occasional cause; he would avoid the mistake of giving to sense objects a power they do not have, or that they have only in relation to the affections of the soul which they represent to us . . .   163

But in this century when people strive to materialize all the operations of the soul, and take away all morality from human feeling, I am deceived if the new philosophy does not become as fatal to good taste as to virtue.   167

XVI. FALSE ANALOGY BETWEEN COLOURS AND SOUNDS

In the harmonic system, no sound is anything naturally. It is neither tonic, dominant, harmonic nor fundamental, because all these properties are only relations . . . But the properties of colours do not consist in relations. Yellow is yellow, independently of red and of blue . . .   173

From this one sees that painting is closer to nature and that music relates more to human art. One also feels that the one is more interesting than the other, precisely because it brings men closer and always gives us some idea of our fellows. Painting is often dead and inanimate. It can transport you to the depths of a desert; but as soon as vocal signs strike your ear, they proclaim to you a being like yourself. They are, so to speak, the organs of the soul. Even if they portray solitude to you they tell you that you are not alone there . . .

It is one of the great advantages of the musician that he can depict things that cannot be heard, while it is impossible for a painter to represent things which cannot be seen. And the greatest prodigy, for an art which only acts through movement, is to be able to go so far as to form the image of rest. Sleep, the calm of night, solitude, even silence, enter into musical pictures. It is known that noise can produce the effect of silence, and silence the effect of noise, as when one falls asleep in an indifferent and monotonous lecture and wakes up the moment it stops. But music acts more intimately on us, arousing through one sense affections similar to those aroused through another . . . Even if the whole of nature were asleep, those who contemplate it would not be. And the musician's art consists of substituting for an impassive image of the object the movements

175–7 which its presence excites in the heart of him who contemplates it.

[In the last two chapters Rousseau describes the degeneration of music, as singing and speech become separated,* and how this reflects and accompanies a social degeneration.]

XX. RELATION OF LANGUAGES TO GOVERNMENT

[Today] public force makes up for persuasion. Neither art nor symbol are needed to say 'such is my pleasure'. What sort of public discourse remains to be given to the assembled people? Sermons . . .

Societies have taken on their final form; no longer is anything exchanged except by cannons and cash. And since there is nothing to say to the people except 'Give money', it is said with posters on street corners or by soldiers in their homes. It is not necessary to assemble anyone for that. On the contrary, the subjects must be kept

197–9 apart. That is the first rule of modern politics.

* The desire to overcome this separation made him pay particular attention to the recitative of his own opera.

III

Rousseau devoted two letters in *The New Heloïse* to music (Part One, Letter 48, on the experience of music, and Part Two, Letter 23, a sardonic description of the Paris Opera), but his most substantial writing on the subject was his *Dictionary of Music*; begun in 1755, finished in 1765, although he did not in fact regard it as complete, and published in Paris at the end of 1767. It is an enormous work, incorporating passages from his earlier writing but with much new material on both the technique and theory of music. It also contains comments on ancient and oriental music and includes a melody from China (transcribed with one alteration or mistake) which later caught Weber's attention. It was used by him in his overture to *Turandot*, and then by Hindemith in his *Symphonic Metamorphoses on Themes by Weber*.[19]

In some of these articles the interconnection between Rousseau's aesthetic writing and his moral and political thought is particularly striking. No one, not even a genius, is an isolated individual. His article on genius, which according to his *Dialogues* aroused much interest,[20] says that genius is a particular gift, a view he had already expressed in the *First Discourse* and *The Social Contract*: 'True genius [does not copy, it] creates and makes everything out of nothing.'[21] But in the article on Taste we read: 'Genius creates, but taste chooses' and taste can benefit a 'too abundant genius'. Taste, moreover, is distinguished from sensibility just as *sentiment* had earlier been distinguished from *sensation*. This leads Rousseau to develop a social sense of aesthetic value that has some affinities with the general will.

In many articles Rousseau continues to stress the cultural (as opposed to natural) aspects of music, while still upholding his belief in the value of what is simple and close to nature. Reading these writings on music we come into closer contact, perhaps, than anywhere else with those emotional forms that sustained all his thought.

Dictionary of Music

Accent . . . The universal accent of nature, which draws inarticulate sounds from every man, is one thing; and the accent of language, which produces the melody particular to a nation, is another . . . The same foundation of passion reigns in [man's] soul; but what a variety of expression [there is] in his accents and his language. Now, it is

to this variety alone, when he is able to imitate it, that the musician
592 owes the energy and grace of his song.

Air . . . An air discovered by genius and composed with taste is the
masterpiece of music . . . After a beautiful air we are satisfied, the
ear desires nothing more. It remains in our imagination, we take it
away with us, we repeat it at our pleasure . . . The heart, impressed
with a very lively feeling, often expresses it more acutely by inarticu-
604 late sounds, than by words.

Baroque. A baroque music is one in which the whole harmony is
confused, filled with modulations and dissonances, the song hard
and unnatural, the intonation difficult, and the movement constrained. It seems evident that this term comes from the baroco of
609 the logicians.

Castrato. Musician deprived in his childhood of the organs of
generation to keep his voice shrill . . . [Let us speak out against]
this horrid custom . . . These men sing well but without fire or
627 passion, [and are] the most miserable actors in the world.

Composer. One who composes music or who knows all the rules
of composition . . . All the knowledge possible is not enough without
643 the genius which puts it into operation . . .

[Composers, wrote Rousseau in the article on Opera, need 'the
fire of invention and the gift of imitation'. (759).]

Genius. Do not seek, young artist, for what genius is. If you have
it you will feel it in yourself. If you do not have it you will never
know it. The genius of a musician subjects the whole universe to his
art. He paints every picture by sounds; he makes even silence speak.
He conveys ideas by feelings, feelings by accents, and the passions
which he expresses he arouses in our hearts. Pleasure through him
takes on new charm; the grief which he expresses draws out our
tears. He is continually burning, but is never consumed. He expresses
with warmth frost and ice. Even in painting the horrors of death he
conveys to the soul that feeling of life which never abandons it, and
which he communicates to hearts made to feel it. But alas! he can
say nothing to those who do not have his seed; and his marvels are
hardly perceptible to those who cannot imitate them. Would you
like to know then if any spark of this devouring fire inspires you?
Run: fly to Naples. Listen to the masterpieces of Leo, Durante,
Jommelli, Pergolesi. [If they move you, then] take Metastasio,* and
work. His genius will inflame yours; you will create after his example.

---

* The leading librettist in eighteenth-century Italy.

It is this which makes genius . . . [But if you are not moved] how do you dare ask what genius is? . . . What does it matter to you to know? You cannot feel it. Make French music.   701–2

Licence. A liberty which the composer takes and which seems contrary to rules, although it is in the principle of the rules. This is what distinguishes licences from faults . . . As most of the rules of harmony are founded on arbitrary principles, and change with custom and the taste of composers, it happens that these rules vary, are subject to fashion, and what is a licence at one time is not so at another.   719

Opera. A dramatic and lyric spectacle in which we strive to bring together all the charms of the fine arts in the representation of a passionate action, and, with the help of pleasant sensations, to excite interest and illusion. The constituent parts of an opera are the poem, the music, and the decoration. By poetry we speak to the mind, by music to the ear, and by painting to the eyes; and the whole ought to be brought together to move the heart and convey to it at one and the same time the same impression through different organs.   755

[Rousseau discusses 'the difficulty of uniting song to speech in our languages' (756), a difficulty which was unknown to the Greeks; 'all their poetry was musical and all their music declamatory, so their song was virtually a sustained speech' (756). Because of this difficulty the first operas had seemed an unnatural mixture, and to make them plausible fantastic subjects were used. But then the musical possibilities were developed.]

As soon as music had learnt to paint and speak, the charms of feeling soon replaced those of fairy tales. The theatre was purged of its jargon of mythology. Interest was substituted for the marvellous . . . The opera became a spectacle equally touching and noble . . . the imitation of nature, often more difficult and always more pleasing than that of imaginary creatures, became more interesting as it became more true to life.   758–60

Sensibility. A disposition of the soul which inspires the composer with the lively ideas which he needs, the performer with the lively expression of those same ideas, and the hearer with the lively impression of the beauties and faults of the music which is being played to him.   798

Taste. Of all natural gifts taste is that which is most felt and least explained. It would not be what it is if it could be defined, for it judges objects where the judgement has no more grasp, and serves, as it were, as the spectacles to reason . . .

[Every man has a particular sense of taste.] But there is also a general taste, on which all well-balanced* people are agreed, and it is only to this that the name of taste can be given absolutely. Let a concert be heard by ears sufficiently exercised and men sufficiently instructed. The greatest number will generally agree on the judgement of the pieces and in what order they prefer them. Ask everyone the reason for his judgement; there are things on which they will give an almost unanimous opinion. These things are those which are found submitted to rules, and this common judgement is then that of the artist and the connoisseur. But among these things . . . there are some on which they cannot come to a judgement by any solid reason, common to all. It is this [kind of] judgement that belongs to the man of taste. If a perfect unanimity is not to be found [among them], it is because all are not equally well balanced, because all are not people of taste, and because the prejudices of habit or education often change the order of natural beauties by arbitrary conventions. With regard to this taste, we may disagree about it, because there is only one [judgement] which can be the true one. But I hardly see any other means of ending the dispute — when we do not even agree about the voice of nature — than that of counting the [human] voices. Here then is what ought to decide the preference of French and Italian music.

As for the rest, Genius creates, but Taste chooses; and a too abundant genius is often in need of a severe censor to prevent it from abusing its wealth. We can do great things without taste, but it is that which makes them interesting. It is taste which makes the composer seize the ideas of the poet; it is taste which makes the performer catch the ideas of the composer. It is taste which provides both with everything that can adorn and show off their subject, and which gives the hearer the sense of its appropriateness. Taste however is not sensibility. We may have much taste with a cold soul; and a man who is carried away by really passionate things is little affected by the gracious. It seems that taste is more readily connected with small expressions, and sensibility with the great.

703–4

Unity of melody. [Rousseau contrasts the four-part singing of psalms with the 'good modern music' of the Opera House in Venice. The former is soon tiring and becomes monotonous; the latter holds continuous and increasing interest.]

* The phrase Rousseau uses — *bien organisé* — means literally 'well-formed organically'.

This difference [in their effects] comes from that of the character of the two [kinds of] music, one of which is only a sequence of chords, and the other a sequence of song. The pleasure of harmony is only a pleasure of pure sensation, and the enjoyment of the senses is always short: satiety and boredom soon follow it. But the pleasure of melody and song is a pleasure of interest and feeling, which speak to the heart . . .

Music must then sing in order to touch, please, and sustain the interest and attention. But how in our system of chords and harmony can the music manage to sing? If each part has its own song, all the songs heard at once will mutually destroy one another, and will make no song. If all the parts make the same song there will be no more harmony, and the concert will be entirely in unison.

The way in which a musical instinct . . . has overcome this difficulty . . . is very remarkable. Harmony, which should stifle the melody, animates it, strengthens it, determines it. The different parts co-operate in the same effect without being confused; and although each of them seems to have its own song, you only hear one and the same song emerging from all these parts. This is what I call unity of melody.   85

8 WAR

The first work Rousseau undertook after his move to the Hermitage in 1756 was a selection from the works of the Abbé de St-Pierre. He had met the Abbé before the latter's death in 1743 and shown interest in his writing. The Abbé's nephew had therefore entrusted Rousseau with the task of editing 'twenty-three volumes of difficult, confused, long-winded and repetitive writings'.[1] Rousseau believed they contained 'treasures',[2] the only problem was that they were so badly expressed that they were very hard to read. In fact he discovered as he worked on them that they were of less value than he had supposed.

> A complete examination of his political works revealed only superficial views, projects which were useful but made impracticable by the one idea the author could never get rid of, that men were motivated more by their intelligence than their passions. The high opinion he had of modern learning had made him adopt the mistaken principle of perfected reason; it was the base of all the institutions he proposed and the cause of all his political errors. This rare man . . . perhaps the only man ever since the human race existed who had no other passion except that of reason . . . wanted to make men like himself, instead of taking them as they are and as they will continue to be.[3]

Rousseau extracted two works from the Abbé's writing, his *Project for Perpetual Peace* and his *Polysynody*; to each extract he also attached a *Judgement*, a commentary of his own. The *Polysynody* was a system of government in which the business of administration was divided into eight councils, each devoted to a particular subject, overseen by a general council; the nine councils together formed the Plurality of Councils described by the title. It was put forward as an alternative to the arbitrary system of monarchical rule. Rousseau had many reservations about this proposal, not least the impossibility of putting it into effect with the monarchy in power; moreover, its implications made it too radical to publish in France.

The *Perpetual Peace*, however, was published, and it also played an important part in the development of Rousseau's thought. The Abbé was one of the first people to tackle the problem of war in a rational way. Instead of lamenting it as endemic to the human condition, or condemning it as morally wrong, he applied himself to finding ways to overcome it. The *Perpetual Peace*, 'the most considerable and developed of all his works',[4] suggested a Confederation of European Heads of State. By uniting them in this common body, in which all would defend the common interest of maintaining peace, he hoped to prevent war.

This idea of a confederation and the attempt to formulate policy in terms of a common interest were both developed by Rousseau. Some of the remarks he attributes to the Abbé are in fact clearly his own: 'Ideas of commerce and money [have] produced a kind of political fanaticism.'[5] 'There is a great difference between being dependent on another [person] and only [being dependent] on a body of which one is a member, and of which everyone is leader in turn; for in this latter case you are only making your freedom certain by the guarantees you give. [Freedom] would be alienated in the hands of a master, but it is affirmed in the hands of associates.'[6]

In his *Judgement*, Rousseau praised the Abbé's proposal, and its cogent reasoning, but he criticized his poor knowledge of men.

Judgement on the Project for Perpetual Peace

The whole occupation of kings, or of those who are charged to carry out their business, is devoted to only two objects: to extend their domination beyond their frontiers and to make it more absolute within. Every other consideration relates to either one or the other of these two, or serves as a pretext for it. Phrases like 'the public good', 'the happiness of the subject', 'the glory of the people', are never permitted in councils and are used so heavy-handedly in public pronouncements that . . . the people groan in anticipation when their masters speak to them of their paternal concern . . .   592

It is easy to see that wars of conquest and the advance of despotism mutually encourage one another . . . That conquering princes make war as much on their subjects as on their enemies . . .   593

[The Abbé had put forward as a reason for peace the fact that the cost of armies would be reduced and commerce would be uninterrupted.]

It is a great mistake to reckon the gains or losses of princes in terms of money. The degree of power they have in mind is not counted by the millions they possess. The prince always makes his schemes rotate: he wants to command to be rich, and to be rich to command. He will sacrifice in turn one or the other in order to acquire whichever of the two he lacks, but it is only in order to possess them both in the end that he pursues each separately; for to be master of men and things he needs both empire and money.

Let us add, on the subject of the great advantages for commerce which should result from a general and lasting peace, that while they are certain and indisputable in themselves, since they are common to everyone they will not be particular to anyone. Such advantages are only felt by their differences; to increase your relative power you should only look for exclusive gains.

594

Constantly misled by the appearance of things Princes will therefore reject this peace; [that is] if they consider their interests themselves What will it be if they are considered by their ministers, whose interests are always opposed to those of the people and almost always to those of the prince? Ministers need war to make themselves necessary, to put the prince in difficulties which he cannot get out of without them, to lose the state, if necessary, rather than their position. They need it to harass the people under the pretext of public necessity. They need it to find jobs for their underlings, to make profits on the market, and create a thousand hateful monopolies. They need it to satisfy their passions, and mutually keep out their rivals. They need it when dangerous intrigues are formed against them, to occupy the prince and keep him away from the court. They would lose all these resources with a perpetual peace, and the public still asks why, if this project is possible, the ministers have not adopted it?

To find a favourable moment to carry out this system [it would be necessary] for the sum of all the private interests not to be greater than the common interest, and for everyone to think he sees in the good of all the greatest good that he can hope for himself. Now that demands a concurrence of wisdom in so many heads, and a concurrence of direction in so many interests, that one should scarcely hope for the chance of such a fortuitous agreement . . .

595

Let us not say then that if [the Abbé's] system has not been adopted it is because it was no good. Let us say rather that it was too good to be adopted. For the evil and the abuses, from which so many people profit, come about by themselves; but what is useful to the public scarcely ever comes about except by force, since private interests are almost always opposed to it . . .   599

Let us admire such a beautiful plan, but let us console ourselves for not seeing it carried out; for that could only be done by violent means, terrible for humanity. We will not see federal leagues established except by revolutions, and on that principle which of us would dare to say whether this European League is to be wished for or to be feared? It would perhaps do more damage in an instant than it would prevent for centuries.   600

Rousseau's writing on war was timely. A month after he had moved to the Hermitage Great Britain declared war on France and three months after this Frederick of Prussia invaded Saxony. The Seven Years' War had begun. At the end of it Britain had gained colonies in both Canada and India, while the European powers had incurred such debts that the resulting need to increase revenue also increased social tensions and hastened the end of the monarchies.

Rousseau had written about war in another manuscript, which is sometimes connected with the works of the Abbé de St-Pierre, though it was probably written earlier. The work, which was left incomplete, is entitled *That the State of War is Born from the Social State*. As this titles indicates, it is principally a polemic against Hobbes. It is not merely a polemic, however.

In these pages, as also in his incomplete writings on luxury and commerce, Rousseau delineates with chilling clarity the condition of men who have lost all sense of limit or humanity. He attacks both the philosophers who use their reason to justify intolerable conditions, and the men whose lust for domination puts them beyond the reach of reason. The condition where the whole universe becomes necessary to each person (see p. 233), because 'he who has much wants everything'. Living in Paris Rousseau had imagined the past history of natural man; living now in the country he suggests the future history of urban man.

The State of War

If it were true that this unlimited and ungovernable greed would be developed in every man to the degree our sophist supposes, it would still not produce that state of universal war of each against all, the hideous picture of which Hobbes dares to draw. This unchecked desire to appropriate everything for oneself is incompatible with that of destroying all one's fellows; and the conqueror, who, having killed everyone, would have the misfortune to remain alone in the world, would enjoy nothing of it for the very reason that he did possess everything. What is wealth itself good for, if not to be communicated? What use will possession of the whole universe be to him, if he is the only inhabitant of it? What? Will his stomach devour all the fruits of the earth? Who will bring him all the products of every region? Who will tell him about his rule over the vast solitudes which he will not inhabit? What will he do with his treasures? Who will consume his provisions? In whose eyes will he display his power? I understand. Instead of massacring everyone he will put them all in chains, so that at least he has slaves. That immediately changes the nature of the question; and since it is no longer a matter of destruction, the state of

601   war is abolished . . .

Man is naturally peaceful and fearful; at the slightest danger his first instinct is to flee; he only becomes warlike through force of habit and experience. However, self-interest, prejudices, revenge, all the passions which can make him brave perils and death, are far from him in the state of nature. It is only when he has made society with some man that he decides to attack another; he only becomes a

601–2   soldier after he has been a citizen . . .

There is therefore no general war of man against man; and the human race was not formed solely to destroy itself . . .

If natural law was only written in human reason it would be little capable of directing most of our actions, but it is rather engraved in the heart of man in ineffaceable characters and there it speaks to him more strongly than all the precepts of philosophers. There it cries out to him that he is not allowed to sacrifice the life of his fellow-man for the preservation of his own, and it makes him horrified to spill human blood without [being carried away by] anger, even when he sees himself obliged to do so . . . There can have been fights

602   and murders, but never, or very rarely, long hostilities or wars . . .

There is no war between men; there is only war between states . . .

Man has a period of strength and greatness fixed by nature, which he cannot pass. However he thinks of it, he finds all his faculties limited. His life is short, his years are finite. His stomach does not grow with his wealth; his passions increase in vain; his pleasures have their measure; his heart is like all the rest; his capacity for enjoyment is always the same. In vain does he have an elevated idea of himself, he always remains small.

The state on the other hand, being an artificial body, has no deter-mined measure; it has no definite size suitable to it, it can always increase; it feels itself to be weak when there are stronger states than itself. Its security and its preservation demand that it makes itself more powerful than all its neighbours. It can only augment, nourish and exercise its strength at their expense . . . The inequality of men has limits set down by the hands of nature, but that of societies can grow constantly, until one alone absorbs all the others . . .   604–5

People have worked hard to reverse the true ideas of things. Everything leads natural man to rest; to eat and sleep are the only needs he knows; and only hunger overcomes his laziness. Out of this he has been made into a madman, always ready to torment his fellows by passions which he does not know. These passions do not exist there; on the contrary, they are aroused in the midst of society by everything which can inflame them. Thousands of writers have dared to say that the body politic is without passions and it has no reason to be, except reason itself. As if we did not see the opposite: that the essence of society consists in the activity of its members and that a state without movement would be a dead body . . .   605

I open the books on right and morality, I listen to the scholars and jurists, and moved by their persuasive words I deplore the miseries of nature. I admire the peace and justice established by the civil order, I bless the wisdom of public institutions and console myself for being a man by seeing myself as a citizen. Well instructed in my duties and my happiness I close the book, leave the classroom and look around me. I see wretched peoples groaning beneath a yoke of iron, the human race crushed by a handful of oppressors; a starving crowd, over-whelmed by hunger and suffering, their blood and their tears being drunk by the rich, and everywhere the strong armed against the weak by the terrible power of the laws . . .   608–9

I raise my eyes and look in the distance. I see fire and flames, the countryside deserted, towns ransacked . . . I hear a terrifying noise. What a tumult! What cries! I approach them. I see a scene of murder, ten thousand men slaughtered, the dead piled up in heaps, the dying trampled underfoot by horse, everywhere the image of death and agony. This then is the outcome of these peaceful institutions!

What man is there whose very entrails would not be moved by these sad sights? But it is no longer permitted to be a man and plead the

cause of humanity. Justice and truth must give way before the
609   interest of the most powerful; that is the rule . . .

Who could have imagined without trembling the mad system of the
natural war of each against all? What strange animal is it who would
think his good attached to the destruction of his whole species!
And how could anyone imagine that such a monstrous and detestable
species could last more than two generations? This is where the desire,
or rather the fury, to establish despotism and passive obedience have
611   led one of the finest geniuses* who has lived . . .

I have already said, and I cannot repeat too often, that the mistake
of Hobbes and the philosophers is to confuse natural man with men
whom they have in front of them, and to transpose into one system a
being who can only survive in another. Man wishes his well-being
and all that can contribute to it. That is indisputable. But this well-
being of man is naturally limited to physical need; when he has a
healthy soul and his body does not suffer, what does he lack to be
happy according to his constitution?

He who has nothing desires few things. He who commands no
one has little ambition. But superfluity awakens greed; the more you
get, the more you want. He who has much wants everything . . . This
is the course of nature, this is the development of the passions. A
superficial philosopher observes souls refashioned a hundred times,
fermented in society, and believes he has observed men. But to know
man well you have to be able to unravel the natural gradations of his
feelings. It is not among the inhabitants of a great city that we must
look for the first features of nature in their imprint on the human
611–12 heart.

So this analytic method produces only horrors and mysteries, where
the wisest understand the least . . . They only know what they see
and they have never seen nature. They know very well what is a
bourgeois of London or Paris, but they will never know what is a
612   man.

* Although Rousseau disagreed radically with Hobbes' view of man, and
detested his defence of absolutism, he admired his ability. It is probable that
he owed some elements of his own concept of sovereignty and of the artificial
nature of political society to his reading of Hobbes.[7]

9 OPTIMISM

In his *Theodicy*, published in 1710, Leibniz argued that everything in creation acts according to its own nature and in agreement with universal harmony; evil is not an active principle but rather a lack, a necessary consequence of our finite condition. Men are free and God 'wills to produce only what is the best among things possible'.[1] This encouraging belief came to be known as 'optimism'; the word first appeared in French in the 1730s and in English in the 1750s. It became widely known and widely shared. In his *Essay on Man* Pope wrote: 'All are but parts of one stupendous whole/ Whose body nature is, and God the soul' . . . 'And, spite of pride, in erring reason's spite,/ One truth is clear, Whatever is, is right.' God provided for the good of man; divine Providence was essentially benevolent.

This belief suffered a shock in 1755 when an earthquake in Lisbon killed twenty thousand people. It was not merely the scale of the disaster but the fact that it had happened on All Saints' Day, when large numbers of the population were in church. How could such an event be reconciled with the optimist philosophy? Was it not rather a sign that God had no hand in the affairs of men, and that there was no divinely-inspired order? That there was no promise of a life to come which could compensate for the miseries and disasters we endured here and now?

This was how it appeared to the ageing Voltaire. In a poem *On the Lisbon Disaster* he attacked the beliefs of Leibniz and Pope. 'The phrase "All is good" is only an insult to the griefs of our life', he wrote.[2] In the summer of 1756 he sent copies, with another poem *On Natural Law* and some additional notes, to Rousseau, Diderot and D'Alembert.

Rousseau had known Pope's *Essay on Man* since his youth, and not long before, in his *Letter to M. Philopolis*, he had taken issue with the optimist philosophy. But his argument there was with the application of optimism to society, with the idea that the social order reflected God's will. Such a view was directly contrary to his own belief, set out in the *Discourse on Inequality*, that it was precisely in the social order that the origin of evil lay. In this context optimism was wrong. Voltaire's comments, however, were not about society but about God, nature and the meaning of life. In this context Rousseau was an optimist.

> Struck by the sight of this poor man overwhelmed, so to speak, by prosperity and glory, yet declaiming bitterly against the miseries of this life and always finding that everything was evil, I formed the mad scheme of making him return to himself and of proving to him that all was good. While always appearing to believe in God, Voltaire has never really believed in anything but the Devil, since his supposed God is only a malicious creature who, according to him, only takes pleasure in doing harm . . . Having more reason than him to weigh up and assess the evils of human life, I examinèd them fairly and I proved to him that of all these evils there is not one that could be blamed on Providence, and not one which did not have its origin in the abuse which man has made of his faculties, rather than in nature herself.[3]

Rousseau made an essential distinction between the natural order and what men have done to it. There are physical evils but there is no general evil; this is a point he was to reiterate again and again — 'In the physical order there is nothing absolutely bad. The whole is good.'[4] Just as there is no original sin in man so there is no general evil in the world.

But how can this belief be sustained in the face of the physical evils we do suffer and have to endure? The optimist's answer was based on the relation of the parts to the whole. In the nature of things the decay of one part makes possible the life of another. The disasters that occur cannot be taken to prove that there is no general sense of order. The irregularities we may find in nature reveal more about the limits of our own faculties than about the true condition of things. 'Nothing is foreign to the universe.'[5]

This view of a harmonious natural order was to be developed later by Rousseau in the *Profession of Faith of a Savoyard Priest*. It was one of his principal reasons for believing in God. Another aspect of his faith that is set out here is his belief in the immortality of the soul. Given the injustices that go uncorrected it seemed to him that if God were just our souls must be immortal, that there must be an afterlife in which the virtuous man would enjoy the happiness that was denied him in this life.

More important than either of these, in that it has parallels and implications in all areas of his thought, is the sense of belonging to a greater whole. We are not isolated, we belong to something which, in so far as it is good, can give us a sense of our own existence that is deeply satisfying. It is this sense that gives Rousseau the confidence that distinguishes this *Letter*. It also enables him, sometimes, to feel hopeful about society. (His thoughts turn naturally to society; the *Letter* contains a first version of the idea of a civil religion, which he was to develop in *The Social Contract*.) Our lives obtain meaning from what relates us to our fellow-men; we are not separate or alone.

At the same time, however, Rousseau was alone. Because the views he put forward in this *Letter* set him apart from both the established Church and his fellow-intellectuals. Here, for the first time, he criticized them both openly. When he developed these criticisms later the consequences for himself were to be disastrous.

Voltaire received Rousseau's reply courteously and said he would answer at length in due course. No such answer came, but it was Rousseau's belief that Voltaire did answer indirectly — by writing *Candide*.[6]

Letter to Voltaire on Optimism, 18 August 1756

[Rousseau thanks Voltaire for the poems, one of which he likes very much.]

All my unhappiness is with your poem *On the Lisbon Disaster*, for I expected effects more worthy of humanity than those which seem to have inspired you. You reproach Pope and Leibniz with insulting our evils by maintaining that all is good, and you indulge yourself so much in portraying our miseries that you exacerbate the feeling [of them]. Instead of the consolation I hoped for, you have given me only affliction . . .

Do not deceive yourself, Sir. What happens is quite the opposite of what you suggest. That optimism which you find so cruel in fact consoles me. Pope's poem softens my ills and brings me patience . . . 'Man, have patience', say Pope and Leibniz to me. 'Your evils are a necessary effect of your nature and of the constitution of this universe. The eternal and benevolent Being who governs you would have wanted to make you secure from them. Of all possible economies he has chosen that which combines the least evil and the most good, or, to put it rather more crudely . . . if he has not done better, it is because he could not do better.' Now what does your poem tell me? 'Suffer for ever, unhappy man. If there is a God who has created you, without doubt he is omnipotent; he could have prevented all your ills; therefore do not hope that they will end; for it is impossible 1060 to see why you exist, if it is not to suffer and die.'

[He reminds Voltaire how he (Rousseau) was taken to task for writing against mankind, and adds:]

My intention in depicting human misery was, I believe, excusable and even laudable; for I showed men how they caused their misfortunes themselves, and consequently how they could avoid them.

I do not see where we can look for the source of moral evil except in man, a free, improved, yet corrupted creature. As for physical evils, if it is a contradiction for matter to be both sensitive and inert, as it seems to me, they are inevitable in every system of which man forms a part. So the question is not 'Why is not man perfectly happy?' but 'Why does he exist?' Moreover, I think I have shown that, except for death, which can be called an evil only from the preparations which go before it, the majority of our physical evils are still our own work. Without leaving your subject of Lisbon, for example, you must agree that nature never collected there twenty thousand houses of six or seven storeys high, and that if the inhabitants of this great town had been more equally spread out, and less elaborately housed, the damage would have been a lot less, and perhaps none at all. All would have fled at the first tremble, and you would have seen them the next day, twenty leagues away, as happy as if nothing had happened. But instead they had to stay, stubbornly, by the ruins, exposed to new shocks, because what they had to leave behind was worth more than what they could take away. How many unhappy people perished in this disaster for wanting to get their clothes, their papers or their money? Is it not well known that the person of each man has become the least part of him, and it is almost not worth 1061–2 the trouble of saving it when everything else is lost? . . .

There are events which often strike us more or less according to the light in which they are seen, and which lose much of the horror which they inspire at first sight when they are more closely examined . . . Among so many men crushed under the ruins of Lisbon, several have undoubtedly avoided worse misfortunes; and despite the

occasion that such a subject affords for poetry and touching description, it is not certain that a single one of those unlucky people would
have suffered more if, in the ordinary course of things, he had
waited in long anguish for the death which has just surprised him . . .
Is there a sadder end than that of a dying man overwhelmed by useless
concerns, not left free to breathe by a notary and heirs, murdered
in his bed by unfeeling doctors and made to relish death by
barbarous priests? . . . For my part I see everywhere that the evils
which nature does to us are a great deal less than those which we
add to her.   1062

But however ingenious we may be in increasing our miseries by
means of beautiful institutions, we have not been able, up to now, to
improve ourselves to the point of making life generally a burden,
and of preferring nothingness to our existence. Otherwise, dis-
couragement and despair would soon get hold of the greatest number
and the human race would not have been able to last very long. Now
if it is better for us to be than not to be, that would be enough to
justify our existence, even when we may have no compensation to
expect for the evils we have suffered, and even if these evils are as
great as you depict them. But it is difficult to find on this subject
good faith among men, or good calculations among philosophers;
because the latter in comparing good and evil always forget the sweet
feeling of existence, which is independent of every other sensation,
and the vanity of scorning death makes the others slander life. Rather
like those women who, with a stained dress and some scissors, claim
to prefer holes to stains.   1062–3

You think with Erasmus that few people would want to be born
again in the same conditions in which they have lived . . . [But, Sir,]
whom am I to believe you have consulted on that? The rich, perhaps,
satiated with false pleasures, but ignorant of true ones, always bored
with life and always afraid to lose it; men of letters perhaps, of all
the orders of men the most sedentary, the most unhealthy, the most
thoughtful and as a result the most unhappy. Do you want to find
men of better temperament, or at least usually more sincere, and,
who, forming the greatest number, ought for that reason at least to
be heard in preference? Consult an honest tradesman who will
have passed an obscure and peaceful life; a good artisan, who lives
comfortably from his business; even a peasant, not in France, where
it is supposed that they must be made to die of poverty in order that
they can make us live, but in the country, for example, where you are,
and generally in any free country. I dare to suggest in fact that in the

High Valais there is perhaps not a single Montagnard* unhappy with his almost automatic existence, who would not willingly agree, even in place of paradise, to be born again continually, to vegetate thus for ever. These differences make me think that it is often the abuse that we make of life which makes it a burden to us . . . and if it is not

1063–4 always an evil to die, it is very rarely an evil to live . . .

Our different ways of thinking on all these matters explain why several of your proofs are far from conclusive for me. For I am not ignorant of how much more easily human reason takes on the pattern of our opinions than that of truth . . .

[The evidence that Voltaire brings forward to demonstrate the irregularities of nature is unconvincing.]

For these apparent irregularities undoubtedly come from some laws which we do not know and which nature follows just as faithfully as those that we do know, from some cause which we do not perceive . . . Otherwise it would clearly be necessary to say that there are actions without principle and effects without cause, which is repugnant to all philosophy . . . [As for mathematical proofs] mathematical figures being only abstractions have no relation to anything except

1065 themselves . . .

Who can know if there are not perhaps a million other laws possible,

1066 without hitting the true one? . . .

As for the good of the whole, in preference to that of a part, you make man say: 'I, a thinking and feeling being, ought to be as dear to my master as the planets, which probably do not feel at all.' Without doubt this material universe ought not to be dearer to its Author than a single thinking and feeling being. But the system of this universe, which produces, preserves and perpetuates all feeling and thinking beings, ought to be dearer to Him than a single one of these beings. He can therefore, in spite of his goodness, or rather through his very goodness, sacrifice something of the goodness of the individuals for the preservation of the whole. I believe and I hope that I am worth more in the eyes of God than the soil of a planet; but if the planets are inhabited, as is probable, why should I be worth more

1067 in His eyes than all the inhabitants of Saturn? . . .

That the corpse of a man nourishes worms, wolves or plants is not, I confess, a compensation for the death of that man; but if, in the system of the universe, it is necessary to the preservation of the human species that there should be a circulation of substance between

* Inhabitant of the High Valais.

men, animals and vegetables, then the particular ill of an individual contributes to the general good. I die, I am eaten by worms; but my children and my brothers will live as I have lived . . .

To return, Sir, to the system which you attack, I believe that it cannot be examined properly without distinguishing carefully between the particular evil of which no philosopher has ever denied the existence, and the general evil which the optimist does deny. It is not a question of knowing if each of us suffers, or not; but if it was good that the universe should be, and if our evils were inevitable in the constitution of the universe. Therefore it seems to me that the addition of a single article would make the proposition more exact; and instead of 'All is good' [*Tout est bien*], it would perhaps be better to say 'The whole is good' [*Le tout est bien*], or 'All is good for the whole' [*Tout est bien pour le tout*]. Then it is very evident that no man would be able to give direct proof for it or against it; for the proof depends on a perfect knowledge of the constitution of the world and the intention of its Author, and this knowledge is undeniably above human intelligence. The true principles of optimism cannot be drawn either from the properties of matter or the mechanism of the universe, but only by induction from the perfections of God who presides over all . . . So that one does not prove the existence of God by the system of Pope, but the system of Pope by the existence of God, and it is beyond doubt that the question of the origin of evil is derived from that of Providence. If neither of these two questions have been better treated, it is because people have always reasoned so badly about Providence; absurd things have been said about it. This great and consoling dogma has been severely obscured by all the corollaries that people have been able to draw from it.

The first to have damaged the cause of God have been the priests and devotees who do not allow that anything is done according to the established order, but always make divine justice intervene in purely natural events.

The philosophers, for their part, scarcely seem any more reasonable when I see them lay the blame on heaven for whatever makes them suffer, crying out that all is lost when they have toothache or they are poor or they are robbed, and charging God, as Seneca says, with looking after their luggage . . .   1068–9

It is to be believed that particular events here below are nothing in the eyes of the Master of the universe, that His Providence is solely universal, that He contents Himself with preserving the genera and the species and with presiding over the whole, without

1069 worrying himself over the way in which each individual spends his short life . . .

To think correctly in this respect it seems that things ought to be considered relatively in the physical order and absolutely in the moral order; so that the greatest idea that I can make of Providence is that each material being is disposed in the best way possible in relation to the whole, and each intelligent and sensitive being in the best way possible in relation to himself. What this signifies, in other terms, is that for him who feels his existence, it is better to exist than not to exist. But it is necessary to apply this rule to the total duration of each sensitive being and not to some particular moments of his duration, such as human life; which shows how much the question of Providence relates to that of the immortality of the soul, which I have the happiness to believe in, not without being aware that reason can doubt it — and to that of the eternity of torments — which neither you nor I, nor any man ever thinking well of God, will ever believe in.

If I bring these different questions down to their common principle, it seems to me that they all relate to that of the existence of God. If God exists, he is perfect; if he is perfect, he is wise, powerful and just; if he is wise and powerful, all is good; if he is just and powerful, my soul is immortal; if my soul is immortal, thirty years of life are nothing for me and are perhaps necessary to the maintenance of the universe. If I am granted the first proposition, the subsequent one can never be shaken; if it is denied, it is unnecessary to argue about

1070 its consequences . . .

[From reading Voltaire's books Rousseau presumes that they are in agreement on the existence of God. There is no point in arguing with the intellectuals who do not agree on this, since the matter is not susceptible to proof. He wishes, though, that they in turn would not argue since they destroy people's peace of mind. He continues:] I think, after your example, that one cannot attack too strongly the superstition which disturbs society, nor respect too much the religion which sustains it.

But I am outraged, as you are, that each man's faith should not be in the most perfect freedom, and that any man dares to control the interior of consciences, which he cannot penetrate — as if it depended on us to believe or not to believe in matters where demonstration has no place — and that one can never subject reason to authority. Do the kings of this world have some insight into another? And do they have the right here below to torment their subjects, to force them to go to paradise? No. Every human government is limited by its nature to civil duties; and whatever that sophist Hobbes might be able to say about it, when a man serves the state well he owes no account to anyone of the way in which he serves God . . .   1072

There is, I admit, a sort of profession of faith that the laws could impose, though outside the principles of morality and natural right it should be purely negative — because there can exist religions which attack the foundations of society, and it is necessary to begin by eradicating these religions in order to ensure the peace of the state. Of the dogmas to proscribe, intolerance is undoubtedly the most hateful; but it must be checked at its source; for the most bloodthirsty fanatics change their language according to their success, and preach only gentleness and patience when they are the strongest. Therefore I call intolerant by principle every man who imagines that one cannot be a good man without believing all that he believes, and who damns pitilessly all those who do not think like him . . . If there were intolerant unbelievers, who wished to force the people to believe nothing, I would not banish them less severely . . . I would like it therefore if one had in each state a moral code, or a sort of profession of civil faith, which would contain positively the social maxims that each should be bound to acknowledge, and negatively the fanatical maxims that each should be bound to reject, not as impious but as seditious. So every religion which could be in agreement with the code would be admitted; every religion which would not be in agreement would be proscribed; and everyone would be free to have no other religion at all other than the code itself. Done with care this work would be, it seems to me, the most useful book that would ever have been composed, and perhaps the only one necessary to men. There, Sir, is a subject for you. I passionately wish you would undertake this work and make it beautiful with your poetry . . . You have given us in your Poem on Natural Religion, the Catechism of Man; give us now, in what I propose to you, the Catechism of the Citizen . . .   1073–4

I cannot help noticing, Sir, a very strange contrast between you and me in the subject of this letter. Satiated with glory, and disabused of vain magnificence, you live freely in the midst of plenty; assured of immortality, you philosophize peacefully on the nature of the soul . . . yet you find only evil on the earth. And I, obscure, poor, and tormented by an incurable disorder, meditate with pleasure in my retreat, and find that all is good. Where do these apparent contradictions come from? You have explained it yourself; you enjoy, but I hope, and hope makes everything beautiful . . .

I have suffered too much in this life not to expect another. All the subtleties of metaphysics will not make me doubt for a moment the immortality of the soul and a benevolent Providence. I feel it, I believe it, I wish it, I hope for it, I will defend it until my last breath. This will be, of the disputes that I will have undertaken, the only one

1075   where my own interest will not be forgotten . . .

10 THEATRE

In 1757 Volume VII of the *Encyclopedia* appeared; it contained an article on Geneva by D'Alembert. Most of his comments on the city were favourable. It was beautifully situated, it was independent, its government had all the advantages and none of the disadvantages of democracy, neither nobility nor wealth brought position or privilege. Its church was so tolerant that many of the clergy did not even believe in the divinity of Christ, worship was simple, and though their singing might be poor, the Genevans were virtually as happy as anyone could expect to be. His only criticism was that no theatre was allowed. He suggested that one should be set up, because 'theatre would form the taste of the citizens and give them a *finesse* in behaviour and a delicacy of feeling which it is very difficult to acquire without its help; literature would profit from it without licentiousness developing, and Geneva would combine the wisdom of Sparta with the refinement of Athens'.[1]

These remarks had been largely inspired by Voltaire. He had entertained D'Alembert while the latter was doing his research and it was his wish that Geneva should have a theatre. His passion for plays and performing had brought him into conflict with the Genevan authorities and was forcing him to move from his original property at Les Délices over the border to Ferney.

The article caused an uproar. Praise from the *Encyclopedia* was anathema to self-respecting Christians, and the suggestion that the Genevan clergy no longer believed in Christ's divinity, a heresy known as Socinianism, provoked so much trouble that it contributed to D'Alembert's resignation as Diderot's co-editor. The Genevans set up a committee to answer the damaging article and they produced a Profession of Faith early the next year.

Rousseau also came to the defence of his native city. His main concern, however, was not with the charge of Socinianism, though he refuted that, but with the idea of setting up a theatre. That was 'the most dangerous advice that could be given us . . . It is not a matter of vain philosophical chatter, but a truth of practical importance to a whole people.'[2] He set aside his other work to explain why; his epigraph was from Virgil: 'May the gods grant better things to the good, and such a mistake to our enemies.'[3]

His opposition to the theatre was entirely consistent with his earlier views on the arts. After his first full-blooded attack on them, in the *First Discourse*, he had developed the view that they could be necessary as palliatives, as medicines were necessary to sick men. He was to write in the Preface to *The New Heloïse*: 'Large cities need theatres, and corrupted people need novels.'[4] But if the people were not yet corrupted, as in his opinion the people of Geneva were not, then theatres were not necessary. Worse, they would be harmful, morally, socially and aesthetically.

Although Rousseau had a puritan streak which set him against the sexuality of theatre, and although his unenlightened attitude to women was offended by their working as actresses (and he made both these criticisms), he disassociated himself from the traditional objections that the church made against the theatre. He focused rather on the moral claims that intellectuals made for it. He did not regard theatre as a necessary element or ornament to a good life. He maintained that the idea that Aristotle had put forward in his *Poetics*, that tragedy was morally purifying, was spurious. Far from correcting us or improving us plays made us feel exempt from actually doing good.* They weakened our respect for virtue and our ability to be virtuous. Instead of forming public opinion or behaviour they merely followed and reflected it.

Theatres were equally undesirable for social reasons. They would disrupt the existing 'circles', the clubs and groups in which Genevans relaxed in one another's company; they would encourage a taste for luxury, and the expense would give rise to more taxes. The theatre proposed was of course the French theatre, which, as Rousseau described it in *The New Heloïse* (Part Two, Letter 17), only concerned itself with the nobility and the wealthy and ignored the rest of society. Such a theatre aggravated social tensions and increased inequalities.

---

* In the Second Preface to *The New Heloïse* Rousseau wrote: 'It is in the most depraved times that people like lessons of the most perfect morality. That exempts them from practising it. A few hours' reading takes care, at no great cost, of their remaining taste for virtue.'[5]

It was this kind of theatre which was being proposed for Geneva. It was the patrician citizens who wanted it and the bourgeoisie who opposed it. Jean-François De Luc, one of the leaders of the democratic movement, who had become a friend of Rousseau's during his visit to the city in 1754, also wrote a pamphlet attacking D'Alembert's article. When a theatre was set up later, in 1766, at the insistence of the French plenipotentiary (who had intervened because of the political deadlock), it was burnt down.

The most far-reaching of Rousseau's objections were aesthetic. When he was preparing his *Letter* he read Plato's criticism of the arts in *The Republic* and the *Laws*, and he collected these criticisms in an essay later published under the title *Theatrical Imitation*. Some of his own remarks were derived from Plato. He shared his belief in the importance of reason in achieving virtue, and reason could never be predominant in so essentially emotional an activity as theatre. He also shared a belief in the inferiority of imitation to reality. But while imitation was bad to Plato because it obscured the ideal, it was inferior to Rousseau because it was a substitute for the actual. Reality for Plato was only an inferior image of the ideal; for Rousseau it was desirable in itself, 'the sweet feeling of existence'. He did not discredit our emotions in order to elevate our reason; the 'sweet feeling' was itself emotional. This is why his comments on the emotional aspects of the theatre are so penetrating. He had an acute sense of the frustrations of the imagination, an awareness of how inadequate its substitute pleasures could be. He had suggested in his *Letter to Voltaire* in 1755 (see p. 69) that the taste for art grew out of an 'inner fault' or weakness. The meaning of this was that art could not overcome the alienation we may feel, but was itself a product of that alienation. 'Become your own entertainment', he says to his fellow-citizens. Far from being a restricted or censorious view of art, as has often been suggested, this was magnificently and profoundly invigorating.

The *Letter to D'Alembert* is an uneven, impulsive work, with long digressions on the people in the mountain valleys round Neuchâtel, and on duelling. Rousseau wrote it in the space of three weeks in the winter of 1758, 'with no protection from the wind and the snow, with no fire except the one that burned in my heart'.[6] It was a time of ill-health when he fully expected to die. When spring came he wrote in a letter: 'During the short period that remains to me I am enjoying the happiness of *living;* my regret is not that of finishing so soon, but of having started so late.'[7] He did not want to write about living, or read about it or see plays about it, he wanted to live in himself. That was also his advice to his fellow-citizens.

Letter to D'Alembert on his Article 'Geneva'

What questions I find to discuss in what you seem to resolve! . . Everything about the true effects of theatre is still a problem because the disputes which it occasions only take place between men of the church and men of the world, each only looking at it through his 64–5 own prejudices . . .

Giving a first glance at these institutions, I see to begin with that a theatre is an amusement; and if it is true that men need amusements, you will at least agree that they are only permissible in so far as they are necessary, and that all useless amusement is an evil for a creature whose life is so short and time so precious. The state of man has pleasures which derive from his nature and which arise from his work, his relationships and his needs; and these pleasures, so much the sweeter if he who tastes them has a healthy soul, make whoever knows how to enjoy them indifferent to all others. A father, a son, a husband, a citizen, have such precious duties to fulfil that they have nothing left to give to boredom. Good use of time makes time still more precious, and the better it is used the less one has to lose. So we constantly see that the habit of work makes inactivity unbearable, and that a clear conscience destroys the taste for frivolous pleasures. It is dissatisfaction with oneself, it is the burden of idleness, it is the forgetting of simple and natural tastes, that makes necessary extraneous amusement. I do not like it at all that we continually need to 65–6 attach our hearts to the stage, as if they were ill at ease in ourselves . . .

To ask if theatre is good or bad in itself is to put too vague a question; it is to examine a relationship before having fixed the terms. Theatre is made for people, and it is only by its effects on you that you can determine its absolute qualities. There can be an infinite number of different kinds of theatre. There is from people to people a prodigious variety of morals, temperaments, characters . . . It is a question of knowing if the morality of the theatre is necessarily loose, if abuses are inevitable, if the drawbacks derive from the nature 66–7 & n. of the thing, or if they come from causes that could be avoided . . .

The stage in general is a portrayal of human passions, the original of which is in every heart. But if the artist does not take care to flatter these passions, the spectators would soon be repelled and would no longer wish to see themselves in a way which made them despise themselves. When he puts some in a bad light it is only those which are not typical and which are naturally hated. The author therefore does nothing except follow public feeling. Moreover, those passions that repel are always used to give greater value to others which are, if not more legitimate, at least more to the spectators' liking. It is only reason which is good for nothing on the stage. A man without passions, or a man who always controlled them, could not be of interest to anyone . . .

The theatre should not therefore be credited with the power of changing feelings or morals which it can only follow and embellish. An author who wanted to go against the prevailing taste would soon be writing only for himself . . .   68–9

It follows from these first observations that the general effect of the theatre is to reinforce national character, to increase natural inclinations and to give new energy to all the passions. In this sense it would seem that as this effect is limited to reinforcing and not changing existing morals, a play would be good to the good and bad to the wicked . . . I know that the aesthetic of the theatre pretends to do the opposite and purge the passions in arousing them; but I have trouble grasping this rule. Would it be that in order to become moderate and wise, it is necessary to begin by being violent and mad? . . . Why should the image of the sufferings produced by the passions efface that of the elements of pleasure and joy which they also produce, which authors take even more care embellishing so as to make their pieces more enjoyable?   71–3

I know only three kinds of instrument by means of which one can act on the morals of a people: namely, the force of the laws, the rule of public opinion, and the appeal of pleasure. Now laws have no effect on the theatre, as the least constraint would make it painful and not amusing.* Opinion is in no way dependent on it, since instead of making rules for the public the theatre receives them from it; and as for the pleasure which one can have there, its whole effect is to lead us back there more often.

Let us see if there could be other means. The theatre, I am told, directed as it could and ought to be, makes virtue lovable and wickedness hateful. What then? Before there were plays did people not love the good and hate the bad? Were these feelings weaker in places

---

* Laws can determine the subjects, the form of the pieces, and the way of playing them; but they cannot force the public to enjoy them. (Note by Rousseau.)

which were deprived of theatre? The theatre makes virtue lovable . . . It works a great miracle to do what nature and reason are doing before it! The wicked are hated on the stage . . . Are they loved in society, when they are known for what they are? . . . I doubt that anyone, to whom you told in advance the crimes of Phaedra and Medea, would not detest them more at the beginning of the play than at the end. And if this doubt is well founded, what must we think of 74–5 this effect that is so boasted about in the theatre?

I should like it to be clearly shown . . . by what means the theatre could produce in us feelings that we do not have, and make us judge moral beings any differently from how we judge them ourselves . . . If the beauty of virtue was the result of art, virtue would have been disfigured long ago. As for me, though I may be treated as wicked once more for daring to maintain that man is born good, I think it and I believe I have proved it. The origin of the concern which attaches us to what is honest, and inspires us with an aversion for evil, is in us and not in the plays. It takes no art to produce this concern, but only to make it prevail. The love of beauty is a feeling as natural to the human heart as self-love. It is not produced by an arrangement of scenery; the author does not bring it there, he finds it there; and from this pure feeling which he gratifies come the sweet tears which he makes flow.

Imagine the most perfect play that you like. Where is the person who, going there for the first time, is not already convinced of what is proved there, and already predisposed to those who are made attractive there? But that is not what is at issue; it is a matter of acting according to one's principles and imitating the people one respects. The heart of man is always right about everything which does not personally involve himself.* In quarrels where we are only spectators, we immediately take the side of justice, and there is no wicked act that does not give us a lively sense of indignation, so long as we draw no profit from it. But when our interest is involved our feelings are soon corrupted; and it is only then that we prefer the wrong that is useful to us, to the good that nature makes us love. Is it not a necessary result of the way things are that the wrongdoer draws a double advantage, first from his injustice, and then from the honesty of others? . . . He loves virtue, no doubt, but he loves it in others, because he hopes to profit from them. He does not wish it for

* In the *Confessions* Rousseau quotes an Italian proverb to this effect: *Ogn'un ama la giustizia in casa d'altrui.*[8]

himself, because it would cost him something. What then is he going to see in the theatre? Precisely what he would like to find everywhere: lessons of virtue for the public, which does not include him, and characters giving up everything for their duty, while nothing is demanded of him.   76–7

I hear it said that tragedy leads to pity through fear; that may be, but what is this pity? A fleeting and vain emotion which lasts no longer than the illusion which produced it; a residue of natural feeling which is soon stifled by the passions; a sterile pity which feeds on a few tears and has never produced the slightest act of humanity . . .

If, as Diogenes Laertius says, the heart is more easily touched by imaginary ills than real ills; if theatrical imitations draw out of us sometimes more tears than the actual presence of the objects being imitated, it is less . . . because the emotions are more feeble and do not amount to grief than because they are pure and not mixed with anxiety for ourselves. In giving tears to these fictions we have satisfied all the rights of humanity without having to give anything more of ourselves. They take the place of unfortunate people in person demanding our concern, consolation, comfort and acts which could involve us in their troubles, which would cost at least something to our indolence, and from which we are very glad to be exempt. One could say that our heart contracts, for fear of being touched at our expense.   78–9

In fact, when a man has gone to admire beautiful deeds in stories and cry for imaginary misfortunes, what more can be asked of him? Is he not pleased with himself? Does he not applaud his beautiful soul? Has he not acquitted himself of all that he owes to virtue by the homage that he has just rendered it? What more could one want him to do? That he practises it himself? He has no rôle to play; he is not an actor. The more I reflect on it, the more I find that everything that is staged in the theatre does not bring it nearer to us but makes it more remote . . . The theatre has its own rules, lore and standards, as well as its language and costume . . . Nothing of all that is right for us; you would be thought as ridiculous adopting the virtues of the heroes as speaking in verse and getting up in Roman costume. This, then, is virtually the only good of all these fine feelings and all these splended maxims, which are boasted about: to be confined for ever to the stage, and to show us virtue as a theatrical game, good to amuse the public, but mad to want to apply seriously to society. So the most forceful effect of the best tragedies is to reduce to a few brief, sterile and useless feelings all the duties of man; to make us applaud our courage in praising that of others, to applaud our humanity in pitying the ills that we might have been able to cure, 79–80 and to applaud our charity in saying to the poor: God will help you.

It is true that the stage could be given a simpler apparatus, and the tone of the theatre could come closer to that of the world. But morals are not corrected in this way, they are only described, and an ugly face does not seem at all ugly to him who wears it. If you want to correct morals by exaggeration you depart from nature and verisimilitude, and the portrayal has no more effect. Exaggeration does not make objects more hateful, it only makes them ridiculous, and ridicule is the favourite weapon of vice. It is through ridicule, attacking in the depths of our heart the respect we owe to virtue, that vice in the end extinguishes the love we ought to have for it. So it is that everything forces us to abandon this vain idea of improvement which people want to give us in the form of theatre aimed at public utility. It is an error . . . to hope that the true relations of things are shown there; for as a rule the poet can only alter these relations to accommodate them to public taste. In comedy he lessens them and puts them beneath man; in tragedy he extends them, and puts them above humanity. They are therefore never in proportion, and all we ever see in the theatre is creatures other than our own 80–1 kind.

[Rousseau turns to the example of the French theatre.]
Most tragedies, being only pure fables, events which are known to be the invention of the poet, do not make much impression on the spectators. By dint of showing them that you wish to instruct them, you no longer instruct them. Moreover, the punishments and rewards are always effected by such unusual means that you expect nothing 83 like them in the normal course of human affairs.

[When the criminal characters are punished 'they are presented in such a favourable light that all sympathy is for them'.[8] Furthermore:]
You will find that all the dreadful monsters and atrocious actions — useful, if you like, to create interest in the plays and give exercise to virtues — are certainly dangerous, in that they accustom the eyes of the people to horrors which they ought not even to know and to 90–1 crimes which they should not suppose possible . . .

Happily tragedy such as it exists is so far from us, it presents us creatures so grotesque, overblown, and fantastic, that the example of their vices is scarcely more contagious than that of their virtues is useful; and the less it wants to instruct us so much the less does it do us any harm. But it is not so with comedy, where the behaviour (*mœurs*) has a more immediate relation to our own, and in which the characters more closely resemble men. All of it is bad and harmful . . .   92

[Take Molière, for example] the most perfect comic writer whose works we have known . . . His greatest concern is to turn goodness and simplicity to ridicule, and to make scheming and lying sympathetic. His honest folk only talk, it is his villiains who act and who are most often favoured with the most shining success. The greatest applause rarely goes to the most deserving, but almost always to the most cunning . . .   93

The general spirit of Molière and his imitators [is that of] people who sometimes attack vices without ever making us love virtue; people who, as an ancient author said, are very good at snuffing out a lamp but never put any oil in it . . .   94

[Rousseau then criticizes at length *The Misanthrope*.]
The desire to make laughter at the expense of the character has forced [Molière] to degrade him, against the truth of his [Alceste's] nature . . .   103

The actions of Philinte and Alceste [are put] in apparent contradiction to their principles and in perfect conformity to their characters . . . The Misanthrope should have been always furious against public vices and always calm to the personal wrongs of which he was the victim. On the other hand, the intellectual Philinte ought to look on all the disorders of society with a stoic indifference, and become furious at the least wrong that was directly done to him. In fact, I notice that these people, so unconcerned at public injustices, are always those who make most noise at the slightest wrong that is done them, and they only keep their philosophy as long as they have no need of it themselves. They resemble that Irishman who did not want to get out of his bed, although the house was on fire. 'The house is burning', they cried out to him. 'What does it matter to me?' he answered, 'I am only the tenant'. Finally the fire reached him. At once he jumps up, runs out, cries out, and gets into a terrible state. He begins to understand that sometimes it is necessary to take an interest in the house in which we live even though it does not belong to us . . .   104–5

[Rousseau admires the play: 'The more you think about it, the more new beautiful things you discover in it.' But, finally:]
Let us agree that as the intention of the author is to please corrupted minds, either his morality leads to evil, or the false good that it preaches is more dangerous than evil itself; in that it seduces by the appearance of reason; in that it makes the habits and maxims of the

world preferable to complete integrity; in that it makes wisdom consist of a middle way between vice and virtue; in that, to the great relief of the spectators, it persuades them that to be an honest man, it
110 is enough not to be an obvious criminal . . .

These faults are so inherent in our theatre that in wishing to be rid of them we disfigure it. Our modern authors, guided by the best intentions, make their plays more 'moral'. But what happens? They are no longer really funny and have no effect. They instruct a great deal, if you like; but they bore a great deal more. One might as
112 well go to a sermon . . .

[Rousseau then criticizes the fact that so many plays are devoted to love and romantic subjects. His objections to this are various. Among them is the way they create harmful expectations.]

The sweet emotions that you feel there do not have in themselves a particular object, but they create the need for one; they do not exactly provide us with love but they prepare us to feel it; they do not choose
119 the person you should love but they force us to make this choice . . .

[Plays may show how love can lead to tragedy, as in Racine's *Bérénice*, but:] the portrayals of love always make more impression than the maxims of wisdom, and the effect of a tragedy is altogether
124 independent of that of its dénouement!

[Rousseau now turns to the social aspects of the theatre. The reason there had been a ban on theatrical activity in the past was because it led to a taste for luxury, extravagance, and dissipation. In a large town where these already exist, a theatre is desirable.]

In a great city, full of scheming, idle people without religion or principles, whose imaginations — depraved by idleness, inactivity, the love of pleasure and great needs — engender only monsters and inspire only crimes; in a great city, where morals and honour are nothing because each person, easily hiding his conduct from the public eye, shows himself only by his reputation and is esteemed only by his wealth, the authorities cannot provide enough permitted pleasures or apply themselves enough to making them attractive, in order to keep individuals away from the temptation of looking for more dangerous pleasures . . . But in small towns, in less populated places, where individuals are always in the public eye, critics of one another from birth, and where the authorities have everyone under their eye,
130–1 completely different rules should be followed . . .

In a small town . . . each person draws more on himself, and puts more of himself into what he does; because the human spirit, being less spread out, less swamped by public opinion, develops and grows better in peaceful solitude; because seeing less you imagine more; because finally, being less pressed for time you have more leisure to extend and digest your ideas . . .   133

[Introducing a theatre would make people lose their taste for work, it would also make them need to work more in order to pay for it, and make taxes necessary. The effect of all that would tend to favour the 'haves' against the 'have-nots' and increase inequality. With regard to the immoral and licentious behaviour of actors and actresses, D'Alembert had suggested that laws could be drawn up to forbid it; Rousseau points out the futility of using laws for this. D'Alembert had also suggested that actors have behaved badly because they have been treated badly.]

I could attribute these prejudices [against actors] to the pronouncements of priests if I did not find them among the Romans before the birth of Christianity, and not only occurring vaguely in the spirit of people, but authorized by specific laws which declared actors infamous, deprived them of the title and rights of a Roman citizen, and put actresses on à level with prostitutes . . .   158

[The only theatre which has been without these and other faults was the Greek theatre.]

The people of the ancient world had heroes and put men on their stages; we, on the other hand, hardly have any men and put heroes on our stages . . .   89

As tragedy had something sacred in its origin their actors were regarded rather as priests than mountebanks. As all the subjects of the plays were drawn from their national history, which the Greeks worshipped, they saw in these same actors less people who played in fables than informed citizens showing the history of their country to their compatriots . . .   160

Their theatres were not raised through interest and avarice; nor were they shut up in dark prisons . . .

These great and magnificent spectacles given under the sky, before the whole people, presented on all sides only struggles, victories, and prizes, subjects able to inspire the Greeks with a keen sense of emulation and warm their hearts with feeling of honour and glory . . .   161

[Another objection to the profession of actors was that the actor spent his life in pretence, he was never himself; his work demanded a 'trading of himself' (163), or even an abolition, a complete denial of himself (165). As for actresses, they filled Rousseau with disgust; the way they had to assert themselves on stage was totally contrary

to the modesty which he regarded as their most important characteristic (170). The way they were on display for money was dishonour-
able to their sex and led to obvious and undesirable consequences
(179). The Greek theatre, he had noted (161), had had no women in it.
Rousseau then develops his argument on the social consequences with
a description of how Genevans relax now, and what effect a theatre
would have on their habits and their economy. He concludes:]
I see only one solution to so many drawbacks; in order to have
dramas suitable for our entertainment we should compose them
ourselves. We should have authors before actors. For it is not good
that we should be shown all kinds of imitation, but only the imitation
225   of honest things, which are agreeable to free men . . .
[He suggests subjects drawn from Genevan history.]
For my part I confess that I would much prefer it if we were able
to do without any of these theatres, and that, young and old, we were
able to draw our pleasures and our duties from our condition and
231   from ourselves . . .
What! Should there then be no entertainment in a republic? On
the contrary, there should be plenty. It is in republics that entertainments are born, it is in their heart that you see them flourish
with a truly festival atmosphere. What people are better suited to
come together often and form among themselves sweet bonds of
pleasure and joy, than those who have so many reasons for loving one
another and for staying always united? We already have several public
festivals; let us have still more, I would be delighted. But let us not
adopt those exclusive entertainments which dismally shut up a small
number of people in a dark cavern; which keep them fearful and
motionless in silence and inactivity; which only display prisons,
swords, soldiers, distressing images of bondage and inequality. No,
happy people, your festivals are not like that! It is in the open air,
under the sky, that you should come together and abandon your-
232–3   selves to the sweet feelings of your happiness.
Do not let your pleasures be affected or mercenary; do not let
them be in any way constrained, nor poisoned by interest. Let them
be free and open-hearted as you are; let the sun shine on your innocent
entertainments; you will make one yourselves, the most creditable
that could be seen.
But what will be the subjects of these entertainments? What will
be shown in them? Nothing, if you like. With liberty, wherever
prosperity reigns, there well-being reigns too. Set up in the middle
of a square a stake crowned with flowers; assemble the people there,

and you will have a festival. Do still better; let the audience be their own play; make them actors themselves, each seeing himself and loving himself in the others so that all are closer to one another.   233–4

There is no pure joy but public joy, and the true feelings of nature only prevail among the people.   249 n.

Rousseau was aware of the contradictions between the views he put forward and his own example. He admitted in a footnote: 'I am passionately fond of plays. Racine delights me and I have never willingly missed a performance of Molière.'[9] Even as he wrote the *Letter to D'Alembert* he was working on his novel *The New Heloïse*, and he was to write more fiction and short plays over the next few years. If he needed to create imaginary worlds, as he evidently did, why should not others do likewise, or if not create them, at least enjoy the creations of others?

Rousseau did not deny this need. Nor did he think that art was always a product of alienation, or only a palliative to soothe the depraved. Our aesthetic sense is an important sense — 'The love of beauty is a feeling as natural to the human heart as self-love' (see above, p. 125). And he was quite aware that our aesthetic faculties function in a distinct way: 'That imitation should only be applied to useful subjects is a good precept in morality but not a rule for poetics. For there are very beautiful pieces about subjects which can be of no use at all — Sophocles' *Oedipus* for example.'[10]

His most extended treatment of this issue, in Book IV of *Emile*, raises more problems than it settles, but his concluding remarks there are important:

> My main aim in teaching [Emile] to feel and love beauty of every kind is to fix his affections and his taste on it, to prevent the alteration of his natural appetites . . . I have said elsewhere* that taste is only the art of being a judge of small things, and that is very true. But since the charm of life depends on a tissue of small things such efforts are not a matter of indifference. Through them we learn how to fill our life with good things that are within our reach, in all the truth they can have for us. I do not mean here the morally good, which relates to a good

* *The New Heloïse:* 'Taste is, in some way, the microscope of judgement; it brings small objects to our view, and its operations begin where those of judgement end.'[11]

disposition of the soul, but only to what relates to [a good disposition of] feeling, and real pleasure.'[12]

Two further comments should be made here. Rousseau did see a fundamental connection between our moral and aesthetic senses. This had been indicated in his *Essay on the Origin of Languages* and was clearly stated in *The New Heloïse*: 'I always believed that the good was only beauty in action, that they were both intimately connected and had a common source in well-ordered nature'[13], and in *Emile*: 'By taste the mind opens itself unawares to ideas of beauty of every kind, and at length to the moral notions that are related to beauty.'[14] This was a belief he shared with Plato.

With the question of imitation, however, Rousseau went beyond his classical predecessors. It is true that, like them, he discusses art in terms of imitation, but he extends the area of discussion. It is this desire for a wider dimension to aesthetic experience that makes the *Letter to D'Alembert* so significant. In a very characteristic way Rousseau attacks the theatre of his time for being both too impersonal, of too little consequence to ourselves — 'the basis for imitation among us always comes from the desire to be carried away outside ourselves'[15] — and at the same time for being too isolated, too separate from other people. Our aesthetic activities should involve both more of ourselves and more of our fellow-men. Art should be less a specialized product, which some consume, and more an active process in which all participate.

11 'THE NEW HELOÏSE'

I

In the summer of 1756 Rousseau found himself in conditions for perfect happiness, 'leading a life to my taste, in a place of my choice, with someone who was dear to me [Thérèse]'.[1] But he was not happy:

> in the middle of so many good things that I had longed for so much, [I found] no pure enjoyment . . . I saw myself already on the decline to old age . . . having scarcely experienced any of the pleasures which my heart so desired, having scarcely given life to the vivid feelings I felt inside me . . . How was it possible that with a naturally expansive soul, for which to live was to love, I had not yet found a friend entirely to myself, a true friend . . . Devoured by this need to love without having been able to satisfy it, I saw myself reaching the gates of old age, and dying without having lived.[2]

'What did I do? [You] will already have guessed . . . The impossibility of reaching real creatures threw me into the land of fantasies . . . which my creative imagination soon populated with creatures after my own heart . . . [I made] an enchanted world.'[3] 'I imagined love and friendship, the two idols of my heart . . . [I imagined] two women friends . . . I gave one of them a lover . . . I identified myself with the lover . . . I needed a lake . . . and I ended up choosing that around which my heart has never ceased to wander',[4] that is, the Lake of Geneva. This was how Rousseau came to write the first three parts of *The New Heloïse* or to give it its full title: '*Julie or the New Heloïse. Letters of Two Lovers, residents of a small town at the foot of the Alps*'. The town was Vevey, the original home of Madame de Warens.

The novel begins as a passionate love story, told in the epistolary form that Richardson had used in *Pamela* and *Clarissa Harlowe*, both of which had been translated into French and were known to

Rousseau. A young man, Saint-Preux, is engaged as a tutor to Julie, the only daughter of the Baron d'Etange. He falls in love with her, and she with him,* but his love does not bring him happiness: 'My heart has more than it could hope for, and it is not content. You love me, and you tell me so . . . [but] this unjust heart dares to want more when there is no more to desire. It afflicts me with its fantasies, it makes me restless in the midst of happiness.'[5]

His unhappiness is in part a matter of temperament, as he recognizes: 'What a fatal gift from heaven is a sensitive soul! Whoever has received one must expect suffering and grief on earth. He will look for the supreme happiness without remembering that he is [only] a man. His heart and his reason will be constantly at war and limitless desires will create an endless [sense of] deprivation.'[6] But it is also caused by the social barrier and differences between them. The barrier is that of their respective classes; the Baron will not allow his daughter to marry a mere tutor; the difference is that Julie belongs to a community, while Saint-Preux is isolated:

> What a difference there is between your condition and mine . . .
> You are surrounded by people whom you cherish and who adore
> you; the concern of a tender mother and father . . . the friendship
> of a cousin . . . a whole family whose ornament you are; a whole
> town proud to have seen you born . . . But I, alas, a wanderer,
> with no family and almost no *patrie*, I have no one but you on
> earth, and possess nothing at all but love.[7]

Saint-Preux, in other words, is that figure who will come to obsess the nineteenth-century imagination, the romantic outcast.

'You despise me as a madman . . . The extravagance of my love frightens you, my frenzy makes you pity me.'[8] Caught in a vortex of violent emotion, where a vivid imagination battles against, and has to compensate for, social exclusion, he will turn towards death as the only way out. Saint-Preux comes to contemplate suicide and at one moment (at the end of Part Four) almost gives in to the temptation to drown both Julie and himself.

He does not do so because there was more to Rousseau than Saint-Preux; the identification was far from complete. Rousseau, well into middle age, was able to show the young man's bad side as

---

* Rousseau's achievement in conveying a woman's feelings, in the letters written by Julie, made a deep impression on women writers from Madame de Staël to George Eliot. To some extent it made up for his unenlightened remarks about women in the *Letter to D'Alembert* and *Emile*.

much as his good. The acute psychological skill with which he does
this is one of the remarkable things about the book. Furthermore,
the character of Julie has a more refined, spiritual dimension, which
not only restrains the impulsive man of feeling, but also reveals his
limitations. She has a sense of calm at the centre: in her 'the heart
does not follow the senses, it leads them'.[9] In her company Saint-Preux
undergoes an *education sentimentale*.

> Tell me, Julie, you who with your own sensibility know so well
> how to judge that of another, do you think that I have ever
> tasted true love? . . . My feelings have greatly changed since
> yesterday. They seem to be less impetuous, but also more soft,
> more tender, more delightful . . . Without losing anything of
> their force, they are multiplied. The tenderness of friendship
> tempers the extravagance of love and I can hardly imagine any
> kind of attachment which does not unite me to you . . .
>
> I must confess a suspicion I have entertained . . . It is that you
> are more capable of love than I. Yes, Julie, my life, my being
> depends on you. I adore you with all my soul. But yours contains
> more love than mine. I see, I feel that love has reached deeper
> into your heart . . . How far am I from that delightful state which
> is sufficient in itself. I want to enjoy your love, you simply
> want to love. The feeling that your heart feeds upon is alone the
> supreme happiness.[10]

The dramatic character of the love story arises from the social
barriers which prevent its easy development or eventual fulfilment.
This conflict between natural feelings and social convention is also
reflected in the locations of the novel. Not that they were mere
reflections. For Rousseau there was an essential connection between
the circumstances surrounding us and the way we feel and behave.

In the Second Part, Saint-Preux has to leave Julie: he goes to
Paris. 'It is with a secret terror that I enter this vast desert of the
world . . . [Here] I find only an empty appearance of feelings and
truth . . . I see only ghosts and phantoms which are glimpsed for a
moment, only to disappear when you try to lay hold on them. Until
now, I have seen many masks, when will I see men's true faces?'[11] In
the First Part, by contrast, he had made a journey into the mountains
of the High Valais.* There he had regained his peace of mind.

---

* One of the most influential aspects of the book was the lyrical feeling of
passages like this — a feeling which needs longer extracts than there is room for
here to do it justice.

PART ONE, LETTER XXIII

I set out, sad with my sufferings . . . I climbed slowly on foot using quite rugged paths, led by a man whom I had hired as a guide but whom, throughout the journey, I found more a friend than a hireling. I wanted to dream, but I was constantly distracted by some unexpected sight. One moment, huge rocks hung in ruins above my head, the next, I was enveloped in a thick mist which rose from thundering cascades . . . Sometimes, I was lost in the obscurity of a dense wood, sometimes I emerged from a deep gorge to be suddenly confronted by a pleasing meadow. An astounding mixture of wild and cultivated nature, which showed everywhere the hand of man, where you would have thought man had never penetrated. Here you see a cavern and alongside it, houses; there are vineyards where one would expect nothing but brambles, vines growing in wind-blown soil; delicious fruit among barren rocks and fields among precipices.

It was not only man's work which made such bizarre contrasts in these strange lands. Nature, too, seemed to take pleasure in contradicting herself, the same place appearing so different under various aspects. To the east, the flowers of spring, to the south, the fruits of autumn and, northwards, the ice of winter. Nature unites all the seasons in the same moment, all the climates in the same place, different soils in the same land, and, with a harmony unknown elsewhere, joins the produce of the plains with that of the Alps. Add to all this the optical illusions, the way the light falls differently on the mountain peaks, the play of sun and shadow, and all the tricks of the light which occur both morning and evening; then you will have some idea of the never-ending spectacle which continually won my admiration, and which seemed to me to be set in a true
76–7 theatre . . .

During the first day I attributed the calm I felt inside me to this pleasing variety of scenes . . . But finding that my tranquillity continued during the night and increased the following day, I soon felt that this was due to some other cause, as yet unknown to me. That day, I came to the lower mountains and, crossing their rugged peaks, attained the highest summit that was within my reach. Having walked a while among the clouds, I reached a more restful spot, from where, at the right time of year, one can observe thunder and
78 storms gathering below . . .

It was here that I discerned in the purity of the air, the true cause of the change in my mood and of the return of that inner peace that I had lost for so long. This, indeed, is a general feeling common to all men, though not all are aware of it. In the high mountains, where the air is pure and rarefied, we breathe more easily, our bodies feel lighter, our minds more serene, our pleasures less keen, our passions more restrained. Our meditations take on an indefinable quality. Something grand and sublime, equal to the sights that surround us, an inexpressible quality of calm delight, with no trace of the sour or the sensual. It seems as if, once lifted above all human society, you leave behind every base and worldly feeling and that as you approach the ethereal regions, the soul absorbs something of their eternal purity. There, you are grave without melancholy, peaceful, but not idle, content simply to exist and to meditate. Our desires lose their violence, they lose that sharpness that makes them painful, leaving the heart with nothing but tender and sweet emotion . . . I am surprised that exposure to the wholesome and beneficial mountain air is not one of the great remedies prescribed by both medicine and morality . . .   78–9

Imagine to yourself all the impressions that I have just described gathered together and you will have some idea of the delightful situation in which I find myself. Imagine the variety, the grandeur, the beauty of a thousand astonishing sights, the pleasure at being surrounded by nothing but new discoveries . . . the spectacle has an indefinable quality of magic, of the supernatural, which delights the mind and the senses. Everything is forgotten, including oneself, and one no longer even knows where one is.

[Rousseau then describes the people Saint-Preux meets, praising] their disinterested humanity and their warm hospitality for all those strangers who may be led to them by chance or curiosity . . .   79

So complete was their magnanimity that throughout the entire journey I was unable to leave a single coin among them. Indeed, how can one spend money in a country where landlords will accept nothing to cover their expenses, and servants nothing for their trouble, and where there is not a single beggar? However, money is very rare in the High Valais; and it is for this very reason that the inhabitants live comfortably: for food is abundant, with no market sale to the outside and no consumption of luxury within, and without the mountain farmer, for whom work is a pleasure, becoming any less industrious. If ever they have more money, they will certainly be poorer . . .   80

II

The initial impulse behind the novel gave the love-scenes in the first three parts an intensity that was at that time astonishing. But that same intensity embarrassed Rousseau, it laid him open to the criticism to which he was most sensitive: that his invective was only a pose and that he was as susceptible to 'civilized' habits, like writing or reading novels, as anyone else. 'I felt this inconsistency in all its force, I reproached myself for it, I blushed from it, I was annoyed at it, but none of that brought me back to reason.'[12]

This problem became acute the following summer, when he fell in love himself with the Comtesse d'Houdetot, 'Sophie'. She was the sister-in-law of Madame d'Epinay (who had invited Rousseau to the Hermitage), and was herself in love with another man. So she did not return his feeling. However, both her husband and lover were away in Germany, fighting in the Seven Years' War, and as she enjoyed walking and Rousseau's company, the two of them spent many days in the summer together. Rousseau found himself in a similar situation to Saint-Preux.

These two factors, the doubt over the novel itself and the need to come to terms with an agonizing situation, combined to alter the character of the book. Virtue replaced passion as its central theme. The ending of the original story of Abelard and Heloïse*, in which passion was fulfilled, had been tragic and violent; in this New Heloïse the lovers find peace and happiness outside, or beyond, their ill-fated passion. Julie marries Baron Wolmar as her father intended, and they have a family. Saint-Preux goes off on a journey to the Pacific and returns a few years later to visit them.

They are living happily at Clarens, an estate by the lake where Julie and Saint-Preux had first kissed. What had once been a scene of violent emotion is now calm and orderly, but it is an order in harmony with nature. The private garden that Julie has made her Elysium is moulded to the natural forms — 'You see nothing laid out in a line, nothing made level . . . Nature plants nothing in a straight line.'[13] — and it has been allowed to grow at its own pace: 'Patience and time had worked this miracle. These are the methods that rich people scarcely think of in their pleasures. Always being in

---

* The *Letters* of Abelard and Heloïse were popular throughout the eighteenth century. Their story was given fresh prominence in 1758 when a French translation of Pope's *Eloisa to Abelard* appeared.

a hurry to enjoy themselves, force and money are the only means they know.'[14]

The domestic economy of Clarens is described in Part Four. We do not have to choose between the remote innocence of the High Valais, or the ugly corruption of Paris. We can develop a man-made world that is balanced, satisfying and complete in itself.

'Authors, men of letters and intellectuals are forever saying that to fulfil your duties as a citizen you should live in the city', wrote Rousseau in his *Second Preface* to the novel:

> country people are nothing in their eyes . . . For the happiness of mankind we should work to stop this flow of poisonous advice . . . It is not a question of creating a world of Arcadian shepherds or worthy peasants cultivating their land with their own hands and philosophizing about nature, nor any other romantic creatures like that, who only exist in books. But of showing people who are comfortably off that country life and agriculture have pleasures that they are unaware of; that these pleasures are not as whimsical, or as coarse, as they think . . .
> that a gifted man who wanted to retire to the country with his family and become a farmer could lead a life there as satisfying as any spent among the amenities of a city . . . and finally that there the most tender feelings of the heart can give life to a society much more attractive . . . than that in which our sour and satirical laughter is the sad substitute for a happiness we no longer know.[15]

His description of Clarens is detailed and evocative. It is a world in which 'all is done through affection'.[16] But it has a serious limitation. It is a static world in which the masters remain in control and the servants must be obedient. Even in the relaxed atmosphere of the wine harvest, a servant must not forget himself: if he does 'he is dismissed, without appeal, first thing the next day'.[17] This comment shows the extent to which, in this book, Rousseau 'maintains social and economic inequality in practice, while denying it in theory'.[18]

The patriarchal community at Clarens bears little relation to the just society Rousseau described in his political writings. But it is wrong to suppose it modifies those writings. *The New Heloïse* operates on a different level; it was written on impulse, not after long consideration, and is concerned more with feelings than with principles. To expect it to be consistent with his other work is to fail to recognize its distinctive character. We may sometimes be surprised by what Rousseau's imagination revealed. But we should also note that at an imaginative level the static nature of Clarens is seen to be limited; for that is a major reason for Julie's dissatisfaction in Part Six.

PART FOUR, LETTER X

[Saint-Preux describes the estate at Clarens.]

Since M. and Mme Wolmar took up residence they have put to use everything which served only for ornament; it is no longer a house for show, but for convenience . . . They have replaced furniture which was old and valuable with pieces that are simple and practical. Everything here is pleasant and cheerful, breathing an air of plenitude and propriety, with no trace of pomp or luxury. There is not one single room where one does not feel oneself in the country, but with, none the less, all the comforts of life in town. Similar changes are to

441   be seen out of doors . . .

Their land is not leased out, they farm it themselves, and this cultivation forms a large part of their activity, their livelihood and their enjoyment . . .

It is a principle with them to exploit their lands to the utmost, not in order to make greater profits, but as a means of feeding more

442   mouths . . .

A man's wealth is not in his coffers, but in the use he makes of what he draws out of them, because one can only own the things one possesses by using them, and abuses are always more inexhaustible than riches; the result is that one's enjoyment is not proportionate to one's expenditure, but depends rather on how well it is managed . . . What if true property is born in the relation between ourselves and our possessions; if it is the use we make of our wealth, rather than its acquisition that gives us riches? What task is there more important for the head of the family than that of domestic economy and the

466   good management of his household? . . .

The great art, by which master and mistress get their servants to behave in the way they want, is to show themselves as they really are. Their behaviour is always frank and open, for they are not afraid that their actions will belie their words. Since their own moral principles are no different from those they wish to give to others, they have no need of circumspection in what they say . . . Since their servants never see their master do anything that is not just, fair and reasonable, they do not regard justice as a tax on the poor, a yoke on

468   the backs of the wretched, or as one of the evils of their condition . . .

470   All is done through affection . . .

PART FIVE, LETTER II

Mme Wolmar's great principle is never to encourage anyone to change his situation but to do all that she can to make everyone happy in his present station and, above all, to prevent the free peasant, the happiest of men, from abandoning his occupation in favour of other employment.

On that, I made the objection that nature seems to have distributed different talents among men in order to fit them for different occupations, without regard to their birth. To this she answered that there were two considerations more important than talent, namely morals and happiness. Man is too noble a being to have to serve simply as an instrument for [the use of] others. We should not give a man tasks for which he is suited without also asking if they suit him. For men are not made for positions, positions are made for them. In the right order of things therefore, we should not seek that employment for which a man is best suited, but that which is most likely to make him good and happy.* It can never be right to ruin one human being for the advantage of others, nor to make a man a criminal in the service of honest people . . .

536

PART FIVE, LETTER VII

[The highlight of the year at Clarens is the autumn wine harvest.]

For a month past the warmth of autumn has been preparing a good grape harvest. [Now] the first frosts have led us to begin. The withered leaves reveal the grapes . . . and seem to invite people to lay hands on them; all the vines [are] loaded down with this bountiful fruit . . . Everywhere there is the sound of barrels and casks being coopered, the hillsides echoing to the songs of the grape-harvesters, the constant to and fro of those who carry the grapes to the press, the hoarse sound of country instruments encouraging the labourers at their work; the pleasant and moving sight of a general cheerfulness, which seems at this moment to spread over the face of the earth. A veil of mist rises, like theatre curtains, with the sun in the morning, revealing to the eye a delightful spectacle. Everything combines to produce a

* In one version of this passage, which Rousseau omitted from the final text, he continued at this point: 'for it is much better for society to be badly ordered and all the citizens happy and honest, than that society be well ordered and [all] the citizens miserable and wicked. This order, about which so much noise is made, is often only an apparent order, and to sacrifice to it the reality of things, (as is done among the majority of peoples), is in fact to destroy it.'[19]

festival [atmosphere]; and this festival becomes even more pleasing, when one reflects that this is the only one in which man has discovered how to join utility with pleasure.

604

You cannot imagine with what eagerness and gaiety all this is done. We sing, we laugh the whole day through, and our work is the better for it. We all live together in the greatest familiarity, everyone is equal, yet no one forgets himself. The ladies are without affectation, the peasants are respectable, the men playful, but not coarse . . .

607

The peaceful equality which reigns recreates the order of nature, and provides instruction for some, consolation for others and ties of friendship for all.

608

Supper is served at two long tables . . . Everyone sits down together, masters, labourers and servants. Everyone, without discrimination or distinction, gets up to serve himself, and it is done graciously and with pleasure. We drink as much as we please; propriety is the only constraint . . .

After supper we sit up for an hour or two stripping hemp. Everyone sings a song in turn. Sometimes the women sing on their own, or one of them sings alone, and the others join in the chorus. Most of the songs are old ballads, and the tunes are not very lively. But they possess an indefinable quality, old-fashioned and gentle. The words are simple, naïve, often sad. None the less they are pleasant to hear . . .

608–9

In this way we spend our evenings. When it is nearly bed-time, Mme Wolmar says: 'Now let us go and set off the fireworks.' At which everyone picks up his bundle of hemp stalks, the worthy sign of his labour: we carry them triumphantly into the middle of the yard, pile them into a heap, like a trophy, and then we set fire to it . . . The stalks flare up into a blaze which reaches to the sky, a real bonfire, around which we laugh and dance. Then everyone is offered a drink . . . and goes to bed content with a day passed in work, good cheer and innocence, and which we would willingly begin again the next day, the day after that, and for the rest of our lives.

610–11

III

Rousseau's affair with Mme d'Houdetot, which did not last beyond the summer of 1757, was one of several things that came between him and Mme d'Epinay. His growing estrangement from Diderot was another. As a result he left the Hermitage at the end of that year and moved to Mont-Louis at Montmorency. Here he completed *The New Heloïse*.

The separation from Diderot affected him as much as the separation from his Sophie. Ever since he had left Paris relations between the two men had been difficult; the more Rousseau developed the implications of his own ideas, the greater became the differences between them. The *Letter to D'Alembert* written in the winter of 1758 made those differences apparent, but he still hoped for some reconciliation.

The bitter quarrel over religion, between the Christians and the *philosophes*, aggravated their differences. Both parties seemed to Rousseau equally fanatical and intolerant. A desire to 'show each party the merit and virtue of the other'[20] lay behind the writing of much of Part Five and Part Six of *The New Heloïse*.

> The intention was to bring the opposing sides together through mutual esteem, to teach the *philosophes* that you can believe in God without being a hypocrite, and to teach the religious that you can be an unbeliever and yet not dishonest. The devout Julie is a lesson for philosophers and the atheist Wolmar one for the intolerant.[21]

The latter, though an atheist, is generous, considerate and humane: he is a cold man perhaps, but he is not a bad man. His lack of faith distresses Julie but causes no problems for anyone else.

Julie's faith is less straightforward. Throughout the book she has been an idealized character and her death in Part Six has Christlike overtones.* She had always been a religious person to some extent; and at her marriage she had had a sort of new baptism, a sense that her decision to marry Wolmar was the right decision in the eyes of God. But this was no more than a reassurance which strengthened her virtue, the quality necessary for a lasting domestic happiness, and committed her more thoroughly to their shared life at Clarens. That life, as Rousseau describes it, is complete and satisfying.

> I am surrounded by all that interests me. The whole universe is here for me. I enjoy, at one and the same time, the regard I have for my friends, theirs for me and that which they have for each other. Their mutual goodwill either comes from, or relates, to me. I see nothing that does not expand my being and nothing that divides it. It is in everything that surrounds me, no part of

---

* The epigraph for the whole book, taken from Petrarch, has a similar suggestion: 'The world possessed her without knowing her and I who knew her remain here below to weep for her.'[22]

it is far from me. My imagination has no more to do, I have nothing to desire. To feel and to enjoy are to me one and the same thing. I live at once in all that I love.[23]

What more can anyone want?

But Julie is not content; what is complete may also be static, and her attention turns from this world to the next. Saint-Preux is alarmed and tells her she is mistaken. Julie is unmoved by this criticism of her. 'Even my husband is happier with my inclination for it. Devotion, he claims, is an opium for the soul: taken in small doses it enlivens, animates and sustains: [only if] the dose is too strong [does it] dull, or drive mad, or make you ill. I hope I will not go that far.'[24]

Julie dies from an illness caught while saving one of her children from drowning. The faith she professes before she dies is far from extreme and the example of her self-sacrifice moves even Wolmar to the possibility of belief. But the religious problem has not been settled, for Rousseau. In the letters from the different characters his mind shifts and turns over the questions. Why should Clarens fail to satisfy? Why do our imaginations demand more? What compensation could there ever be for the pain of unfulfilled love? Julie's last message to Saint-Preux is one saying that her love for him had never ended and that she is sure they will be re-united in the next world. Does that mean that her faith was at heart no different from Saint-Preux's own previous longing for death?

It is an indication of Rousseau's imaginative genius that these questions should still remain open, that his fictional world stands independent of his own intentions. We never lose sight of the writer but the tensions that fired his imagination are so fully realized that they become vividly alive for us. We experience the tensions between passion and virtue, nature and man, and none of them exists in isolation.

For many readers today *The New Heloïse* is overwritten and overlong. Its descriptive passages often seem more accessible than the declarations of love, guilt, doubt or despair which fill many of its pages, and it is these which have recently received more attention. But the personal drama at the centre of the book remains interesting because it reveals so much of the problems which obsessed Rousseau: the problem above all of happiness. From the passionate unhappiness of Saint-Preux in Part One to the religious contentment of Julie in Part Six, this question is always before us. It was a problem to which Rousseau could find no single solution.

The book was completed in September 1758 and published at the beginning of 1761. Its success was astonishing, and completely altered Rousseau's reputation. Up till then he had been generally regarded as a 'man of paradox' who had put forward bizarre ideas in order to shock. Now he became known as the 'Socrates of the Century', 'an Apostle of Virtue'.[25] The scenes of passion caught everyone's interest and the triumph of virtue won their admiration. Not only that, by arousing in others a sense of the intense inner life that he experienced himself, Rousseau brought about a new awareness of our moral and emotional needs. We can only be complete by fulfilling these aspects of our personality; they are an essential part of us, and they are essentially interlinked.

The book went through seventy-two French editions and ten English editions before the end of the century, reaching a very wide public. Even a Wolmar was impressed: 'I consider this work his masterpiece', wrote Hume, 'though he himself told me that he valued most his *Social Contract;* which is as preposterous a judgement as that of Milton, who preferred the *Paradise Regained* to all his other performances.'[26]

12 'THE SOCIAL CONTRACT'

INTRODUCTION

When Rousseau left Paris in 1756 the work that attracted him and preoccupied him most was his *Political Institutions*. The idea for this book had first come to him in Venice, thirteen years earlier, 'when I had had some opportunity to see the failings of that highly praised government'.

> Since then my awareness had been greatly developed by studying morals in history. I had seen that everything depended radically upon politics, and that, however one looked at the subject, no people could ever be other than what the nature of their government made them. So this great question of the best possible government seemed to me to come down to this: what is the nature of the government suitable to form the most virtuous, most enlightened and wisest people, the best people, taking this word in its broadest sense? I thought I had seen that this question related very closely to another, which was almost the same: what is the government which by its nature keeps closest to the law? Then, what is the law? And a sequence of questions of this importance. I saw that all this led me to great truths, useful to the happiness of the human race, but especially that of my *patrie*. I had not found their ideas of law and liberty to be just enough or as clear as I would have liked, on the journey I had recently made there [in 1754].[1]

He wanted to spend the rest of his life working on this book; he believed it would put the seal on his reputation. But although he had already been thinking about it for some years, it had not made much progress.

> Works of this kind demand meditation, leisure, tranquillity. Furthermore, I was doing it undercover, as it were; I had not

wanted to tell anyone about the project, not even Diderot. I was afraid that it would seem too bold for the century and the country in which I was writing, and that the alarm of my friends might prevent my carrying it through. [Moreover] my discussions with Diderot always tended to make me more satirical and sarcastic than I was by nature. That was what dissuaded me from consulting him on an enterprise where I wanted to employ only the power of reasoning, without any trace of temperament or partiality.[2]

At the Hermitage Rousseau continued working on the book but other concerns interrupted him — the writings of the Abbé de St-Pierre, *The New Heloïse*, and the *Letter to D'Alembert*. When he moved to Montmorency at the end of 1757 he reconsidered his plans.

I examined the state of this book and found that it still needed several years' work. I did not have the strength to go on with it. I therefore gave it up. I decided to take from it what could be detached, and then burn the rest. Pushing ahead enthusiastically with the writing, without interrupting that of *Emile*, I brought to completion in less than two years *The Social Contract*.[3]

The Social Contract, therefore, is a part of what Rousseau intended to be a much larger work. It has also come down to us in two versions, the second of which — the one we know as *The Social Contract* — is more condensed, emphatic and self-contained than the first. This accounts for its unique character among Rousseau's writings. Its closely argued manner was to have been common to all parts of the *Political Institutions*, but its particularly concentrated character, which has made it so difficult a text, arises from the way it was successively revised and polished.

The first version, generally known as *The Geneva Manuscript*, is not complete; it breaks off at the beginning of Book III. (There is also an early version of the chapter on Civil Religion, Bk IV, Ch. 8.) The material in Books I and II of *The Geneva MS* does not differ substantially from that in *The Social Contract*. It is presented differently, it is argued in a more relaxed manner but, with one exception, it was almost all incorporated into the definitive version.

The one exception is the second chapter, The General Society of the Human Race, which was omitted altogether from the later work. This chapter, however, serves as an excellent introduction to the later work, because it makes clear the development of Rousseau's thought, from the criticism of existing societies in his earlier work to the prescription for future societies in *The Social Contract*. It was written in reply to Diderot's article on Natural Right which had appeared in Volume V of the *Encyclopedia* in 1755. Diderot had argued that 'in the condition of independence' (that is, before social organizations arose), 'reason leads us to co-operate in the common good by making us aware of our own interest'.[4] He maintained that we had at that time a sense of common humanity — the general society of the human race — and that a rational consideration of our interests in relation to that sentiment gave rise to our sense of natural law and justice.

Rousseau argued the exact opposite. Only in our own particular societies do we even develop our reason in the first place. Only after we have developed a sense of the good for our own society, and established laws for that, can we have any sense of a general society and the good for the whole human race. The chapter is a forceful statement of the positive view of society he now held; only in society do we develop, and only by remaking society will we develop more satisfactorily.

The Geneva Manuscript

BK I, CH. 2. THE GENERAL SOCIETY OF THE HUMAN RACE

Let us begin by finding out where the need for political institutions is born.

The strength of man is so proportioned to his natural needs and his primitive condition that when this condition changes and his needs increase, however slightly, the assistance of his fellow-men becomes necessary to him; when at length his desires extend over the whole of nature the co-operation of the whole human race is scarcely enough to gratify them. So it is that the same causes which make us wicked also make us slaves, and we are subjected as we become depraved. The feeling of our weakness comes less from our nature than from our greed. Our needs bring us together to the same extent that our passions divide us, and the more we become enemies of our fellows the less we are able to escape from them. Such are the first bonds of 281–2 general society . . .

[Then] the sweet voice of nature is no longer an infallible guide for us, nor the independence we received from her a desirable state. Peace and innocence left us for ever before we tasted their delights . . .

The happy life of the golden age was always foreign to the human race, either through not having known it when they could have enjoyed it, or through having lost it when they might have been able to know it.

[Rousseau adds that primitive freedom and innocence] would always have had an essential fault . . . the lack of that binding of the parts which makes up the whole. The earth would have been covered with men among whom there would have been almost no communication . . . Everyone would have remained isolated among the others, everyone would only have thought of himself. Our understanding would not have been able to develop; we would have lived without feeling anything, we would have died without having lived. All our happiness would have consisted in not knowing our misery . . .   283

[Rousseau argues against Diderot:] It is not true that in the state of independence reason leads us to agree to the common good through a consideration of our interests. Private interest and the general good, far from being allied, are mutually exclusive in the natural order of things . . .   284

Moreover, the art of generalizing ideas is one of the most difficult exercises of the human understanding and one of the last to develop . . .   286

It is only from the social order established among us that we derive the ideas of the social order that we imagine. We have a [conception of] society in general only [in the light of] our particular societies, and we only really start to become men after we have [first] been citizens . . .   287

Yet although there is no natural and general society among men, although they become unhappy and wicked in becoming sociable, although the laws of justice and equality are nothing for those who live at the same time in the liberty of the state of nature and subjected to the needs of a state of society, nevertheless we should not think that there is no virtue or happiness for us . . . Let us strive to draw from the ill itself the remedy which could cure it. Let us correct, if we can, the lack of a general association by making new associations . . . The ills which art initially did to nature can be made good by improved art . . .   288

THE NATURE OF THE CONTRACT (BOOK I)

The task, therefore, is that of 'making new associations'. More specifically, it is to make legitimate associations. *The Social Contract* is subtitled 'Principles of Political Right'; its central theme is right, legitimacy, legality.* Book I opens: 'I want to find out if, in political society, there can be any legitimate and sure rule of administration, taking men as they are and laws as they might be.'⁵ This opening statement is very important. Firstly, Rousseau is not trying to portray a single political model which could be universally or uniformly imposed on any society. He is setting out the 'rule of administration', that is, the essential principles which any constitution should observe if it is to be legitimate. In practice a constitution can take various forms, as he makes clear in Books II and III. Secondly, Rousseau takes 'men as they are'. In this sense his principles are not utopian, and he himself later distinguished *The Social Contract* from utopian 'fantasies' (see p. 244). One of the notable features of his political theory is precisely its psychological insight, its emotional realism. Thirdly, he is discussing 'laws as they might be'. He is talking about rights, not facts.

Rousseau regarded himself as without predecessors in this task. '[The science of] political right is still to be born', he says in *Emile*. He dismisses the work done by Grotius and Hobbes and continues:

> The only modern writer able to create this great and useless science has been the illustrious Montesquieu. But he was not concerned with the principles of political right; he was content to deal with the positive laws of established governments, and nothing in the world could be more different than these two branches of study.⁷

This distinction is crucial. Rousseau is not discussing how things are, but how they ought to be. What is a just basis for civil society and political organization?

Different writers had put forward different suggestions for the basis of civil society — the family, the right of the strongest,† slavery — all of which Rousseau rejects (Bk I, Chs 2, 3, and 4). Any legitimate association must be made between free people. In his chapter on slavery Rousseau writes:

---

* The epigraph for the work, from Virgil's *Æneid*, reads: 'Let us make equal laws for a treaty'; the passage continues: 'and call our companions into one rule of government.'⁶

† In a footnote in *The Geneva MS* Rousseau refers to contemporary colonization as an example: 'I have seen in [a paper], called . . . the *Dutch Observer*, a rather charming principle: it is that all land inhabited only by the savages ought to be considered vacant, and that one can legitimately deprive them of it and chase out the inhabitants without doing them any wrong according to natural law.'

To renounce freedom is to renounce being a man, one's rights of
humanity and equally one's duties. There is no possible compensation for one who renounces everything. Such a renunciation
is incompatible with man's nature; to take away all freedom of
his will is to remove all morality from his acts . . .   356

The direction of his argument is continually to assert the importance
of this freedom. In *The Geneva MS* this emphasis is even more
apparent:

There are a thousand ways of gathering men together, but there
is only one way of uniting them . . . What can have committed   297
men to come together willingly in a social body, if it is not for
their common utility? Common utility is therefore the foundation
of civil society. That agreed, what can distinguish legitimate
states from forced groupings, which nothing authorizes, unless
it is by considering their object or purpose? If the form of
society tends to the common good, it follows the spirit of its
institution: if it only takes into account the interest of the leaders,
it is illegitimate by right of reason and humanity. For even if the
public interest were in agreement sometimes with that of tyranny,
that temporary agreement could not be sufficient to authorize a
government of which it was not the principle . . . It is not a
question of what is, but of what is appropriate and just; not
of the power which one is forced to obey, but the power one is
obliged to recognize.   304–5

Rousseau is arguing here against earlier versions of the contract
theory, the type he had referred to in the *Discourse of Equality* (see
p. 63).

The theory of the social contract has a long history in political
theory. It had become particularly important in the seventeenth
century, when it had been developed by Hobbes, Locke and such
legal theorists as Grotius and Pufendorf, all of whom Rousseau
had studied. It put forward a contractual basis for political organization, a covenant or pact between men which established the state
and authorized law; this replaced theories like the Divine Right of
Kings which had relied on divine intervention into human affairs
to create legality and sanction authority.

Rousseau altered this theory in several crucial ways. The fundamental problem was to reconcile liberty and obedience, the rights of
the individual and the needs of society. For Locke, men entered into

the social contract to secure their rights and protect their possessions; his overriding concern was to minimize interference from other people, freedom to him was freedom *from* society. Rousseau did not see society as essentially hostile. He had developed a forward-looking view which he had set out clearly in *The Geneva MS* (in the chapter on The General Society of the Human Race), and elsewhere: 'It is only in mutual association that the most sublime faculties are developed and the excellence of our nature is revealed.'[8] 'Affectionate feelings nourish the soul, the communication of ideas sharpens the mind. Our sweetest existence is relative and collective,* and our true ego is never entirely in ourselves.'[10] He therefore believed that our freedom is realized *in* society. If we all equally participate in the making of our society we will all accept what the common good demands. The covenant that establishes a legitimate state is one in which everyone freely commits himself fully to the community, in order to receive back from it his legal rights.

It is important to understand that the phrase Rousseau uses to describe this act of covenant — 'total alienation' — does not mean a complete expropriation or loss of freedom. The act is a recognition by the individual that he owes his rights to the society in which he participates and to which he belongs. Rousseau points out that if the alienation were not total everyone would not be equal. What he does not say, in this chapter, is that these rights must include certain specific rights; but he has made it clear, in his remarks on freedom, quoted above, that he regards freedom and humanity as indissoluble. In Bk I, Ch. 9 he also says that everyone 'naturally has a right to what he needs', in terms which he then defines. In Bk II, Ch. 4 he sets out the limits of the sovereign's power over the individual, and elsewhere† he made it clear that the laws of the state must not infringe the 'natural laws', by which he means the sense of justice which we all have naturally — the social aspect of our conscience.‡ (This

---

* Rousseau saw our collective experience as an extension and development of our individual experience, and not as a restriction or negation of it. He was opposed to any possible denial of our sense of ourselves, which is why he wrote elsewhere: 'The French have no personal existence; they only think and act as a mass, each of them on his own is nothing. Now in such collective bodies there is never any disinterested love of justice; that has been engraved by nature only on the hearts of individuals.'[9]

† See the *Letters from the Mountain*, p. 175. Also, Rousseau's remarks in *The State of War*, p. 107, and the *Considerations on the Government of Poland*, p. 298.

‡ See the *Profession of Faith*, p. 227.

sense does not, of course, exist in a state of nature; it develops in society, but it is, like conscience, innate.)

The Social Contract

BK I, CH. 1. SUBJECT OF THE FIRST BOOK

Man was born free;* and everywhere he is in chains. One thinks himself the master of others, and still remains a greater slave than they. How did this change come about? I do not know. What can make it legitimate? That question I think I can answer.

If I took into account only force, and the effects derived from it, I should say: 'As long as a people is compelled to obey, and obeys, it does well; as soon as it can shake off the yoke, and shakes it off, it does still better; for, regaining its liberty by the same right as took it away, either it is justified in resuming it, or there was no justification for those who took it away.' But the social order is a sacred right which is the basis of all other rights. Nevertheless, this right does not come from nature, and must therefore be founded on conventions . . .   351–2

[Rousseau discusses other theories of the origin of society (Chs. 2, 3 and 4,) and concludes in Ch. 5: 'that we must always go back to a first covenant'.† He then outlines his theory of the social contract.]

BK I, CH. 6. THE SOCIAL PACT

I suppose men to have reached the point at which the obstacles in the way of their preservation in the state of nature show their power of resistance to be greater than the resources at the disposal of each individual for his maintenance in that state. That primitive condition can then subsist no longer; and the human race would perish unless it changed its manner of existence.

But, as men cannot engender new forces, but only unite and direct existing ones, they have no other means of preserving themselves than the formation, by aggregation, of a sum of forces great enough to overcome the resistance. These they have to bring into play by means of a single motive power, and cause to act in concert.

This sum of forces can arise only where several persons come to-

---

* This sentence — *L'homme est né libre* — can equally well be translated 'Man is born free'.

† In *Emile* he wrote: 'Take away the primitive law of conventions, and the obligations which it imposes, [and] all is illusory and vain in human society.'[11]

gether: but, as the force and liberty of each man are the chief instruments of his self-preservation, how can he pledge them without harming his own interests, and neglecting the care he owes to himself? This difficulty, in its bearing on my present subject, may be stated in the following terms: 'The problem is to find a form of association which will defend and protect with the whole common force the person and goods of each associate, and in which each, while uniting himself with all, may still obey himself alone, and remain as free as before.' This is the fundamental problem to which the social contract provides the solution.

360

The clauses of this contract are so determined by the nature of the act that the slightest modification would make them vain and ineffective; so that, although they have perhaps never been formally set forth, they are everywhere the same and everywhere tacitly admitted and recognized, until, on the violation of the social pact, each regains his original rights and resumes his natural liberty, while losing the conventional liberty in favour of which he renounced it.

These clauses, properly understood, may be reduced to one — the total alienation of each associate, together with all his rights, to the whole community; for, in the first place, as each gives himself absolutely, the conditions are the same for all; and, this being so, no one has any interest in making them burdensome to others.

361

Moreover, the alienation being without reserve, the union is as perfect as it can be, and no associate has anything more to demand: for, if the individuals retained certain rights, as there would be no common superior to decide between them and the public, each, being on one point his own judge, would ask to be so on all; the state of nature would thus continue, and the association would necessarily become inoperative or tyrannical.

Finally, each man, in giving himself to all, gives himself to nobody; and as there is no associate over whom he does not acquire the same right as he yields others over himself, he gains an equivalent for everything he loses, and an increase of force for the preservation of what he has.

If then we discard from the social pact what is not of its essence, we shall find that it reduces itself to the following terms: 'Each of us puts his person and all his power in common under the supreme direction of the general will, and, in our corporate capacity, we receive each member as an indivisible part of the whole.'

At once, in place of the individual personality of each contracting party, this act of association creates a corporate and collective body, composed of as many members as the assembly contains voters, and receiving from this act its unity, its common identity, its life, and its will. This public person, so formed by the union of all other persons, formerly took the name of city, and now takes that of *republic* or body politic; it is called by its members *state* when passive, *sovereign* when active, and *power* when compared with others like itself. Those who are associated in it take collectively the name of *people*, and severally are called *citizens*, as sharing in the sovereign authority, and *subjects*, as being under the laws of the state . . .   361–2

BK I, CH. 7. THE SOVEREIGN

This formula shows us that the act of association comprises a mutual undertaking between the public and the individuals, and that each individual, in making a contract, as we may say, with himself, is bound in a double relation; as a member of the sovereign he is bound to the individuals, and as a member of the state to the sovereign. But the maxim of civil right, that no one is bound by undertakings made to himself, does not apply in this case; for there is a great difference between incurring an obligation to yourself and incurring one to a whole of which you form a part . . .   362

As soon as this multitude is so united in one body, it is impossible to offend against one of the members without attacking the body, and still more to offend against the body without the members resenting it. Duty and interest therefore equally oblige the two contracting parties to give each other help; and the same men should seek to combine, in their double capacity, all the advantages dependent upon that capacity . . .   363

Each individual, as a man, may have a particular will contrary or dissimilar to the general will which he has as a citizen. His particular interest may speak to him quite differently from the common interest: his absolute and naturally independent existence may make him look upon what he owes to the common cause as a gratuitous contribution, the loss of which will do less harm to others than the payment of it is burdensome to himself . . . he may wish to enjoy the rights of citizenship without being ready to fulfil the duties of a subject. The continuance of such an injustice could not but prove the undoing of the body politic.

In order then that the social pact may not be an empty formula, it tacitly includes the undertaking, which alone can give force to the rest, that whoever refuses to obey the general will shall be compelled to do so by the whole body. This means nothing less than that he will be forced to be free;* for this is the condition which, by giving each citizen to his country, secures him against all personal dependence.† In this lies the key to the working of the political machine; this alone legitimizes civil undertakings, which, without it, would be absurd, 364 tyrannical and liable to the most frightful abuses.

BK I, CH. 8. THE CIVIL STATE

The passage from the state of nature to the civil state produces a very remarkable change in man, by substituting justice for instinct in his conduct, and giving his actions the morality they had formerly lacked. Then only, when the voice of duty takes the place of physical impulses and right of appetite, does man, who so far had considered only himself, find that he is forced to act on different principles, and to consult his reason before listening to his inclinations. Although, in this state, he deprives himself of some advantages which he got from nature, he gains in return others so great, his faculties are so stimulated and developed, his ideas so extended, his feelings so ennobled, and his whole soul so uplifted, that, did not the abuses of this new condition often degrade him below that which he left, he would be bound to bless continually the happy moment which took him from it for ever, and, instead of a stupid and unimaginative animal, made him an intelligent being and a man.

Let us draw up a simple comparison of all that is involved. What man loses by the social contract is his natural liberty and an unlimited right to everything he tries to get and succeeds in getting; what he gains is civil liberty and the proprietorship of all he possesses. If we are to avoid mistakes in weighing one against the other, we must clearly distinguish natural liberty, which is bounded only by the strength of the individual, from civil liberty, which is limited by the general will; and possession, which is only the result of force or the

---

* The general will is not external to us; it is something each of us possesses — a sense of common interest we share with others, as opposed to the self-interest concerned only with ourself. To make someone obey the general will, to 'force him to be free', means therefore no more than to make him recognize that he is a social being, and has obligations to his society. Without such a recognition, Rousseau says, no society can justly continue.[12]

† See Rousseau's important remarks about 'dependence on men' in *Emile*, p. 189.

right of the first occupier, from property, which can be based only on a positive title.

We might, over and above all this, add, to what man acquires in the civil state, moral liberty, which alone makes him truly master of himself; for the mere impulse of appetite is slavery, while obedience to a law which we prescribe to ourselves is liberty. But I have already said too much on this head,* and the philosophical meaning of the word liberty is not what concerns us here.   364–5

BK I, CH. 9. PROPERTY

. . . The right of the first occupier, though more real than the right of the strongest, becomes a real right only when the right of property has already been established. Every man has naturally a right to everything he needs; but the positive act which makes him proprietor of one thing excludes him from everything else. Having his share, he ought to keep to it, and can have no further right against the community. This is why the right of the first occupier, which in the state of nature is so weak, claims the respect of every man in civil society. In this right we are respecting not so much what belongs to another as what does not belong to ourselves.

In general, to establish the right of the first occupier over a plot of ground, the following conditions are necessary: first, the land must not yet be inhabited; secondly, a man must occupy only the amount he needs for his subsistence; and, in the third place, possession must be taken, not by an empty ceremony, but by labour and cultivation, the only sign of proprietorship that should be respected by others, in default of a legal title . . .   365–6

I shall end this chapter and this book by remarking on a fact on which the whole social system should rest, i.e. that, instead of destroying natural equality, the fundamental pact substitutes, for such physical inequality as nature may have set up between men, an equality that is moral and legitimate, and that men, who may be unequal in strength or intelligence, become every one equal by convention and legal right.†

* This is a reference to *Emile* (see page 206).

† Under bad governments this equality is only apparent and illusory; it serves only to keep the pauper in his poverty and the rich man in the position he has usurped. In fact, laws are always of use to those who possess and harmful to those who have nothing: from which it follows that the social state is advantageous to men only when all have something and none too much. (Note by Rousseau.)   367

THE SOVEREIGN, THE GENERAL WILL, THE LAW
(BOOK II)

The state, in Rousseau's terms, is purely passive, the collection of its members. What makes it act is the sovereign, everyone participating in the determination and pursuit of the common good. The decisions of the sovereign are the source of public authority. There is no higher authority, which is what Rousseau means when he calls the sovereign 'absolute'. He does not mean by this that its authority is arbitrary, and he indicates specific limits to its power (Ch. 4).

The sovereign involves all of us, acting together for the good of the whole. This is why it is 'indivisible' (Ch. 2). Since it is only through our participation that we can all accept what the common good demands, we cannot allow deputies or representatives to take our place. We may not all agree about the common good, our decisions need not be unanimous,* but as long as we have been present when a decision is made we will feel under obligation to abide by it. Our participation is a condition of our freedom. We can only be free if we live under laws which we have made ourselves. This is what Rousseau means when he says that the sovereign is 'inalienable' (Ch. 1).

The decisions of the sovereign are embodied in the general will. Rousseau had first discussed this concept in the *Discourse on Political Economy* (see p. 76). He now develops it as a central feature of his political theory, defining it specifically and carefully. It is not an average or an aggregate of what everyone wants for himself; that would only be the product of our individual private wishes. Acting together like that, motivated only by self-interest, we would only produce what Rousseau calls the 'will of all' (Ch. 3). The 'general will' is what people want when they set aside their self-interest and choose for the common good, on the basis of shared interest. 'As the will always tends to the good of the being who wills, the individual will always has private interest as its object, and the general will has the common interest; it follows that this last alone [the common interest] is, or should be, the real motive force of the social body' (*The Geneva MS*: 295).

The sovereign, acting according to the general will, makes the laws. (Rousseau makes a distinction between 'laws', which involve everyone, and 'decrees' — those acts which are only binding on a particular number of people and which are determined by the

---

* The one exception is the initial social covenant; everyone who enters into the civil state made by the pact must do so voluntarily (Bk IV, Ch. 2).

government.) The first laws to be made are the political or fundamental laws, those which fix the actual conditions of the constitution.
To make these laws well two considerations must be taken into account — first, the spirit and intelligence with which the project is
carried out, and second, the character of the people (that is, the
nation), and the conditions in which they live.

The second of these — which is more a matter of fact than of right
— presents no problems. Rousseau discusses a number of conditions
which will affect the possibility of a people adopting just laws. These
include such items as their history, geography, economy, and
size — 'for the constitution of a state to be at its best it is possible to
fix limits that will make it neither too large for good government,
nor too small for self-maintenance' (Ch. 9).

With the first of these two considerations, however, Rousseau
faces what seems an insurmountable problem. If people are only
what their governments make them, as he had written previously
elsewhere (see pp. 48 and 79), how could any people create a
better government? He was trapped in a logical impasse, as he himself recognized:

> For a young people to be able to grasp the principles of political
> theory and follow the fundamental rules of statecraft, the effect
> would have to become the cause; the social spirit, which should
> be created by these institutions, would have to preside over their
> very foundation; and men would have to be before the law what
> they should become by means of the law.

383

To overcome this difficulty Rousseau introduces the lawgiver,* 'the
engineer who invents the machine'. He is neither the founder of a
state nor its governor; he is merely an adviser. He has no power
whatsoever: if he prescribed 'anything to individuals without first
having received the sanction of general consent [he would] destroy
at the very beginning the essence of the very thing that one wished
to form, and would break the social bond while believing it was being
strengthened' (*The Geneva MS*: 316). He must be not only a man of
feeling, aware of human passions, but also a 'superior intelligence',
with a 'great soul'. To these attributes Rousseau adds a semi-mystical
quality.

To some people the lawgiver is a major weakness in Rousseau's
political theory. Where could such a desirable and considerate

---

* *Législateur*, translated as legislator when it refers to a body of people rather
than a single person (see pp. 247 and 300).

superman be found? The examples Rousseau gives, like Lycurgus or Moses, seem hopelessly remote; and despite the many detailed safeguards Rousseau sets out, to prevent a lawgiver abusing his position, there is a frequent tendency to see him as an authoritarian figure.

This is to misunderstand the function he has in *The Social Contract*. To a large extent he is a metaphor for the moral transformation that can alone bring about a just society. He is 'supreme reason', a personification of the super-ego present in each one of us. This is why he should not be seen as authoritarian.* In several ways he resembles the tutor in *Emile*, who is likewise in some respects a fictional creation, a means of demonstrating in direct and immediate terms a complex and difficult process.

This process could well be compared with the production of a play, and the function of the lawgiver compared with that of a director in the modern theatre. The actors only come to have a sense of the play as a whole through the process of rehearsal. The director helps them in this process. To do this well he needs to understand how each of them feels, while never losing sight of the overall view that they initially will not possess. Only the process of rehearsal brings alive in the actors the qualities, both in themselves and between one another, which give life to the play. When the process of rehearsal is completed the director's work is finished. He has nothing to do with the actual performance that the actors give to the audience, which is the purpose of the whole enterprise.

The position of a director is of course open to abuse. But the success of performances, like the success of laws (as Rousseau describes it at the end of Bk II), does not lie in force or authority, but in the extent to which the people, like the actors, believe in them. 'The most important kind [of law] is not engraved on marble or brass but in the hearts of the citizens. This forms the real constitution of the state' (Ch. 12).

BK II, CH. 1. THAT SOVEREIGNTY IS INALIENABLE

The first and most important deduction from the principles we have so far laid down is that the general will alone can direct the state

* Critics tend to be obsessed with Rousseau's occasional severity or rhetorical excess, and to forget that for him ultimate authority always remains with the sovereign, which is all the people, everyone of whom has the right to speak freely and openly against any proposed law.

according to the object for which it was instituted, i.e. the common good: for if the clashing of particular interests made the establishment of societies necessary, the agreement of these very interests made it possible. The common element in these different interests is what forms the social tie; and, were there no point of agreement between them all, no society could exist. It is solely on the basis of this common interest that every society should be governed.

I hold then that sovereignty, being nothing less than the exercise of the general will, can never be alienated, and that the sovereign, who is no less than a collective being, cannot be represented except by himself: the power indeed may be transmitted, but not the will . . . 368

BK II, CH. 2. THAT SOVEREIGNTY IS INDIVISIBLE

Sovereignty, for the same reason as makes it inalienable, is in-divisible; for will either is, or is not, general;* it is the will either of the body of the people, or only of a part of it. In the first case, the will, when declared, is an act of sovereignty and constitutes law; in the second, it is merely a particular will or act of magistracy — at the most a decree . . . 369

BK II, CH. 3. WHETHER THE GENERAL WILL IS FALLIBLE

It follows from what has gone before that the general will is always upright and always tends to the public advantage; but it does not follow that the deliberations of the people always have the same rectitude. Our will is always for our own good, but we do not always see what that is; the people is never corrupted, but it is often deceived, and on such occasions only does it seem to will what is bad.

There is often a great deal of difference between the will of all and the general will; the latter considers only the common interest, while the former takes private interest into account, and is no more than a sum of particular wills: but take away from these same wills the pluses and minuses that cancel one another,† and the general will remains as the sum of the differences . . . 371

---

* To be general, a will need not always be unanimous; but every vote must be counted: any formal exclusion is a breach of generality. (Note by Rousseau.)

† 'Every interest', says the Marquis d'Argenson, 'has different principles. The agreement of two particular interests is formed by opposition to a third.' He might have added that the agreement of all interests is formed by opposition to that of each. If there were no different interests, the common interest would be barely felt, as it would encounter no obstacle; all would go on of its own accord, and politics would cease to be an art. (Note by Rousseau.)

It is essential, if the general will is to be able to make itself known, that there should be no partial society in the state and that each citizen should express only his own opinion . . . But if there are partial societies, it is best to have as many as possible and to prevent them from being unequal . . . These precautions are the only ones that can guarantee that the general will shall be always enlightened, and 372   that the people shall in no way deceive itself.

BK II, CH. 4. THE LIMITS OF SOVEREIGN POWER

If the state is a corporate body* whose life is in the union of its members, and if the most important of its cares is the care for its own preservation, it must have a universal and compelling force, in order to move and dispose each part as may be most advantageous to the whole. As nature gives each man absolute power over all his members, the social pact gives the body politic absolute power over all its members also; and it is this power which, under the direction of the general will, bears, as I have said, the name of sovereignty.

But, besides the public person, we have to consider the private persons composing it, whose life and liberty are naturally independent of it. We are bound then to distinguish clearly between the respective rights of the citizens and the sovereign, and between the duties the former have to fulfil as subjects, and the natural rights they should enjoy as men.

Each man alienates, I admit, by the social pact, only such part of his powers, goods, and liberty as it is important for the community to control; but it must also be granted that the sovereign is sole judge of what is important.

Every service a citizen can render the state he ought to render as soon as the sovereign demands it; but the sovereign, for its part, cannot impose upon its subjects any fetters that are useless to the community, nor can it even wish to do so; for no more by the law of reason than by the law of nature can anything occur without a cause.

The undertakings which bind us to the social body are obligatory only because they are mutual; and their nature is such that in fulfilling them we cannot work for others without working for ourselves.

---

* The phrase Rousseau uses here — *personne morale* — is a legal term for an entity brought into being by the union of its members, which has capacities and can function like a single person.

Why is it that the general will is always upright, and that all continually will the happiness of each one, unless it is because there is not a man who does not think of 'each' as meaning him, and consider himself in voting for all? This proves that equality of rights and the idea of justice which such equality creates originate in the preference each man gives to himself, and accordingly in the very nature of man. It proves that the general will, to be really such, must be general in its object as well as its essence; that it must both come from all and apply to all; and that it loses its natural rectitude when it is directed to some particular and determinate object, because in such a case we are judging of something foreign to us, and have no true principle of equity to guide us . . .   372–3

We can see from this that the sovereign power, absolute, sacred, and inviolable as it is, does not and cannot exceed the limits of general conventions, and that every man may dispose at will of such goods and liberty as these conventions leave him; so that the sovereign never has a right to lay more charges on one subject than on another, because, in that case, the question becomes particular, and ceases to be within its competency.

When these distinctions have once been admitted it is seen to be so untrue that there is, in the social contract, any real renunciation on the part of the individuals, that the position in which they find themselves as a result of the contract is really preferable to that in which they were before. Instead of a renunciation they have made an advantageous exchange: instead of an uncertain and precarious way of living they have got one that is better and more secure; instead of natural independence they have got liberty, instead of the power to harm others, security for themselves, and instead of their strength, which others might overcome, a right which social union makes invincible. Their very life, which they have devoted to the state, is by it constantly protected; and when they risk it in the state's defence, what more are they doing than giving back what they have received from it? . . .   375

[Bk II, Ch. 5 discusses the death penalty; Bk II, Ch. 6 discusses the law, which presents a major difficulty.]

BK II, CH. 6. LAW

. . . Laws are, properly speaking, only the conditions of civil association. The people, being subject to the laws, ought to be their author: the conditions of the society ought to be regulated solely by those who come together to form it. But how are they to regulate them? Is it by common agreement, by a sudden inspiration? . . . Of itself the people always wills the good, but of itself it by no means always sees it. The general will is always upright, but the judgement which guides it is not always enlightened . . . [The people] must be taught to know what it wills. If that is done, public enlightenment leads to the union of understanding and will in the social body: the parts are made to work exactly together, and the whole is raised to its highest 380   power. This makes the lawgiver necessary.

BK II, CH. 7. THE LAWGIVER

. . . He who dares to undertake the making of a people's institutions ought to feel himself capable, so to speak, of changing human nature, of transforming each individual, who is by himself a complete and solitary whole, into part of a greater whole from which he in a manner receives his life and being; of altering man's constitution for the purpose of strengthening it; and of substituting a partial and moral existence for the physical and independent existence nature has conferred on us all. He must, in a word, take away from man his own resources and give him instead new ones alien to him, and incapable of being made use of without the help of other men. The more completely these natural resources are annihilated, the greater and the more lasting are those which he acquires, and the more stable and perfect the new institutions; so that if each citizen is nothing and can do nothing without the rest, and the resources acquired by the whole are equal or superior to the aggregate of the resources of all the individuals, it may be said that legislation is at the highest possible point of perfection.

The lawgiver occupies in every respect an extraordinary position in the state. If he should do so by reason of his genius, he does so no less by reason of his office, which is neither magistracy, nor sovereignty. This office, which sets up the republic, nowhere enters into its constitution; it is an individual and superior function, which has nothing in common with human empire; for if he who holds command over men ought not to have command over the laws, he who has command over the laws ought not any more to have it over men; or else his laws would be the ministers of his passions and would often merely serve to perpetuate his injustices: his private aims would 381–2   inevitably mar the sanctity of his work . . .

[Bk II, Chs. 8, 9 and 10 discuss the people, the different characteristics which determine what kind of constitution is appropriate and possible.]

BK II, CH. 9.

In every body politic there is a maximum strength which it cannot exceed and which it only loses by increasing in size. Every extension of the social tie means its relaxation; and, generally speaking, a small state is stronger in proportion than a great one.

A thousand arguments could be advanced in favour of this principle. First, long distances make administration more difficult . . . Administration therefore becomes more and more burdensome as its stages are multiplied . . .

The people has less affection for its rulers, whom it never sees, for its *patrie*, which to its eyes seems like the world, and for its fellow citizens, most of whom are unknown to it . . . The leaders, overwhelmed with business, see nothing for themselves; the state is governed by clerks. Finally, the measures which have to be taken to maintain the general [i.e. sovereign] authority, which all these distant officials wish to escape or exploit, absorb all the energy of the public, so that there is none left for the happiness of the people . . . 386–7

All peoples have a kind of centrifugal force that makes them continually act against one another and tend to expand at their neighbours' expense . . . There are reasons for expansion and reasons for contraction . . . [But] it may be said that the former, being merely external and relative, ought to be subordinate to the latter, which are internal and absolute. A strong and healthy constitution is the first thing to look for; and it is better to count on the vigour which comes of good government than on the resources provided by a large territory . . . 388

BK II, CH. 11. THE VARIOUS SYSTEMS OF LEGISLATION

If we ask in what precisely consists the greatest good of all, which should be the end of every system of legislation, we shall find it reduces itself to two main objects, liberty and equality — liberty, because all particular dependence means so much force taken from the body of the state, and equality, because liberty cannot exist without it.

I have already defined civil liberty; by equality we should understand not that the degrees of power and riches are to be absolutely identical for everybody; but that power shall never be great enough for violence, and shall always be exercised by virtue of rank and law; and that, in respect of riches, no citizen shall ever be wealthy enough to buy another, and none poor enough to be forced to sell himself:* which implies, on the part of the great, moderation in goods and position, and, on the side of the common people, moderation in avarice and covetousness.

Such equality, we are told, is an impractical ideal that cannot actually exist. But if its abuse is inevitable, does it follow that we should not at least make regulations concerning it? It is precisely because the force of circumstances tends continually to destroy equality that the force of legislation should always tend to its maintenance.

But these general objects of every good legislative system need modifying in every country in accordance with the local situation and the temper of the inhabitants; and these circumstances should determine, in each case, the particular system of institutions which is 391–2 best, not perhaps in itself, but for the state for which it is destined . . .

THE GOVERNMENT (BOOK III)

The political or fundamental laws establish the form of the state, with the sovereign as supreme authority. The sovereign, acting according to the general will, then makes the civil and criminal laws under which everyone lives. But it does not administer the laws, nor does it conduct the business of the state. That is the function of government (Ch. 1).

In earlier versions of the contract theory there was a contract between the governors and the governed.† To Rousseau that type of contract does not and cannot exist (Ch. 16). The government is not an equal party with the people: it is their instrument. It is not enough that the government shall have the tacit consent of the people: it must have their active approval. 'Those in whom executive power is

---

* If the object is to give the state consistency, bring the two extremes as near to each other as possible; allow neither rich men nor beggars. These two estates, which are naturally inseparable, are equally fatal to the common good; from the one come the friends of tyranny, and from the other tyrants. It is always between them that public liberty is put up to auction; the one buys, and the other sells. (Note by Rousseau.)

† This is sometimes referred to as a contract of submission. Rousseau's contract, by contrast, is a contract of association.

entrusted are not the people's masters but their officers; they can appoint them or dismiss them as they please' (Ch. 18).

In Bk III (Chs. 2, 3, 4, 5, 6 and 7) Rousseau discusses at length the different forms government can take. His own preference is not for democratic government; for everyone to participate in the actual administration of the state there would have to be 'a people of gods' (Ch. 4). The best in his view is an 'elective aristocracy',* one in which a small number of magistrates are elected to carry out the necessary business (Ch. 5). But it is not a simple matter of preference. Different governments suit different kinds of country (Ch. 8).

Two of Rousseau's constant preoccupations come to the surface in this book. Both are fundamental to his political theory, but because of the abstract nature of its presentation they are often overlooked. The first is the sense of belonging and of sharing, so that we feel dependent only on what we know and are part of, and our freedom is constrained only by what we can understand to be a reasonable constraint. This concern is manifest in Rousseau's objections to deputies or representatives: 'Sovereignty cannot be represented . . . Every law which the people has not ratified in person is void; it is not law at all . . .' (Ch. 15).

The criticism is often made that this insistence on direct participation means that Rousseau's principles can only be applied to small states. That is correct, but Rousseau would not regard it as a criticism. Because his principle is based on the way we are, the way we feel. His insistence on such an aspect is an example of his awareness of real limits that do exist, and must be recognized. The difficulties we face in applying his principles to our own society are our problem, not his failure.

Rousseau's other preoccupation is the danger of concentrations of power and arbitrary authority. The government will always tend to usurp power (Ch. 10). It must therefore be continually under the eye of the sovereign, and one way of doing this is to have periodic assemblies of the people — 'the shield of the body politic and the brake on the government'. Considerable attention is given to this matter (Chs. 12, 13, 14 and 18). Rousseau's overriding concern is that the executive should be 'always ready to sacrifice the government to the people, and never to sacrifice the people to the government' (Ch. 1).

* This is what we usually call a democracy nowadays.

BK III, CH. 1. GOVERNMENT IN GENERAL

. . . What then is government? An intermediate body set up between the subjects and the sovereign, to secure their mutual correspondence, charged with the execution of the laws and the maintenance of liberty, both civil and political . . . I call *government*, or supreme administration, the legitimate exercise of the executive power, and *prince* or *magistrate* the man or the body entrusted with that administration . . .

The government gets from the sovereign the orders it gives to the people, and, for the state to be properly balanced, there must, when everything is taken into account, be equality between the product or power of the government, taken in itself, and the product or power of the citizens, who are on the one hand sovereign and on the other subject.

Furthermore, none of these three terms can be altered without the balance being instantly destroyed. If the sovereign desires to govern, or the magistrate to give laws, or if the subjects refuse to obey, disorder takes the place of rule, force and will no longer act together, and the state is dissolved and falls into despotism or anarchy. Lastly, as there is only one mean proportional between each relation, there is also only one good government possible for a state. But, as countless events may change the relations of a people, not only may different governments be good for different peoples, 396–7 but also for the same people at different times . . .

[The two foremost considerations in deciding which government is appropriate to a people are the size of the state and its economy.]

BK III, CH. 3. THE DIVISION OF GOVERNMENTS

. . . Generally, democratic government suits small states, aristocratic 403–4 government those of middle size, and monarchy great ones . . .

BK III, CH. 8. THAT ALL FORMS OF GOVERNMENT DO NOT SUIT ALL COUNTRIES

. . . In all the governments there are, the public person consumes without producing. Whence then does it get what it consumes? From the labour of its members. The necessities of the public are supplied out of the superfluities of individuals . . . The amount of this excess 414 is not the same in all countries . . .

BK III, CH. 10. THE ABUSE OF GOVERNMENT AND ITS
TENDENCY TO DEGENERATE

As the particular will acts constantly in opposition to the general will, the government constantly exerts itself against the sovereignty. The greater this exertion becomes, the more the constitution changes; and, as there is in this case no other corporate will to create an equilibrium by resisting the will of the prince, sooner or later the prince must inevitably suppress the sovereign and break the social treaty. This is the unavoidable and inherent defect which, from the very birth of the body politic, tends ceaselessly to destroy it, as age and death end by destroying the human body.

There are two general courses by which government degenerates: that is, when it undergoes contraction, or when the state is dissolved.

Government undergoes contraction when it passes from the many to the few, that is, from democracy to aristocracy, and from aristocracy to royalty. To do so is its natural propensity . . .   421

The dissolution of the state may come about in either of two ways.

First, when the prince ceases to administer the state in accordance with the laws, and usurps the sovereign power . . .

[Or] when the members of the government severally usurp the power they should exercise as a body; this is as great an infraction of the laws, and results in even greater disorders . . .   422–3

BK III, CH. 11. THE DEATH OF THE BODY POLITIC

. . . The body politic, as well as the human body, begins to die as soon as it is born, and carries in itself the causes of its destruction. But both may have a constitution that is more or less robust and suited to preserve them a longer or a shorter time. The constitution of man is the work of nature; that of the state the work of art. It is not in men's power to prolong their own lives; but it is for them to prolong as much as possible the life of the state, by giving it the best possible constitution . . .

The life-principle of the body politic lies in the sovereign authority . . . The state subsists by means not of the laws but of the legislative power. Yesterday's law is not binding today . . .   424

BK III, CH. 12. HOW THE SOVEREIGN AUTHORITY
MAINTAINS ITSELF

The sovereign, having no force other than the legislative power, acts only by means of the laws; and the laws being solely the authentic acts of the general will, the sovereign cannot act save when the people is assembled. The people in assembly, I shall be told, is a mere chimera. It is so today, but two thousand years ago it was not so. Has man's nature changed?

The bounds of possibility, in moral matters, are less narrow than we imagine; it is our weaknesses, our vices, and our prejudices that
425   confine them . . .

BK III, CH. 13

It is not enough for the assembled people to have once fixed the constitution of the state by giving its sanction to a body of law; it is not enough for it to have set up a perpetual government, or provided once for all for the election of magistrates. Besides the extraordinary assemblies unforeseen circumstances may demand, there must be fixed periodical assemblies which cannot be abrogated or prorogued, so that on the proper day the people is legitimately called together by law, without need of any formal summoning . . .

Generally speaking, the stronger the government the more often the
426   sovereign should show itself . . .

BK III, CH. 14

The moment the people is legitimately assembled as a sovereign body, the jurisdiction of the government wholly lapses, the executive power is suspended, and the person of the meanest citizen is as
427   sacred and inviolable as that of the first magistrate . . .

BK III, CH. 15. DEPUTIES OR REPRESENTATIVES

As soon as public service ceases to be the chief business of the citizens, and they would rather serve with their money than with their
428   persons, the state is not far from its fall . . .

The better the constitution of a state, the more does public business take precedence over private in the minds of the citizens. Private affairs are even of much less importance, because the aggregate of the happiness furnishes a greater proportion of that of each individual,
429   so that he has less need to seek it in private interests . . .

Sovereignty, for the same reason as makes it inalienable, cannot be represented; it lies essentially in the general will and will does not admit of representation; it is either the same, or other; there is no intermediate possibility. The deputies of the people, therefore, are not and cannot be its representatives; they are merely its agents, and can carry through no definitive acts. Every law the people has not ratified in person is null and void — is, in fact, not a law. The people of England regards itself as free; but it is grossly mistaken; it is free only during the election of members of parliament. As soon as they are elected, slavery overtakes it and it is nothing. The use it makes of the short moments of liberty it enjoys shows indeed that it deserves to lose them . . .   429–30

The moment a people allows itself to be represented, it is no longer free; it no longer exists.

[In Bk III, Chs. 16 and 17 Rousseau elucidates his important principle that the government is subordinate to the sovereign.]

BK III, CH. 18. HOW TO CHECK THE USURPATION OF THE GOVERNMENT

What we have just said . . . makes it clear that the institution of government is not a contract, but a law; that those in whom executive power is entrusted are not the people's masters, but its officers; that it can set them up and pull them down when it likes; that for them there is no question of contract, but of obedience . . .

It is true that such changes are always dangerous, and that the established government should never be touched except when it comes to be incompatible with the public good; but the circumspection this involves is a maxim of policy and not a rule of right, and the state is no more bound to leave civil authority in the hands of its rulers than military authority in the hands of its generals . . .   434–5

CIVIL RELIGION (BOOK IV)

Most of Book IV is taken up with a discussion of political organization drawn from Roman history, but in the penultimate chapter Rousseau makes a proposal for another safeguard against the decay of the state — an open and unequivocal commitment to the common good made by all the citizens, a civil profession of faith.

The chapter on civil religion takes up the suggestion he had first made in his *Letter to Voltaire on Optimism* (see p. 118). Like many of his contemporaries Rousseau was horrified by the persecutions and intolerance of established churches. For men to live peacefully in society there can only be one source of authority, which should be civil authority; the church should be subordinate to the state.

At the same time, he felt that religion was a necessary part of human life, and, more than that, it was necessary to the life of society. In the first version of the chapter on civil religion he had written: 'As soon as men live in society they need a religion which keeps them together in it. No people has ever or will ever last without religion' (*The Geneva MS*: 336).

Christianity was not suitable as a religion for a state because 'it preaches only servitude and dependence'; men whose thoughts are turned to heaven do not make good citizens. Rousseau therefore proposes a civil religion which would both support the sense of the common good and provide a basic religious faith on which everyone could agree.

His proposal has aroused, and did arouse, much criticism, because the conditions accompanying it involve severe penalties. Although the punishment is for anti-social conduct, and not belief, it would seem difficult for a sincere atheist to be sincere in his unbelief and not be punished. This seems an uneasy accompaniment to the one negative dogma of no intolerance.

Rousseau was not alone in excluding atheists from his state. Locke had done the same in his *Essay on Toleration*. But in *The New Heloïse* he had set out to show, in the character of Wolmar, that it was possible to be an atheist and a good man. He had also written, in a footnote: 'If I was a magistrate, and the law carried the death penalty against atheists, the first person I would have burnt would be anyone who came to denounce someone else.'[13] By the time he came to write this chapter of *The Social Contract* his attitude seems to have hardened, and his remarks do seem, as one judicious critic has described them, 'unfortunate'.[14] But it should be pointed out that they are not an integral part of his political theory and, furthermore, that in the discussion of the death penalty earlier in *The Social Contract* (Bk II, Ch. 5) he had written: 'The state has no right to put to death, even for the sake of making an example, anyone whom it can leave alive without danger.'

BK IV, CH. 8. THE CIVIL RELIGION

... The right which the social pact gives the sovereign over the subjects does not, we have seen, exceed the limits of public utility.* The

---

* 'In the republic', says the Marquis d'Argenson, 'each man is perfectly free in what does not harm others.' This is the invariable limitation, which it is impossible to define more exactly. (Note by Rousseau.)

subjects then owe the sovereign an account of their opinions only to such an extent as they matter to the community. Now, it matters very much to the community that each citizen should have a religion. That will make him love his duty; but the dogmas of that religion concern the state and its members only so far as they have reference to morality and to the duties which he who professes them is bound to do to others. Each man may have, over and above, what opinions he pleases, without its being the sovereign's business to take cognizance of them; for, as the sovereign has no authority in the other world, whatever the lot of its subjects may be in the life to come is not its business, provided they are good citizens in this life.   467–8

There is therefore a purely civil profession of faith of which the sovereign should fix the articles, not exactly as religious dogmas, but as social sentiments without which a man cannot be a good citizen or a faithful subject. While it can compel no one to believe them, it can banish from the state whoever does not believe them — it can banish him, not for impiety but as an anti-social being, incapable of truly loving the laws and justice, and of sacrificing, at need, his life to his duty. If anyone, after publicly recognizing these dogmas, behaves as if he does not believe them, let him be punished by death: he has committed the worst of all crimes, that of lying before the law.

The dogmas of civil religion ought to be few, simple, and exactly worded, without explanation or commentary. The existence of a mighty, intelligent, and beneficent Divinity, possessed of foresight and providence, the life to come, the happiness of the just, the punishment of the wicked, the sanctity of the social contract and the laws: these are its positive dogmas. Its negative dogmas I confine to one, intolerance, which is a part of the cults we have rejected . . .

Now that there is and can be no longer an exclusive national religion, tolerance should be given to all religions that tolerate others, so long as their dogmas contain nothing contrary to the duties of citizenship.   468–9

The short last chapter of *The Social Contract* (Bk IV, Ch. 9) describes the subjects Rousseau would have dealt with in other parts of his *Political Institutions:* 'the law of nations, commerce, right of war and conquests, international law, alliances, negotiations and treaties, etc.' A fuller description is given in the summary of the whole work that occurs in Book V of *Emile.* It is evident both there and from a footnote to *The Social Contract* (Bk III, Ch. 15) that among the alliances and treaties there would have been a discussion of confederations, the way small states could remain small in themselves but find a means of common defence to protect themselves from large states.

SUMMARY

The most succinct account Rousseau ever made of his political theory is contained in the Sixth Letter of the *Letters from the Mountain*. Here is the synopsis of *The Social Contract* given there:

What is it that makes a state one? It is the union of its members. And where does that union come from? From the obligation which binds them. So far everyone is agreed.

But what is the basis of that obligation? This is where writers disagree. According to some, it is force; according to others, paternal authority; according to others, the will of God. Each sets up his own principle and attacks that of others. I have done the same myself, and following the soundest school among those who have discussed these matters, I have laid down as the foundation of the body politic the covenant of its members. I have refuted the principles that are

806   different from mine.

Quite apart from the truth of this principle it is preferable to all the others in that it provides a solid foundation; for what more reliable foundation can there be to the obligation among men than the free commitment of those who put themselves under this obligation? Every other principle can be disputed: this cannot.

But by this condition of liberty, which incorporates others, all kinds of commitment are not valid, even before human tribunals. In order to determine this one must explain its nature; one must discover its use and its end, one must prove that it is suitable for men and that it is not contrary to natural laws. For it is no more permissible to violate the natural laws by the social contract than it is to violate the positive laws [of the state] by private contracts, and it is only through these same laws that the liberty exists which gives force

806–7   to the commitment.

I concluded from this analysis that the institution of the social contract is a pact of a special kind, by which each commits himself to all, from which follows the reciprocal commitment of all to each, which is the immediate purpose of the union.

I say this commitment is of a special kind in that being absolute, unconditional, and without reservation, it can nevertheless be neither unjust nor susceptible to abuse; since it is not possible that the body wishes to harm itself, so long as the whole only wills for all.

It is also of a special kind in that it binds the contracting parties without subjecting them to anyone, and that, in giving them no more than their own will to rule them, it leaves them as free as they were before.

The will of all* is therefore the order, the supreme rule, and this general and personified rule is what I call the sovereign.

It follows from this that the sovereignty is indivisible, inalienable, and resides essentially in all the members of the body.

But how does this abstract and collective being act? It acts through laws, and it cannot act in any other way.   807

And what is a law? It is a public and solemn declaration of the general will on a matter of common interest.

I say on a matter of common interest; because the law would lose its force and would cease to be legitimate if the matter did not concern everyone.

By its nature the law cannot have any particular and individual object; although the application of the law falls on particular and individual objects.

The legislative power which is the sovereign therefore needs another power which executes, that is to say, which reduces the law into particular acts. This second power must be set up in such a way that it always executes the law, and never anything but the law. Hence arises the institution of the government.

What is the government? It is an intermediary body set up between the subjects and the sovereign for their mutual communication, charged with the execution of the laws and the maintenance of both civil and political liberty.   807–8

The government as an integral part of the body politic participates in the general will which constitutes it; as a separate body it has a will of its own. These two wills are sometimes in agreement and sometimes in conflict. It is from the combined effect of this agreement and conflict that the whole play of the machine results.

The principle which determines the different forms of the government consists in the number of members which compose it. The smaller the number, the greater the force of the government; the

---

* This is an inconsistency on Rousseau's part: he should have written 'the general will'. It is not the only instance of such an inconsistency.

larger the number, the feebler the government; and as the sovereignty tends always to grow weak the government tends always to grow strong. Thus the executive body must in time prevail over the legislative body, and when the law is finally subjected to men there are only slaves and masters left; the state is destroyed.

Before this destruction, the government must in its natural course change its form and pass by stages from the greater number to a 808   lesser.

The different forms which the government may take can be reduced to three main kinds.* Having compared their advantages and disadvantages I choose as preferable the one which is intermediary between the two extremes and which is called aristocracy. At this point it should be remembered that the constitution of the state and that of the government are two quite distinct things, and that I have not confused them. The best of governments is aristocratic; the worst of sovereignties is aristocratic.

These discussions lead on to others about the way in which the government degenerates and about the means of retarding the destruction of the body politic.

Finally in the last book I examine, by way of comparison with the best government that has existed, which is that of Rome, the form of discipline which best contributes to the working of the state. Then I end this book and the whole work with some investigations into the way in which religion can and should be a constituent part of the 808–9   composition of the body politic.

Rousseau hoped that *The Social Contract* would be 'a book for all times.'[15] At the same time he did not expect it to reach a wide public. In a letter to his printer in Holland he wrote that it was 'difficult material, fit for a few readers'.[16] In Geneva he was proved wrong, but as far as France was concerned he was right. Its circulation there was made more difficult by the Censor's refusal to allow it entry. Copies did come in and were read, but not widely. Only with the French Revolution did it become generally known. One commentator wrote in 1791: 'Formerly it was the least read of all Rousseau's works. Today all the citizens think about it and learn it by heart.'[17]

A similar observation had been made earlier that year by another writer, though in a somewhat different mood:

* Democracy, aristocracy and monarchy.

Him they study; him they meditate; him they turn over in all the time they can spare from the laborious mischief of the day, or the debauches of the night. Rousseau is their canon of holy writ . . . he is their standard figure of perfection. To this man and this writer, as a pattern to authors and Frenchmen, the foundries of Paris are now running for statues, with the kettles of their poor and the bells of their churches.

That was Edmund Burke.[18]

13 'EMILE'

Emile, which Rousseau considered 'his greatest and best work'[1] and which he also intended should be his last book, took him 'twenty years of meditation and three years' labour'.[2] He had written about education when he had been a tutor in Lyons, before he came to Paris. When he left the city in 1756 he had been asked by Mme Dupin to write something for her son, but it seems it was not until the end of 1758 that he began work. Two letters in *The New Heloïse* (Part V, Letters 2 and 3), had meanwhile been devoted to the education of Wolmar and Julie's children in very similar terms to *Emile*.

The book was first intended as a 'memoir of a few pages'.[3] But Rousseau became carried away by the subject and it expanded to its present length. What happened was that he began writing a treatise but then introduced a fictional element, the characters of the Tutor, Emile and Sophie, to give examples, and the fiction took over. At Montmorency the Duke of Luxembourg had made available to him some rooms in an isolated building in a beautiful garden. 'It was in that deep and wonderful solitude, among woods and water, with the sounds of birds of every kind and the smell of the orange blossom, that I wrote in a state of continual ecstasy Book V of *Emile*. To a large extent I owed the fresh colouring of it to the vivid effect of the place in which I wrote it.'[4]

In addition Rousseau had wanted to work out his religious faith. In *Emile* he had an opportunity to include the result of his inquiry since some religious instruction was necessary for his pupil; hence the long episode of the *Profession of Faith of a Savoyard Priest*, which is dealt with in the next chapter.

The result of all this is a book which is at first sight very difficult to read, a 'collection of reflections and observations without order and almost without continuity'.[5] On further acquaintance, however, its richness and significance become clear. What begins as an essay on education turns into a prolonged discussion of human nature and the human condition; it includes passages on a great variety of subjects — language, history, aesthetics, politics, society, religion, and time — which intersperse and exemplify the central obsession of the relation of nature to culture, of natural goodness to the good life. With *The Social Contract*, which it complements, *Emile* is Rousseau's most important work.

It has sometimes been thought that the two works contradict one another. This is due to a misunderstanding. In Book I Rousseau distinguishes between public education and private education; he then says that there can be no public education 'because where there is no *patrie* there can be no more citizens'.[6] What he is saying is that as almost all current governments are corrupt, none can provide a legitimate public education; any education aimed at producing the sort of citizen those states wanted would be as bad as the states themselves. Given these circumstances he puts forward a plan for private or domestic education, which is what Emile receives. It is a plan for growing up well in unfavourable social conditions, so that while you may not have social freedom you will have an inner freedom — 'liberty is not in any form of government, it is in the heart of a free man, he carries it everywhere with him'.[7]*

Parallel with this, however, coming in Book V as the culmination of Emile's development, is his social and political education. 'A father has only done a third of his task when he begets children and feeds them. He owes men to humanity, sociable men to society, and he owes citizens to the state.'[10] Emile learns that it is not enough to be a man, he must also be a citizen; he is therefore taught the principles of *The Social Contract* and he travels to see how different societies operate and different people live.

Furthermore, the kind of person Emile has been brought up to be is precisely the kind of person who, if he was living with people of similar character, would form a state like that in *The Social Contract*: people who have a sense of social commitment and concern for the common good because they have achieved a moral freedom from

---

* In 1758 Rousseau believed that in Geneva there could be an education 'midway between the public education of the Greek republics and the domestic education of monarchies'.[8] After the political turmoil and disillusion of 1762–5, however, he wrote to his friend Deluc — 'A people ceases to be free when the law has lost its force. But virtue never loses its force and the virtuous man remains always free.'[9]

obsessive private appetites and desires, and realize that they belong
to a wider world. This is why Rousseau maintained that the two
works formed a complete whole. 'If there is any reform to be attempted in public morals it must begin with domestic morals.'[11]

This aspect of *Emile* is not, of course, what made it and has
continued to make it so influential. The most original part of the
book is the treatment of the child. Believing, as he did, that 'all
the first impulses of nature are good and right',[12] Rousseau set out to
show how a child could be allowed to grow up according to its own
nature. Instead of being treated as a miniature adult, with vices to be
curbed and controlled, the child should be given freedom to discover
the world for himself, in his own time and in his own way. This
freedom is not unlimited; quite the reverse, the child has to learn
that we are all dependent in various ways and in various degrees.
We all depend on the laws of nature, which in themselves can be
harsh, and we all depend on our fellow-men in society. At the same
time the child has to learn that every desire or whim — *fantaisie* is the
word Rousseau uses — will not be gratified, because the sense of
unlimited desire is the greatest cause of unhappiness, as well as the
most persistent obstacle to any moral behaviour.

The child should be given freedom, but it is 'freedom well-
regulated'.[13] He is not limited by instructions, however, or by
reading the right books. He is limited by things; he learns by his
own experience, not by being told. Rousseau was strongly opposed
to book-learning in childhood. He believed we develop our mental
faculties only through and after our senses; we have to learn to feel
before we are able to think. The child has a 'sensitive reason' before
he has an 'intellectual reason'.[14]

This view not only relates to a theory of knowledge, which Rousseau
derived from Locke and Condillac, it also reflects an essential aspect
of his view of a happy life. His preference for Sparta, rather than
Athens, his enthusiasm for the simplicity he associated with Geneva,
and the puritan streak* that was in him, have led people to suppose
that he favoured an austere, ascetic way of life. The truth is otherwise.
He favours simplicity in material things, certainly, but as far as the
personality is concerned he wants an emotional plenitude, a fullness

---

* This puritan streak was confined to sex. Rousseau was never able to come to
terms with sexuality. His own personality, the experience he had with women,
and possibly his illness as well, combined to make it a problem for him. He
never satisfactorily united sex and love, and the result was that he elevated a
purified kind of love and denigrated an ordinary kind of sex.

and richness of feeling which must not be stunted or stifled by excessive intellectualization. 'To exist for us is to feel'[15] says the Savoyard priest. Only if we develop our ability to feel when we are children will we be able to realize our full emotional potential as adults.

In a note in the margin of the first version of *Emile* Rousseau delineated the stages he thought an education should follow: 'The age of nature — [up to the age of] twelve. The age of reason — fifteen. The age of strength — twenty. The age of wisdom — twenty-five. The age of happiness — all the rest of life.'[16] Book I covers infancy, Book II covers boyhood, both forming the age of nature; Book III is the age of reason, when Emile reads his first book; Book IV takes him through adolescence, and includes the *Profession of Faith;* in Book V he learns about love and society.

Book V opens with a section called 'Sophie, or Woman' devoted to female education. It is the least satisfactory in the book.* Although sensitive to the different characteristics often shown by men and women, Rousseau believed a woman's place in the home and in society should be subordinate to that of man. It is true to say, in fact, that 'his plan for the instruction of a woman is as dead as his scheme for musical notation'.[19]

Book V ends, after Emile's travels and political education, with his happy marriage and his resolution to bring up his own children in the way that his tutor has brought up him. The epigraph for the whole work is taken from Seneca: 'We suffer from a curable ill, and since we are born upright nature helps us if we wish to correct ourselves.'[20]

PREFACE

. . . The literature and learning of our day tend rather to destroy than to build up. We find fault after the manner of a master; to make proposals we must adopt a different style, a style less in accordance with the pride of the philosopher . . . We know nothing of childhood; and with our mistaken notions the further we advance the further we go astray. The wisest writers devote themselves to what

---

* It was also the aspect of the book which was least individual, that had most in common with the period in which it was written. D'Alembert wrote: 'Almost everything he says on the subject [of female education] is true, well thought out, and practicable.'[17] Another contemporary, Bachaumont, described this part of *Emile* as 'a masterpiece'.[18]

a man ought to know, without asking what a child is capable of learning. They are always looking for the man in the child, without considering what he is before he becomes a man. It is to this study 241–2 that I have chiefly devoted myself . . .

BOOK ONE

Everything is good coming from the hands of the Author of things, everything degenerates in the hands of man. He forces one soil to yield the products of another, one tree to bear another's fruit. He mixes and confuses climates, elements, seasons. He mutilates his dog, his horse and his slave. He overturns and disfigures everything, he loves deformity, monsters. He does not want anything as nature made it, not even man himself; he must learn his paces like a saddle-horse; he must be shaped to his master's taste like a tree in his garden.

Yet without that everything would be still worse, and mankind cannot be made by halves. Under the condition things are in now, a man abandoned from his birth to himself among others would be the most disfigured of all. Prejudices, authority, necessity, example, all the social institutions in which we find ourselves buried, would stifle nature in him, and would put nothing in its place. It would be like a sapling which chance had sown in the middle of a road, bent hither 245 and thither and soon destroyed by the passers-by . . .

Plants are fashioned by cultivation, men by education . . . We are born weak, we need strength; we are born deprived of everything, we need help; we are born stupid, we need judgement. All that we do not have at birth and that we need when we have grown up is given to us by education. This education comes to us by nature or men or things. The internal development of our faculties and organs is the education of nature; the use which we learn to make of this development is the education of men; and the fruit of our own experience from the objects which affect us is the education of things.

Thus each of us is formed by three sorts of masters. The pupil in whom their different lessons conflict is badly brought up and will never be in agreement with himself; he in whom they all agree on the same points, and tend to the same ends, goes straight to his 246–7 goal and lives accordingly. Only he is well brought up . . .

Since all three modes of education must work together the two that we can control must follow the lead of that which is beyond our control. Perhaps this word 'nature' has too vague a meaning. Let us try to define it. Nature we are told is merely habit. What does that mean?

Are there not habits formed under compulsion, habits which never stifle nature? Such, for example, are the habits of plants trained horizontally. The plant keeps its artificial shape, but the sap has not changed its course and any new growth the plant may make will be vertical. It is the same with a man's disposition; while the conditions remain the same, habits, even the least natural of them, hold good; but change the conditions, habits vanish, nature reasserts herself . . . We are born sensitive and from our birth onwards we are affected in various ways by our environment. As soon as we become conscious of our sensations we tend to seek or shun the things that cause them, at first because they are pleasant or unpleasant, then because they suit us or not and finally because of judgements formed by means of the ideas of happiness and goodness which reason gives us. These tendencies gain strength and permanence as we come to feel more and become more enlightened, but hindered by our habits they are more or less warped by our prejudices. Before this change they are what I call nature in us.

It is therefore to these primitive inclinations that everything should relate . . .   247–8

Whether my pupil is destined for the sword, the church or the bar matters little to me. Before the vocation of the parents, nature calls him to human life. To live is the career that I would teach him . . . Our true study is that of the human condition. He among us who best knows how to endure the good and the bad in this life is to my mind the best brought up; from which it follows that the true education consists less in precepts than in practice. We begin to instruct ourselves when we begin to live . . . Living is not breathing, it is acting; it is making use of our organs, our senses, our faculties, every aspect of ourselves which gives us the feeling of our existence. The man who has lived the most is not he who has counted most years, but he who has felt most life . . .   252–3

Our wisdom is slavish prejudice, our customs consist in control, constraint and compulsion. Civilized man is born and dies a slave. The infant is bound up in swaddling clothes, the corpse is nailed down in his coffin. All his life long man is imprisoned by our institutions. . . .   253

[Children need freedom; it will not harm them. And mothers should feed their children themselves.]

If the voice of instinct is not strengthened by habit and care, it grows weak in the first years, and the heart dies before it is born . . .   259

[But children should not be over-protected; they have to learn to be strong. The father's rôle is as important as the mother's.]

[Good health is essential. Keep away from doctors.] By nature man bears pain bravely and dies in peace. It is the doctors with their rules, the philosophers with their precepts, the priests with their exhortations, who debase the heart and make us afraid . . . The only useful part of medicine is hygiene, and hygiene is less a science than a virtue. Moderation and work are the true medicines for man; work sharpens his appetite, and moderation prevents him from abusing it . . .

270–1

Men are not made to be crowded together in ant-hills, but scattered over the earth to till it. The more they are massed together, the more corrupt they become . . . Men are devoured by our towns. In a few generations the species perishes or degenerates; it must be renewed, and it is always the country which provides this renewal. Send your children to regain in the open fields the vigour that is lost in the foul air of our crowded cities . . .

276–7

Man's education begins at birth; before he can speak or understand he is learning. Experience precedes instruction; when he recognizes his nurse he has learnt much. The knowledge of the most ignorant man would surprise us if we had followed his course from birth to the present time. If all human knowledge were divided into two parts, one common to all, the other peculiar to the learned, the latter would seem very small compared with the former. But we scarcely heed this general experience, because it is acquired without our thinking about it, before the age of reason; because knowledge is only made remarkable by its differences; and because as in algebraic equations, common factors count for nothing. Even animals learn a lot . . .

281

Reason alone teaches us to know good and evil. Therefore conscience, which makes us love the one and hate the other, though it is independent of reason, cannot develop without it. Before the age of reason we do good or ill without knowing it, and there is no morality in our actions, although there is sometimes in our feeling, with regard to other people's actions in relation to ourselves . . .

288

[A child's destructiveness comes not from sinfulness but eagerness.]

As the child grows it gains strength and becomes less restless and unquiet and more independent. Soul and body become better balanced and nature no longer asks for more movement than is required for self-preservation. But the love of commanding does not die with the need that aroused it; power arouses and flatters self-interest, and habit strengthens it; thus whim follows upon need and the first seeds of prejudice and opinion are sown. The principle once known, we see clearly the point where one departs from the way of nature; let us see what must be done to stay on it.

First maxim. Far from being too strong children are not strong enough for all the claims of nature. Give them full use of such strength as they have; they will not abuse it.

Second maxim. Help them and supply the experience and strength they lack whenever the need is physical.

Third maxim. In the help you give them confine yourself to what is really needful, without granting anything to whim or unreasonable desire; for they will be not tormented by whim if you do not call it into existence, seeing it is no part of nature.

Fourth maxim. Study carefully their speech and gestures, so that at an age when they are incapable of deceit you may discriminate between those desires which come from nature and those which spring from opinion.

The spirit of these rules is to make children more in accord with real liberty and less with power, to let them do more for themselves and demand less of others; so that by teaching them from the first to confine their wishes within the limits of their powers they will scarcely feel the want of whatever is not in their power . . .   289–90

From the very first children hear spoken language; we speak to them before they can understand or even imitate spoken sounds . . . I object to [a nurse] bewildering the child with a multitude of vain words of which it understands nothing but her tone of voice . . . That unhappy facility in the use of words we do not understand begins earlier than we think. In the schoolroom the scholar listens to the verbiage of his master as he listened in the cradle to the babble of his nurse. I think it would be a very useful education to leave him in ignorance of both . . . Restrict as much as possible the vocabulary of   293 the child. It is very undesirable that he should have more words than ideas, that he should be able to say more than he thinks. One of the reasons why peasants are generally shrewder than townsfolk, I think, is that their vocabulary is smaller. They have few ideas, but those few are thoroughly grasped . . .   298

BOOK TWO

. . . I shall not take pains to prevent Emile hurting himself; far from it, I should be vexed if he never hurt himself, if he grew up unacquainted with pain. To bear pain is his first and most useful lesson. It seems as if children were small and weak on purpose to teach them these valuable lessons without danger . . . So far as I know, no child, left to himself, has ever been known to kill or maim itself . . . unless it has been foolishly left on a high place or alone near the fire, or 300 within reach of dangerous weapons . . .

What is to be thought of that cruel education which sacrifices the present to an uncertain future, that burdens the child with all sorts of restrictions and begins by making him miserable, in order to prepare him for some far-off happiness which he may never enjoy? . . . The age of enjoyment is spent in tears, punishments, threats and slavery . . . Who can say how many children fall victims to the excessive care of their fathers and mothers? . . . Men, be humane, that is your first duty; be so for every age and station, kind to all that is not foreign to humanity. What wisdom can you find that is greater than humanity? Love childhood, indulge its sports, its pleasures, its delightful instincts . . . Why rob these little innocents of the joys which pass so quickly, of that precious gift which they cannot abuse? . . . How people will cry out against me! I hear from afar the shouts of that false wisdom that is ever dragging us out of ourselves, counting the present as nothing, and pursuing without a pause a future which flies as we approach, that false wisdom which removes us 301–2 from our place and never brings us to any other . . .

Wretched foresight, which makes someone miserable now in the hope, well or badly founded, of making him happy one day . . . Humanity has its place in the order of things; childhood has its place in the order of human life. The man must be considered as a man, and the child as a child. To assign each his place and fix it there, to order human passions according to the way man is made, is all that we can do for his well-being. The rest depends on foreign causes which are not in our power.

Absolute good and evil are unknown to us. In this life they are blended together; we never enjoy any perfectly pure feeling, nor do we remain for more than a moment in the same state. The feelings of our souls, like the changes in our bodies, are in a continual flux. Good and ill are common to all, but in varying proportions. The happiest is he who suffers least, the most miserable is he who enjoys least. Ever more sorrow than joy — this is the lot of all of us. Man's happiness in this world is but a negative state; it must be reckoned 303 by the fewness of his ills.

Every feeling of hardship is inseparable from the desire to escape from it; every idea of pleasure from the desire to enjoy it. All desire implies a want and all wants are painful; hence our wretchedness

consists in the disproportion between our desires and our powers.
A conscious being whose powers were equal to his desires would be
perfectly happy. What then is human wisdom? Where is the path of
true happiness? The mere limitations of our desires is not enough, for
if they were less than our powers, part of our faculties would be idle,
and we should not enjoy our whole being. Neither is the mere extension of our powers enough, for if our desires were also increased
we should only be the more miserable. True happiness consists in
decreasing the difference between our desires and our powers, in
establishing a perfect equilibrium between the power and the will.
Then only, when all our forces are employed, will the soul be at rest
and man will find himself in good order . . .

As soon as the potential powers of man's mind begin to function,
imagination, more powerful than all the rest, awakes and precedes
all the rest. It is imagination which enlarges the bounds of possibility
for us, whether for good or ill, and therefore stimulates and feeds
desires by the hope of satisfying them. But the object which seemed
within our grasp flies quicker than we can follow . . . we exhaust our
strength, yet never reach our goal, and the nearer we are to pleasure,
the further we are from happiness . . . The world of reality has its
bounds, the world of imagination is boundless; as we cannot enlarge
the one, let us restrict the other; for all the sufferings which really
make us miserable arise from the difference between the real and the
imaginary . . .   303–5

Man is very strong when he is content to be himself; when he
strives to be more than man he is weak indeed. But do not imagine
you can increase your strength by increasing your powers. Not so;
if your pride increases more quickly your strength is diminished. Let
us measure the extent of our sphere and remain in its centre like the
spider in its web . . . By striving to increase our happiness we change it
into wretchedness . . .   305

Foresight! Foresight which is ever bidding us look forward into
the future, a future which in many cases we shall never reach. Here
is the real source of all our troubles! How mad it is for so short-lived
a creature as man to look forward into a future which he rarely attains,
while he neglects the present which is his! This madness is all the
more fatal since it increases with years; the old, always timid,
miserly, and looking ahead, prefer to do without necessaries today
that they may have luxuries at a hundred. Thus we grasp everything,
we cling to everything; we are anxious about time, place, people,
things, all that is and will be; we ourselves are but the least part of

ourselves. We spread ourselves, so to speak, over the whole world, and all this vast expanse becomes sensitive. No wonder our woes increase when we may be wounded on every side. How many princes make themselves miserable for the loss of lands they never saw, and how many merchants lament in Paris over some misfortune in the

307 Indies! . . .

We no longer live where we are, but where we are not . . . Oh man! Keep your life within you and you will no longer be wretched. Keep to the place which nature has assigned you in the chain of beings, and nothing can tear you from it. Do not kick against the stern law of necessity nor waste the strength given to you by heaven by wanting to resist it [or] to prolong or extend your existence, but [rather] to preserve it so far and so long as heaven pleases. Your freedom and your power extend as far and no further than your natural strength.

308 Anything more is but slavery, trickery and deceit . . .

The only man who achieves what he wants is he who does not need to put himself into the hands of another in order to achieve it; from which it follows that the first of all goods is not authority but liberty. The truly free man only wills what he can do, and does what pleases him. This is my fundamental maxim. It is only a question of applying it to childhood and all the rules of education spring from

309 it . . .

These considerations . . . provide a solution to all the contradictions of the social system. There are two kinds of dependence: dependence on things, which is the work of nature; and dependence on men, which is the work of society. Dependence on things, being non-moral, does no injury to liberty and begets no vices; dependence on men, being no part of the [natural] order,* gives rise to every kind of vice, and through this master and slave become mutually depraved. If there is any cure for this social evil, it is to be found in the substitution of law for the individual; in arming the general will with a real strength beyond the power of any individual will. If the laws of nations, like the laws of nature, could never be broken by any human power, dependence on men would become dependence on things; all the advantages of a state of nature would be combined with all the advantages of the civil state in the republic. The liberty which preserves a man from vice would be united with the morality which raises him to virtue.

* In my *Principles of Political Right* it is demonstrated that no private will can be part of the order of the social system. (Note by Rousseau.) This is a reference to *The Social Contract* Bk I, Ch. 7.

Keep the child dependent on things only. By this course of education you will have followed the order of nature. Let his unreasonable wishes meet only with physical obstacles, or with the punishment which results from his own actions. These lessons will be recalled when the same circumstances occur again. It is enough to prevent him from wrongdoing without forbidding him to do wrong. Experience or lack of power should take the place of law. Give him, not what he wants, but what he needs. Let there be no question of obedience for him or tyranny for you. Let him feel his freedom in his actions and yours equally. Supply the strength he lacks just so far as is required for freedom, not for power, so that he may receive your services with a sort of shame, and look forward to the time when he may dispense with them and may achieve the honour of self-help.   311–12

Nature provides for the child's growth in her own fashion and this should never be thwarted. Do not make him sit still when he wants to run about, nor run about when he wants to be quiet . . . All their own activities are instincts of the body for its growth in strength; but you should regard with suspicion those wishes which they cannot carry out for themselves, those which others must carry out for them. Then you must distinguish carefully between natural and artificial needs, between the needs of budding whim and the needs which flow from the overflowing life just described . . .   312

Do you know the surest way to make your child miserable? Let him have everything he wants; for as his wants increase in proportion to the ease with which they are satisfied you will be compelled, sooner or later, to refuse his demands, and this unexpected refusal will hurt him more than the lack of what he wants . . . Man naturally considers all that he can get as his own. In this sense Hobbes' theory is true to a certain extent: multiply both our wishes and the means of satisfying them, and each will be master of all. Thus the child who has only to want in order to have thinks himself the master of the universe; he considers all men as his slaves; and when you are at last compelled to refuse, he takes your refusal as an act of rebellion for he thinks he has only to command . . . How should I suppose that such a child can ever be happy? He is the slave of anger, a prey to the fiercest passions. Happy! He is a tyrant, at once the basest of slaves and the most wretched of creatures . . .   314

The very words obey and command will be excluded from his vocabulary, still more those of duty and obligation; but the words, strength, necessity, weakness and constraint must have a large place in it. Before the age of reason it is impossible to form any idea of moral

316 beings or social relations; so avoid as far as possible the use of words which express these ideas . . .

Of all man's faculties reason which is, so to speak, compounded of all the rest is the last and choicest growth . . . To make a man reasonable is the coping stone of a good education . . . You begin at

317 the wrong end if you make the end the means.

If children understood reason they would not need education . . . Childhood has its own ways of seeing, thinking and feeling; nothing is more foolish than to try and substitute our ways; and I should no more expect judgement in a ten-year-old child than I should expect him to be five feet high. Indeed, what use would reason be to him at that age? It is the curb of strength, and the child does not

319 need the curb . . .

Give your scholar no kind of verbal lesson; he should only receive that of experience . . . The perpetual restraint imposed upon your scholars stimulates their activity; the more subdued they are in your presence the more boisterous they are as soon as they are out of your sight. They must make amends . . . for the harsh restraint to which you subject them. Two schoolboys from the town will do more

321–2 damage in the country than all the children of the village . . .

Let us lay it down as an incontrovertible rule that the first impulses of nature are always right; there is no original perversity in the human heart, the how and the why of the entrance of every vice can be traced. The only natural passion is self-love or self-interest taken in a wider

322 sense. This selfishness is good in itself and in relation to ourselves . . .

The first education should be merely negative. It consists not in teaching virtue or truth but in preserving the heart from vice and from the spirit of error . . . Exercise his body, his limbs, his senses, his strength, but keep his mind idle as long as you can . . . allow childhood to ripen in your children . . . There is another point to be considered which confirms the suitability of this method; it is the child's individual genius, which must be thoroughly known before we can choose the fittest moral training. Every mind has its own form, in accordance with which it must be governed; and the success of the pains taken depends largely on the fact that it is governed in this way and no other. Oh wise man, take time to observe nature; watch your scholar well before you say a word to him; first leave the germ of his character free to show itself, do not constrain him in anything,

323–4 the better to see him as he really is . . .

Our first duties are to ourselves; our first feelings are centred on ourselves; all our natural impulses are at first directed to our own preservation and our own welfare. Thus the first feeling of justice springs not from what we owe to others, but from what is due to us. If you talk to children of their duties and not of their rights, you are beginning at the wrong end, and, telling them what they cannot understand, cannot be of any interest to them.

If I have to train a child . . . I should say to myself: 'A child never attacks people, only things; and he soon learns by experience to respect those older and stronger than himself. Things however do not defend themselves. Therefore the first idea he needs is not that of liberty but of property, and that he may get this idea he must have something of his own' . . . We must go back therefore to the origin of property for that is where the first idea of it must begin . . .   329–30

[Rousseau suggests a way in which Emile can learn by experience the meaning of property: similarly, he will learn of charity by seeing his tutor give, not by being told to give himself.]

The only moral lesson which is suited for a child — the most important lesson for every time of life — is this: 'Never hurt anybody.' The very rule of well-doing, if not subordinated to this rule, is dangerous, false and contradictory. Who is there who does no good? Everyone does some good, the wicked as well as the righteous; he makes one happy at the cost of the misery of a hundred and hence spring all our misfortunes. The noblest virtues are negative; they are also the most difficult, for they make little show and do not even make room for that pleasure so dear to the heart of man, the thought that someone is pleased with us . . .   340

Give nature time to work before you take over her business, lest you interfere with her dealings. You assert that you know the value of time and are afraid to waste it. You fail to perceive that it is a greater waste of time to use it ill than to do nothing . . . What would you think of a man who refused to sleep lest he should waste part of his life? You would say: 'He is mad; he is not enjoying his life, he is robbing himself of part of it; to avoid sleep he is hastening his death.' Remember that these two cases are alike, and that childhood is the sleep of reason . . .   343–4

[Rousseau argues against book-learning — languages, history and geography.]

Without the study of books such a memory as the child may possess is not left idle; everything he sees and hears makes an impression on him, he keeps a record of men's sayings and doings and his whole environment is the book from which he unconsciously enriches his memory, till his judgement is able to profit by it . . .   351

Reading is the curse of childhood . . .   357

357 If children are not to be required to do anything as a matter of obedience it follows that they will only learn from what they perceive to be of real and present value, either for use or enjoyment; what other motive could they have for learning? . . .

The lessons the scholars learn from one another in the playground are worth a hundred times more than what they learn in the classroom.

Watch a cat when she comes into a room for the first time; she goes from place to place, she sniffs about and examines everything, she is never still for a moment; she is suspicious of everything till she has examined it and found out what it is. It is the same with the child when he begins to walk and enters, so to speak, the room of the world around him . . . Since everything that comes into human understanding enters through the senses, man's first reason is a sensitive reason. It is this that serves as a foundation for intellectual reason; our first teachers in natural philosophy are our feet, hands and eyes. To substitute books for them does not teach us to reason, it teaches us to use the reason of others rather than our own; it teaches us to believe much and know little. Before you can practise an art you must first get your tools; and if you are to make good use of those tools, they must be fashioned sufficiently strongly to stand use. To learn to think we must therefore exercise our limbs, our senses, and our bodily organs, which are the tools of the intellect; and to get the best use out of these tools, the body which supplies us with them must be strong and healthy. Not only is it a mistake that true reason is developed apart from the body, but it is a good bodily con-

369–70 stitution which makes the workings of the mind easy and correct . . .

To train the senses it is not enough merely to use them; we must learn to judge well by them, to learn to feel, so to speak; for we cannot touch, see, or hear, except as we have been taught . . . Do not merely exercise the strength, exercise all the senses by which it is guided; make the best use of every one of them, check the results of one by the

380 other . . .

Let a man always be forearmed against the unforeseen. Let Emile run about barefoot all the year round, upstairs, downstairs and in the garden . . . Let him learn to perform every exercise which en- courages agility of body . . . Children will always do anything that

390–2 keeps them moving freely . . .

We must never forget that all this should be play, the easy and voluntary control of the movements which nature demands of them, the art of varying their games to make them pleasanter, without the

403 least bit of constraint to transform them into work . . .

[To a child of ten or twelve] work or play are all one, his games are his work; he knows no difference. He brings to everything the cheerfulness of interest, the charm of freedom, and shows the bent of his mind and the extent of his knowledge . . . He has reached the maturity of childhood, he has lived the life of a child; his progress has not been bought at the price of his happiness. He has gained both . . .   423

[Rousseau has discussed in this book how all the five senses can and should be developed. He adds:]

In the following books I have still to speak of the training of a sort of sixth sense, called common-sense, not so much because it is common to all men, but because it results from the well-regulated use of the other five, and teaches us the nature of things by the sum total of their external aspects. So this sixth sense has no special organ, it has its seat in the brain, and its sensations, which are purely internal, are called perceptions or ideas. The number of these ideas is the measure of our knowledge; exactness of thought depends on their clearness and precision; the art of comparing them one with another is called human reason. Thus what I call sensitive reason, or the reasoning of the child, consists in the formation of simple ideas through the association of several sensations; what I call intellectual or human reason consists in the formation of complex ideas by the association of several simple ideas.

If my method is indeed that of nature, and if I am not mistaken in my application of that method, we have led our pupil through the region of sensation to the bounds of the child's reasoning; the first step we take beyond these bounds must be the step of a man.   417–18

BOOK THREE

When we can do more than we want, we have strength enough and to spare; we are really strong. This is the third stage of childhood. At about twelve or thirteen the child's strength increases far more rapidly than his needs. He is approaching adolescence, though he has not yet reached puberty . . .   426

Children are first restless, then curious; and this curiosity, rightly directed, is the means of development for the age with which we are dealing . . .   429

What a sudden change, you will say. Just now we were concerned with what touches ourselves, with our immediate environment, and all at once we are exploring the whole world and leaping to the bounds of the universe. This change is the result of our growing strength and of the inclination of our mind . . . Let us transform our sensations into ideas, but do not let us jump all at once from the objects of sense to objects of thought. The latter are attained by means of the former. Let the senses be the only guide for the first workings of the mind. No book but the world, no teaching but that of facts. The child who reads ceases to think, he only reads. He is acquiring

430 words, not knowledge . . .

Never tell the child what he cannot understand; no descriptions, no eloquence, no figures of speech, no poetry. The time has not

432 come for feeling or taste . . .

Never substitute the sign for the thing [signified], unless it is impossible to show the thing itself; for the child's attention is so

434 taken up with signs that he will forget what it represents . . .

This is also the time to train him gradually to prolonged attention to a given object; but this attention should never be the result of

436 constraint but of interest or desire . . .

[Science:] We shall make all our apparatus ourselves; I would not make it beforehand, but having caught a glimpse of the experiment we shall invent step by step an instrument for its verification. I would rather our apparatus was somewhat clumsy and imperfect but our ideas clear as to what the apparatus ought to be, and the results to be obtained by means of it . . . Undoubtedly the notions of things thus acquired for oneself are clearer and much more convincing than those acquired from the teaching of others; and not only is our reason not accustomed to a slavish submission to authority, but we develop greater ingenuity in discovering relations, connecting ideas and inventing apparatus, than when we merely accept what is given us and allow our minds to be enfeebled by indifference, like the body of a man whose servants always wait on him, dress him and put on his shoes, whose horse carries him, till he loses the strength and use of his limbs . . . The more ingenious our apparatus, the coarser and more unskilful are our senses. We surround ourselves with tools

441–3 and fail to use those with which nature has provided us . . .

As soon as he has sufficient self-knowledge to understand what constitutes his well-being, and as soon as he can grasp such far-reaching relations as to judge what is good for him and what is not, then he is able to discern the difference between work and play, and to consider the latter as merely relaxation. Then objects of real utility may be introduced into his studies and may lead him to more pro-

444 longed attention than he gave to his games . . .

'What is the use of that?' In future this is the sacred formula, the
formula by which he and I test every action of our lives . . .   446

It is easy to convince a child that what you wish to teach him is
useful, but it is useless to convince him if you cannot also persuade.
Pure reason may lead us to approve or censure, but it is passion which
leads to action, and how shall we care about that which does not
concern us? . . .   453

I hate books; they only teach us to talk about things we know
nothing about . . . [However] There is one book which, to my thinking, supplies the best treatise on an education according to nature . . .
It will be a text to which all our talks about natural sciences are but a
commentary . . . What is it? . . . *Robinson Crusoe*.   454–5

The exercise of the natural arts, which may be carried on by one
man alone, leads on to the industrial arts which call for the co-
operation of many hands . . . The value set by the general public on
the various arts is in inverse ratio to their real utility. They are even
valued directly according to their uselessness. This might be expected.
The most useful arts are the worst paid, for the number of workers
is regulated by the demand, and the work which everybody requires
must necessarily be paid at a rate which puts it within the reach of the
poor. On the other hand, those great people who are not artisans
but called artists . . . who labour only for the rich and idle, put a
fancy price on their trifles; and as the real value of this vain labour
only relies on opinion, the price itself adds to their market value, and
they are valued according to their costliness. The rich think so much
of these things, not because they are useful, but because they are
beyond the reach of the poor . . .   456–7

Agriculture is the earliest and most honourable of arts; metal
work I put next, then carpentry, and so on. This is the order in which
the child will put them, if he has not been spoilt by vulgar prejudices.

What valuable considerations Emile will derive from his Robinson
in such matters!   460

[The discussion of work leads Rousseau on to teach Emile about
exchange — 'There can be no society without exchange' (461) —
and how exchange operates in our society through money.]

Be content with this, and do not touch upon the moral effects of
this institution. In everything you must show clearly the use before
the abuse. If you attempt to teach children how the sign has led to
the neglect of the thing [signified], how all the fantasies of opinion
grow out of money, how countries rich in silver must be poor in
everything else, you will be treating these children not only as

philosophers but as wise men, for you are professing to teach them
462 what very few philosophers have grasped.

The teacher's art consists in this: to turn the child's attention from
trivial details and to guide his thoughts continually towards relations
of importance which he will one day need to know, that he may judge
462–3 rightly of good and evil in civil society.

The man who clearly sees the order of the whole, sees where each
part should be; the man who sees one part clearly and knows it
thoroughly may be a learned man, but the former is a judicious man;
and you remember that it is judgement rather than knowledge that we
466 intend to acquire . . .

When we leave the state of nature we compel others to do the same;
no one can remain in a state of nature in spite of his fellow-creatures,
and to try to remain in it when it is no longer practicable would really
be to leave it, for self-preservation is nature's first law. Thus the idea
467 of social relations is gradually developed in the child's mind . . .

Hitherto I have made no distinction of condition, rank or fortune;
nor shall I distinguish between them in the future, since man is the
same in every condition; the rich man's stomach is no bigger than
the poor man's, nor is his digestion any better; . . . the natural needs
are the same to all, and the means of satisfying them should be
equally within the reach of all. Fit a man's education to his real self,
468 not to what is no part of him . . .

You reckon on the present order of society, without considering
that this order is subject to inevitable revolutions, and that you can
neither foresee nor provide against the one which may affect your
children. The great become small, the rich poor, the king a commoner.
Does fate strike so seldom that you can count on immunity from her
blows? We are approaching a state of crisis and a century of revolutions. I believe it impossible that the great monarchies of Europe
468 & n. have much longer to last . . .

Who can answer for your fate? What man has made, man may
destroy. Nature's characters alone are ineffaceable and nature makes
neither the prince, the rich man, nor the nobleman . . .

Let men praise as they will that conquered monarch who like a
madman would be buried beneath the fragments of his throne; I
despise him; to me he is merely a crown, and when that is gone he is
nothing. But he who loses his crown and lives without it, is more than
a king; from the rank of a king, which may be held by a coward, a
villain or madman, he rises to the rank of a man, a position few
can fill. Thus he triumphs over fortune, he dares to defy her; he

depends on himself alone, and when he has nothing left to show but
himself he is not nothing, he is something . . .   468–9

The man and the citizen, whoever he may be, has no goods to
invest in society but himself; all his other goods belong to society in
spite of himself, and when a man is rich, either he does not enjoy
his wealth, or the public enjoys it too; in the first case he robs others
as well as himself; in the second he gives them nothing. Thus his
debt to society is still unpaid, while he only pays with his goods . . .
[If] you are born under favourable conditions you owe more to others
than if you had been born with nothing. It is not fair that what
one man has done for society should pay another's debt, for since
every man owes all that he is he can only pay his own debt, and
no father can transmit to his son any right to be of no use to mankind . . . The man who eats in idleness what he has not himself earned
is a thief, and in my eyes the man who lives on an income paid him by
the state for doing nothing, differs little from a highwayman who
lives on those who pass by . . . Man in society is bound to work;
rich or poor, weak or strong, every idle citizen is a thief.   469–70

Now of all the pursuits by which a man may earn his living, the
nearest to a state of nature is manual labour; of all stations that of
the artisan is least dependent on fortune or men . . .   470

I want to give my pupil a rank that he cannot lose, a rank which will
always do him honour. Stoop to the position of an artisan, to rise
above your own . . .   471

I do not like those stupid trades in which the workmen mechani-
cally perform the same action without pause and almost without
mental effort . . . The trade I should choose for my pupil, among
the trades he likes, is that of the carpenter. It is clean and useful;
it may be carried on at home; it gives enough exercise; it calls for
skill and industry, and while fashioning articles for everyday use, there
is scope for elegance and taste . . .   477–8

Having entered into possession of himself our child is now ready
to cease to be a child. He is more than ever conscious of the necessity
which makes him dependent on things. After exercising his body and
his senses you have exercised his mind and his judgement. Finally
we have joined together the use of his limbs and his faculties. We have
made him an active and thinking creature; all that remains to finish
the man is to make a loving and sensitive creature, to perfect reason
through feeling . . .   481

BOOK FOUR

We are born, so to speak, twice over; born into existence, and born
into life; born into our species, and born into our sex . . .

Man is not meant to remain a child. He leaves childhood behind
him at the time ordained by nature; and this critical moment, short
enough in itself, has far-reaching consequences. As the roaring of
the waves precedes the tempest, so the murmur of rising passions
announces this tumultuous change; a suppressed excitement warns
us of the approaching danger. A change of temper, frequent outbreaks
of anger, a perpetual stirring of the mind, make the child almost
ungovernable. He becomes deaf to the voice he used to obey; he is a
489–90 lion in a fever; he distrusts his keeper and refuses to be controlled . . .

This period, when education is usually finished, is just the time to
begin . . . Our passions are the chief means of self-preservation; to
try to destroy them is therefore as absurd as it is useless; this would
be to overcome nature and reshape God's handiwork. If God told
men to abolish the passions which he has given them . . . he would
contradict himself.

But should we reason rightly if, from the fact that the passions are
natural to man, we inferred that all the passions we feel in ourselves
and behold in others are natural? Their source indeed is natural;
but they have been swollen by a thousand other streams; they are a
great river which is constantly growing, one in which we can scarcely
find a single drop of the original stream. Our natural passions are very
limited; they are the instruments of our freedom, they tend to self-
preservation. All those which enslave and destroy us have another
source; nature does not bestow them on us; we seize on them to her
cost. The source of our passions, the origin and principle of all the
others, the only one which is born with man and never leaves him
while he lives, is self-love; it is original, innate, and precludes all
other passions; all the others are in a sense only modifications of it.
But most of these modifications are the result of external influences,
without which they would never occur and such modifications, far
from being advantageous to us, are harmful. They change the original
purpose and work against its end; then it is that man finds himself
490–1   outside nature and in contradiction with himself . . .

The child's first sentiment is self-love, his second, which is derived
from it, is love of those about him; for in his present state of weakness
he is only aware of people through the help and attention received
from them . . . So a child is naturally disposed to good-will because

he sees that everyone about him is inclined to help him, and from this experience he gets the habit of a kindly feeling towards his species; but with the expansion of his relations, his needs, and his dependence, active or passive, the consciousness of his relations to others is awakened and leads to the sense of duties and preferences.

Then the child becomes masterful, jealous, deceitful and vindictive . . . Self-love, which concerns itself only with ourselves, is content to satisfy our own needs. But self-interest, which is always comparing self with others, is never satisfied and never can be; for this feeling, which prefers ourselves to others, demands that they should prefer us to themselves, which is impossible. Thus the tender and gentle passions spring from self-love, while the hateful and angry passions spring from self-interest. So it is the fewness of his needs, and the less he compares himself with others, that makes a man really good; what makes him really bad is a multiplicity of needs and relying on the opinions of others . . .   492–3

Man's proper study is that of his relationships. When he only knows himself through his physical being, he should study himself in relation to things; this is the business of his childhood. When he begins to feel his moral being, he should study himself in relation to his fellow-men; this is the business of his whole life and we have now reached the time when that study should be begun . . .   493

Do you want to give order and regulation to the emerging passions? Prolong the period of their development so that they may have time to find their proper place as they arise. Then they are ordered by nature herself, not by man; your task is merely to leave it in her hands. If your pupil were alone you would have nothing to do; but everything which surrounds him inflames his imagination. He is swept along by the torrent of prejudices; to rescue him you must urge him in the opposite direction. Imagination must be curbed by feeling, and reason must silence the opinions of men. The source of all the passions is sensibility, imagination determines their inclination . . . It is the errors of imagination which transform into vices the passions of all limited creatures . . .   500

Man's weakness makes him sociable. Our common sufferings draw our hearts to our fellow-creatures; we should have no duties to mankind if we were not men. Every affection is a sign of insufficiency; if each of us had no need of others, we should hardly think of associating with them . . .

Hence it follows that we are drawn towards our fellow-creatures less by our feelings for their joys than their sorrows; for in them we discern more plainly a nature like our own, and a pledge of their affection for us. If our common needs create a bond of interest our common sufferings create a bond of affection. The sight of a happy man arouses in others envy rather than love, we are ready to accuse him of usurping a right which is not his, of seeking happiness for himself alone, and our self-interest suffers an additional pang in the thought that this man has no need of us. But who does not pity the unfortunate when he beholds his sufferings? Who would not deliver him from his woes if a wish could do it? Imagination puts us more readily in the place of the miserable man than of the happy man; we feel that the one condition touches us more nearly than the other. Pity is sweet, because, when we put ourselves in the place of one who suffers, we are aware, nevertheless, of the pleasure of not suffering like him. Envy is bitter, because the sight of a happy man, far from putting the envious in his place, inspires him with regret that he is not

503–4   there . . .

What should we do to stimulate and nourish this growing sensibility, to direct it, and to follow its natural inclination? Should we not present to the young man objects on which the expansive force of his heart may take effect, objects which dilate it, which extend it to other creatures, which take him outside himself? Should we not carefully remove everything that narrows him, concentrates him, and tends to strengthen his ego? That is to say, we should arouse in him kindness, goodness, pity, and beneficence, all the gentle and attractive passions which are naturally pleasing to man, and prevent the birth

506   of envy, greed and hate . . .

We never pity another's woes unless we know we may suffer in like manner ourselves . . . Why have kings no pity on their people? Because they never expect to be ordinary men. Why are the rich so hard on the poor? Because they have no fear of becoming poor . . . So do not train your pupil to look down from the height of his glory upon the sufferings of the unfortunate, the labours of the wretched, and do not hope to teach him to pity them while he considers them so

507   far removed from himself . . .

The pity we feel for others is proportionate not to the amount of the evil, but to the feelings we attribute to the sufferers. We only pity the wretched in so far as we think they feel the need of pity. The bodily effect of our sufferings is less than one would suppose; it is memory that prolongs the pain, imagination which projects it into the future and makes us really to be pitied. This is, I think, one of the reasons why we are more callous to the sufferings of animals than

of men, although a fellow feeling ought to make us identify ourselves
equally with either . . . In this way we become callous to the fate of
our fellow-men, and the rich console themselves for the harm done
by them to the poor, by the assumption that the poor are too stupid
to feel . . .   508–9

It is the people who make up [the body of] humanity. Those who
do not belong to the people are so few in number that they are not
worth counting. Man is the same in every station of life; if that be
so, those ranks to which most men belong deserve most honour . . .
Have respect then for your species; remember it consists essentially
of the people, that if all the kings and intellectuals were removed
they would scarcely be missed, and things would go none the worse.
In a word, teach your pupil to love all men, even those who fail to
appreciate him; act in such a way that he is not a member of any class,
but takes his place in all alike; speak in his hearing of the human race
with tenderness, and even with pity, but never with scorn. Man,
do not dishonour mankind . . .   509–10

We are coming at last to the moral order . . . Hitherto my Emile
has only thought of himself . . . [Now] we must know what he believes
his place among men to be . . . This is the time for taking account of
inequality, natural and civil, and for the picture of the whole social
order. Society must be studied in the individual and the individual
in society; those who desire to treat politics and morals apart from
one another will never understand either . . .   522–4

Let him know that man is naturally good, let him feel it, let him
judge his neighbour by himself; but let him see how men are depraved
and perverted by society; let him find the source of all their vices in
their prejudices; let him be disposed to respect the individual, but to
scorn the multitude; let him see that all men wear almost the same
mask, but let him also know that some faces are fairer than the mask
that conceals them . . .   525

This is the time for history; with its help he will read the hearts of
men without lessons in philosophy.   526

[It is only now that Rousseau comes to religious education.] If I
had to depict the most heart-breaking stupidity I would paint a
pedant teaching children the catechism; if I wanted to drive a child
crazy I would set him to explain what he learned in his catechism . . .

'We must believe in God to be saved.' This doctrine wrongly
understood is the reason for the bloodthirsty intolerance and the
cause of all the futile teaching which strikes a deadly blow at human
reason, by training it to cheat itself with mere words. No doubt

there is not a moment to be lost if we would deserve eternal salvation;
but if the repetition of certain words is enough to obtain it, I do not
see why we should not people heaven with starlings and magpies
as well as children . . . The faith of children and of many men is a
matter of geography. Will they be rewarded for having been born
554–5   in Rome rather than in Mecca ? . . .

556   Let us beware of proclaiming the truth to those who cannot as
yet comprehend it, for to do so is to want to inculcate error . . .

[What religion shall Emile be taught now ? As an example Rousseau
recounts his own experience in the section known as the *Profession
of Faith of the Savoyard Priest*; this is dealt with in the next chapter.
After the *Profession*, Rousseau deals with Emile's sexual feelings.]

As a somnambulist, wandering in his sleep, walks along the edge
of a precipice, over which he would fall if he were awake, so my
Emile, in the sleep of ignorance, escapes the perils which he does not
see; were I to wake him with a start, he might fall. Let us first try to
withdraw him from the edge of the precipice, and then we will
643   awaken him to show him it from a distance . . .

If [in this way] we bide our time, if we prepare the way for hearing,
if we then show him the laws of nature in all their truth . . . [and] the
sanction of these laws in the physical and moral evils which overtake
those who neglect them, then while we speak to him of this great
mystery of procreation, we will join to the idea of the pleasure, which
the Author of nature has given to this act, the idea of the exclusive
affection which makes it delightful, the idea of the duties of faithful-
ness and modesty which surround it, and redouble its charm while
650   fulfilling its purpose . . .

Do not coldly oppose his wishes; do not stifle his imagination,
but guide it lest it should bring forth monsters. Speak to him of love,
651   of women, of pleasure . . .

Those who desire to guide young people rightly and to preserve
them from the snares of the senses give them a disgust for love, and
would willingly make the very thought of it a crime at their age, as
if love was made for the old. All these mistaken lessons have no effect;
the heart gives the lie to them. The young man, guided by a surer instinct, laughs to himself over the gloomy maxims which he pretends
to accept, and only awaits the chance of disregarding them. All that is
contrary to nature. By following the opposite course I reach the same
end more safely. I am not afraid to encourage in him the tender
feeling for which he is so eager, I shall paint it as the supreme joy of
life, as indeed it is; when I picture it to him, I desire that he shall give

himself up to it; by making him feel the charm which the union of
hearts adds to the delights of the senses, I shall inspire him with a
disgust for debauchery; I shall make him a lover and a good man.

How narrow-minded to see nothing in the rising desires of a young
heart but obstacles to the teaching of reason. In my eyes these are
the right means to make him obedient to that very teaching. Only
through passion can we gain the mastery over passions; their tyranny
must be controlled by their legitimate power, and nature herself must
furnish us with the means to control her.   653–4

[Rousseau has suggested that sexual desire should neither be indulged nor struggled against, but rather associated with the idea of
love, which to him takes the form of an ideal woman. He then discusses Emile's aesthetic education, and Book Four concludes:]

Pleasure is ours when we want it; it is only prejudice which makes
everything hard to obtain, and drives pleasure from us. To be happy
is a hundred times easier than it seems. If he really desires to enjoy
himself the man of taste has no need for riches; all he needs is to be free
and to be his own master. With health and daily bread we are rich
enough . . .   691

Book Five of *Emile* opens with a long section on female education,
entitled 'Sophie, or Woman'. Rousseau's concern is 'Always to
follow the indications of nature. Everything that characterizes the
sex should be respected as established by nature.'[21] He regards the
sexes as being complementary:

> The search for abstract and speculative truths, for principles
> and axioms in science, for all that tends to wide generalization,
> is beyond a woman's grasp; their studies should be thoroughly
> practical. It is their business to apply the principles discovered
> by men, it is their place to make the observations which lead
> men to discover those principles . . . The men will have a better
> philosophy of the human heart, but women will read more
> accurately in the hearts of men.[22]

Man and woman together form a miniature society, and Rousseau
uses the same phrase to describe them as he has used elsewhere for
the formation of the body politic[23] — *personne morale*, translated
here as 'corporate body'. The corporate body is something more
than the sum of its parts; it is a new entity, in which we realize aspects
of our personality that are otherwise unfulfilled.

The social relation of the sexes is a wonderful thing. This relation produces a corporate body of which woman is the eye and man the hand, but the two are so dependent on one another that the man teaches the woman what to see, while she teaches him what to do. If women could discover principles and if men had as good heads for detail, they would be mutually independent, they would live in perpetual strife, and there would be an end to all society. But in the mutual harmony each contributes to a common purpose, each follows the other's lead, each commands and each obeys.[24]

After the discussion of female education that follows these remarks Rousseau returns to Emile, who is now travelling. Emile, however, does not travel like most of his contemporaries:

BOOK FIVE

Men say life is short, and I see them doing their best to shorten it. As they do not know how to spend their time they lament the swiftness of its flight, and I perceive that for them it goes only too slowly. Intent merely on the object of their pursuit, they behold unwillingly the space between them and it; one desires tomorrow, another looks a month ahead, another ten years beyond that. No one wants to live today, no one contents himself with the present hour; all find it passing too slowly . . .

770–1
A man spends half his life rushing from Paris to Versailles, from Versailles to Paris, from town to country, from country to town, from one district of the town to another . . .

[Emile and I] do not travel like couriers but like explorers. We do not merely consider the beginning and the end, but the space between. The journey itself is a delight. We do not travel sitting dismally imprisoned, so to speak, in a tightly closed cage . . . We do not deprive ourselves of the fresh air, nor the sight of the things about us, nor the
771
opportunity of examining them at our pleasure.

[Emile and Sophie meet and fall in love. The boy has grown into a man and now reaches the final stage of his education, which is to learn the meaning of virtue and of justice. Only when he has come to experience the strongest emotions is he in a position to understand that all desires, even those of the heart, sometimes need to be controlled:]

You have not yet learnt to give a law to the desires of your heart; and the difficulties of life arise rather from our affections than from our needs. Our desires are vast, our strength is little better than nothing. In his wishes man is dependent on many things; in himself he is dependent on nothing, not even on his own life; the more his connections are multiplied, the greater his sufferings . . . [If you are] a slave to your unbridled passions, how greatly are you to be pitied! . . . You will possess nothing because of the fear of losing it; you will never be able to satisfy your passions, because you desired to follow them continually. You will always be seeking that which will fly before you; you will be miserable and you will become wicked . . .   816–17

What crime will stop a man who has no law but his heart's desires, who does not know how to resist his own passions? My son, there is no happiness without courage, nor virtue without a struggle. The word virtue is derived from a word signifying strength, and strength is the foundation of all virtue . . . What is meant by a virtuous man? He who can conquer his affections; for then he follows his reason, his conscience; he does his duty; he is his own master and nothing can turn him from the right way. So far you have had only the semblance of liberty, the precarious liberty of the slave who has not received his orders. Now is the time for real freedom; learn to be your own master; control your heart, my Emile, and you will be virtuous . . .   817–18

Do not expect me to supply you with lengthy precepts of morality, I have only one rule to give you which sums up all the rest. Be a man; restrain your heart within the limits of your manhood. Study and know these limits; however narrow they may be, we are not unhappy within them; it is only when we wish to go beyond them that we are unhappy, only when, in our mad passions, we try to attain the impossible . . .   819

In this way Emile learns the meaning of moral freedom. He now has to learn about social freedom, how to be a citizen. 'The greatest difficulty in the way of throwing light upon these important matters is to interest an individual in discussing them and in answering these two questions: "How does it concern me; and what can I do?" '[25] Given that this difficulty is overcome, the next stage is a consideration of the principles on which social justice should be based, and an examination of the actual societies and governments that exist. 'Before beginning our observations we must lay down rules of procedure; we must find a scale with which to compare our measurements. Our principles of political right are our scale. Our actual measurements are the civil laws of each country . . .'[26]

The principles are, of course, those set out in *The Social Contract*,* a summary of which Rousseau now gives. At the end of this he writes:

I should not be surprised if my pupil, who is a sensible young man, should interrupt me saying, "One would think we were building our edifice of wood and not of men; we are putting everything so exactly in its place!" That is true; but remember that the law does not bow to the passions of men, and that we have first to establish the true principles of political right. Now that our foundations are laid, come and see what men have built upon them; and you will

849   see some strange sights!

[The task now is to see if you have a *patrie*, a just and legitimate state to which you can belong. Émile and his tutor travel in search of one, but with no success. That does not mean, however, that he should not care for the public good, or work for the common interest, wherever he is.]

He who has no *patrie* has, at least, the land in which he lives. There is always a government and certain so-called laws under which he has lived in peace . . . Where is the good man who owes nothing to his country? Whatever that country may be he owes it what is the most precious thing a man has, the morality of his actions and the love of virtue . . . The public good, which to others is a mere pretext, is a real motive for him. He learns to fight against himself and to prevail, to sacrifice his own interest to the common interest. It is not true that he gains nothing from the laws; they give him courage to be just, even among the wicked. It is not true that they have failed to make him free; they have taught him to rule himself. Do not say therefore, 'What does it matter where I am?' It does matter that you should be where you can best do your duty; and one of these duties is to love the place where you were born. Your fellow-countrymen protected you in childhood; you should love them in your manhood. You should live among them, or at least you should live where you can serve them to the best of your power, and where they know where

858   to find you if ever they are in need of you . . .

Men say the golden age is a fable; it always will be for those whose feelings and taste are depraved. People do not really regret the golden age, for they do nothing to restore it. What is needed for its re-

* In the letter to his Paris publisher where Rousseau refers to the two works as forming 'a complete whole' he says that *The Social Contract* 'should be considered as a sort of appendix' to *Emile*.[27]

storation? One thing only, and that is an impossibility; we must love
the golden age.   859

Emile was published in Paris in 1762. The publisher, Duchesne,
worried that the work would cause trouble, pretended that it had
been printed in Holland. The manœuvres this involved led Rousseau
to think that attempts were being made to cut or alter the work.
These suspicions, aggravated by ill-health, made him very troublesome to both Duchesne and the censor, Malesherbes. The latter
exercised his powers with flexibility and had always been generous
and helpful to Rousseau. It was partly to explain and apologize for
his behaviour over *Emile* that Rousseau wrote his four long *Letters
tc Malesherbes*.

Emile* was banned on publication but it was widely read and extremely influential. Twenty-five years later Madame de Staël was
able to write: 'He has succeeded in restoring happiness to childhood.'[28]

Rousseau later began a sequel, called *Emile and Sophie or the
Solitary Ones*. Through a variety of circumstances the marriage has
broken up, and Emile's happiness is destroyed. The book sets out
to show how he restores his peace of mind by finding a new self-
reliance, but only two chapters were written and how it was to end
is uncertain.

14 PROFESSION

'In my childhood I believed by authority, in my youth I believed by feeling; when I became mature I believed by reason.'[1] Rousseau's passage from youth to maturity was a long one, and longest of all in the matter of religion. When he came to Paris at the age of thirty it is probable that he had no strong feelings about the subject. In the company of Diderot, Holbach and other atheists, any faith he might have retained was shaken. He described how his belief then developed in the Third Walk of *The Reveries of the Solitary Walker*.

> The ardent missionaries of atheism . . . did not persuade me, but they made me uneasy. Their arguments shook me, but never convinced me. I did not find any good reply but I felt that there must be one . . . Finally I said to myself . . . their philosophy is for others; I need another. Let me search then with all my strength, while there is still time, to find a steady rule of conduct for the rest of my life . . . This is the moment of my external and material reform, let it also be that of my intellectual and moral reform. Let me fix once and for all my opinions and my principles . . .
>
> I carried out this work slowly, at different intervals, but with all the effort and concentration of which I was capable. I felt acutely that the peace of mind of the rest of my life and indeed my whole fate depended on it. I found myself at first in such a labyrinth of obstructions, difficulties, dead-ends, turnings and darkness that I was tempted to abandon it all twenty times . . . I persisted; for the first time in my life I had courage . . . After the most ardent and sincere researches that have perhaps ever been made by any human being, I decided on the feelings which it was important for me to have for the rest of my life . . .

I confess that I had not always removed all the difficulties I had found in my way . . . But resolving finally to come to a decision on matters where human intelligence has so little grasp, and finding on all sides impenetrable mysteries and insoluble objections, I adopted on each question the feeling which seemed to me the most directly established, the most believable in itself; and I did not stop at objections which I could not resolve but which were contradicted by other objections no less strong in the opposite system . . .

You must have a feeling for yourself and choose it with all the maturity of judgement that you can bring. If, in spite of that, we fall into error we cannot in good faith be blamed, since we are not guilty. This is the unshakeable principle on which my sense of security is based. The result of my painful researches was almost exactly what I put down in the *Profession of Faith of a Savoyard Priest*, a work . . . which one day could cause a revolution among men if good sense and good faith were ever to be born again.[2]

The *Profession* is therefore the culmination of the process that first began publicly in the *Letter to Voltaire on Optimism*, which had continued in the six letters written to Mme d'Houdetot, known as the *Letters to Sophie* or the *Moral Letters*, and which had also been evident in the passages on Julie's faith in *The New Heloïse* (Part VI, Letters 7, 8 and 11). It is Rousseau's most complete religious statement and one he worked on with great care and deliberation. The result is a work of unusual lucidity, which makes Rousseau's thought immediately accessible and reveals some of its most characteristic features.

The work is in two sections. In the first Rousseau establishes the principles of his natural religion, which is based not on revelation or Scripture but on our experiences of the world and ourselves; an experience that arises out of feeling and is confirmed by reason — 'my reason chooses the feeling that my heart prefers'.[3] The foundations of his faith are the beauty and order of nature, and the unequivocal sense of conscience. These are common to all men and equally accessible to them, since they do not begin with reasoning, which only some carry out, but with experience.

In his attitude to both nature and man Rousseau is arguing against the materialist views that had been championed by La Mettrie, Holbach and above all Helvétius. He rejects the possibility that matter can have movement or order of its own accord; there must be an independent source of life and intelligence. The world is more than a fortuitous collection of atoms. Similarly, men are more than a bundle of impulses and desires; they are also more than just another animal. They have free will and they have conscience. Our experience and our rational consideration of both world and man therefore leads to a sense of some life, intelligence and good that is outside the world and ourselves, namely, God.

Although he uses two of the traditional arguments in favour of God's existence — the argument of first cause, and the argument of design — he uses them for negative purposes, to argue against the materialists. His faith does not rest on intellectual foundations but on 'the spectacle of nature'* and 'the inner voice'.

This kind of belief set Rousseau apart from the Christianity of his time and indeed from almost all Christian teaching from St Paul onward. He had already, in the *Discourse on Inequality* and in Book Two of *Emile*, rejected original sin; he now rejected the revelation itself. His admiration for Jesus was uncompromising, he was 'like a God', but he was not God. Nor could Rousseau accept a religion that relied on Scripture, or miracles, or which acted with such intolerance. These criticisms are made explicit in the second part.

It is clear from this that Rousseau's faith was, as he himself wrote in a letter, 'not so much metaphysical as moral'.[5] It was not a systematic set of beliefs based on reason, but the realization of the spiritual element in our nature, a matter of experience rather than argument. This experience leads him to believe in the immortality of the soul, and divine justice, and there were occasional hints in it of transcendence. But it did not remove him from this world. Rousseau did not reject the world, as most Christian teaching had done. On the contrary, he directed his attention to 'the pure pleasure that is born from happiness in oneself',[6] a sense of wholeness in oneself and with the natural world, guided by the moral teaching of the Gospel.

This emphasis on belonging — on being part of a greater whole — and on right conduct has obvious links and similarities with his political thought. So also has his refusal to accept authority for its own sake. A legitimate belief is one which he can experience as legitimate, one that evidently involves him, not one that he must

---

* 'I understand how city-dwellers have little faith', he wrote in the *Confessions*, 'they see only walls and streets and crimes.'[4]

accept because he is told to accept it. We start with ourselves. But that self is not a narrow self-interested self; it has an ability to expand. And its true nature and full potential is only realized in the participation and interplay with something greater than itself.

The Savoyard priest is based on two men Rousseau had known in his youth, the Abbé Gaime in Turin, and the Abbé Gâtier in Savoy. The form of the work is that of the priest meeting a young man in distress; he becomes acquainted with him and, when he feels the right time has come, opens his own heart to him, to show how he himself moved from doubt to a secure faith. The episode begins in the fictional manner used in the rest of *Emile* — 'Thirty years ago there was a young man in an Italian town . . . an exile from his native land . . . reduced to the depths of poverty' — but then Rousseau drops the third person and admits that he was the young man in question. This sudden move into autobiography heightens the mood and gives the piece that sincerity and directness which made it so influential in its time.

Emile, Book IV

[The priest] was attracted by the young fugitive and he questioned him closely. He saw that ill-fortune had already seared his heart, that scorn and disgrace had overthrown his courage, and that his pride, transformed into bitterness and spite, led him to see nothing in the harshness and injustice of men but their evil disposition and the vanity of all virtue . . .   560

There is a stage of degradation which robs the soul of its life; and the inner voice cannot be heard by one whose whole mind is bent on getting food. To protect the unlucky youth from the moral death which threatened him [the priest] began to revive his self-esteem and his good opinion of himself . . .   562

I am weary of speaking in the third person, and the precaution is unnecessary; for you are well aware, my dear friend, that I myself was this unhappy fugitive . . .   563

The most difficult fault to overcome in me was a certain haughty misanthropy, a certain bitterness against the rich and successful, as if their wealth and happiness had been gained at my own expense, and as if their supposed happiness had been unjustly taken from my own. The foolish vanity of youth, which kicks against humiliation, made me only too inclined to this angry temper; and the self-esteem,* which my mentor strove to revive, led to pride, which made men still more vile in my eyes, and only added scorn to my hatred.

Without directly attacking this pride, he prevented it from developing into hardness of heart; and without depriving me of my self-esteem, he made me less scornful of my neighbours. By continually drawing my attention from the vain appearance [of things] and showing me the real ills that it covered, he taught me to deplore the faults of my fellows and feel for their sufferings, to pity rather than envy them . . .

564

'I will open my whole heart to yours,' he said, embracing me. 'You will see me, if not as I am, at least as I seem to myself. When you have heard my whole profession of faith, when you really know the condition of my heart, you will know why I think myself happy, and if you think as I do, you will know how to be happy too . . .'

The meeting was fixed for the very next morning. It was summer time; we rose at daybreak. He took me out of the town on to a high hill above the river Po, whose course we beheld as it flowed between its fertile banks; in the distance the landscape was crowned by the vast chain of the Alps; the beams of the rising sun already touched the plains and cast across the fields long shadows of trees, hillocks, and houses enriching with a thousand gleams of light the fairest picture which the human eye can see. You would have thought that nature was displaying all her splendour before our eyes to furnish a text for our conversation. After contemplating this scene for a while in silence, the man of peace spoke to me.

565

PROFESSION OF FAITH OF A SAVOYARD PRIEST

My child, do not look to me for learned speeches or profound arguments. I am no great philosopher, nor do I desire to be one. I have, however, a certain amount of commonsense and a constant devotion to truth. I have no wish to argue with you nor even to convince you; it is enough for me to show you what I think in the simplicity of my heart. Consult your own heart while I speak; that is all I ask. If I am mistaken, I am honestly mistaken, and therefore my error will not be counted to me as a crime; if you, too, are honestly mistaken, there is no great harm done. If I am right, we are both endowed with reason, we have both the same motive for listening to the voice of reason. Why should you not think as I do? . . .

566

---

* Rousseau uses the phrase *amour-propre* here, but not in the specific and pejorative sense he normally intends.

['I too,' he explains, 'was once in distress like you.']

I felt that the evidence on which my principles rested was being weakened; at last I knew not what to think . . .

I was in that state of doubt and uncertainty which Descartes considers essential to the search for truth. It is a state which cannot continue, it is disquieting and painful . . .

I pondered, therefore, on the sad fate of mortals, adrift upon this sea of human opinions, without compass or rudder, and abandoned to their stormy passions with no guide but an inexperienced pilot who does not know whence he comes or whither he is going. I said to myself, 'I love truth, I seek her, and cannot find her. Show me truth and I will hold her fast; why does she hide her face from the eager heart that would worship her?' . . .   567

I cannot understand how anyone can be a sceptic sincerely and on principle. Either such philosophers do not exist or they are the most miserable of men. Doubt with regard to what we need to know is a condition too violent for the human mind; it cannot long be endured; in spite of itself the mind decides one way or another, and it prefers to be deceived rather than to believe nothing . . .

I consulted the philosophers, I searched their books and examined their various theories; I found them all alike proud, assertive, dogmatic, professing, even in their so-called scepticism, to know everything, proving nothing, scoffing at each other . . . I could find no way out of my uncertainty by listening to them.   567–8

I suppose this prodigious diversity of opinion is caused, in the first place, by the weakness of the human intellect; and, in the second, by pride. We have no means of measuring this vast machine, we are unable to calculate its relations; we know neither its first laws nor its final purpose; we do not know ourselves, we know neither our nature nor the principle that moves us; we scarcely know whether man is a simple or compound creature; we are surrounded by impenetrable mysteries. These mysteries are beyond the region of sense; we think we can penetrate them by the light of reason, but we only have our imagination. Through this imagined world each forces a way for himself which he holds to be right; none can tell whether his path will lead him to the goal. Yet we long to know and understand it all. The one thing we do not know is the limit of the knowable. We prefer to trust to chance and to believe what is not, rather than to admit that not one of us can see what really is. A fragment of some vast whole whose bounds are beyond our gaze, a fragment abandoned by its Creator to our foolish quarrels, we are vain enough to want to

568–9

determine the nature of that whole and our own relations with regard to it . . .

The first thing I learned from these considerations was to restrict my inquiries to what directly concerned myself, to rest in profound ignorance of everything else, and not even to trouble myself to doubt anything beyond what I required to know.

I also realized that the philosophers, far from ridding me of my vain doubts, only multiplied the doubts that tormented me and failed to remove any one of them. So I chose another guide and said, 'Let me follow the inner light; it will not lead me so far astray as others have done, or if it does it will be my own fault, and I shall not go so

569   far wrong if I follow my own illusions as if I trusted to their deceits.' . . .

Bearing thus within my heart the love of truth as my only philosophy, and as my only method a clear and simple rule which dispensed with the need for vain and subtle arguments, I returned with the help of this rule to the examination of such knowledge as concerned myself; I was resolved to admit as self-evident all that I could not honestly refuse to believe, and to admit as true all that seemed to follow directly from this; all the rest I determined to leave undecided, neither accepting nor rejecting it, nor yet troubling myself to clear up difficulties which did not lead to any practical ends.

But who am I? What right have I to decide? What is it that determines my judgements? If they are inevitable, if they are the results of the impressions I receive, I am wasting my strength in such inquiries; they would be made or not without any interference of mine. I must therefore first turn my eyes upon myself to acquaint myself with

570   the instrument I desire to use, and to discover how far it is reliable.

I exist, and I have senses by which I am affected. This is the first truth that strikes me and I am forced to accept it. Have I any independent knowledge of my existence, or am I only aware of it through my sensations? This is my first difficulty, and so far I cannot solve it. For I continually experience sensations, either directly or indirectly through memory, so how can I know if the feeling of self is something beyond these sensations and if it can exist independently of them?

My sensations take place in myself, for they make me aware of my own existence; but their cause is outside me, for they affect me in spite of any need I have for them, and they are produced or destroyed independently of me. So I clearly perceive that my sensation, which is within me, and its cause or its object, which is outside me, are different things.

Thus, not only do I exist, but other entities exist also, that is to say, the objects of my sensations; and even if these objects are merely ideas, still these ideas are not me.

Now everything outside myself, everything which acts upon my senses, I call matter, and all the particles of matter which I suppose to be united into separate beings I call bodies. Thus all the disputes of the idealists and the materialists have no meaning for me; their distinctions between the appearance and the reality of bodies are wholly fanciful.

I am now as convinced of the existence of the universe as of my own. I next consider the objects of my sensations, and I find that I have the power of comparing them, so I perceive that I am endowed with an active force of which I was not previously aware.

To perceive is to feel; to compare is to judge; to judge and to feel are not the same. Through sensation objects present themselves to me separately and singly as they are in nature; by comparing them I rearrange them, I shift them so to speak, I place one upon another to decide whether they are alike or different, or more generally to find out their relations. To my mind, the distinctive faculty of an active or intelligent being is the power of understanding this word 'is' . . .   571

This power of my mind which brings my sensations together and compares them may be called by any name; let it be called attention, meditation, reflection, or what you will; it is still true that it is in me and not in things, that it is I alone who produce it, though I only produce it when I receive an impression from things. Though I am compelled to feel or not to feel, I am free to examine more or less what I feel.

I am not therefore simply a feeling and passive being, but an active and intelligent being, and whatever philosophy may say about it I will dare to presume to the honour of thinking. I only know that truth is in things, and not in my mind which judges them, and that the less of myself that I bring to my judgements about them, the more I am sure of approaching the truth; so my rule of delivering myself to feeling more than to reason is confirmed by reason itself.   573

Being now, so to speak, sure of myself, I begin to look at things outside myself, and I behold myself with a sort of shudder flung at random into this vast universe, plunged as it were into the immensity of beings, knowing nothing of what they are in themselves or in relation to me. I study them, I observe them; and the first object which suggests itself for comparison with them is myself.

All that I perceive through the senses is matter, and I deduce all the essential properties of matter from the sensitive qualities which make me perceive it, qualities which are inseparable from it. I see it sometimes in motion, sometimes at rest, hence I infer that neither motion nor rest is essential to it, but motion, being an action, is the result of a cause of which rest is only the absence. When, therefore, there is nothing acting upon matter it does not move, and for the very reason that rest and motion are indifferent to it, its natural state is a state of rest . . .

573–4

I feel myself so thoroughly convinced that the natural state of matter is a state of rest, and that it has no power of action in itself, that when I see a body in motion I at once assume that it is either a living body or that this motion has been imparted to it. My mind declines to accept in any way the idea of inorganic matter moving of its own accord, or giving rise to any action.

Yet this visible universe consists of matter, matter diffused and dead,* matter which has none of the cohesion, the organization, the common feeling of the parts of a living body, for it is certain that we who are parts have no consciousness of the whole. This same universe is in motion, and in its movements, ordered, uniform, and subject to fixed laws, it has none of that freedom which appears in the spontaneous movements of men and animals. So the world is not some huge animal which moves of its own accord; its movements are therefore due to some external cause, a cause which I cannot perceive. But the inner voice makes this cause so apparent to me that I cannot watch the course of the sun without imagining a force which drives it, and when the earth revolves I think I see the hand that sets it in motion . . .

574–5

The first causes of motion are not to be found in matter; matter receives and transmits motion, but does not produce it. The more I observe the action and reaction of the forces of nature playing on one another, the more I see that we must always go back from one effect to another, till we arrive at a first cause in some will; for to assume an infinite succession of causes is to assume that there is no first cause. In a word, no motion which is not caused by another motion can take place, except by a spontaneous, voluntary action; inanimate bodies have no action but motion, and there is no real action without

---

* I have tried hard to grasp the idea of a living molecule, but in vain. The idea of matter feeling without any senses seems to me unintelligible and self-contradictory. To accept or reject this idea one must first understand it, and I confess that so far I have not succeeded. (Note by Rousseau.)

will. This is my first principle. I believe, therefore, that there is a will which sets the universe in motion and gives life to nature. This is my first dogma, or the first article of my creed.   576

The doctrine I have just laid down is indeed obscure; but at least it suggests a meaning and there is nothing in it repugnant to reason or experience; can we say as much of materialism? . . .   576-7

Far from being able to picture to myself an entire absence of order in the fortuitous concurrence of elements, I cannot even imagine such a strife, and the chaos of the universe is less conceivable to me than its harmony. I can understand that the mechanism of the universe may not be intelligible to the human mind, but when a man sets to work to explain it, he must say what men can understand.   578

If matter in motion points me to a will, matter in motion according to fixed laws points me to an intelligence; that is the second article of my creed. To act, to compare, to choose, are the operations of an active, thinking being; so this being exists. Where do you find him existing, you will say? Not merely in the revolving heavens, nor in the sun which gives us light, not in myself alone, but in the sheep that grazes, the bird that flies, the stone that falls, and the leaf blown by the wind.

I judge of the order of the world, although I know nothing of its purpose, for to judge of this order it is enough for me to compare the parts one with another, to study their co-operation, their relations, and to observe their united action. I do not know why the universe exists, but I see continually how it is changed; I never fail to perceive the close connection by which the beings of which it consists lend their aid one to another. I am like a man who sees the works of a watch for the first time; he is never weary of admiring the mechanism, though he does not know the use of the instrument and has never seen its face. I do not know what this is for, says he, but I see that each part of it is fitted to the rest, I admire the workman in the details of his work, and I am quite certain that all these wheels only work together in this fashion for some common end which I cannot perceive.

Let us compare the special ends, the means, the ordered relations of every kind, then let us listen to the inner voice of feeling; what healthy mind can reject its evidence? Unless the eyes are blinded by prejudices, can they fail to see that the visible order of the universe proclaims a supreme intelligence? . . .   578-9

There is not a being in the universe which may not be regarded as in some respects the common centre of all the others, around which they are all ordered, so that they are all reciprocally end and means in relation to each other. The mind is confused and lost amid these innumerable relations, not one of which is itself confused or lost in the crowd. What absurd assumptions are required to deduce all this harmony from the blind mechanism of matter set in motion by chance! . . . It is not in my power to believe that passive and dead matter can have brought forth living and feeling beings, that blind chance has brought forth intelligent beings, that that which does not think has brought forth thinking beings.

580   I believe, therefore, that the world is governed by a wise and powerful will; I see it or rather I feel it, and it is a great thing to know this. But has this same world always existed, or has it been created? Is there one source of all things? Are there two or many? What is their nature? I know not; and what concern is it of mine? When these things become of importance to me I will try to learn them; till then I abjure these idle speculations, which may trouble my pride, but cannot affect my conduct nor be comprehended by my reason.

Recollect that I am not preaching my own opinion but explaining it. Whether matter is eternal or created, whether its origin is passive or not, it is still certain that the whole is one, and that it proclaims a single intelligence; for I see nothing that is not part of the same ordered system, nothing which does not co-operate to the same end, namely, the preservation of all within the established order. This being who wills and can perform his will, this being active through his own power, this being, whoever he may be, who moves the universe and orders all things, is what I call God. To this name I add the ideas of intelligence, power, will, which I have brought together, and that of goodness, which is their necessary consequence; but for all this I know no more of the being to which I ascribe them. He hides himself alike from my senses and my understanding; the more I think of him, the more perplexed I am; I know full well that he exists, and that he exists of himself alone; I know that my existence depends on his, and that everything I know depends upon him also. I see God everywhere in his works, I feel him within myself, I behold him all around me; but if I try to ponder him himself, if I try to find out where he is, what he is, what is his substance, he escapes me and my troubled spirit finds nothing.

Convinced of my unfitness, I shall never argue about the nature of God unless I am driven to it by the feeling of his relations with myself. Such reasonings are always rash; a wise man should venture on them with trembling, he should be certain that he can never sound their depths; for the most insolent attitude towards God is not to abstain from thinking of him, but to think evil of him.   581

After the discovery of such of his attributes as enable me to know of his existence, I return to myself, and I try to discover what is my place in the order of things which he governs, and I can myself examine. At once, and beyond possibility of doubt, I discover my species; for by my own will and the instruments I can control to carry out my will, I have more power to act upon all bodies about me, either to make use of or to avoid their action at my pleasure, than any of them has power to act upon me against my will by mere physical impulsion; and through my intelligence I am the only one who can examine all the rest. What creature here below, except man, can observe others, measure, calculate, foresee their movements, their effects, and unite, so to speak, the feeling of a common existence with that of his individual existence? What is there so absurd in the thought that all things are made for me when I alone can relate all things to myself?

It is true, therefore, that man is lord of the earth on which he dwells; for not only does he tame all the beasts, not only does he control its elements through his industry; but he alone knows how to control it; by contemplation he takes possession of the stars which he cannot approach. Show me any other creature on earth who can make a fire and who can behold with admiration the sun . . .

I am not puffed up by this thought, I am deeply moved by it; for this state was no choice of mine, it was not due to the deserts of a creature who as yet did not exist. Can I see myself distinguished in this way without taking pleasure in this post of honour, without blessing the hand which bestowed it? The first return to self has given birth to a feeling of gratitude and thankfulness to the author of my species, and this feeling calls forth my first homage to the benevolent Divinity. I worship his almighty power and my heart acknowledges his mercies. I do not need to be taught this worship, it is suggested to me by nature herself.   582–3

But when, in my desire to discover my own place within my species, I consider its different ranks and the men who fill them, where am I now? What a sight meets my eyes! Where is now the order I perceived? Nature showed me a scene of harmony and proportion; the human race shows me nothing but confusion and disorder. The elements agree together; men are in a state of chaos. The beasts are happy; their king alone is wretched. Oh Wisdom, where are your laws? Oh Providence, is this your rule over the world? Benevolent God, where is your power? I see the earth, and there is evil upon it.

Would you believe it, dear friend, from these gloomy thoughts and apparent contradictions, there was shaped in my mind the sublime idea of the soul, which all my seeking had hitherto failed to discover? While I meditated upon man's nature, I seemed to discover two distinct principles in it; one of them raised him to the study of the eternal truths, to the love of justice, and of true morality, to the regions of the world of thought, which the wise delight to contemplate; the other led him downwards to himself, made him the slave of his senses, of the passions which are their instruments, and opposed everything suggested to him by the former principle. When I felt myself carried away, distracted by these conflicting motives, I said: No; man is not one; I will and I will not; I feel myself at once a slave and a free man; I perceive what is right, I love it, and I do what is wrong; I am active when I listen to the voice of reason; I am passive when I am carried away by my passions; and when I yield, my worst suffering is the knowledge that I might have resisted . . .

583

[Not only does man have an active will, but this will is free.]

No material being is in itself active, and I am active. In vain do you argue this point with me; I feel it, and it is this feeling which speaks to me more forcibly than the reason which disputes it. I have a body which is acted upon by other bodies, and it acts in turn upon them; there is no doubt about this reciprocal action. But my will is independent of my senses; I consent or I resist; I yield or I win the victory, and I know very well in myself when I have done what I wanted and when I have merely given way to my passions . . .

585–6

Man is therefore free to act, and as such he is animated by an immaterial substance; that is the third article of my creed. From these three you will easily deduce the rest, so that I need not enumerate them.

If man is at once active and free, he acts of his own accord; what he does freely is no part of the system marked out by Providence and it cannot be imputed to Providence. Providence does not will the evil that man does when he misuses the freedom given to him; neither does Providence prevent him doing it, either because the wrong done by so feeble a creature is as nothing in its eyes, or because it could not prevent it without doing a greater wrong and degrading his nature. Providence has made him free that he may choose the good and refuse the evil. It has made him capable of this choice if he uses rightly the faculties bestowed upon him, but it has so strictly limited his powers that the misuse of his freedom cannot disturb the general order. The evil that man does reacts upon himself without affecting the system of the world, without preventing the preservation of the human species in spite of itself. To complain that God does not prevent us from doing wrong is to complain because he has made man of so excellent a nature, that he has endowed his actions with that morality by which they are ennobled, that he has made virtue man's birthright. Supreme happiness consists in self-content; that we may gain this self-content we are placed upon this earth and endowed with freedom, we are tempted by our passions and restrained by conscience. What more could divine power itself have done on our behalf? Could it have made our nature a contradiction, and have given the prize of well-doing to one who was incapable of evil? To prevent a man from wickedness, should Providence have restricted him to instinct and made him an animal? Not so, God of my soul, I will never reproach you that you created me in your own image, that I may be free and good and happy like you!

It is the abuse of our powers that makes us unhappy and wicked. Our cares, our sorrows, our sufferings are of our own making . . .   587

If we were but content to be ourselves we should have no cause to complain of our lot; but in the search for an imaginary good we find a thousand real ills. He who cannot bear a little pain must expect to suffer greatly. If a man injures his constitution by dissipation, you try to cure him with medicine; the ill he fears is added to the ill he feels; the thought of death makes it horrible and hastens its approach; the more we seek to escape from it, the more we are aware of it; and we go through life in fear of death, blaming nature for the evils we have inflicted on ourselves by our neglect of her laws.

Oh Man! seek no further for the author of evil; you are he. There is no evil but the evil you do or the evil you suffer, and both come from yourself. Evil in general can only spring from disorder, and in the system of the world I find a never-failing order . . .   588

Where all is well, there is no such thing as injustice. Justice and goodness are inseparable; now goodness is the necessary result of boundless power and of that self-love which is innate in all feeling creatures. The omnipotent projects himself as it were into the being of his creatures . . .

The omnipotent can only will what is good. Therefore he who is supremely good, because he is supremely powerful, must also be supremely just, otherwise he would contradict himself; for that love of order which creates order we call goodness, and that love of order which preserves order we call justice.

Men say God owes nothing to his creatures. I think he owes them all he promised when he gave them their being. Now to give them the idea of something good and to make them feel the need of it, is to promise it to them. The more closely I study and consider myself, the more plainly do I read these words written in my soul, 'Be just and you will be happy.' It is not so, however, in the present condition of things; the wicked man prospers and the oppression of the righteous continues. Observe how angry we are when this expectation is disappointed. Conscience revolts and murmurs against her Creator; she exclaims with cries and groans, 'You have deceived me.'

'I have deceived you, rash soul! Who told you this? Is your soul destroyed? Have you ceased to exist?' . . .

One might judge from the complaints of impatient men that God owes them the reward before they have deserved it, that he is bound to pay for virtue in advance. Oh! let us first be good and then we shall be happy. Let us not claim the prize before we have won it, nor demand our wages before we have finished our work . . .

589

If the soul is immaterial, it may survive the body; and if it so survives, Providence is justified. Had I no other proof of the immaterial nature of the soul, the triumph of the wicked and the oppression of the righteous in this world would be enough to convince me. I should seek to resolve so appalling a discord in the universal harmony. I should say to myself, 'All is not over with life, everything finds its place at death' . . . My vices make me only too well aware that man is but half alive during this life; the life of the soul only begins with the death of the body.

But what is that life? Is the soul of man in its nature immortal? My finite understanding cannot conceive the infinite; what is called eternity eludes my grasp. What can I assert or deny, how can I reason with regard to what I cannot conceive? . . .

590

In this world our inner feeling is absorbed by a thousand eager passions . . . But when, freed from the illusions of the bodily senses, we will enjoy the contemplation of the supreme Being and the eternal truths which flow from him; when all the powers of our soul are alive to the beauty of order and we are wholly occupied in comparing what we have done with what we ought to have done, then it is that the voice of conscience will regain its strength and sway; then it is that the pure delight which springs from self-content, and the sharp regret for our own degradation of that self, will decide by means of overpowering feeling what shall be the fate which each has prepared for himself. My good friend, do not ask me whether there are other sources of happiness or suffering; I cannot tell. What I imagine is enough to console me in this life and to bid me look for a life to come. I do not say the good will be rewarded, for what greater good can a truly good being expect than to exist in accordance with his nature? But I do assert that the good will be happy, because their maker, the author of all justice, who has made them capable of feeling, has not made them that they may suffer . . .   591

Do not ask me whether the torments of the wicked will endure for ever. I cannot tell, and I have no empty curiosity for the investigation of useless problems. How does the fate of the wicked concern me? I take little interest in it. All the same I find it hard to believe that they will be condemned to everlasting torments. If the supreme justice calls for vengeance, it claims it in this life. The nations of the world with their errors are its ministers. Justice uses self-inflicted ills to punish the crimes which have deserved them. It is in your own insatiable souls, devoured by envy, greed, and ambition, it is in the midst of your false prosperity, that the avenging passions find the due reward of your crimes. What need to seek a hell in the future life? It is here in the breast of the wicked . . .   592

God is good; this is certain. But man finds his happiness in the love of his fellows and God's happiness consists in the love of order; for it is through order that he maintains what is, and unites each part in the whole. God is just; of this I am sure, it is a consequence of his goodness; man's injustice is not God's work, but his own; that moral disorder which seems to the philosophers a presumption against Providence is to me a proof of its existence. But man's justice consists in giving to each his due; God's justice consists in demanding from each of us an account of that which he has given us . . .   593

Having thus deduced from the perception of objects of sense and from my inner consciousness, which leads me to judge of causes by my native reason, the principal truths which I require to know, I must now seek such principles of conduct as I can draw from them, and such rules as I must lay down for my guidance in the fulfilment of my destiny in this world, according to the purpose of my Maker. Still following the same method, I do not derive these rules from the principles of the higher philosophy, I find them in the depths of my heart, traced by nature in characters which nothing can efface. I need only consult myself with regard to what I wish to do; what I feel to be right is right, what I feel to be wrong is wrong; conscience is the best casuist . . . Conscience is the voice of the soul, the passions are the voice of the body. Is it strange that these voices often contradict each other? And then to which should we give heed? Too often does reason deceive us; we have only too good a right to doubt her; but conscience never deceives us; she is the true guide of man; it is to the soul what instinct is to the body; he who obeys his conscience is following nature and he need not fear that he will go 594–5 astray . . .

My young friend, let us look within, let us set aside all personal prejudices and see whither our inclinations lead us. Do we take more pleasure in the sight of the sufferings of others or their joys? Is it pleasanter to do a kind action or an unkind action, and which leaves the more delightful memory behind it? . . . They say we are indifferent to everything but self-interest; yet we find our consolation for our sufferings in the charms of friendship and humanity, and even in our pleasures we should be too lonely and miserable if we had no one to share them with us . . . Take from our hearts this love of what is noble and you rob us of the joy of life. The mean-spirited man, in whom these delicious feelings have been stifled among vile passions, who by thinking of no one but himself comes at last to love no one but himself, this man feels no raptures, his cold heart no longer throbs with joy, and his eyes no longer fill with the sweet tears of sympathy, he delights in nothing; the wretch has neither life nor feeling, he is already dead.

There are many bad men in this world, but there are few of these dead souls, alive only to self-interest, and insensible to all that is right and good. We only delight in injustice so long as it is to our own advantage; in every other case we wish the innocent to be protected . . . We do not hate the wicked merely because of the harm they do to ourselves, but because they are wicked. Not only do we wish to be happy ourselves, we wish others to be happy too, and if this happiness does not interfere with our own happiness, it increases it. In conclusion, whether we will or not, we pity the un- 596–7 fortunate; when we see their suffering we suffer too . . .

There is therefore at the bottom of our hearts an innate principle of justice and virtue, by which, in spite of our maxims, we judge our own actions or those of others to be good or evil; and it is this principle that I call 'conscience'.

But at this word I hear the murmurs of all the wise men so-called. Childish errors, prejudices of our upbringing, they exclaim in concert! There is nothing in the human mind but what it has gained by experience; and we judge everything solely by means of the ideas we have acquired. They go further; they even venture to reject the clear 598 and universal agreement of all peoples . . .

Self-interest, so they say, induces each of us to agree for the common good. But how is it that the good man consents to this to his own cost? Does a man go to death from self-interest? No doubt each man acts for his own good, but if there is no such thing as moral good to be taken into consideration, self-interest will only enable you to account for the deeds of the wicked. Possibly you will not attempt to do more. Such a philosophy which could find no place for good deeds would be too detestable . . .   598

I have told you already that I do not wish to philosophize with you, but to help you to consult your own heart. If all the philosophers in the world should prove that I am wrong, and you feel that I am right, that is all I ask.

For this purpose it is enough to lead you to distinguish between our acquired ideas and our natural feelings; for feeling precedes knowledge, and since we do not learn to want what is good for us and avoid what is bad for us, but get this desire from nature, in the same way the love of good and the hatred of evil are as natural to us as our self-love. The decrees of conscience are not judgements but feelings. Although all our ideas come from without, the feelings by which they are weighed are within us, and it is by these feelings alone that we perceive the fitness or unfitness of things in relation to ourselves, which leads us to seek or shun these things.   599

To exist for us is to feel; our feeling is undoubtedly earlier than our intelligence, and we had feelings before we had ideas. Whatever may be the cause of our being, it has provided for our preservation by giving us feelings suited to our nature; and no one can deny that these at least are innate. These feelings, so far as the individual is concerned, are self-love, the fear of pain, the dread of death, the desire for well-being. Again, if, as it is impossible to doubt, man is by nature sociable, or at least made to become sociable, he can only be so by means of other innate feelings, relative to his kind; for if only physical need were considered, men would certainly be scattered rather than brought together. Now the motive power of conscience is derived from the moral system formed through this twofold relation to himself and to his fellow-men. To know good is not to love it; this knowledge is not innate in man; but as soon as his reason leads him to know it, his conscience impels him to love it; it is this feeling which is innate . . .   600

Conscience! Conscience! Divine instinct, immortal voice from heaven; sure guide for a creature who is certainly ignorant and finite, yet also intelligent and free; infallible judge of good and evil, making man similar to God! In you consists the excellence of man's nature and the morality of his actions. Apart from you I find nothing in myself to raise me above the beasts — nothing but the sad privilege of wandering from one error to another, with the aid of an understanding without rule and a reason without principle.

Thank heaven we have now got rid of all that alarming show of philosophy; we may be men without being scholars; now that we need not spend our life in the study of morality, we have found a less costly and surer guide through this vast labyrinth of human thought. But it is not enough to be aware that there is such a guide; we must know her and follow her. If she speaks to all hearts, how is it that so few give heed to her voice? She speaks to us in the language of nature, which everything leads us to forget. Conscience is timid, she loves

601   peace and retirement; she is startled by noise and numbers . . .

We have any number of reasons for refusing to follow the inclinations of our heart; false caution restricts the heart within the limits of the human ego; a thousand efforts are needed to break these bonds. The joy of well-doing is the prize of having done well, and we must deserve the prize before we win it. There is nothing sweeter than virtue; but we do not know this till we have tried it . . .

Reason alone is not a sufficient foundation for virtue; what solid ground can be found for it? Virtue we are told is love of order. But can this love prevail over my love for my own well-being, and ought it so to prevail? Let them give me clear and sufficient reason for this preference. Their so-called principle is in truth a mere playing with words; for I also say that vice is love of order, taken in a different sense. Wherever there is feeling and intelligence, there is some sort of moral order. The difference is this: the good man orders his life with regard to the whole; the wicked orders everything with regard to himself. The latter centres all things round himself; the other measures his radius and remains on the circumference. Thus his order relates to the common centre, which is God, and to all the concentric circles which are His creatures. If there is no God, the wicked is

602   right and the good man is nothing but a fool.

Oh my child! May you feel one day what a burden is removed when . . . you find at last so close at hand the path of wisdom, the prize of this life's labours and the source of that happiness you had despaired of. All the duties of natural law which had almost been effaced from my heart by the injustice of men are engraved there in the name of that eternal justice which lays these duties on me and sees me fulfil them. I feel myself merely the work and the instrument of the Great Being, who wills what is good, who performs it, who will bring about my own good through the co-operation of my will with his own, and by the right use of my liberty. I acquiesce in the order he establishes, certain that one day I shall enjoy that order and find my happiness in it. For what sweeter joy is there than this, to feel oneself a part of a system where all is good? A prey to pain, I bear it in patience, remembering that it will soon be over, and that it results from a body which is not mine. If I do a good deed in secret, I know that it is seen, and my conduct in this life is a pledge of the life to come. When I suffer injustice, I say to myself, the Almighty who does all things well will compensate me for it. My bodily needs, my poverty, make the idea of death less intolerable. There will be all the fewer bonds to be broken when my hour comes... 603

[The priest reiterates his belief that God 'has given me conscience to love the good, reason to know it, and freedom to choose it' (605); he repeats his trust in divine justice and the first part of the *Profession* comes to a close. Rousseau says that his beliefs are very like natural religion. The priest agrees:]

Behold the spectacle of nature; listen to the inner voice. Has not God spoken it all to our eyes, to our conscience, to our reason? What more can men tell us? Their revelations only degrade God, by investing him with passions like our own. Far from throwing light upon the ideas of the Supreme Being, special doctrines seem to me to confuse those ideas ... they add absurd contradictions, they make man proud, intolerant, and cruel; instead of bringing peace on earth they bring fire and the sword. I ask myself what is the good of it, and I find no answer. I see only the crimes of men and the misery of mankind.   607–8

[He then attacks the doctrine of the revelation and beliefs based on Scripture or miracles.]

The best of religions must be the clearest. He who hides the religion he preaches under mysteries and contradictions teaches me to distrust that religion ... The minister of truth does not tyrannize over my reason, he enlightens it.   614

[He adds, however] that the holiness of the Gospel speaks to my heart ... Is it possible that he whose history is contained in this book is no more than a man? ... What gentleness and purity in his actions, what a touching grace in his teaching; how lofty his sayings, how profoundly wise his preaching; what presence of mind, what finesse and justice in his replies.   625–6

[He compares Jesus with Socrates.]

If the life and death of Socrates are those of a philosopher, the life and
626 death of Christ are those of a God.

[He concludes:]

I serve God in the simplicity of my heart; I only seek to know what
affects my conduct. As to those dogmas which have no effect on
627 action or morality . . . I give no heed to them.

[His closing advice to the young Rousseau is to] remember that the
real duties of religion are independent of human institutions; that
in every land, in every sect, to love God above all things and to love
our neighbour as ourself is the whole law. Remember there is no religion which absolves us from our moral duties; that these alone are
really essential, that the service of the heart is the first of these duties,
632 and that without faith there is no true virtue.

Dare to confess God before the philosophers; dare to preach
humanity to the intolerant . . . Self-interest misleads us; the hope of
633–5 the just is the only sure guide . . .

15 TO THE ARCHBISHOP

Rousseau had intended *Emile* to be his last work. He never expected the official outcry against it. He believed that the statement of faith that the dying Julie made in *The New Heloïse* (Part Six, Letter 11) 'was exactly the same as that of the Savoyard priest. All that was bold in *The Social Contract* had been previously in the *Discourse on Inequality:* all that was bold in *Emile* was previously in *The New Heloïse.*'[1]

While this may have been essentially true for Rousseau, it was not evidently so to his readers. *The Discourse on Inequality* had put forward a secular version of the Fall of man, the implications of which would inevitably bring him into conflict with the church. But the process of working out those implications had taken several years. His principles may have remained the same but his arguments had certainly not. Only in the *Social Contract* and *Emile* had he fully elaborated his views; only in the *Profession of Faith* had he made plain his criticism of Christianity.

When both *Emile* and *The Social Contract* were condemned by the Small Council in Geneva, in June 1762, Rousseau expected his supporters to speak up in his defence. They did not do so. His religious views alarmed them. The rejection of the doctrine of revelation, the doubt about Christ's divinity, was exactly the heretical belief of Socinianism which D'Alembert had claimed to find among the Genevan clergy, a claim they had rigorously denied. Rousseau himself had opposed D'Alembert, but now he seemed to have dissociated himself from that opposition and to have set out a faith that was as contrary to the Protestant Church as it was to the Catholic. In addition, he had made hostile remarks about Christianity in *The Social Contract*.

Then, in August 1762, the Archbishop of Paris, Christophe de

Beaumont, issued a Mandate against *Emile*. He condemned the book for its 'abominable doctrines' and prohibited the inhabitants of his diocese from reading or keeping the book. His Mandate was the most extended and clearly argued of all the condemnations and it therefore provided an excellent opportunity for Rousseau to answer the charges made against him.

It was an opportunity he seized. By demonstrating his differences with the head of the Catholic Church in France he would show his doubting supporters in Geneva where he stood, and reassure them that he was still a Christian. By revealing the flaws in the Archbishop's arguments he would reassert his own faith in the goodness of man, against the doctrine of original sin, and he would vindicate his *Profession*. He was himself now a victim of the intolerance and fanaticism he had condemned. Both church and state had made him an outcast from society. What he had previously written in the cause of justice, he now wrote in his own defence: a man alone, as he indicated in his title-page, against a man of position, title, and authority.

The *Letter to Christophe de Beaumont* is one of Rousseau's most vigorous and fluent works. He had brought his life's work to completion with *Emile;* the years of tortuous thinking were over. He could now look back and point out the unity that no one else had been able to see. The great labour is over, and there is a sense of release, a sense of complete confidence in the coherence and validity of what he had written.

Letter to Christophe de Beaumont

JEAN-JACQUES ROUSSEAU
Citizen of Geneva
to
CHRISTOPHE DE BEAUMONT
Archbishop of Paris
Duke of St Cloud, Peer of France
Commander of the Order of the Holy Spirit
Master of the Sorbonne, etc.

I have written on various subjects, but always with the same principles, the same morality, the same faith, the same maxims and, if you will, the same opinions. People, however, have made very diverse judgements on my books, or rather on the author of my books; because I have been judged rather from the subjects I treated than from my opinions. After my *First Discourse*, I was [said to be] a man of paradox, who amused himself in proving things he did not believe; after my *Letter on French Music* I was a professed enemy of that nation and was very near being treated as a conspirator; one would have thought that the fate of the French monarchy depended on the glory of the opera; after my *Discourse on Inequality* I was an atheist and a misanthrope; after my *Letter to D'Alembert* I was the defender of Christian morality; after *The New Heloïse* I was passionate and tender; now I am impious; soon, perhaps, I shall be devout.   928

Thus public opinion about me fluctuates foolishly. It knows as little why it detests me now as why it loved me before. As for myself, I have always remained the same: more zealous than enlightened in my researches, but sincere in everything, even against myself; simple and good, yet sensitive and weak; often doing evil and always loving good; bound by friendship, never by things, and holding more to my feelings than to my interests; not demanding anything from others and not wishing to be dependent on them; no more yielding to their prejudices than to their will, and preserving my own [will] as free as my reason; fearing God without being afraid of hell; reasoning about religion without irresponsibility; loving neither impiety nor fanaticism, but hating those who are intolerant still more than zealots . . .   928–9

[At last he had put down his pen. What happened?]

A citizen of Geneva gets a book printed in Holland; and by a decree of the *Parlement* of Paris this book is burnt. A Protestant proposes, in a Protestant country, certain objections against the Church of Rome; and he is condemned by the *Parlement* of Paris. A republican makes objections in a republic against monarchy; and he is condemned by the *Parlement* of Paris. The *Parlement* of Paris must have strange ideas of their empire and must believe themselves the rightful judge of the whole human race . . .   929

The fundamental principle of all morality — that on which I have reasoned in all my writings and which I developed in my last work with all the clarity at my command — is this: That man is a naturally good being, who loves justice and order; that there is no original perversity in the human heart and that the first movements of nature are always right. I have shown that the only passion which is born in man, namely self-love, is in itself indifferent either to good or evil; that it becomes good or evil only by accident, and according to the circumstances in which it is developed. I have shown that none of the vices imputed to the human heart is at all natural to it. I have described the manner in which they arise; I have traced, as it were, their genealogy and have shown how, by successive deviations from their original goodness, men finally become what they are.

I have explained further what I understand by this original goodness, which does not seem to flow from that indifference to good and evil which is natural to self-love. Man is not a simple being; he is made up of two elements . . . Self-love is not a simple passion, but has two principles, namely, the intelligent being and the sensitive being, whose well-being is not the same. The appetite of the senses tends to that of the body and the love of order to that of the soul. This second love, when developed and made active, is called conscience; but conscience is only developed and only acts from enlightenment. It is only by acquiring enlightenment that man succeeds in knowing order; and it is only when he knows it that his conscience leads him to love it. The man who has made no comparisons and has seen no relationships has no conscience. In such a state as this a man only knows himself; he does not see his own well-being to be identified with or contrary to that of anyone else; he neither hates anything nor loves anything; but limited to no more than physical instinct, he is no one, he is animal. This is what I have demonstrated in my *Discourse on Inequality*.

935-6

When by a development — the stages of which I have shown — men begin to look round at their fellows, they begin also to see their relationships with men and with things, to get their ideas of consistency, of justice and of order. They begin to become sensitive to moral beauty and conscience becomes active. Then they have virtues; and, if they have vices as well, it is because their interests grow and their ambition awakens in proportion as their knowledge expands. But as long as there is less opposition of interests than agreement of ideas, men are essentially good. This is the second state.

Finally all the individual interests are aroused and come into conflict. Self-love is fermented into self-interest. Then opinion, by making the whole universe necessary to each man, makes them all born enemies; each finds his good only in the misfortune of others; then conscience, weaker than the aroused passions, is stifled by them and is in men's mouths no more than a word made for mutual deceit. Then each pretends to sacrifice his own interests to those of the public and all lie. No one wants the public good except when it agrees with his own; hence this agreement is the purpose of that true plan which seeks to make people happy and good. But I am now beginning to talk a strange language, as little known to my readers as to you.

This, my lord, is the third and last state, beyond which nothing remains to be done; and this is how, man being good, men become wicked. I have devoted my book to finding out how one ought to set about preventing them from becoming wicked. I did not assert that it was definitely possible as things are, but I certainly asserted, and still do, that there are no other means of effecting it than those I have proposed . . .

936–7

You say that my plan of education, 'far from being consistent with Christianity, is not even fit to make citizens or men'; and your only proof is to quote original sin against me. Baptism, my lord, is the only way of being cleansed from original sin and its effects. From which it would follow, according to you, that only Christians have ever been citizens or men. You must either deny this consequence or agree that you have proved too much.

You go so far back for your proofs that you force me to go just as far to look for my replies. First, it appears to me that this doctrine of original sin, subject to such terrible difficulties, is not to be found in the Scriptures so clearly or so harshly expressed as the elaborate Augustine and our theologians have been pleased to maintain. How also can one conceive that God should create so many innocent and pure souls expressly to join them to sinful bodies, to make them contract moral corruption from them, and to damn them all to hell for no other crime than that union which was his own work? I shall not say whether you clarify the mystery of the human heart by this system — as you have boasted — but I see that you greatly obscure the justice and goodness of the Supreme Being. If you take away one objection, it has only been to substitute others which are a hundred times stronger.

But after all, what has this doctrine to do with the author of *Emile*? Although he believed his book useful to the human race, it is for Christians that he intended it; it is for men cleansed from original sin and its effects, at least with regard to their souls, by the sacrament instituted for that purpose. According to that same doctrine we have all recovered our primitive innocence in our infancy. We have all come out of baptism as pure in heart as Adam came out of the hands of God . . . You attribute to original sin the faults of people whom you acknowledge to have been cleansed of original sin, and then you blame me for having given another origin to those vices . . .

938

It could be said, it is true, that the effects which I attribute to baptism do not appear by any external signs; that Christians are not seen to be less prone to evil than infidels: whereas, according to me, the innate evil of sin should be apparent in the latter through visible differences. It could be further argued that with the assistance of gospel morality, in addition to baptism, all Christians ought to be angels, while infidels, who, in addition to their original corruption, are given over to false religions, ought to be demons. I can imagine that if this difficulty were pressed, it could become embarrassing . . .

939   Original sin explains everything except its own principle and this is the very thing [that has] to be explained . . .

  You can only see man in the hands of the devil, and I see how he fell there . . . Man was created good, we are both agreed, I think, on that; but you say he is wicked *because* he has been wicked and I show *how* he has been wicked. Which of us, do you think, gets closest

940 to first principles? . . .

  [You say:] 'Man feels himself to be drawn down a fatal slope, and how would he stand firm against it, if he was not in his infancy directed by teachers, full of virtue, wisdom and vigilance, and if, during the whole course of his life, he did not himself, under the protection and with the grace of God, make continual and powerful efforts?' This is as much as to say, We see men wicked, although they are constantly tyrannized from their infancy; if therefore they are not tyrannized from that time, how would one succeed in making them wise, since even by this constant tyrannizing over them it is impossible to make

941 them so? . . .

  [You say:] 'Alas, my dear brethren, in spite of the principles of the soundest and most virtuous education, and in spite of the most magnificent promises of religion and the most terrible threats, the errors of youth are still only too frequent, only too widespread.' But I have proved that the education which you call the soundest is the most senseless, that the education which you call the most virtuous gives children all their vices. I have proved that all the glory of paradise tempts them less than a lump of sugar and that they are much more afraid of being bored at vespers than of burning in hell. I have proved that all the errors of youth, which you complain cannot be repressed by these means, are really the result of them. 'Into what errors and excesses would not youth rush, if abandoned to itself?' [you say]. Youth, my lord, never goes astray by itself; all its errors come from being badly led. Companions and mistresses complete what priests and teachers have begun: I have proved this. [When you say:] 'It is a torrent that pours out in spite of the most powerful dykes that can be raised against it; what would happen then if no obstacle checked its flood and broke its flow?' I could reply: 'It is a torrent which breaks down your feeble dykes and shatters everything. Enlarge its bed and let it flow without any obstacle and it will never do any harm' . . .   943

I lay down negative education as the best, or rather as the only one that is good. I prove that all positive education, however one sets about it, follows a route away from its own goal and I show how one moves towards the same goal and how one arrives there by the method that I have traced. I call that education positive which tends to form the mind prematurely and to give the child knowledge of the duties of a man. I call that education negative which tends to perfect the bodily organs, the instruments of our knowledge, before giving us that knowledge and which prepares us for reasoning by exercising our senses. Whatever else, however, negative education is not idle. It does not give virtue, but it prevents vice. It does not teach truth, but it prevents error. It disposes the child towards everything that can lead him to truth, when he is ready to hear it; and to good, when he is ready to love it . . .   945

The order of the universe — admirable as it is — does not move everyone equally. The [common] people pay little attention to it, as they lack the knowledge which makes that order visible and as they have not learned at all to reflect on what they see. It is neither perversity nor obstinacy; it is ignorance and dullness of the mind. The least study tires such people, just as the least manual labour tires the student. They have heard talk of the works of God and the wonders of nature. They repeat the same words, indeed, but without connecting the same ideas to them; and they are little affected by everything that can lift up the wise man to his Creator. Now if even among us the people, who are within reach of so much instruction, are still so stupid, what will be the case with those poor people who being left to themselves from their infancy have never learnt anything from others? . . . What shall we do with such people, the Eskimos, for example? Shall we make theologians of them? . . .   951–2

Neither the burning [of my books] nor the decrees [against me] will ever make me change my language. The theologians, in ordering me to be humble, will never make me be false and the philosophers, by taxing me with hypocrisy, will never make me profess unbelief. I will speak my religion because I have one; and I will speak it loudly, because I have the courage to speak it; and it were to be wished, for the good of mankind, that it were that of the whole human race.

My lord, I am a Christian, a sincere Christian, according to the doctrine of the Gospel. I am a Christian, not as a disciple of priests, but as a disciple of Jesus Christ. My Master laid little stress on the subtleties of dogma, but put great emphasis on duties. He prescribed fewer articles of faith than good works; he only ordered us to believe what was necessary in order to be good. When he summed up the law and the prophets, it was much more in acts of virtue than in articles of belief. And he has told me himself and through his apostles

960 that whosoever loves his brother has fulfilled the law . . .

As soon as I was able to observe mankind, I watched them do things and heard them say things. Then as I saw that what they did bore no resemblance to what they said, I tried to find out the reason for this difference. I discovered that, as being and appearing were for them two things as different as acting and speaking, this latter difference was the cause of the former and had itself a cause which

966 remained to be discovered.

I found that cause in our social order. It is in every respect contrary to nature, which nothing can destroy. It incessantly tyrannizes over her and forces her to claim her rights. I followed all the results of this contradiction and saw that it was alone sufficient to explain all the vices of men and all the evils of society. From this I concluded it was unnecessary to suppose men naturally wicked when I could thus trace the origins and progress of their wickedness. These reflections naturally led me to further researches into the human mind, considered in the civil state [as opposed to the state of nature]. I found that enlightenment and vice always developed at the same rate — not indeed in individuals, but in peoples: a distinction which I have always been careful to make, though none of my opponents has ever been able to grasp it.

I sought the truth in books; I only found lies and errors. I consulted the authors; I only found charlatans who made a game of deceiving people — with no law but their interest, with no god but their reputation . . .

By listening to those who were permitted to speak in public I found they were either afraid or unwilling to say anything disagreeable to those in authority and, being paid by the strong to preach to the weak, they could only speak to the latter of their duties and to the former of their rights. All public instruction will always tend to lies, so long as those who administer it find their interest in lying and they alone are exempt from speaking the truth. But why should I be an

967 accomplice to men like that?

Are there prejudices which ought to be respected? That may be
when everything else is so bound up [with them] that one cannot
remove these prejudices without also removing what compensates
for them. Then one leaves evil for love of the good. But when the state
of things is such that any change must be for the better, can there
be any prejudices so worthy of respect that we must sacrifice to them
reason, virtue, justice and all the benefits which the truth could give
to men? . . .   967

I have seen the same falseness in religion as in politics, and I have
been outraged by it, for the faults of government can only make its
subjects unhappy on earth; but who knows how harmful mistakes of
conscience can be to unhappy mortals? I have seen that people follow
faith, doctrine and worship without believing in them; and I have
seen that none of it reaches their heart or their reason and has
scarcely any influence on their conduct. I must be direct, my lord.
The true believer cannot accommodate himself to all these pretences.
He is aware that man is an intelligent being, who needs a reasonable
religion and that man is a sociable being, who needs a morality made
for humanity. First, let us find this religion and this morality which
will be applicable to all men. Then, when national forms are needed,
we will examine their foundations, relations and suitability, and after
having said what is [right] for man, we will then say what is [right]
for the citizen . . .   968–9

It appears certain, in my opinion, that if man is made for society,
the truest religion must be also the most social and humane; for God
wishes that we are as he made us; and if it was true that he had made
us wicked, it would be to disobey him to wish to cease to be so . . .   969

I neither say nor think that there is no good religion on earth;
but I do say, and it is too true, that there is no religion among those
which are or have been dominant which has not given the most
cruel wounds to humanity . . .   970

The less reasonable a religion, the more people try to establish it by
force. He who professes a senseless doctrine cannot bear that others
should dare to see it as it [really] is. Reason then becomes the greatest
of crimes. It must be removed at any price from others because of
the shame of being seen to be without it. Thus inconsistency and
intolerance have the same source. Men must be constantly intimidated
and terrified. If you leave them for one moment to their reason, you
are lost.

From this alone it follows that when people are in this madness it
is a great good to teach them to reason about religion. It brings them

back to their duty; it removes the dagger from intolerance and restores to humanity all its rights. But one must go back to principles that are general and common to all men; for if, when you want to reason, you leave any hold for the authority of priests, you give a weapon

970–1 back to fanaticism and provide it with what will make it more cruel...

Most new religions are established by fanaticism and maintained by hypocrisy; hence they offend reason and do not lead to virtue. Enthusiasm and frenzy never reason; so that while they last, anything is acceptable and there is little haggling about dogmas of faith. Besides, is not that convenient? Doctrines cost so little to follow and morality costs so much to practise that by taking the easiest path one can redeem good works by the merit of a great faith. But after all, fanaticism is a state of crisis which cannot last forever. It has its fits which are long or short, frequent or rare; and it also has its pauses when calm reappears. Then, returning to oneself, one is astonished to find oneself entangled in so many absurdities. But the religion is settled, the forms prescribed, the laws established and transgressors punished. Will anyone on his own protest against all that, challenge the laws of his country and deny the religion of his

972–3 father? Who would dare. One submits in silence ... [So most people behave] and that is the key to the inconsistency between their morality and their actions ...

As for opinions which have no bearing on morality, which have no influence in any way on one's actions and which do not tend at all towards breaking the laws, everyone has only his judgement for master on these matters, and no one has either the right or the

973 interest to prescribe to others how to think ...

Is it so essential for each religion to hate the others, so that if you

983 take away the hate, you take away everything? ...

[Surely] it is less important to men to hold on to the opinions which divide them than those which unite them ... [Why do we spend] our lives in disputing, wrangling, tormenting, persecuting, and fighting over the things we understand the least and which it is least

984 necessary [for us] to understand?

Doctrines which lead to crime and murder and which make fanatics are abominable. Ah! what can be more abominable in the world than to reduce violence and injustice to a system and make them proceed

985 from the mercy of God? ...

You treat me as impious. Of what impiety can you accuse me, I, who have never spoken of the Supreme Being but to give him the glory that is due to him, nor of my neighbour but to lead everyone to love him? The impious are those who unworthily profane the cause of God in making him serve the passions of men. The impious are those who daring to stand as interpreters of the Divinity, as arbiters between it and man, demand for themselves the honours which are owed to it. The impious are those who arrogate to themselves the right of exercising the power of God on earth and want to open and shut the gates of heaven at their pleasure . . .   1006

You who are set up in dignity can talk away at your ease. Acknowledging no other rights than your own, no other laws than those which you impose, far from making it your duty to be just, you do not even think yourselves obliged to be humane. You proudly crush the weak without accounting for your iniquities to anyone; [the cries of] outrage cost you no more than the [acts of] violence, and for the slightest expedience of interest or of state you sweep us before you like dust . . .   1006–7

You hold a rank where you can dispense with being just: and I am nothing. Yet you who profess the Gospel, you, Prelate, created to teach others their duty, you know yours . . . For my part, I have done mine. I have nothing further to say to you and I am silent.   1007

16 GENEVA

The citizenship that Rousseau renounced in May 1763 was not something that all the inhabitants of Geneva shared. The population was divided into four orders — citizens, bourgeois, inhabitants, and natives. The citizens and bourgeois had political rights and economic privileges denied to the inhabitants, who were foreigners who been allowed to settle in the city, and the natives, who were descendants of the inhabitants. Only adult males over the age of twenty-five, from families who were already citizens or bourgeois, could belong to the General Council. This amounted to about fifteen hundred men, out of a total population of between twenty and twenty-five thousand. Rousseau identified with the bourgeoisie, and accepted their exclusion of the inhabitants and the natives from political activity. This is one of his most obvious historical limitations.

At the same time, however, the bourgeoisie themselves had been effectively excluded from participation by the patrician élite among the citizens, and when he articulated their cause he provided some of the arguments that would eventually lead to the emancipation of the lower orders.

Rousseau's mistreatment by the oligarchic Small Council brought to the surface for the third time that century the conflicts between the patricians and the bourgeoisie. The previous conflict had been re-solved by the mediation of France, Berne and Zurich; the Act of Mediation in 1738 had established a new constitution which all parties had accepted. In effect, however, the Small Council, elected from members of a few families, continued to act as they wished.

The patricians lived in the upper town and were mostly occupied in banking and finance. They had close links with both French culture and the French authorities. They enjoyed Voltaire's enter-tainment and hospitality at Ferney, and they had supported the idea for a theatre to be built in the city. This was the project that Rousseau had opposed in his *Letter to D'Alembert* and it was this *Letter* that allied him publicly with the bourgeoisie.

The latter were mostly occupied in watch-making and jewellery. Their numbers and their wealth had increased during the century and their sense of grievance accordingly. When *The Social Contract* first appeared it was recognized by both parties as having special meaning for Geneva. The book, wrote one of Rousseau's supporters, is 'the arsenal of liberty'.[1] The Genevan government was the only government in Europe to ban the book on publication.

Neither this ban nor the prohibition on the reprinting of the *Letter to Christophe de Beaumont* aroused the bourgeoisie to action. But when Rousseau renounced his citizenship they acted. Forty of them made a representation to the Small Council protesting against the injustices and illegalities in the way he had been treated. The Small Council rejected their complaint. (The two parties were known as the *Représentants* and the *Négatifs*.) A second representation was made, this time by a hundred men; it was also unsuccessful. Opposition grew. The third representation was made by five hundred men, who demanded that the whole question should be discussed by the General Council. Yet again the Small Council rejected their protest. Then, in justification of this policy, the Procurator-General, Jean-Robert Tronchin, wrote a pamphlet called *Letters from the Country*. Posing as an impartial observer — the pamphlet appeared anonymously — he put forward arguments that were so clearly and forcefully expressed that the bourgeoisie were silenced.

Rousseau watched these activities from Môtiers, sixty miles away, and was kept informed by his friends. He was reluctant to intervene, but the *Letters from the Country* cried out for a reply. In December 1764 his answer appeared — the *Letters from the Mountain*.

The work is made up of nine letters. They are written with the same energy that was displayed in the *Letter to Christophe de Beaumont*, and the work forms another superb polemic against injustice. 'My *patrie* has not become so foreign to me,' he wrote in his Introduction, 'that I can watch with equanimity its citizens being oppressed, especially when they have risked their rights in defending my cause ... Religion, liberty, justice! Whoever you are, these subjects should not be beneath you.'[2]

The first five letters are written in defence of *Emile*. In the First Letter he attacked intolerance and 'Christians who are like St Paul, who was a natural persecutor and did not hear Jesus Christ himself'.[3] In the Second Letter he asserted that the Protestant faith, having arisen in opposition to established authority, was 'tolerant by principle, it is essentially tolerant, it is as tolerant as it is possible to be';[4] and he showed how the persecuted had then become persecutors themselves. Calvin was included in his criticism: 'Calvin was undoubtedly a great man but he was, in the end, [only] a man, and what is worse, a theologian. He had, besides, all the pride of a genius who feels his superiority and who is outraged that anyone disputes it with him.'[5] In contrast he cited the peaceful and loving ethic put forward by the Savoyard priest. In the Third Letter he attacked the weakness of any faith based on miracles, and once again expressed his admiration for Jesus, whose personality was in no way austere or harsh. In the Fourth and Fifth Letters he enumerated the illegalities in the condemnation of his books — 'the Council has as its model the judicial forms of the Inquisition' — and pointed out that 'condemning a book does not destroy its arguments'.[6]

In the Sixth Letter Rousseau defended *The Social Contract* and in the last three Letters he takes up the cause of the bourgeoisie and asserts their political rights. His arguments are based both on a close analysis of Genevan history and on the essential principles laid out in *The Social Contract*. There are qualifications to these, not only in the limitation of the suffrage, but also in the way that only the Small Council could initiate legislation in Geneva; and the accuracy of his analysis of the city's history is a matter of dispute. Moreover, his attitude to the bourgeoisie is equivocal. Sometimes he praises them as the one class who cares for freedom, giving them capacities and a rôle which had previously been given to the aristocracy and were later to be given to the proletariat. At other times he criticizes them for being narrow minded, selfish, and caring only for profit.

These qualifications, however, are less significant than Rousseau's central argument. In *The Social Contract* he had written of the abuse of government. He was obsessed with a terrible sense of political decay: 'the body politic, as much as the body of man, begins to die from the day of its birth and carries in it the causes of its own destruction'.[7] Once corruption sets in, a terminal process has begun. Now Geneva itself, the very city he had proclaimed as a model and uncorrupted state, was revealed as unjust and tyrannical. And he himself was the victim of that injustice. It is this sense of a prophecy fulfilled, combined with a deep personal bitterness, that gives these Letters their force and vitality.

Rousseau fights against the injustice he has suffered, and for the cause of the bourgeoisie. But he is also fighting for the ideal Geneva he had believed in, and for the hope that that ideal could be achieved.

Letters from the Mountain

SIXTH LETTER

I am not only accused, but judged and condemned, for having published two works which are 'rash, scandalous, impious and tending to destroy the Christian religion and all governments' . . . 804

Of the two books of mine that were burnt . . . there is only one which deals with political right and matters of government. If the other deals with them it is only in an extract from the first. So I suppose that the accusation is levelled only at the former. 806

[Rousseau therefore outlines *The Social Contract*, as quoted in Chapter 12; see page 175.]

What do you think, Sir, when you read this short and faithful analysis of my book? I can guess. You say to yourself: this is the history of the government of Geneva. The same has been said, when they read this work, by all those who know your constitution.

And in fact, this primitive contract, this essence of sovereignty, this rule of laws, this setting up of government, this way of restraining it in various degrees to counterbalance authority by force, this tendency to usurp, these regular assemblies, this haste to do away with them, and, finally, this approaching destruction which threatens you and which I wanted to prevent; is this not the very picture of your republic, from its birth up to now?

I have therefore taken your constitution, which I found beautiful, as a model of political institutions; and by putting it forward as an example to the rest of Europe, far from seeking your destruction I was indicating the means of preserving it . . . 809

If I had only made an [ideal] system, you can be quite sure that no one would have said a thing. *The Social Contract* would have been cheerfully consigned to the land of fantasies along with Plato's *Republic* and More's *Utopia* . . . But I portrayed something that exists; people wanted to change its face. My book bore witness against the outrage they were going to commit. That is what is unforgivable . . . 810

The result of unwise prohibitions is that they are not observed at all and they weaken the force of authority. My book is in everyone's hands in Geneva; would that it were equally in everyone's heart! Read, Sir, this book so attacked, but so necessary; throughout it you will see the law put above men; you will see liberty called for, but always under the authority of the laws, without which liberty cannot exist, and under which one is always free, however one is governed. It may be said that I do not pay due respect to the powers that be; so much the worse for them; for I know their true interests, if they could see them and follow them. But passions blind men to their own good. Those who subject the laws to human passions are the true destroyers of governments; these are the people who should be punished.

The foundations of the state are the same in all governments, and these foundations are better set out in my book than in any other. When it is a question of comparing the different forms of government, one cannot avoid weighing separately the advantages and inconveniences of each; this is what I believe I have done with impartiality. All in all I have given the preference to the government of my own country. That was natural and reasonable; I would have been criticized if I had not done so. But I have not excluded other governments; on the contrary, I have shown that each has its reason which can make it preferable to every other, depending on the people, the time and the place. Therefore, far from destroying all govern-
810–11 ments, I have established them.

SEVENTH LETTER

Nothing is more free than your legitimate state; nothing is more
813 servile than your actual state . . .

What has happened to you is what happens to all governments like yours. At first the legislative power and the executive power which constitute the sovereignty are not distinct from it. The sovereign people wills by itself, and by itself it does what it wills. Soon the inconvenience of everyone deciding on everything forces the sovereign people to charge a few of its members with the execution of its wishes. These officers, having fulfilled their commission, give an account of it and return to the common equality. Little by little these commissions become frequent, finally permanent. Imperceptibly, a body grows up which acts the whole time. A body which acts the whole time cannot give an account of every action; it only gives an account of the main ones; soon it ends up by giving an account of none. The more the power which acts is active, the more it enervates

the power which wills. The will of yesterday is presumed to be also
that of today; whereas the act of yesterday does not take care of the
need to act today. Finally, through its inactivity the power which
wills is submitted to the power which executes; the latter makes
[first] its actions more and more independent, soon its wishes;
instead of acting for the power which wills it acts for itself. There
then is left in the state only one acting power, it is the executive.
The executive power is only force, and where force alone reigns the
state is dissolved. That, Sir, is how all democratic states finally perish.   815

The General Council of Geneva is sovereign in its own right; it is the
living and fundamental law which gives life and force to all the rest,
and recognizes no other rights beyond its own. The General Council
is not an order in the state, it is the state itself . . .   824

When will men realize that there is no disorder as deadly as the
arbitrary power which they think can be its remedy? This power
is itself the worst of all disorders. To use such a means to prevent
disorders is to kill people to prevent them from getting the fever.   828

EIGHTH LETTER

The democratic constitution has up to now been poorly analysed.
All those who have spoken of it either did not know it, or took
too little interest in it, or were interested in presenting it in a false
light. None of them has sufficiently distinguished the sovereign from
the government, the legislative power from the executive. There is no
state where these two powers are so separate [as in democracy], and
where they have not been more frequently confused. Some imagine
that a democracy is a government in which the whole people is
magistrate and judge. Others, who only see liberty in the right of
electing their leaders and not being subject to princes, believe that he
who commands is always the sovereign. The democratic constitution
is certainly the masterpiece of political art; but the more admirable
its construction, the less accessible is it for everyone to understand.   837–8

People have wanted, unsuccessfully, to confuse independence and
liberty. These two things are so different as to be mutually exclusive.
When each does what he pleases, he often does what displeases others,
and one cannot call that a free state. Liberty consists less in doing your
will than in not being submitted to the will of another; it consists
further in not subjecting another's will to our own. Whoever is master
cannot be free and to reign is to obey. Your magistrates know that
better than anyone, they who do anything, however servile, in order to

command.* The only true free will I know of is that to which no one has the right to oppose resistance; in the common liberty no one has the right to do what the liberty of another forbids him, and true liberty is never self-destructive. Thus liberty without justice is a complete contradiction; for, however the matter is dealt with, every-

841   thing is disrupted in the execution of a disordered will.

There is thus no liberty without laws, nor where anyone is above the law; even in the state of nature man is only free through the favour of the natural law which commands us all. A free people obeys, but it does not serve; it has leaders but not masters; it obeys the laws but it only obeys the laws, and it is through the force of the laws that it does not obey men. All the obstacles that one gives in republics to the powers of magistrates are only set up to safeguard from their attacks the sacred compass of the laws; they are the ministers, not the arbiters of the laws, they must keep them, not violate them. A people is free, whatever form its government takes, when it sees in him who governs it not a man but the organ of the law. In a word, liberty always follows the fate of the laws, it reigns or perishes with them; I know nothing more certain. Your laws are good and wise, either in themselves, or simply from the fact that they are laws. Every condition imposed on each through all cannot be onerous to anyone, and the worst of laws is worth more than the best master; for every master has his favourites, and the law has none.

Since the constitution of your state has taken a fixed and stable

842–3   form, your functions as legislator are finished . . .

The work is complete, it is only a question of keeping it from changing. Now the work of the legislator is only ever altered and destroyed in one way: it is when the people to whom the constitution is entrusted abuse that trust, and make themselves obeyed in the name of the law while disobeying it themselves.† Then the worst

---

* There are few men with a heart sound enough to be able to love liberty. All want to command, at that price none is afraid to obey. A little upstart gives himself a hundred masters to acquire ten servants. You only have to look at the pride of nobles in monarchies; with what emphasis they pronounce these words of 'service' and 'to serve'; how great and admirable they consider themselves when they can have the honour to say 'the king my master'; how they scorn the republicans who are only free and who are certainly more noble than they are. (Note by Rousseau.)

† The people have only ever rebelled against the laws when the leaders have begun to violate them in some way. According to that reliable principle, when there is a rebellion in a province in China they always begin by punishing the governor. In Europe the kings constantly follow the opposite course, and see how their states prosper! (Note by Rousseau.)

thing is born from the best, and the law which serves as a safeguard
against tyranny is more deadly than tyranny itself. This is exactly
what the right of representation as stipulated in your edicts prevents...
This right gives you inspection . . . of the administration; and your
magistrates, all-powerful in the name of the laws, sole masters in
proposing new laws to the legislator, are subjected to its judgements
if they deviate from the laws that are established. By this single
article your government, otherwise marred by several considerable
faults, becomes the best that has ever existed; for what better
government [can there be] than one where all the parties are balanced
in perfect equilibrium, where individuals cannot break the laws
because they are subject to the judges, and no more can the
judges break them, because they are under the scrutiny of the
people? . . .   843–4

In a state such as yours, where the sovereignty is in the hands of
the people, the legislator exists the whole time, though not always
visibly. It only assembles and speaks authentically in the General
Council; but outside the General Council it is not abolished; its
members are scattered but they are not dead; they cannot speak
through laws but they can always watch over the administration of
the laws; it is a right, it is even a duty attached to their persons, and
it cannot be separated from them at any time. Hence the right of
representation.   845

[Rousseau points out the distinction between the initiation of
legislation and the conduct of existing legislation.]

These representations can concern two main subjects; the distinction
between these subjects decides in what different way the [Small]
Council must grant the right of these same representations. Of these
two subjects one is to make some change in the law, the other to
repair some breach of the law . . .

Once this distinction [between the two subjects] has been made,
the Council, to whom the representations are made, ought to consider
them very differently according to which of the two subjects they
belong. In states where the government and the laws are already
settled, one should as much as possible avoid touching them, above
all in small republics where the least disturbance pulls everything
apart. The aversion for novelty is then generally well founded; it is
particularly so for you, who can only lose by it, and the government
cannot bring to bear too great an obstacle to its establishment; for
however useful new laws may be, the advantages of them are almost
always less certain than the dangers are great. In this respect when

the citizen or the bourgeois has expressed his opinion he has done his duty. He should have enough confidence in his magistrate to judge him capable of weighing the advantage of what he has put forward to him and be disposed to approve it, if he thinks it useful to the public good. The law has therefore very wisely provided that the setting up and even the proposal of such novelties cannot happen without the consent of the [Small] Council, and it is in this that the negative right which they call for, and which in my opinion should un-

846–7 doubtedly belong to them, should consist.

But the second subject, having a quite contrary principle, should be seen quite differently. It is not a question here of innovation; it is, rather, a question of preventing innovation; it is a question not of setting up new laws but of maintaining old ones. When things tend to incline towards change fresh care is constantly necessary to stop them . . . The legislator, which is in existence the whole time, sees the effect or abuse of its laws; it sees if they are followed or broken, interpreted in good faith or bad; it watches over them; that is its right, its duty, even its pledge. It is this duty which it fulfils in the representations; it is this right, then, which it is exercising; and it would be against all reason, it would even be indecent, to wish to

847 extend the negative right of the [Small] Council to that subject . . .

[Rousseau now compares the right of representation to similar procedures in other countries, and locates its place in Genevan history; if it was not expresssly restated by the Act of Mediation in 1738, that was because it was already accepted by the mediators, based on an Edict of 1707 and on 'immemorial right'.]

There is no state in the world where a person injured by an unjust magistrate cannot by some means carry his complaint to the sovereign, and the fear which this resource inspires is a curb which prevents many iniquities. Even in France, where the *Parlements* are extremely eager to apply the laws, the judicial channels in many cases are open against them through requests for appeal against the judgement. The Genevans are deprived of such an advantage. A party condemned by the councils can no longer, whatever the case, have any recourse to the sovereign. But what an individual cannot do for his private interest, all can do for him in the common interest; for every breach of the laws, being an infringement of liberty, becomes a public affair, and when the public voice is raised the complaint must be brought to the sovereign. Without that there would not be a *Parlement* or senate or tribunal on earth which would not be armed with the deadly power which your magistrature dares to usurp. In no state would there be a fate as hard as yours. You must admit that that would be a strange liberty!

The right of representation is intimately bound to your constitution; it is the only possible means of uniting liberty and subordination, and of maintaining the magistrate dependent on the laws without affecting his authority over the people. If the complaints are clearly based, if the reasons are evident, one should presume the Council to be just enough to comply with them. If it was not, or if the complaints were not so obvious as to put them beyond any doubt, that would be a different matter, and it would then be for the general will to decide; for in your state this will is the supreme judge and only sovereign. Now as this will, from the beginning of the Republic, has always had the means of making itself heard, and these means were part of your constitution, it follows that the edict of 1707, founded as it was on an immemorial right and on the constant use of this right, did not need any further elaborate explanation. The mediators, having laid it down as a fundamental rule to deviate as little as possible from the former edicts, have left it as it was before . . . So by their ruling your right on this point has remained exactly the same . . .   849–50

[But the mediators had made other changes, including the suppression of assemblies, i.e. they had upheld the right but had omitted to provide for it. It was this defect which the magistrates had picked on:] They raise a thousand imaginary difficulties about the authority which can oblige them to assemble the General Council. There is no authority at all which can make that possible outside that of the laws, when they observe them; but the authority of the law which they break returns to the legislator; and [the magistrates], not daring to deny completely that in such a case this authority is in the greatest number, focus their objections on the means of ascertaining it. Such means will always be easy, as soon as they are allowed, and they will be no trouble, since it is easy to anticipate abuse.   851

There would be no question then of uproar or violence; there would be no question of those measures, sometimes necessary but always terrible, which you have very wisely been forbidden; not that you have ever abused them, since you have only ever employed them in the last resort, only for your defence, and always with a moderation which perhaps ought to have kept you the right of arms, if any people could have had it without danger. Yet I will bless heaven, whatever happens, that the terrifying apparatus [of arms] is no longer seen in your midst.

The author of the *Letters from the Country* says several times: 'Everything is permissible in extreme trouble.' Even were that true, 'everything' would not be expedient. When excess of tyranny puts him who suffers above the laws, what he attempts in order to destroy it must leave him some hope of success. Would you want to be reduced to this extremity? I cannot believe it, and [even] if you were I think it still less likely that any course of action could ever get you out of it. In your position every false step is fatal, everything which induces you to do it is a trap, and were you to be masters but for a moment, in less than a fortnight you would be crushed for ever. Whatever your magistrates may do, whatever the author of the *Letters* may say, violent means are never suitable for a just cause.

Without thinking that anyone wants to force you to such measures, yet I believe that they would see you take them with pleasure. I also believe that you should not be made to think of a measure that can only deprive you of all other remedies. Justice and the laws are on your side. These I know are but feeble supports against interest and intrigue; but they are all you have to trust to. Rely on them and persevere in your peaceful resolutions to the end.

Ah! How could I approve of anyone wanting to disturb the civil peace, for whatever interest; I who have sacrificed to it all that was dearest to me? . . . I have renounced everything, even hope, rather than threaten public tranquillity. I have earned the right to be thought sincere, when I speak in its favour. But why suppress peaceful and purely civil assemblies, which could only have one legitimate subject, since they would remain always under the due subordination of the magistrate? . . .

851–2

[Rousseau suggests that the article preventing assemblies should be repealed: 'However you take them, contradictory rules can never be observed at the same time' (853). Or, another remedy would be:] . . . to re-establish the periodical General Councils, and to limit them to complaints brought to their notice during the interval that has elapsed from one [assembly] to another, without their being allowed to bring any other matter before it. These assemblies, by a very important distinction,* should not have the authority of the sovereign but that of the supreme magistrate. So far from being able to innovate, they can only prevent any innovation on the part of the Councils, and restore everything related to the legislation which the body entrusted with the public force [i.e. the government] can at the

* See *The Social Contract*, Bk III, Ch. 17. (Note by Rousseau.)

moment discard without hindrance as much as it pleases. So that to put an end to these assemblies the magistrates will have nothing to do but to follow the laws exactly. For the convocation of a General Assembly will be useless and ridiculous when there is nothing to be brought before it; and that was very probably the case when the general periodical councils were dissolved in the sixteenth century . . . It was for this purpose . . . that they were re-established in 1707 . . .   854–5

[But they had then been suspended again in 1712. Rousseau continues to make the case for them: 'In the most stormy times frequent General Councils have been the salvation of the Republic' (856). He continues:]

Read the records of your town during the sixteenth century. How did it save itself from the twofold yoke which was crushing it? How did it stifle the factions which were tearing it apart? How did it resist the greedy neighbours who were only helping it in order to enslave it? How did it establish in its heart evangelical and political freedom? How did its constitution achieve coherence? How did its system of government grow up? The history of these memorable times is a sequence of prodigious achievements. Tyrants, neighbours, friends, subjects, citizens, war, plague, famine, all conspired to ruin our unfortunate town. It is hardly possible to see how a state already formed could have escaped all these dangers. Not only did Geneva escape them, but it was during these terrible crises that the great work of its legislation was brought to completion. It was through frequent General Councils; it was through the prudence and firmness which its citizens brought to them, that they finally overcame the obstacles and made their town free and peaceful . . .   859–60

Injustice and fraud often find protectors; they never find them among the public; in this respect the voice of the people is the voice of God. But unfortunately this sacred voice is always weak in human affairs beside the clamour of power; the complaint of oppressed innocence is breathed out in groans which tyranny treats with scorn.   862

NINTH LETTER

The people of the ancient world are no longer a model for modern people. They are too different in all respects. You Genevans above all, keep your place, and do not go after elevated goals which are presented to you to hide from you the abyss that is being dug in front of you. You are neither Romans or Spartans; you are not even Athenians. Leave these great names which are not for you. You are merchants, artisans, bourgeoisie, always concerned with their private interests, their work, their trade, their profit; people for whom even liberty is only a means of acquiring without obstacle and possessing in security.

This situation requires special advice for you. Not having the leisure that the people in the ancient world had you cannot continually occupy yourselves like them with government; but inasmuch as you are less able to keep watch all the time, it should be arranged in such a way that it is more convenient for you to see its goings-on and attend to abuses. Every public office which your interest demands [that you undertake] ought to be made so much the easier to fulfil as it is at your expense and you do not undertake it willingly. To want to be rid of it, is to want to cease to be free. You must choose . . . and those who cannot bear the burden will only find rest in servitude.

I know that there is a need to restrain a restless, idle, turbulent people, who, having no concerns of their own, are always ready to get mixed up in those of the state. But . . . is the bourgeoisie of Geneva a people like that? No one could be less like it; they are the exact opposite. Your citizens, always absorbed in their domestic affairs, and always cold to anything else, only think about the public interest when their own interest is attacked. Not being sufficiently concerned to investigate the conduct of their leaders, they only see the chains that are being prepared for them when they feel the weight of them. Always distracted, always deceived, always preoccupied with other things, they allow themselves to be misled on the most important things, and are always going about looking for the remedy through having failed to foresee the evil.

881

[Rousseau then contrasts the situation of the *Représentants* with that of the *Négatifs*, see p. 242.]

Let us for a moment compare the two parties to judge which of their activities is most to be feared and where the negative right should be placed to moderate that activity.

One one side I see a people who are not very numerous, peaceful and cold, composed of hard-working men, lovers of gain, seeing it to be in their interest to obey the laws and the ministers. They are completely occupied with their trade or their crafts. Being all equal in their rights, and more or less similar in their wealth, they do not have among them either leaders or followers. Tied by their commerce, their condition and their goods to an utter dependence on the magistrate they are all obliged to humour him. They are all afraid to displease him. If they want to become involved with public matters

it is always to the prejudice of their own. On one side they are diverted
by things of more consequence to their family; on the other side they
are halted by considerations of prudence, by all past experience
which teaches them that in a state as small as yours, where every
individual is continually under the eyes of the Council, it is dangerous
to offend it. So they are led by the strongest reasons to sacrifice
everything to peace; for only that way are they able to prosper.
And in this state of things everyone, misled by his private interest,
greatly prefers to be protected than to be free, and pays his due respect
in order to make his living.   888

On the other side I see a small town, whose affairs at bottom do
not amount to much, an independent and perpetual body of magistrates, with virtually nothing to do, making into their main occupation an interest of great consequence which is very natural to those
who command; that is, constantly to increase their empire. For
ambition like avarice is fed by its gains, and the more your power
grows the more you are consumed by the desire for complete power.
Vigilant at all times to indicate scarcely visible distinctions among
their equals by birth, they see in them only their inferiors, and burn
to see them their subjects. Armed with the whole of the public
force, entrusted with all authority, interpreters and dispensers of the
laws which restrain them, they are provided with a weapon that is
both offensive and defensive; a weapon which makes them powerful,
respectable, and sacred to all those whom they wish to attack. It is
in the very name of the law that they can break it with impunity.
They can attack the constitution while pretending to defend it; they
can punish as a rebel whoever dares in fact to defend it. All the
schemes they have become easy for them; they do not allow anyone
to stop them or to know about them. They can act, defer, suspend;
they can seduce, frighten, punish those who resist them, and if they
condescend to find pretexts for that, it is more for the sake of appearance than from necessity. So they have the will to extend their power,
and the means to achieve all that they want.

Such is the relative position between the bourgeoisie and the
Small Council of Geneva. Which of these two bodies ought to have
the negative power to stop the schemes of the other? The author of
the *Letters* asserts that it is the latter. In the majority of states internal   889
troubles come from a brutalized and ignorant populace, first driven
on by unbearable grievances, then secretly whipped up by skilful
troublemakers, who are dressed up with some authority which they
want to extend. But is anything more false than to apply such an

idea to the bourgeoisie of Geneva, at least to that section who stand up to power to maintain the laws? At all times this party has always been the middle order between the rich and the poor, between the leaders and the people. This order, composed of men more or less equal in wealth, position and intelligence, is neither too elevated to have pretensions, or too low as to have nothing to lose. Their great interest, their common interest, is that the laws are observed and the magistrates respected, that the constitution is upheld and the state is peaceful. In this order nobody enjoys in any respect such a superiority over the others that he can set them to work for his private interest. It is the soundest party in the Republic. It is the only one which you can be assured is not able in its behaviour to have any other purpose in view than the good of all. And you see always in their common dealings the decency, modesty, respectful firmness, and reliable seriousness of men who feel that they are in the right and are sticking to their duty.

See, on the other hand, what the other party consists of: folk who are swimming in opulence, and the most abject populace. Is it in these two extremes, one made to buy, the other to sell itself, that one must look for love of justice and laws? It is always through them that the state degenerates; the rich keep the law in their pocket and the poor prefer bread to liberty. It is enough to compare these two parties to judge which of them must first infringe the laws. Look indeed at your history: have not all the plots always come from the side of the magistrature, and have the citizens ever had recourse to 890 force except when they needed it as a safeguard?

[Rousseau then tackles the problem that the right of representation might be abused.]

To suppose that all the abuses are in the party one attacks and there are none in one's own is a very common and coarse fallacy, which every intelligent man should avoid. Abuses must be expected on all sides, because they creep in everywhere; but that is not to say that they are equal in their effects. Every abuse is an evil, often inevitable, and for which it would not be always proper to administer a remedy. But compare them, and you will find on one side certain and terrible wrongs, without limit or end; and on the other side, an abuse which is itself difficult to perpetrate, which if great will be temporary, and which, when it does occur, always carries its own solution. For, once again, there is no possible liberty except in the observance of the laws or the general will, and it is no more in the general will to harm everyone than it is in the individual will to harm oneself.

But let us suppose that the abuse of liberty is as natural as the abuse of power. There will [still] always be this difference between them, that the abuse of liberty rebounds on the people who abuse it, and, punishing them with their own wrong, forces them to look for a remedy. So in this case the evil can only be a crisis, it cannot be a permanent state.

Whereas the abuse of power never rebounds on the powerful but on the weak, and is by its nature without measure, without check, without limits; it only ends with the destruction of him who alone experiences its evil effect. Let us admit therefore that the government concerns a small number, while the inspection of the government concerns everyone, and if abuse is inevitable on one side or the other, it is much better that a people should be miserable through their own fault than oppressed by the hand of another.   890–1

The first and greatest public interest is always justice. All want conditions to be equal for all, and justice is no more than this equality. The citizen only wants laws and the observation of the laws. Each individual among the people knows well that if there are exceptions they will not be in his favour. Thus all fear exceptions, and he who fears exceptions loves the law. Among leaders it is completely different; their very position is one of preference, and they look for preferences everywhere.* If they want laws, it is not to obey them, it is to be the arbiters of them. They want laws to raise themselves up and make their names fearful. Everything looks favourably on this project. They use rights that they have, to take over without risk those that they do not have. As they always speak in the name of the law, even while violating it, whoever dares to defend it against them is seditious and a rebel; he must perish. They are always certain of impunity in their schemes; the worst that can happen to them is not to succeed. If they need support they find it everywhere. It is a natural league, in that it is a league of the strong, and what makes the weakness of the weak is not being able to form such a league . . .   891–2

Equity, virtue, even interest amount to nothing before the love of domination, and he who will be just when he is master will spare no injustice to become one.

The true road to tyranny is not in attacking directly the public

---

* Justice among the people is a virtue of their condition; similarly, violence and tyranny among leaders is a vice of their condition. If we were in their position we would become like them violent, presumptuous and wicked. (Note by Rousseau.)

good; that would be to awaken the whole world to defend it. It is rather in attacking successively all its defenders, and in frightening anyone who would still dare to aspire to defend it. Persuade everyone that the public interest belongs to no one and by that means alone servitude is established. For when everyone is under the yoke where will the common liberty be? If anyone who dares to speak is crushed at that very instant, where will be those who will want to imitate him, and what will be the voice of the whole when each individual stays

893   silent? . . .

How will it be, [if the Small Council] become sole and absolute master [by denying the right of representation]? If they are no longer held back by anything in their conduct, and find no further obstacle to their passions? In such a small state, where no one can hide himself in the crowd, who will not then live in perpetual fear, and will not feel at each moment of his life the misery of having his equals as master? In large states individuals are too far from the prince and the leaders to be seen by them, their littleness saves them; provided the people pay, they are left in peace. But you will not be able to walk a step without feeling the weight of your chains. The relatives, friends, dependants, and spies of your masters will be more your masters than they are; you will neither dare to defend your rights nor reclaim your goods, for fear of making enemies. The darkest corners will not be able to hide you from the tyranny, you will inevitably have to be satellite or victim. You will feel at one and the same time political

894   and civil slavery, you will scarcely dare to breathe in freedom.

This state being the worst in which it is possible to fall has only one advantage; it is that it can only be changed for the better. This is the only resort in extreme troubles; but it is always a great resort if men of sense and heart feel it and are able to take advantage of it. How the certainty of not being able to fall any lower should make you resolute in your proceedings! But be sure, you cannot get out of the abyss while you are divided, while some want to act and others

895   to remain idle . . .

More than anything else, you must all become united. You are lost without resort if you stay divided. And why should you be like that, when such great common interests unite you? In a danger like this how do base jealousy and petty passions dare to make themselves heard? Are they worth so much that they must be indulged at so high a price, and must your children say one day, weeping in their chains: this is the outcome of the quarrels of our fathers? In a word, it is less a matter of discussion here than of agree-

258

The Indispensable Rousseau

ment. The choice of the party which you take is not the greatest matter. If it were bad in itself, take it unanimously; by that means alone it will become the best, and you will always do what needs to be done, provided that you do it in concert. This is my opinion, Sir, and I finish where I began. In obeying you I have fulfilled my last duty to my *patrie*. Now I take leave of those who live there; they can do me no more wrong, and I can do them no more good.   897

The publication of the *Letters from the Mountain* caused a furore in Geneva. (It was later burnt in both Paris and The Hague.) Voltaire's doctor, Theodore Tronchin, cousin of the Procurator-General who had written the *Letters from the Country*, described Rousseau as 'a devil more diabolical than the demons'.[8] Voltaire's reaction was the malicious *Sentiment of the Citizens*.

The bourgeoisie burnt this pamphlet. They were confident that their cause would prevail and that the Small Council would give way. But they did not sustain their momentum through the prevarications that followed and the elections that took place. The victory which seemed within their grasp was denied them. In February 1765 the Small Council made a final ruling against Rousseau.

At this point Rousseau withdrew from the conflict. 'I consider your situation decided', he wrote to Deluc, one of the leaders of the bourgeoisie. 'You are too good as people to push things to extremes and not to prefer peace to liberty . . . I do not wish to hear any more talk of Geneva.'[9]

That Rousseau should let the matter drop in this way was partly a result of his character. 'I have a bold nature, but a timid character', he told Bernardin de St-Pierre. [10] In his *Confessions* he wrote of 'the inaptitude and aversion that I have always had for the active life . . . I was not made to speak or act or deal with affairs among men, but to meditate at ease in solitude. In giving me one talent nature denied me the other.'[11]

But his withdrawal was also a matter of principle. Rousseau refused to countenance the use of force or violence. He had made this clear to his fellow-citizens. He made it more emphatically in a letter the following year.

He was asked his opinion about a young man who suppressed every feeling for the sake of liberating his country. Rousseau replied:

> Your young man is not of this century; he is a prodigy or a monster . . . It is very noble that he is occupied with the sublime

task of delivering his *patrie*, and I would like to think it useful.
But why does he not allow himself any feeling that is foreign to
this duty? Don't all the virtuous feelings support one another?
And can you destroy one without weakening them all?... There
may be sad situations and cruel duties in our lives which sometimes force us to sacrifice one duty to the others ... But is there,
can there ever be, duties which force us to overcome such
legitimate feelings as those of filial, conjugal and paternal
love? And how does any man who makes a specific rule of no
longer being a son, husband or father, dare to usurp the name
of citizen? How does he dare to usurp the name of man?

Reading your letter, Madame, one would say that it was a
question of a conspiracy. Conspiracies can be heroic acts of
patriotism, and there are some that are so ... Let us suppose
that this great enterprise is a sacred duty which should prevail
over all other duties. Must it for that reason abolish them? Are
these different duties so incompatible in this respect that you
cannot serve your *patrie* without renouncing your humanity?...
To renounce for ever — knowingly, willingly, deliberately, cheerfully, and inhumanely — all that should be dear to us ... is
something that no imaginable situation can authorize, or even
suggest, to a man in his right mind who is not a monster ...[12]

17 NATURE

Everything in Rousseau relates to nature.* 'All false religion is opposed to nature',[2] he had written in *The New Heloïse*, and the belief he set out in the *Profession of Faith* was based on the spectacle of nature and our inner nature. The whole of *Emile*, in which the *Profession* occurs, is concerned with developing our personality in harmony with nature. One of his unwritten projects was a work he called *The Sensitive Morality, or The Wise Man's Materialism*. It was intended to show how 'climates, seasons, sounds, colours, darkness, light, the elements, food, noise, silence, movement and rest, all act on our machine and therefore on our soul'.[3] By discovering how we are affected by the world around us he hoped to show how we could relate to it more beneficially. In the passage in *The New Heloïse* on Saint-Preux's visit to the High Valais (see p. 137) he gave an example of this.

To stay in the country was a source of endless pleasure to him. He loved walking.

> I can hardly think at all when I stay in one place; my body needs to be active to make my mind active. The sight of the country-side, the succession of pleasant views, the open air, the healthy appetite and the good health which I get from walking, the freedom of an inn, the distance from everything which makes me feel my dependence, from everything that reminds me of

---

* For Rousseau, as for us, *nature* could mean several things — the physical environment, the living force in the world and in a person, what is original or inherent or spontaneous, what is manifest and what is potential. As one Rousseau scholar has written: 'He plays with the word nature without precision, he delights in her wealth and never agreed to be bound by one definition.'[1] This chapter is concerned with nature in the sense of the natural world around us.

my situation, all of that releases my soul, makes me think more boldly, and throws me somehow into the immensity of beings, to combine them, choose them, take hold of them as I will, without trouble or fear. I grandly dispose of the whole of nature. My heart moves from object to object. It unites itself and identifies with those that please it, becoming surrounded with lovely images, becoming intoxicated with wonderful feelings.[4]

In one of his *Letters to Malesherbes* he gave a vivid account of the way he experienced nature in his youth and middle age.

Third Letter to Malesherbes, 26 January 1762

[I liked] to look for some wild spot in the forest [of Montmorency], somewhere deserted where nothing showed the hand of men or spoke of servitude or domination, some sanctuary which I could think I was the first person to reach, where no annoying third person would come between nature and myself. There nature seemed to unfold before my eyes an ever-new magnificence. The gold of the broom and the purple of the heather struck my eyes with a richness that moved my heart. Majestic trees covered me with their shade, delicate shrubs surrounded me; the astonishing variety of herbs and flowers which I trod underfoot kept my mind continually alternating between observation and admiration. The co-existence of so many interesting objects — clamouring for my attention, constantly attracting me one from another — promoted my dreamy and lazy mood, and often made me repeat to myself: 'No, Solomon in all his glory was not arrayed like one of these' . . .

1139–40

[He is led to imagine 'a golden age', but then feels 'the nothingness of [his] fantasies' and 'an inexplicable void which nothing could fill; a certain pain in the heart for another kind of joy which I had no idea of, and yet for which I felt the need'.]

Soon I lifted up my ideas from the surface of the earth to all the beings of nature, to the universal system of things, to the incomprehensible Being who encompasses all. My mind was then lost in that immensity; I did not think, I did not reason, I did not philosophize. With a sort of pleasure I felt overwhelmed by the weight of the universe; with delight I gave myself up to the confusion of these great ideas; in imagination I loved to lose myself in space. My heart felt confined by the limits of beings, it was too narrow. I stifled in the universe, I would have liked to soar out into the infinite. If I had unveiled all the mysteries of nature I think I would have felt myself to be in a situation less delicious than that nervous, dizzy ecstasy to which my mind surrendered without reserve, and which sometimes made me cry out in passionate excitement: 'Oh Great Being! Oh Great Being!' without being able to say or think anything more.   1141

These extracts describe two different kinds of experience; a general enjoyment of the natural world of trees, plants and flowers, and a sort of mystical euphoria. They were distinct and separate moods. Rousseau was not satisfied just to enjoy the natural world, he was led on to imagine an ideal land of 'people according to my own heart . . . a beautiful society . . . a golden age',[5] with which he was then disillusioned. The main reason he was not satisfied with the first experience was that it was so vague and generalized. It had no focus.

When he was living at Môtiers Rousseau found a focus for his love of nature. He became passionately interested in botany: 'I know of no study in the world better suited to my natural tastes than that of plants.'[6] It was exactly the occupation to fill 'the emptiness of my leisure, leaving no room for the boredom of complete inactivity or the restlessness of the imagination'.[7] His attention to nature became specific and precise.

> However elegant, admirable and diverse the structure of plants may be, it is not striking enough to hold the interest of the ignorant eye. The constant similarity, and at the same time extraordinary variety, which plants possess, only affects those who have some knowledge of them. [Those who do not have this knowledge] have only a stupid and monotonous admiration, when they look on these treasures of nature. They see nothing in detail, they do not even know what they ought to look at. Nor are they aware of the whole, because they have no idea of the relations and combinations which overwhelm with their marvels the mind of the observer.[8]

This passage, like the description of the pleasures of walking quoted above, comes from the *Confessions*, written between 1765 and 1770; and he says there that he would have come to botany earlier if it had not been associated with pharmacy.[9] In his last work, the *Reveries*, he attacked the 'habit of seeking in plants nothing but drugs and remedies',[10] and 'these tendencies of the mind that always relate everything to our material interest, that look for remedies or profit everywhere, and that would make us look on the whole of nature with indifference as long as we are in good health'.[11]

He compared the plant kingdom with the mineral kingdom and the animal kingdom. The first filled him with thoughts of 'quarries, pits, forges, furnaces, an apparatus of anvils, hammers, smoke and fire . . . [and] the emaciated faces of the unhappy people who waste away in the poisonous air of mines'.[12] The second made him think of caging animals, of anatomy and dissection. Only in the plant kingdom did he find satisfaction. 'Attracted by the lovely objects which surround me, I consider them, contemplate them, compare them and finally learn to classify them, and suddenly here I am as much a botanist as anyone needs to be who only wants to study nature constantly to find new reasons for loving her.'[13]

He not only observed and studied plants, he also made herbaria, wrote eight *Letters on Botany*, which were later collected, and compiled a *Dictionary of Botanical Terms*. 'By fixing my attention on the objects which surrounded me' the subject had made him 'become aware of the detail in the spectacle of nature for the first time'.[14] He was no longer led on to imaginative fantasies, or the sense of emptiness or yearning that they produced.

His experience of nature became one of association, participation, identification. And this experience now incorporated something of that expansion of the soul, that mystical euphoria that had previously been accompanied by a sense of anguish and longing. Instead of being overwhelmed by the weight of the universe, he was now overwhelmed by the marvels of the natural world. What had previously been two incomplete experiences now became one complete and satisfying experience.

He realized this most fully in the six weeks he spent on the island of Saint-Pierre, where he took refuge with Thérèse in September 1765 after fleeing from Môtiers. In his *Confessions* he described how 'the different soils that were found on the island, small though it was, offered enough variety of plants for my study and amusement all the rest of my life'. In addition,

> I have always loved water passionately and the sight of it throws me into delicious reverie, often about nothing in particular. On getting up when the weather was fine I never failed to run out on to the terrace to breathe in the fresh, healthy morning air,

and to gaze on the horizon of that beautiful lake; the shores and mountains which bordered it delighted my eyes. I cannot think of a more worthy homage to the divinity than this silent admiration of his works . . .[15]

He liked to spend his days botanizing, or helping in the garden, or drifting in a boat on the lake.

Often leaving my boat to the direction of the wind or the water, I gave myself up to reveries that had no aim but which, stupid though they were, were no less sweet for that. Sometimes, deeply affected, I cried out: 'Oh Nature! Oh my mother! Here I am under your sole protection. Here there is no cunning or mischievous man who can come between you and me.' So I would drift up to half a league from the land. I would have liked that lake to have been the ocean.[16]

He wrote at greater length about his stay on the island in his last work, the *Reveries*.

The Reveries of the Solitary Walker (Fifth Walk)

Of all the homes I have lived in . . . none has made me so truly happy and left me such tender regrets as the island of Saint-Pierre in the middle of the Lake of Bienne . . .

The banks of the Lake of Bienne are wilder and more romantic than those of the Lake of Geneva, because the rocks and woods skirt the water more closely; but they are no less attractive. There is less cultivation of fields and vines, fewer towns and houses, but there are more meadows, more hidden corners shaded by trees, more contrasts and undulations . . . The country is rarely visited by travellers, but it appeals to those solitary contemplatives who love to drink in peacefully the charms of nature and give themselves up to meditation in a silence undisturbed by any sound, except the cry of eagles, the chirping of birds, and the flow of the waterfalls which come off the mountain . . . For all its smallness the island is so varied in its soil and its surface that it provides all kinds of site and allows all kinds of growth. There you find fields, vines, woods, orchards, and rich pastures bordered by all sorts of tree and shrub, kept fresh by the nearby water . . .

1040–1

I undertook to make the *Flora petrinsularis* and describe all the plants of the island, every one, in such detail that it would keep me busy for the rest of my life. They say that a German has written a

book about lemon-peel. I would have done one on each grain of the
fields, each moss of the woods, each lichen that covers the rocks. I
did not want to leave a blade of grass, not an atom of plant, that was
not fully described. In pursuit of this beautiful project I set out each
morning after breakfast, which we all took together. With a magnify-
ing glass in my hand and my *Systema naturae** under my arm I
visited a section of the island . . . Nothing is more remarkable than
the delights and ecstasies I experienced with each study I made of
the structure of plants, and of the play of the sexual parts in bringing
forth fruit . . . The forking of the two long stamens of the Prunella,
the springing of those of the Nettle and the Wallflower, the bursting
of the fruit of the Garden-Balsam and of the capsule of the Box-tree,
a thousand little tricks of fructification which I observed for the
first time and filled me with joy . . .

1043   [In the afternoon] when the water was calm I would row to the
middle of the lake. Stretching myself out full length in the boat and
looking up into the sky, I let myself float and drift slowly with the
flow of the water, immersed in a thousand confused but delicious
reveries . . .

When the lake was too rough for me to go on it I spent the afternoon going over the island, botanizing to the right and left; sometimes
I settled myself in the most attractive and remote corner to dream at
my leisure; sometimes from a terrace or a hillock I gazed out over
the superb and magnificent sight of the lake and its banks, on one
side crowned by nearby mountains, on the other side enlarged by
rich and fertile plains over which the view extended to the distant
blue mountains on the skyline.

When the evening approached I went down from the top of the
island and happily sat on the shore beside the lake, in some hidden
spot. There the sound of the waves and the agitation of the water
captivated my senses; they drove every other agitation from my
soul and plunged it into a delicious reverie; the night often
surprised me without my having noticed it. The ebb and flow of the
water, with its continuous sound, rising and falling, constantly struck
my ears and my eyes; they made up for the internal movements which
the reverie had extinguished inside me; they were enough to make
me feel my existence with pleasure, without taking the trouble to
think. Sometimes some weak and brief reflection was born on the
instability of earthly things, the image of which was on the surface

---

* By Linnaeus.

of the water. But soon these light impressions were erased in the uniformity of continuous movement which lulled me and held me, without any active help from my soul, to such an extent that, when called by the hour and the signal agreed upon, I could not tear myself away from there without effort.

After fifteen years it is impossible for me to think of this beloved place without feeling carried away by impulses of desire . . .   1044–5

The continuation of this passage, in which Rousseau reflects on his experience, is given in Chapter 22 (see p. 307).

18 CORSICA

'There is still one country in Europe suitable for legislation', wrote Rousseau in *The Social Contract*, 'it is the island of Corsica. The courage and tenacity with which these brave people have been able to recover and defend their liberty certainly deserves [the attention of] some wise man who would teach them to preserve that freedom. I have a presentiment that one day this little island will astonish Europe.'[1]

Since the middle ages Corsica had been under the rule of Genoa. In 1729 and then again in 1755 the Corsicans had risen up against their masters: the second rising, under the charismatic Pasquale Paoli, was successful. The island recovered its independence and won the admiration of the rest of Europe.

Rousseau's remarks in *The Social Contract* came to the attention of a Corsican, M. Buttafuoco, who wrote to him in August 1764 asking him to draw up a constitution for the island. Rousseau agreed to do that and worked on the project during his last year at Môtiers. He asked Buttafuoco for extensive details about the geography, natural history, economy, population and culture, and at one stage he even toyed with the idea of visiting the island to see it for himself. He estimated that at least half of the period he thought necessary for the work would have to be spent in this examination and research. For his suggestions to have value they had to relate closely to the people for whom they were intended.

He did not finish his work, but the proposals he drew up are no less interesting for being incomplete. He paid particular attention to the economy: it is his main preoccupation. His suggestion that the island should remain basically agricultural has often been criticized, since he denies the islanders the benefits that commerce and industry would bring. But to Rousseau these 'benefits' were not at all beneficial.

He had read the economic arguments for commerce and seen its effects. Commerce and luxury went together and the results of both were disastrous. They promoted self-interest in the individual and inequality in the society. 'Commerce produces wealth: but agriculture assures freedom.'[2] He writes of the corruption that money brings and attacks 'the mad pride of the bourgeoisie . . . given up to a lifetime of luxury, and the passions it excites . . . they sell themselves to satisfy it'.[3] Rousseau's preference for an agricultural economy was therefore quite consistent with his earlier criticisms of his own society. Moreover, it was a preference that Pasquale Paoli himself shared.

As for industry, Rousseau did not oppose it. The mineral resources of the island should be used, but they must not 'be exploited indifferently'.[4] Industries must be carefully sited, away from good agricultural land and away from any centres of population: only that will keep them in balance with agriculture and prevent the imbalance that otherwise arises, to the harm of the latter. Rousseau's model is Switzerland, where agriculture and small-scale manufacture were satisfactorily mixed.

The short section on industry in this work is very significant, for it indicates that Rousseau was well aware of industry's potential as a source of wealth. He nevertheless considered that unless developed with great care that potential would be more disruptive than productive. Extra wealth would not solve the problems that the young Corsican nation faced. On the contrary, the solutions to social problems lay in the people themselves, in what they were and could be. New economic possibilities would not necessarily alter, and could easily damage, the essential human resources.

Not that he wanted to keep the island poor. A constant theme in Rousseau's writing is that no one can be free where poverty exists — 'The poor prefer bread to liberty' (see pp. 158, 167 and 255). But he makes an equally constant distinction between prosperity and wealth. The latter set everyone against one another and, by arousing a multitude of unnecessary needs, satisfied no one. Wealth, in other words, could also destroy freedom. The best economy must therefore keep a balance, a just mean — 'Everyone should make a living and no one should grow rich; that is the fundamental principle of the prosperity of the nation.'[5]

Among the other interesting aspects of the *Project* are the remarks on property, and the idea of the state being established by an oath: 'the first act in the establishment of the projected system should be a solemn oath sworn by all Corsicans, twenty years of age or older: and all those who swear it should without distinction be enrolled as citizens.'[6]

In one of the fragments attached to the work Rousseau gave further details of this actual social contract.

I. The whole Corsican nation will be united by a solemn oath in a single political body, of which as many of the bodies which should constitute it as the individuals [themselves] will henceforth be members.

II. This act of union will be celebrated the same day in the whole island and all the Corsicans will take part, as many as possible, each in his town, village, or parish according to how it will be decided.

III. Formula of the oath taken in the open air and with a hand on the Bible: In the name of the all-powerful God and the holy Gospels, by a sacred and irrevocable oath, I unite myself, body, goods, will and all my power, to the Corsican nation, to belong to it in all property, I and all who depend on me. I swear to live and die for it, to observe all the laws and obey its legitimate leaders and magistrates in all that conforms to the laws. So God help me in this life, and have mercy on my soul. Long live liberty, justice and the Republic of the Corsicans. Amen. And all holding up their right hand will reply, Amen.[7]

In Geneva, Rousseau had been bitterly disillusioned. With Corsica he saw new ground for hope.

Constitutional Project for Corsica

The first thing [the Corsican nation] has to do is to give itself, by its own efforts, all the stability of which it is capable. No one who depends on others, and lacks resources of his own, can ever be free. Alliances, treaties, and trust in men may bind the weak to the strong, but never the strong to the weak. Leave negotiations, then, to the 903 powers, and depend on yourselves alone . . .

The island of Corsica, not being able to grow rich in money, should try to grow rich in men. The power derived from the population is more real than that derived from finance, and is more certain in its effects. Since the use of manpower cannot be concealed from view, it always reaches its public objective. It is not so with the use of money, which flows off and is lost in private destinations; it is collected for one purpose and spent for another; the people pay to be protected, and their payments are used to oppress them.* That is why a state rich in money is always weak, and a state rich in men is always strong . . .

[Rousseau therefore favours an agricultural economy] one which will lead a people to spread out over the whole extent of its territory [and] make it love country life and labour, finding in them so much of the necessities and pleasures of life that it will have no desire to leave them . . .   904

The administration most favourable to agriculture is the one where power, not being entirely concentrated at any one point, does not carry with it an unequal distribution of population but leaves people dispersed throughout the territory; such is democracy.   906

[Rousseau's model is the democracy of the rural cantons of Switzerland.]

What is suitable for Corsica is a mixed government, where the people assemble by sections rather than as a whole, and where those who are entrusted with power are changed at frequent intervals . . . This form of government will produce two great advantages. First, by confining the work of administration to a small number only, it will permit the choice of enlightened men. Secondly, by requiring the co-operation of all members of the state in the exercise of the supreme authority, it will place all on a plane of perfect equality . . .   907

[Rousseau points out two favourable legacies of Genoese rule: the lack of commerce, and the eradication of the nobility.]

If foreign trade existed, it would be necessary to prohibit it until your constitution had become firmly established and domestic production was supplying all it could . . .

[The Genoese] sought only to degrade the nobility, while you seek to ennoble the nation . . . It is confusing shadow with substance to identify the dignity of a state with the titles of some of its members . . .   908

The fundamental law of your new constitution must be equality. Everything must be related to it, including even authority, which is established only to defend it. All should be equal by right of birth; the state should grant no distinctions except to merit, to virtue, and to services done for the *patrie*.   909–10

[He opposes the prejudice that favours town-life at the expense

---

* In one of the fragments attached to the *Project* Rousseau wrote: 'Wherever money reigns the money people give to maintain their liberty is always the instrument of their enslavement, and what they pay voluntarily today is used tomorrow to make them pay by force' (941).

of country life, and condemns the bourgeoisie for their self-interest and idleness. He suggests as capital a town in the middle of the island, Corte, which is central but which does not have such natural advantages that it will easily grow over-large. Furthermore:]

If you take the further precaution of making none of the great offices of state hereditary, or even tenable for life, it may be assumed that public men, being no more than transient residents in the capital, will not soon give it that fatal splendour which is the ornament and
912–13   ruin of states.

[Rousseau makes a long comparison between Corsica and Switzerland. He concludes:]

Poverty did not make itself felt in Switzerland until money began to circulate there; money created inequalities both in resources and in fortunes. It became a great instrument of acquisition which was
916   inaccessible to those who had nothing . . .

We must set it down as a certain rule that wherever money is a prime necessity, the nation will abandon agriculture to throw itself into more lucrative professions; the condition of a labourer is then either an article of commerce and kind of manufacture for the powerful farmer, or else the last resource of poverty for the mass of the peasantry. Those who grow rich in commerce and industry invest their money, when they have made enough, in landed properties which others cultivate for them; thus the whole nation finds itself divided into rich idlers, who own the land, and wretched peasants who starve while tilling it.

The more necessary money is to private citizens, the more necessary is it to the government; whence it follows that the more commerce flourishes, the higher the taxes, and the peasant must sell the produce of the land if he is to get any good out of tilling it . . . He must turn himself into a petty trader, petty salesman, petty thief . . . The poverty of the general public increases along with the opulence of private individuals; and both of these lead in conjunction to all those
920   vices which cause the ultimate ruin of a nation . . .

Everyone should make a living and no one should grow rich; that is the fundamental principle of the prosperity of the nation; and the system I propose . . . proceeds as directly as possible towards that
924   goal.

[Rousseau discusses in detail the way the economy can remain agricultural, with money playing a very small part, exchange being in kind wherever possible, and with work on the land being given the highest esteem. He then turns to the raw materials of the island;

the forests should not be cut down indiscriminately — 'a strict system of forest control must be set up early, and cutting so regulated that reproduction equals consumption' (927). Mines also should not 'be exploited indifferently' (927).]

The same attention will be paid to manufactures of all sorts, each with reference to its own particular needs, in order to facilitate labour and distribution as much as possible. Care will be taken, however, not to set up establishments of this sort in the most populous and fertile sections of the island. On the contrary, other things being equal, you will choose the most arid sites, sites which, unless they were peopled by industry, would remain desert. This will cause some difficulties in the matter of supplying necessary provisions; but the advantages gained and the disadvantages avoided ought infinitely to outweigh this consideration . . . If you were to found such establishments in fertile places the abundance of provisions and the profits of labour, profits necessarily greater in the [manufacturing] arts than in agriculture, would divert farmers or their families from rural care and would gradually depopulate the countryside . . . The transportation of foodstuffs, by rendering them more costly in the factories, will diminish the profit of the workers, and, by keeping their condition closer to that of the farmers, will better maintain the balance between them.

This balance can never be such, however, that the advantage will still not lie with industry, partly because it attracts a larger share of the money circulating in the state, partly because wealth provides opportunities for the effects of power and inequality to be felt, and partly because increased strength accrues to large numbers of men gathered together in one place, a strength which the ambitious know how to combine to their own advantage. It is therefore important that this too-favoured part should remain dependent for its livelihood on the rest of the nation. In the case of internal conflict, it is in the nature of our new constitution that the farmer should be the one to lay down the law to the worker.

927–8

[He now comes to the question of public revenue; how will the state provide for what it needs if such a small part of the economy is in money and currency?]

I want to see a great deal spent on state service; my only quarrel, strictly speaking, is with the choice of means. I regard finance as the fat of the body politic, fat which when clogged up in certain muscular tissues, overburdens the body with useless obesity, and makes it heavy rather than strong. I want to nourish the state on a more

salutary food, which will add to its substance; food capable of turning into fibre and muscle without clogging the vessels; which will give vigour rather than grossness to the members, and strengthen the body
930–1 without making it heavy.

[He suggests three ways of achieving this: setting up a public domain, having a tax which operates like the ecclesiastical tithe, and having the people themselves carry out public works.]

Far from wanting the state to be poor, I should like, on the contrary, for it to own everything, and for each individual to share in the common property only in proportion to his services . . . [My idea] is not to destroy private property absolutely, since that is impossible, but to confine it within the narrowest possible limits; to give it a measure, a rule, a rein which will contain, direct and subjugate it, and keep it ever subordinate to the public good. In short, I want the property of the state to be as large and strong, that of the citizens
931 as small and weak as possible* . . .

[He then suggests the setting up of the public domain and the tax based on the ecclesiastical tithe. He continues:]
I derive a third sort of revenue, the best and surest of all, from men themselves, using their labour, their arms and their hearts, rather than their purses, in the service of the *patrie*, both for its defence . . . and
932 for its utility . . .

Let everything that is done for the public good be always honourable. Let the magistrate, though busy with other concerns, show that the rest are not beneath him, like those Roman consuls who, to set an example to their troops, were the first to put their hands to the
932–3 construction of field-works.

[He also suggests that the office of collecting public funds should always be temporary, a proving ground for young men, not a career or profession which will inevitably bring abuse. Since payments can always be in money or in kind, the 'chamber of accounts . . . will be the centre of affairs, the motive power behind the whole administration' (935), because the balance between the two elements in the

---

* Rousseau was opposed to retroactive legislation. He writes later: 'No lands legitimately acquired, no matter how great the quantity, can be confiscated by virtue of a subsequent law forbidding the ownership of so much. No law can despoil any private citizen of any part of his property; the law can merely prevent him from acquiring more' (936). Further details of what he envisaged come in one of the Fragments attached to the *Project*, where he suggests a register of land in each area and writes: 'No one will be able to posess land outside his area. No one will be able to posses more than —— land' (942). He left the amount blank.

economy will be the key to the nation's well-being. Rousseau's draft ends with some general reflections:]

Fear and hope are the two great instruments with which one governs men; but instead of using both indiscriminately you must use each according to its own nature. Fear does not stimulate, it restrains; and its use in penal laws is not to make men do good, but to prevent them from doing evil . . . To stimulate the activity of a nation, therefore, you must offer it great hopes, great desires, great motives for positive action . . .   937

The most general and certain of all possible means to the satisfaction of your desires, whatever they may be, is power. Thus, to whatever passions a man or a people inclines, if those passions are vigorous they will vigorously aspire to power, either as an end, if they are proud or vain, or as a means, if they are vindictive or pleasure-loving.

It is therefore in the skilful and economical management of civil power that the great art of government consists; not only to preserve the government itself, but also to diffuse life and activity throughout the state, and to render the people active and industrious.

Civil power is exercised in two ways: the first legitimate, by authority; the second abusive, by wealth.

Wherever wealth dominates, power and authority are ordinarily separate; for the means of acquiring wealth and the means of attaining authority are not the same, and thus are rarely employed by the same people. Apparent power, in these cases, is in the hands of the magistrates, and real power in those of the rich. In such a government everything proceeds in response to the passions of men; nothing aims towards the goal set by the original constitution.

Under these conditions the goal of ambition becomes twofold; some aspire to authority in order to sell the use thereof to the rich and thus themselves grow rich; the rest, the majority, go directly after wealth, with which they are sure one day of having power, either by buying authority for themselves or by buying those who are entrusted with it . . .   938–9

[The *Project* ends a few lines after this, but the direction of Rousseau's thought continues in two of the Fragments:]

People will be industrious when work is honoured; and it always depends on the government to make it so. When esteem and authority are within the reach of the citizens, they will try to attain them; but if they see that they are too far removed they will not stir a step.   940

You will ask me if it is by working a field that one acquires the talents needed for governing. I answer yes, in a government as simple and upright as ours. Great talents are a substitute for patriotic zeal; they are necessary to lead a people which does not love its country and does not honour its leaders. But make the people love the public thing,* seek virtue, and do not concern yourself with great talents; they would do more harm than good. The best motive force for a government is love of the *patrie* and this love is cultivated with the land. Good sense is enough to govern a well-constituted state; and good sense develops as much in the heart as in the head. Men who are not blinded by their passions always do well.

940–1

* In *The Social Contract* (Bk II, Ch. 6) Rousseau had written: 'I call a republic every state ruled by laws, whatever the form of its constitution. For only then does the public interest govern, and the public thing [the *res publica*] is a reality'.

19 PESSIMISM

A sense of pessimism was ever-present in Rousseau's work. The wrong in the world sometimes seemed to him incurable: 'In the social state one man's good is necessarily another man's evil. This relation is in the essence of the thing and nothing can change it.'[1] 'The universal spirit of the laws of all countries is always to favour the strong against the weak, and he who has, against him who has nothing. This defect is inevitable and without exception.'[2]

When he was young he might have thought that these faults could have been remedied. A sense of change was central to his thinking, and he had enjoyed the friendship of Diderot, a man who was always bringing up new ideas and who rarely accepted the *status quo*. But it became acutely and painfully clear to Rousseau that the changes that Diderot and the *philosophes* would bring about were as unsatisfactory as what they would replace. The *philosophes* in general were of course far from being agreed among themselves about these changes, and Diderot in particular was almost as comprehensive in his views and as many-sided in his personality as Rousseau. But as time went by the latter came to regard them all as a common enemy.

The argumentative philosophic spirit assaults and enfeebles life, degrades the soul, and concentrates all the passions in the lowest self-interest, in the meanness of the human ego. Thus it eats away quietly at the very foundations of all society. For what is common to these private interests is so small that it will never balance what they oppose to it . . . If atheism does not lead to bloodshed, it is less from love of peace than from indifference to what is good . . . The principles [of the *philosophes*] detach men from their fellows [and] reduce all their affections to a secret egoism . . . [It is all very well] to display fine maxims in books, but the real question is whether they relate to the doctrine, whether they are a necessary consequence of it . . . It remains to be seen whether philosophy, at its ease and on its throne, would successfully control men's petty vanity, self-interest and ambition . . . and if it would practise that sweet humanity which it boasts of, pen in hand.[3]

Even where it did not exalt self-interest, philosophy left it unaffected. Because the very method by which it proceeded did not relate to our whole experience.

The method of generalizing and abstracting is very suspect to me, because it is too little proportioned to our faculties. Our senses only show us individuals, attention comes to separate them, judgement can compare them one by one, but that is all. To wish to unite everything goes beyond the strength of our understanding, it is to want to push the boat we are in without touching anything outside . . . The analytic method is good in geometry but in philosophy it seems to me worthless; it leads to absurdity by false principles by not being related enough to feeling.[4]

This is what Rousseau was attacking when he wrote: 'The rage for systems has got hold of everyone; no one tries to see things as they are, but as they agree with his system.'[5]

He had referred to his own work as a 'system', but that was 'the true system of nature', or 'the true moral system of the human heart'.[6] What he meant by that was something more comprehensive and less abstract, rigid, or dogmatic. This is evident from an evocative comparison which he made in a footnote to *Emile:*

[The *philosophes*] no longer study, they no longer observe; they dream, and the dreams of a few bad nights are solemnly given to us as philosophy. You will say to me that I dream too. I agree with you. But unlike the others I give my dreams as dreams, leaving the reader to search if there is anything in them [that would be] useful to people awake.[7]

Once again it must be stressed that Rousseau was not opposed to reason. We cannot achieve either justice or morality without reason; his own attempt to set out the conditions for a just society, in *The Social Contract*, was developed on strenuously rational lines. But a

sense of justice or morality is not and cannot be based on reason;
it must be based on feelings — either of self-interest — 'Do unto
others as you would have them do unto you' — or, as Rousseau
himself wanted, on the teaching of the Gospel — 'love your neighbour as yourself'.

> Justice and goodness are not at all mere abstract words, pure
> moral concepts formed by the understanding, but true affections
> of the soul, enlightened by reason . . . By reason alone, inde-
> pendent of conscience, we cannot establish any natural law . . .
> All natural right is a fantasy if it is not founded on a natural
> need of the human heart.[8]

What alarmed Rousseau about the *philosophes* was that they made
no allowance for the needs of the heart. 'Oh Philosophy! How much
trouble you take to contract our hearts.'[9] They looked at the universe
and saw only 'the outside of this immense machine . . . Always
grossly limited by their senses [they] had never been able to see
anything but matter.'[10] They made no allowance for our inner
needs because they had no awareness of the inadequacy or distortion
of their own view. This lack of awareness made their systems seem
sufficient and complete, and they therefore had an equally complete
self-confidence. That confidence was frightening. 'The indifference of
the philosopher resembles the tranquillity of the state under despotism; it is the tranquillity of death; it is more destructive than war
itself.'[11]

The *philosophes* were, in fact, far from being indifferent to the
conditions of their time; they were as concerned as Rousseau at
injustice. But instead of beginning by asking what we *are*, they
developed systems and prescribed rules based on what we have
become.* An example of this was the economic and political thought
of the Physiocrats. They were a group of men who had developed a
systematic model of economic laws on an agricultural basis and in
support of free trade — *laissez-faire* was first used as an economic
slogan by them. Quesnay, the leading Physiocrat, had produced a
Tableau économique, which set out these laws in columns of figures
and geometric lines. They believed them to be natural laws and
expounded them in an extremely doctrinaire way.

For Rousseau the 'natural laws' of the Physiocrats were as unacceptable as the 'natural man' of Hobbes. But this was not all.

---

* See his remarks in the Preface to the *Discourse on Inequality*, quoted on p. 53.

Their indifference to the truth of human nature, as he saw it, was accompanied by a willingness to make compromises with the *status quo*. In this respect too they were typical of the *philosophes*, who attacked intolerance and injustice but who could not envisage the radical transformation that alone, in Rousseau's view, could bring about true justice. For the Physiocrats any government that put their laws into practice would be a good one. This view was put forward by one of the Physiocrats, Mercier de la Rivière, in 1767, in a work entitled *The Natural and Essential Order of Political Societies*. He believed that the best government was despotic, and distinguished between 'arbitrary despotism' and 'legal despotism'. He gave Euclid as an example of the latter, a model ruler whom everyone obeyed: 'Euclid is a true despot.'[12] Rousseau had already expressed his opinion on a figure like Euclid being a political leader — 'Geometrical precision has no place at all in moral calculations'[13] — but this phrase 'legal despotism' was new. When he was sent de la Rivière's pamphlet by Mirabeau (the father of the Mirabeau who became prominent in the French Revolution), he wrote in reply.

Letter to Mirabeau, 26 July 1767

I have never been able to understand very well what evidence can act as a basis for 'legal despotism', and nothing seemed less evident to me than the chapter which deals with the evidence. This is similar to the system of the Abbé de St-Pierre who supposed that human reason would always go on being improved; he expected each century to add its enlightenment to that of the previous centuries. He did not see that human understanding always has the same scope, and a very narrow one. It loses on one side as much as it gains on another,* prejudices constantly being renewed take away from us as much acquired enlightenment as cultivated reason can replace . . .

159

How can philosophers . . . not be aware that each of us acts very rarely on his knowledge and very often according to his passions? You prove that the real interest of the despot is to govern legally. That is recognized all the time, but who is there who does act according to his real interests? Only the wise man, if he exists . . . Almost all men know their real interests [but] do not follow them any better

---

* In *Emile* Rousseau had also written: 'There is no real progress in reason among the human race, because what is gained on one side is lost on the other . . . The time we spend learning what others have thought cannot be spent in learning to think for ourselves.'[14]

because of that. The prodigal who spends his capital knows perfectly well that he is ruining himself, but does not change his ways. What is the use of reason enlightening us, if it is passion that leads us? . . . 'I see and I recognize the best; I follow the worst.'* That is what your despot will do, being ambitious, prodigal, greedy, indulgent, vindictive, jealous and weak. For that is what they all do, and all of us likewise . . . You give too much weight to your calculations and not enough to the inclinations of the human heart and the play of the passions. Your system is very good for the people of Utopia; it is worthless for the children of Adam.

This is, as I used to see it, the great problem of politics, which I compare to that of squaring the circle in geometry and [the problem] of longitude in astronomy: to find a form of government that puts the laws above man.   160

If such a form can be found, let us find it and try to establish it . . . If unfortunately it cannot be found — and I confess frankly that I believe that it is not to be found — I believe we must pass to the other extreme, and immediately put man as far as possible above the law; to establish, therefore, arbitrary despotism, and the most arbitrary possible. I wish that the despot might be God. In a word, I do not see any tolerable mean between the most austere democracy and the most perfect Hobbesism. For the conflict of men and laws, which puts the state into a continual civil war, is the worst of all political states.   160–1

But a Caligula, a Nero, a Tiberius . . . My God . . . I groan at being a man . . .

Whatever happens, do not talk to me any more of your legal despotism. I could not fancy it or even understand it. I only see in it two contradictory words which when put together mean nothing . . .

* A quotation from Ovid's *Metamorphoses*.[15]

20 CONFESSION

When he was a young man, Rousseau had become 'embittered by the injustices he had experienced, and by those he had witnessed...'

> I came to despise my century and my contemporaries ... and little by little detached myself from the society of men ... I tried to break the bonds which kept me attached to this society ... and which chained me to occupations less by inclination than by needs which I thought were those of nature, but in fact were only those of opinion. Suddenly a happy accident revealed to me what I had to do for myself, and what I should think of my fellow-men. My heart had been in constant contradiction with my mind about them, because I had still felt drawn to love them, while having so many reasons to hate them.[1]

Now the 'happy accident', which was his 'illumination', brought his mind and his heart together. What had been revealed to him he now revealed to his fellow-men.

He did this not only by what he wrote but by his attitude to writing. Since his belief in the truth of what he wrote was total, that belief could not be compromised in any way.

> I have always felt that the state of a writer is, and can only be, illustrious and respectable in so far as it is not a career. It is too difficult to think nobly when you are only thinking for a living. To be able, and to dare, to speak great truths you must not depend on your success. I threw my books to the public in the certainty of having spoken for the common good, without any concern for anything else.[2]

An essential part of this total commitment therefore was that he displayed the truth not only in what he wrote but also in his way of life, his 'reform'. He threw away the clothes that made him acceptable to a society he condemned; he took to earning his living copying music. He wrote in *Emile:* 'Teach by doing whenever you can',[3] and in the *Essay on Languages:* 'What the people of the ancient world said most vividly they did not express through words, but through signs. They did not say it, they showed it.'[4]

At first his example was not taken seriously; he was 'a man of paradox', who enjoyed controversy and provocation. But with *The New Heloïse* he came to be regarded as the 'friend of truth' he proclaimed himself to be. The immense success of the novel made people aware of a new sense of themselves, their inner feelings and their moral life. Rousseau became 'the apostle of truth and virtue'.

When *Emile* appeared the apostle became a martyr. This book not only extended the area of awareness made vividly alive in *The New Heloïse*, it also brought disaster on its author. He was driven from Paris, Berne and Geneva. His books were burnt, he was condemned without trial, he was banished from his native city. The treatment confirmed his reputation and the value of what he had written. Had not Socrates and Jesus been treated likewise?

But then his reputation was shattered, and the value of his example called into question. The secret of the abandonment of his children became known. The man who claimed to be the most virtuous and upright was shown to be callous and inhuman. Rousseau was not alone in sending his children to the Foundlings' Hospital, by any means. But it was generally only the poor and the needy who did so, not the educated who read his books, let alone the man of virtue who wrote those books.

No one had been more radical than he in criticism of existing society and of the way people lived. At the centre of his criticism was the distinction he made between 'nature' and 'opinion', between being and appearance: 'all look for happiness in appearance, none care for reality. All put their being into appearing; slaves and dupes of self-interest, none of them live in order to live but [only] to make believe they have lived.'[5] But now the nature and very being of the man who could write such words were shown to be no better than anyone else's.

The shock of this revelation, first made by Voltaire in his *Sentiment of the Citizens*, gave new impetus to a project Rousseau had been considering for some time; this was to write his memoirs. His publisher in Amsterdam had asked him to do this several years previously, and he had been gathering material in the meantime.

In the crisis that preceded the publication of *Emile*, when he had thought he was going to die, he had made a first draft summary of an autobiography, in his four long *Letters to Malesherbes*. (The passage at the opening of this chapter comes from the second of these letters.) They show a similar combination of self-justification and self-analysis to that found later in the *Confessions*. But both these writings also contain another quality, which might be called self-evocation.

Our nature is in ourselves, and to realize our nature we must become what we have in us to be. 'Let us begin by becoming ourselves once more; by concentrating ourselves inside us; by circumscribing our soul within the same limits that nature has given our being. Let us begin, in a word, by bringing ourselves together where we are; so that as we seek to know ourselves, everything that makes up what we are will come to present itself to us.'[6] 'I know of no happiness or peace of mind in being distant from oneself. Rather do I feel . . . that we are only happy on earth in so far as we move further away from things and come closer to ourselves.'[7]

'What am I?' This was the question he set out to answer in a way no one had done before him. The attention and concern he had previously given to his society and his fellow-men he now turned on himself. His political theory was remarkable for its refusal to make compromises with the *status quo*. His *Confessions* were remarkable for their revelation of a world beneath the evident facts of his life — 'a man such as he was within'.[8] 'What is seen is the least part of what is';[9] his epigraph, from Persius, was 'In the interior, under the skin'.[10]

This exploration of himself was conducted with extraordinary sensitivity and written in some of his most beautiful prose. In its own way it was to be as influential as anything else Rousseau wrote. This was not only because of its evocative introspection but also its astonishing frankness. 'I have always laughed at the false naïvety of Montaigne. While appearing to admit his faults he took great care to give himself only likeable ones. I believe, though . . . that there is no human being whose interior, however pure it might be, does not conceal some horrible vice'.[11] He wrote without hesitation about masochism, exhibitionism, masturbation, and stealing. 'Nothing of me must remain obscure or hidden from [the reader]; I must keep myself continually in front of him, he must follow me into all the disorders of my heart, into all the innermost recesses of my life.'[12]

'I may make omissions in the facts, or errors in dates, or put things out of sequence. But I cannot be wrong about what I have felt, nor about what my feelings have made me do. That is principally what I am writing about. The real aim of my confessions is to provide an exact account of my inner life, in all the events that I have experienced. It is the history of my soul that I have promised.'[13] '[This history] is the key to the tissue of events which are well known to everyone but which will never be reasonably explained without it.'[14]

Rousseau believed that for all his failings, and they were numerous, there was an essential consistency in his life, as there was an essential coherence in his thought. The faults, mistakes and wrongs he had done did not invalidate the truths he had upheld; nor did they justify the charges made against him, of being a hypocrite or a charlatan. He attempted to grasp this underlying consistency, to reach the inner truth of his character which he knew to exist. His belief in this truth reassured him, but because by its very nature it could not be confirmed by anyone else, he was also, in this act of writing about it, seeking reassurance.

At the same time, though, Rousseau did believe that his *Confessions* could have a more than personal significance. In depicting himself as vividly and comprehensively as he did, he hoped to make so complete a portrait of a man's nature that it could 'serve as the first piece of comparison for the study of men, [a subject] which has certainly still to begin'.[15] As a rule we judge others by ourselves, and we never discover what they really are. In reading this work, he hoped, 'everyone might be able to know [both] himself and another, and that other will be me'.[16] In characteristic fashion Rousseau felt himself to be at one and the same time both unique and typical.

The First Part of the *Confessions* covers his boyhood, youth and early manhood, beginning with his birth and ending with his departure for Paris in 1741. It provides a vivid and unforgettable picture of these early years and experiences — Geneva, Italy, his travels, his time with Madame de Warens, the people he met, his first loves, his irregular education. The Second Part, which he himself felt 'could only be inferior to the First in every way',[17] contains a detailed record of the years from his arrival in Paris in 1741 to his expulsion from Switzerland in 1765. It is also essential reading for an understanding of Rousseau's life and character but it has an element of self-justification which is absent from Part One — except, that is, for the very opening. When he came to put the whole book together Rousseau wrote a new defiant beginning to Part One. It is this statement which now opens the book.

Confessions

PART ONE

I am undertaking an enterprise which is without precedent and which, when finished, will have no imitator. I want to show my fellow-men a man in all the truth of nature; and that man, he will be me.

Myself alone. I understand my heart and I know men, I am not made like anyone else I have seen. I dare to suppose that I am not made like anyone else who exists. If I am no better, at least I am different. Whether nature did good or ill, in breaking the mould in which she formed me, is something that can only be decided after reading this book.

Let the trumpet of the Last Judgement sound when it will. I will come to present myself before the Supreme Judge with this book in my hand. I will say out loud: 'This is what I have done, what I have thought, what I have been. I have recounted good and bad with equal frankness. I have neither excluded anything bad, nor added anything good. If I have ever happened to use some irrelevant decoration, it has only ever been to fill a gap caused by a fault in my memory. I have put forward as true what I know to have been true, never what I know to have been false. I have shown myself as I was — despicable and vile when I have been that; good, generous and sublime when I have been that. I have revealed what is within me as You have seen it Yourself. Eternal Being, gather around me the numberless crowd of my fellows. Let them hear my confessions, let them groan at my baseness, let them blush at my distress. Let each of them in turn reveal his heart at the foot of Your throne with the same sincerity. And then let a single one of them say to You, if he
5   dare: "I was a better man than he." '

[After an account of his childhood with his father, and his first memories, which were of reading, Rousseau describes the two years he spent outside Geneva at Bossey.]

My way of life in Bossey suited me so well that if only it had lasted longer it would have fixed my character for ever. It was based on tender, affectionate and peaceful feelings . . . My most vivid desire was to be loved by everyone who came near me. I was gentle, so was my cousin Bernard, so were those who looked after us. For two whole years I was neither witness nor victim of any violent feeling. Everything encouraged in my heart the disposition it had received
14   from nature . . .

Mademoiselle de Lambercier had a mother's love for us. She also had a mother's authority, and that sometimes led her to give us a child's punishment, when we deserved it . . . For a long time she did no more than threaten us . . . But after I had been smacked I found the event less terrible than the anticipation, and, what is even stranger, I found that the punishment increased my affection for the person who was inflicting it. I needed all the honesty of this affection, and all my natural gentleness, not to look for a way of earning a repetition of the same treatment. For I had found in the grief, in the very shame, an element of sensuality which gave me less fear than a desire to experience it once more from the same hand . . .

Who would imagine that this child's punishment, by a thirty-year-old woman on an eight-year-old boy, would have decided my tastes, desires and feelings, my very self, for the rest of my life, exactly contrary to what they should have been naturally? . . .   15

To be kneeling before a masterful mistress, to obey her orders, and to have to ask her forgiveness, have been for me the sweetest pleasures; the more my vivid imagination excited my blood, the more like an enraptured lover I looked. As can be imagined, this way of making love does not lead to very rapid progress; nor is it very dangerous to the virtue of the desired person. I have therefore possessed very few women. Nevertheless, I have not lacked enjoyment in my own way, that is, in my imagination . . .   17

I have made the first and most painful step in the dark and murky labyrinth of my confessions. It is not what is criminal that is hardest to speak of, but what is ridiculous and shameful. From now on, after what I have just dared to describe, I feel sure of myself. Nothing can stop me now . . .   18

[Another episode at Bossey which had an enduring effect on the young Jean-Jacques was when he was wrongly accused, and severely punished, for having broken a comb.]
It is now almost fifty years since this event and I am not afraid now of being punished again for what happened. Nevertheless, I declare before Heaven that I was innocent, that I did not touch the comb nor break it, I did not go near [the place it had been left] nor even so much as thought of doing so. Do not ask me how the damage was done. I do not know and have never been able to understand. What I do know for certain is that I was innocent.   19

Think of a person who is shy and amenable in ordinary life, but who is proud, ardent and unconquerable when aroused. A child who has always been ordered by the voice of reason, always treated with gentleness, fairness and kindness, who has no idea even of injustice.

And who then experiences injustice so terribly for the first time, from the very people whom he most loved and respected. What an upheaval in his ideas, what chaos in his feelings, what bewilderment in his heart and brain, in all his limited intellectual and moral being! . . .

This first feeling of violence and injustice has remained so deeply engraved on my soul that every idea which relates to it brings back my first emotion to me. The feeling was originally confined to myself, but it has become so consistent in itself, and so detached from any personal interest, that my heart rises up at the sight or account of any unjust action, whatever its object and wherever it is committed, just as if I was involved myself. When I read of the cruelties of a fierce tyrant, or the subtle plots of a two-faced priest, I would willingly set out to stab those wretches, even if I were to perish a hundred
20 times over . . .

[Book One ends with Rousseau's departure from Geneva.]
Nothing was more fitted to my temperament nor more suited to make me happy than the quiet and obscure life of a good artisan, especially if it was like that of an engraver in Geneva . . . I would have been a good Christian, good citizen, good father, good friend,
43 good workman, a good man in everything . . .

[Book Two describes his first meeting with Madame de Warens, his journey to Italy and his stay in Turin. Among the people he describes in Book Three is the Abbé Gaime, a Savoyard priest who was later one of the models for the Savoyard priest in *Emile*.]
In the succession of my tastes and ideas I had always been too high or too low, now Achilles, now Thersites, hero or good-for-nothing. M. Gaime took the trouble to put me in my place and show me to myself without sparing me or discouraging me. He spoke to me very directly about my nature and my talents, but he added that he saw obstacles arising from them which would prevent my benefiting from them. In his view I should make use of them less as steps on which to climb to fortune than as resources to manage without it.

[Till then] I had only had false ideas of human life, he drew me a true picture. He showed me how, when fate is against him, the wise man can always seek happiness and sail against the wind to achieve it; how there is no true happiness without wisdom, and how wisdom can be found in all situations. He very much reduced my admiration for greatness by proving to me that those who dominate others are no wiser or happier. He told me something which has often come back to my mind: if every man could read into the heart of everyone else
91 there would be more people wanting to descend than wanting to rise . . .

Although the sensibility of the heart which makes us really enjoy ourselves is the work of nature, and perhaps the product of our constitution, it needs situations to develop it. However sensitive a man may be, he would feel nothing without the right circumstances; he would die without having known his true being. That is virtually how I was [on my return from Italy], and how I would always have been, if I had never known Madame de Warens or, even having known her, if I had not lived long enough in her company to pick up the sweet habit of affectionate feelings which she inspired in me...   104

[He writes about all his early experiences of, and feelings for, women.]

Seamstresses, servant-girls or shop-girls hardly tempted me. I needed young ladies. Everyone has his fantasies — they have always been mine ... However, it is in no way the pride of rank or class which attracts me. It is a better-preserved complexion, more beautiful hands, more lovely ornaments, a general air of delicacy and refinement ... I myself find this preference quite ridiculous. But my heart gives it to me in spite of me ...   134

My passions have made me live and my passions have killed me. What passions? you may ask. Nothings, the most childish things in the world. But they have affected me as if it was a matter of the possession of Helen or the throne of the Universe. First of all, women. When I possessed one my senses were quiet, but my heart was never quiet. In the midst of pleasure I was devoured by the needs of love ...

Music was another passion, less impetuous but no less consuming ... [And then there were] all the mad ideas which passed through my changeable head, the fleeting desires of a single day — a journey, a concert, a meal, a walk to take, a novel to read, a play to see. Whatever was least premeditated among my pleasures or my affairs became the most violent passion for me ...   219–20

[He writes about his travelling.]

Of the details of my life that I have forgotten the thing I most regret is not to have made accounts of my journeys. Never have I thought so much, existed so much, lived so much, been so much myself — if I can say that — as in those journeys I made alone on foot ... You will ask: why did I not write them down? And I will reply: why should I write them down? Why should I deprive myself of the actual pleasure of enjoyment, for the sake of telling others what I have enjoyed? What did readers, the public, the whole earth, matter to me, when I was soaring in heaven? Besides, should I have carried pen and paper with me? If I had thought of all that, nothing would have come to me. I do not foresee the ideas that I have. They come when it pleases them, not when it pleases me. They either do not come at all, or they come in a mass, they overwhelm me with their number and strength. Ten volumes a day would not have been enough. Where could I have found time to write them down? When I arrived I only thought of having a good meal. When I set off I only thought of having a good journey. I felt that a new paradise was waiting close 162–3 by; my only thought was to go off in search of it . . .

[Among the many revealing insights into himself are the following:] None of my dominant tastes is for things that can be bought. I need only pure pleasures and money poisons everything . . . Money has never seemed to me as precious as other people find it. In fact, it has never seemed to me very useful. It is no use by itself. It has to be transformed to be enjoyed. You have to buy and sell, be cheated, at 36 great cost, or badly served . . .

I love liberty; I detest trouble, constraint, restriction. While the money in my purse lasts it guarantees my independence; it relieves me of scheming to find more, a need I have always hated. But for fear of seeing it come to an end I take great care of it. The money you possess is an instrument of freedom; the money you pursue is an 38 instrument of slavery . . .

It is a very peculiar thing that my imagination never becomes more pleasantly alive than when my situation is least pleasant, and vice versa; it is never less happy than when everything is happy around me. My poor head cannot be subjected to things; it cannot embellish [what is], it wants to create. Real objects it depicts more or less as they are; it can only embellish objects that are imaginary. If I want to depict spring it must be winter; if I want to describe a beautiful landscape, I must be indoors. And I have said a hundred times that if 171–2 ever I was shut up in the Bastille I would paint the picture of liberty . . .

[Rousseau ends Book Four with the following remarks:] These long details of my early youth may have seemed very childish, and I regret that. Although in some respects I was born a man, for a long time I was a child, and in many ways I still am a child. I did not promise to show the public a great person. I promised to depict myself as I am. To know me in my later years you need to have a good knowledge of me in my youth . . . There is a certain succession of affections and ideas which modify those that follow; it is necessary to know these to be able to come to a fair judgement. I am trying to set out everywhere the first causes so as to make evident the sequence of effects.

Somehow I would like to be able to make my soul transparent to the eyes of the reader. To do that I am trying to show it to him from all points of view, in all kinds of light, so that there is not a single movement it makes, which he does not see. That way he may judge for himself of the principle which produces them . . . It is not for me to judge of the importance of the facts; I must tell them all and leave the reader the task of selection . . . I have only one thing to fear in this enterprise; it is not of saying too much or of telling lies, it is rather of not saying everything, and [thus] of concealing the truth . . .   174–5

[The last two books of Part One describe the years spent with Madame de Warens. She had moved from Annecy to Chambéry, and there Jean-Jacques became her lover.]

At Annecy I was intoxicated [with love for her]; at Chambéry I was no longer so. I loved her all the time with the utmost passion, but now I loved her less on my own account and more for herself, or at least, I looked for happiness rather than pleasure in her company. She was more to me than a sister, a mother, a friend, more even than a mistress, and it is for this reason that she was not a mistress. In the last resort I loved her too much to lust after her . . .   196

[Madame de Warens also had another lover, Claude Anet.]

Between the three of us there grew up a society which was perhaps without precedent on earth. All our thoughts and cares and feelings were in common, none went beyond this little circle. The habit of living together, and exclusively so, became so strong that if one of the three of us was missing, or if a fourth person came along, everything was upset. In spite of our individual relationships even our tête-à-têtes were not as sweet as when all three of us were together . . .   201–2

[Claude Anet died young but Jean-Jacques' happiness with Madame de Warens continued. They spent idyllic summers together at Les Charmettes. See p. 20.]

True happiness is not described, it is felt; because it is not the result of a collection of facts but is a permanent state . . .   236

[He describes a day, getting up before sunrise, going out for a walk to admire and contemplate the beauty of nature, going to wake Maman, enjoying a leisurely breakfast with her, spending the morning in study and the afternoon likewise, or else working in the garden.] I had another little family at the end of the garden; it was some bees . . . I became very interested in their work. I had endless pleasure seeing them return from their foraging, their little thighs so loaded down sometimes that they had difficulty walking . . . Sometimes I was surrounded by them; I had them on my face and my hands without ever being stung. All animals distrust men, and they are not wrong. But once they are sure that we mean them no harm their confidence becomes so great that you would have to be worse than a barbarian to abuse it . . .

The feeling which continually dominated my soul was the enjoyment of the present . . . My heart, still new, gave itself to everything with the pleasure of a child, or rather, if I may say so, with the rapture of an angel. For these quiet kinds of enjoyment do indeed have the serenity of the joys of paradise. Picnics at Montagnole, suppers in the arbour, the fruit-picking, the grape-harvest, the evenings stripping hemp with our servants — all these were so many festivals which Maman enjoyed as much as I did. Our solitary walks had an even greater charm, because there our hearts overflowed even more freely . . .

So my happy days flowed by . . .

239–40

244

245

Most of Part One of the *Confessions* was written in Môtiers or in England. There was then a two-year gap before Rousseau continued the work, and there is a noticeable difference of mood in Part Two. This was partly due to the subject-matter, but also to the fact that the quarrel with Hume had further damaged his reputation. Hume had published an account of it, in his own defence, and Rousseau's behaviour seemed ungrateful and dishonest. The man of virtue looked even less virtuous. The impulse to justify himself was correspondingly greater.

> Here begins the work of darkness in which I have been buried for the last eight years . . . In the abyss of evils in which I am sunk, I feel the injuries of blows struck against me, and I see the instrument which causes them. But I cannot see the hand which wields it, nor the means by which that hand is put to work. Disgrace and misfortunes fall on me, as if of their own accord, invisibly.[18]

So opens the last book of the *Confessions*. Rousseau is not guilty of the charges that are now made against him, he is the victim of a plot.

The comment was once made 'Rousseau was the worst kind of paranoid and hypochondriac, the type who does in fact suffer persecution and is in fact constantly ill'.[19] This is true. The accusations he makes in Part Two of the *Confessions*, and subsequently, were not the mad delusions they were once thought to be. They had some basis in fact.

In 1770, when he had returned to Paris, he completed the work. (He hoped to write a Part Three, but did not do so.) Once finished he wanted to read it to people he knew, not only to restore his reputation in their eyes, but also to re-establish the validity of his ideas. He had not written in vain, his work should not be disregarded. At the beginning of 1771 he gave these readings. Then they were stopped by the authorities. This was not because of official disapproval, but at the request of Diderot and Mme d'Epinay. His former friends had indeed combined against him.

Rousseau did not give up. He began writing another autobiographical work, the *Dialogues: Rousseau Judge of Jean-Jacques*. His epigraph was the same line from Ovid he had used on the *Discourse on the Arts and Sciences*, the work which had first made his name: 'I am a barbarian here, because men do not understand me.'

The work takes the form of three conversations between Rousseau and a Frenchman. The latter holds the common opinion of Jean-Jacques (who does not appear), that he is a charlatan, troublemaker and imposter. Rousseau suggests that the Frenchman should read Jean-Jacques' books for himself, and he (Rousseau) will go and visit the man Jean-Jacques, to see if he is indeed the monster he is made out to be. Rousseau makes his visit, the Frenchman reads the books, and each reports back to the other. Rousseau's account of the man is a brilliant self-portrait, and the Frenchman's account of the works is an invigorating summary of his ideas. The work concludes with the Frenchman agreeing with Rousseau that the common opinion of Jean-Jacques is wrong.

The *Dialogues* are an uneasy mixture, pages clouded with a sense of persecution alongside passages of great lucidity, moments of pessimism among others of hope. Rousseau himself was aware of the 'longueurs, repetitions, wordiness and disorder' of 'these formless essays'.[20] Their unevenness was due to the way they were written, piecemeal, one short passage at a time, and also to their subject-matter; 'Anger sometimes animates talent, but disgust and the contraction of the heart stifle it.'[21]

Nevertheless, the work does redefine and give extra clarity to some of his earlier statements. His 'two great lessons', he concluded, were 'to have less rash confidence in the pride of human knowledge, [and] to learn . . . to respect natural right in everything and at all times'.[22] 'He had worked for his *patrie* and small states constituted like it. If his doctrine could be of some use to others it was [not to lead them back to their original simplicity but] in changing the objects of their esteem.'[23]

Despite its underlying despair a sense of hope sometimes breaks through:

> The innate feelings that nature has engraved in all the hearts [of men] . . . may be stifled in individuals because of art, intrigues and sophisms, but they will at once be reborn in the following generations. They will always lead man back to his original disposition, as the seed of a grafted tree always produces the original stock. This inner feeling . . . cries out to all hearts that justice has another basis than self-interest . . . The voice of conscience can no more be stifled in the human heart than the voice of reason can be stifled in the understanding . . . Nature will imperceptibly take back her empire.[24]

As this passage suggests, Rousseau no longer expected to be treated fairly by his contemporaries. He was appealing to posterity. When he had finished the work he tried to place it on the high altar of Notre-Dame, but access to the altar was barred. He gave the manuscript to Condillac, who had been a friend since he had first come to Paris, thirty-four years previously. But Condillac was unenthusiastic. He handed it to an Englishman, Brooke Boothby, for safe-keeping, and then tried to distribute a handbill to passers-by which called attention to his treatment. No one was interested.

Both the *Confessions* and the *Dialogues* had failed to reach the audience for whom they were intended. Rousseau made no further attempts to break out of his isolation. In the last two years of his life he withdrew into the solitude he describes in the *Reveries*.

Part One of the *Confessions* was published in 1782, four years after Rousseau's death; Part Two followed in 1789. The book made an immediate and lasting impact. Its influence on the Romantic movement in particular, and subsequent writers in general, was immense. It is, in fact, the one work of Rousseau's on which almost all readers have been agreed. However hostile, bewildered or exasperated the reactions to his other works may be, the *Confessions* is recognized as a masterpiece.

21 POLAND

Rousseau's last political work was his *Considerations on the Government of Poland and on its Projected Reform*. Poland had suffered from internal quarrels and foreign interference for a number of years. In 1769 a Convention called by a large number of landowners decided to ask for advice and proposals for a new constitution. Rousseau was one of several writers who were approached with this request. He worked on his *Considerations* from the autumn of 1770 to the spring of 1771 but they were not published until after his death.

The task before him was different from that on Corsica. This was not a matter of setting up a new state, but of reforming an existing one. The reforms he put forward are mostly in keeping with the principles laid down in *The Social Contract* and he refers to the work several times. But there are some deviations. The most notable of these is that he allows representatives in the legislative body, a practice he had strongly opposed in *The Social Contract* (Bk III, Ch. 15). He sets strict limits on their powers and tries to ensure that the constituents will still feel involved, but the suggestion is a serious modification to his previous view. However, it should not be seen as a contradiction of his earlier position. Nor should it be taken, along with his guarded remarks about the emancipation of the peasantry, as indicating a failure of nerve, the reactionary old age of a former revolutionary.

Rousseau had always been afraid of change, not because he was conservative and wanted to keep things as they were but because he saw most development and change in his lifetime as harmful. An awareness of change runs through all his work: one of his most original aspects is precisely this sense of human and social evolution. But his general view was that change was for the bad rather than the good. The failure of the bourgeoisie to achieve their due rights in

Geneva, and the annexation of Corsica by the French in 1769 only confirmed these feelings. He writes with foreboding in the opening chapter of the *Considerations*. 'I see all the States of Europe rushing to their ruin. Monarchies, republics, all these nations so magnificently established, all these beautiful governments so wisely considered, have fallen into decay and threaten soon to die.'[1] There may be some irony in these words: there is certainly no joy.

This is because Rousseau was also afraid of change for what it could involve. His own experience with Geneva had brought him face to face with a problem he could not solve, a problem which has troubled a great many people since. The demands of right were clear and unequivocal but how do you effect those demands if others do not agree to them? In the *Letters from the Mountain* he argued forcefully for the right; at the same time, and more emphatically in his later letters to his friends among the bourgeoisie, he refused to countenance any violence, any use of force. 'In the misery of human affairs what good is worth being bought with the blood of our brothers? Even liberty is too dear at this price.'[2]

His *Considerations on Poland* are therefore quite consistent with his earlier writing. He examines the condition of the country, sets out what should rightfully be done, and suggests reforms that could achieve them peacefully. 'Never shake the machine too brusquely . . . Since new citizens cannot be created all at once you must begin by making use of those who exist.'[3]

That is the advice with which Rousseau ends the work. More significant, to my mind, are his remarks at the beginning, his preoccupation in the first chapters. This is not with constitutional practice, as in the *Letters from the Mountain*, or with the economy, as in the *Project* for Corsica, both of which are dealt with later. It is rather with the attitude and feelings of the citizens of Poland. No amount of administrative change or well-meaning laws will have any value unless the people believe in and care for their country themselves. The fundamental problem is 'how can the hearts be reached?'

Rousseau therefore turns to education, as he had previously done in the *Discourse on Political Economy* (see p. 83). He also suggests the institution of public games as an opportunity for people to become aware of the pleasure there can be in public activities. With games and festivals, like those he had suggested in the *Letter to D'Alembert* (see p. 131), the people would not only 'have less time and opportunity to grow rich, but they would also have less desire and need to do so.

Their hearts would learn to know other pleasures than those of wealth.'⁴ These passages provide one of the few instances where Rousseau himself used the word 'fraternity'. (It is also interesting to note that in this context, unlike any other, competition is seen as desirable.) In his enthusiasm for these ideas Rousseau's language is sometimes excessive, but that should not obscure or distract from his central and constant preoccupation, which is how to animate a just and free society.

Freedom is not easily achieved or maintained. 'You love liberty, you are worthy of it. You have defended it against a powerful and cunning aggressor [Russia] . . . Now, tired of the troubles of your *patrie* you long for tranquillity. I believe that can easily be found, but it seems to me difficult to preserve it alongside liberty . . . Rest and liberty seem to me incompatible. You must choose.'⁵ The choice will only be for freedom if people care for justice and 'the public thing' (see p. 275).

Considerations on the Government of Poland

There will never be a good and solid constitution unless the law reigns over the hearts of the citizens; as long as the power of legislation is insufficient to accomplish this, laws will always be evaded. But how can hearts be reached? That is the question to which our law-reformers, who never look beyond coercion and punishments, pay hardly any attention; and it is a question which material rewards would perhaps be no better solving. Even the most upright justice is insufficient; for justice, like health, is a good which is enjoyed without being felt, which inspires no enthusiasm, and the value of which is felt only after it has been lost. How then is it possible to move the hearts of men, and make them love the *patrie* and the laws?

955

[Rousseau puts forward a number of suggestions. First, he describes the civic games, festivals and drama of the ancient world which were 'bonds which attached the citizens to the *patrie* and to one another' (958). Second, he suggests an emphasis on what is distinctly Polish.]

It is national institutions which shape the genius, the character, the tastes and morals of a people; which give it an individuality of its own; which inspire it with that ardent love of the *patrie* based on ineradicable habits . . . Given this sentiment alone, legislation, even

if it were bad, would make good citizens; and it is always good citizens
alone that constitute the power and prosperity of the state* . . .

960-1

[However] the immense disparities of fortune which divide the
magnates from the lesser nobility constitute a great obstacle to the
reforms needed to make love of the *patrie* the dominant passion. As
long as luxury reigns among the great, greed will reign in all hearts.
The object of public admiration and the desires of private individuals
will always be the same; and if one must be rich in order to shine,
to be rich will always be the dominant passion. This is a great source

964

of corruption, which must be diminished as much as possible. . .

Where inequality reigns, I must confess, it is very hard to eliminate
all luxury . . . [Laws will not get rid of it.] It is from the depth of the
heart itself that you must uproot it by impressing men with healthier

965

and nobler tastes . . .

[Rousseau therefore turns to education:]
This is the important matter. It is education that must give souls a
national strength, and so direct their opinions and their tastes that
they will be patriotic by inclination, passion and necessity . . . Every
true republican sucks in with his mother's milk the love of the
patrie, that is to say the love of the laws and liberty. This love is his
whole existence; he sees only the *patrie*, he lives only for it; when he
is alone he is nothing . . .

National education is only suitable to free men; it is only they who
enjoy a common existence and are truly bound by law . . . All, being
equal under the constitution of the state, ought to be educated together
and in the same fashion; and if it is impossible to set up an absolutely
free system of public education, the cost must at least be set at a

966-7

level the poor can afford to pay . . .

In every school a gymnasium, or place for physical exercise,
should be established for the children. This much neglected provision
is, in my opinion, the most important part of education, not only
for the purposes of forming robust and healthy physiques, but even
more for moral purposes . . . [The children] should not be allowed
to play separately, at whim, but all together and in public, so that
there will always be a common goal towards which they all aspire, and
which will excite competition and emulation. Parents who prefer
domestic education, and have their children brought up under their

* Later in the work he writes: 'Each country has advantages which are peculiar
to itself, and which should be extended and fostered by its constitution. Husband
and cultivate those of Poland, and she will have few other nations to envy'
(1018-19).

own eyes, ought nevertheless to send them to these exercises. Their instruction may be domestic and private, but their games ought always to be public and common to all; for . . . [this will] accustom them at an early age to rules, to equality, to fraternity, to competition, to living under the eyes of their fellow-citizens and to desiring public approbation. . . .   967–8

[The people of the ancient world had a] vigour of soul, a patriotic zeal, and an esteem for truly personal and properly human qualities, which are without precedent among us. But the leaven exists in the hearts of all men and is ready to ferment if only it is stimulated by suitable institutions. Direct in this sense the usages, customs and morals of the Poles. In them you will develop that leaven, the very existence of which has not been so much as suspected by our corrupt maxims, our outworn institutions, and our egotistical philosophy which preaches what kills.   969

[Rousseau now turns to the constitution itself.]
What is the enterprise, gentlemen, that concerns you at the moment? That of reforming the government of Poland; that is to say, of giving the constitution of a great kingdom the vigour and stability of that of a small republic. Before working towards the execution of this project we must ask first of all whether it is capable of realization. The size of nations, the extent of states; this is the first and principal source of the misfortunes of the human race, and above all of the innumerable calamities that sap and destroy civilized peoples. Practically all small states, no matter whether they are republics or monarchies, prosper merely by reason of the fact that they are small; that all the citizens know and watch over one another; that the leaders can see for themselves the evil that is being done, the good they have to do, and that their orders are carried out before their eyes. All great peoples, crushed by their own mass, suffer either from anarchy, like you, or from subordinate oppressors through whom, by the necessities of devolution, the king is obliged to rule.   970

[The only solution to this problem for Poland is to break down the country into small units, all united by common legislation, all subordinate to the body of the republic.]

In a word, devote yourselves to extending and perfecting the system of federal government . . . the only one that can answer to your purposes . . .   971

[The next problem is the way so many of the population are excluded from legislation.]
The law of nature, that holy and inalienable law, which speaks to the

heart and reason of man, does not permit legislative authority to be so restricted, nor does it allow laws to be binding on anyone who has not voted for them in person . . . or at least through representatives . . . This sacred law cannot be violated with impunity; and the state of weakness to which so great a nation now finds itself reduced is the fruit of that feudal barbarism which serves to cut off from the body of the state that part of the nation which is the most numerous, and sometimes the soundest.

God forbid that I should think it necessary at this point to prove something that a little good sense and compassion will be enough to make everyone feel! . . . . Polish nobles, be more; be men. Then only will you be happy and free. But never flatter yourselves that you 973–4 will be so, while you hold your brothers in chains.

I feel the difficulty of the project of freeing your common people. I am afraid not merely of the badly understood self-interest, self-conceit and the prejudices of the masters; if these were surmounted I should also fear the vices and the cowardice of the serfs. Liberty is a food easy to eat, but hard to digest; it takes very strong stomachs to stand it. I laugh at those debased peoples, who, allowing themselves to be stirred up by troublemakers, dare to speak of liberty without having the slightest idea of its meaning, and who, with their hearts full of all the servile vices, imagine that in order to be free it is enough to be mutinous . . .

To free the common people of Poland is a great and noble operation, but bold, perilous and not to be lightly attempted. Among the precautions to be taken there is one which is indispensable and requires time: it is, before everything else, to make the serfs who are to be freed worthy of liberty and capable of sustaining it . . . Whatever happens, remember that your serfs are men like you, that they have in themselves the capacity to become all that you are. Work first of all to develop that capacity, and do not free their bodies until after you 974 have freed their souls.

[Later in the work, Rousseau outlines a way in which emancipation could take place and everyone be brought into the business of the state.] This will be effected by two methods, the first being to ad-minister justice scrupulously, so that the serf and the commoner, never having to fear unjust harassment by the noble, will be cured of the aversion in which they must naturally hold him. This calls for a great reformation of the courts of law and particular care in the formation of the body of lawyers.

The second method, without which the first is useless, is to open the

way to the serfs to become free, and to the bourgeoisie to become
nobles.   1024

[He suggests for this purpose that once every two years a committee
should be formed in each district to carry out three main functions.
First, to administer charity to those in need;* secondly, to award
scholarships, honours, and grants; thirdly, to recommend for emancipation peasants 'who were distinguished for good conduct, education
and morals, for their devotion to their families and the proper
fulfilment of all the duties of their state' (1026).]

When a certain number of families in a canton had been successively
freed you could proceed to free whole villages, to unite them gradually into communes, to assign them a certain amount of communal
property . . . and to give them communal officers . . . and, finally, to
give them back their natural right to participate in the administration
of their country by sending deputies to the assemblies . . .   1026–7

In executing this plan . . . you would kindle in all the lower orders
an ardent zeal to contribute to the public welfare . . . [you would]
succeed in animating all parts of Poland, and in binding them together
in such a way that they would no longer be anything more than a
single body whose vigour and strength would be at least ten times
greater than is now possible; and this with the inestimable advantage
of having avoided all abrupt and rapid changes, and the danger of
revolutions.   1028

[Rousseau now analyses the current condition of the legislator —
the diets — and the executive, which resided in ministers and officials,
and to some extent the king, all of whom acted independently of
one another and regardless of the law. The legislative power existed,
but was disregarded; the executive power acted, but in disarray.]

You should arm with full executive power a respectable and permanent body, such as the senate, which by its firmness and authority
would be capable of holding to the line of duty those magnates who
are tempted to depart from it . . .   977

If the administration is to be strong and good, and accomplish
its purpose well, the whole executive power should be vested in the
same hands. But it is not enough for those hands to change; if possible
they should act only under the eyes of the legislator, and with its
guidance . . .   978

---

* This would be the only charity allowed, 'for beggars and poor-houses ought
not to be tolerated anywhere in Poland. The priests will no doubt raise a great
outcry for the preservation of the poor-houses; and this outcry is simply one
more reason for destroying these institutions' (1025).

It is to be expected that the king, or the senate, or both together, will make great efforts to rid themselves of the diets and to make them as infrequent as possible. That above all is the thing to be forestalled and prevented. The method I propose is the only one; it is simple and cannot fail to be effective. It is most remarkable that before I set it out in *The Social Contract* [Bk. III, Chs. 12, 13 and 14] no

978   one had ever thought of it.

[He now turns to the problem of the legislator.]

One of the greatest disadvantages of large states, the one which above all makes liberty most difficult to preserve in them, is that the legislative power cannot manifest itself directly, and can only act by delegation. That has its good and evil side; but the evil outweighs the good. A legislator in a body is impossible to corrupt, but easy to deceive. Representatives are hard to deceive, but easily corrupted, and it is rare that they are not so corrupted . . .

I see two means of preventing this terrible evil of corruption . . . The first . . . is the frequency of the diets which, if they change their representatives often make them more costly and more difficult to seduce . . . The second means is to bind the representatives to follow their instructions exactly, and to render their constituents a strict

978–9   account of their conduct in the diet . . .

[He elaborates in detail ways in which this second method can be applied, so that:]

. . . with each word the deputy speaks in the diet, and with every move

980   he makes, he must see himself under the eyes of his constituents.

[He discusses how the diets should conduct their business, how frequently they should last, the possibility of extraordinary diets, and related matters. He then turns to the senate. At the moment members were appointed by the king; that practice should stop. Some of the senators could hold their position for life, others should be elected for a short term. As for the king, he should be elected, and the office should not be hereditary — 'Heredity in the crown and freedom in the nation will always be incompatible' (992). He should honour merit, but not be able to confer power.]

[In the ancient world] citizens were neither lawyers nor soldiers nor priests by profession; they were all [these] by duty. That is the real secret of making everything proceed to the common goal . . .

The office of judge, both in the highest and local courts, should be a temporary employment by which the nation may test and evaluate the merit and integrity of a citizen, to raise him later to those more

1000   important positions of which he has been found capable . . .

[We want] few laws, but well thought out, and above all well
enforced . . .   1002

The choice of an economic system to be adopted by Poland depends on the purposes she has in view in reforming her constitution.
If your only wish is to become noisy, brilliant and fearsome, and to
influence the other peoples of Europe, their example lies before you;
devote yourselves to following it. Cultivate the arts and sciences,
commerce and industry; have professional soldiers, fortresses and
academies; above all have a good system of public finance which
will make money circulate rapidly, and thereby multiply its effective-
ness to your great profit; try to make money very necessary, in order
to keep the people in a condition of great dependence; and with that
end in view, encourage material luxury, and the luxury of spirit which
is inseparable from it. In this way you will create a scheming, ardent,
avid, ambitious, servile and dishonest people, like all the rest; one
given to the two extremes of opulence and misery, of licence and
slavery, with nothing in between. But you will be counted as one of
the great powers of Europe; you will be included in all diplomatic
combinations; in all negotiations your alliance will be courted; you
will be bound by treaties; and there will be no war in Europe into
which you will not have the honour of being plunged. If you are
lucky you will be able to recover your ancient possessions, perhaps
conquer new ones, and be able to say, like Pyrrhus or the Russians,
that is to say, like children: 'When the whole world is mine I will
eat lots of sweets.'   1003

But if, by chance, you would prefer to create a free, wise and peaceful nation, one which has no fear or need of anyone but is self-
sufficient and happy, then you must adopt wholly different methods;
you must preserve and revive in your people simple customs and
wholesome tastes, and a hardy spirit without ambition; you must
create courageous and unselfish souls.

[For this an agricultural economy of the kind he had suggested
for Corsica was necessary. The country will not be famous:]
Philosophers will burn you no incense, poets will not sing your
praises . . . but you will live in true prosperity, justice and liberty . . .

[But] do not try to combine these two objectives, for they are too
contradictory . . .   1004

It is heads, hearts and arms that . . . make the strength of a state
and the prosperity of a people. Financial systems make venal souls;
and when profit is the only goal it is always more profitable to be a
rascal than an honest man. The use of money is devious and secret . . .

[and] of all the incentives known to me, money is both the weakest and the most useless for the purpose of driving the political machine towards its goal, and the strongest and most reliable for turning it away from it.

I know that men can only be made to act in terms of their own interest; but pecuniary interest is the worst, the basest and most corrupting of all, and even, as I confidently repeat and shall always maintain, the least and weakest in the eyes of those who really know the human heart. In all hearts there is naturally a reserve of great passions; when greed for gold alone remains, it is because all the rest, which should have been stimulated and developed, has been enervated and stifled . . . Learn how to nurture and satisfy them directly, without the use of money, and money will soon lose its value.

1005

[Discussing the need for an army, Rousseau opposes the idea of a professional force.]

Regular troops, the plague and depopulators of Europe, are good for two purposes only, to attack and conquer neighbours, or to bind and enslave citizens.

1013–14

[All citizens should compose the nation's army. To make this possible more esteem should be given to being a soldier. But that must not be done by glorifying war, or indulging in conquests.]

Whoever wants to deprive others of their freedom almost always ends up losing his own. This is true even of kings, and very much more of people.

1017(a)

[He then puts forward his plan for promotion and emancipation, described above, and for the election of kings. He concludes:]

As for the manner of tackling the work in question, I have no taste at all for the subtle schemes that have been suggested to you for the purpose of surprising and, in a sense, deceiving the nation with regard to the changes to be introduced into its laws. I should only advise that, while revealing your plan in its full extent, you should not begin putting it into operation abruptly, in such a way as to fill the republic with malcontents . . .

Never shake the machine too brusquely. I have no doubt that a good plan, once adopted, will change the spirit even of those who played a part in government under another system. Since new citizens cannot be created all at once, you must begin by making use of those who exist. To offer a new road for their ambition is the way to make them want to follow it.

1040–1

22 REVERIES

As a young man Rousseau had come to Paris full of youthful enthusiasm, energy and ambition; the city was the capital of the civilized world and there he would make his name. As an old man he came back to Paris. He had become famous, but his name now aroused more distrust than admiration. 'Here I am in Paris, alone, alien, without support, or friend, or relative, or advice.'[1] In reading his *Confessions*, and then in writing the *Dialogues*, he had tried to break through this distrust and isolation, to show that he was not the monster he was presumed to be and vindicate his ideas for happiness, justice, and a better way of life.

Rousseau needed this contact with other people. He needed it not just for the sake of a reputation, but because his sense of himself, of what a person was, depended on his *concours* with his fellow-men. By laying bare his inner self he hoped it would be possible for others to see what he and they had in common. He had tried to show himself as he was: 'I am an observer and not a moralist. I am the botanist who describes the plant.'[2] He had made himself accessible, so that society might become accessible once more to him. But he had failed; he had been rejected. His isolation was now complete.

It was in this situation that he wrote his last work, *The Reveries of the Solitary Walker*, a series of chapters or walks composed in the last two years of his life and left unfinished at his death. He described it as

> a formless journal of my reveries. There will be a lot about myself, because a solitary who reflects is inevitably occupied a lot with himself. As for the rest, all the strange ideas which pass through my head when I am walking will find an equal place. I will say what I have thought as it comes to me, and with as little

connection as the ideas of yesterday usually have with those of the next day . . . I will apply the barometer to my soul . . . [and] be content to register its operations, without trying to reduce them to a system.[3]

These reveries are not meditations or reflections. He is not trying to think. 'I have sometimes thought profoundly, but rarely with pleasure, and almost always against my inclination, as by force. Reverie refreshes me and amuses me, reflection tires me and makes me sad.'[4] Nor is he trying to justify himself in any way: 'I neither argue nor prove, because I am not seeking to persuade anyone. I am writing only for myself.'[5] He is merely trying to record what passes through his mind, a kind of mental browsing, in which his attention is held by something and then passes on, in which his thoughts collect round one subject, as if of their own accord, and then disperse.

This activity is one that Rousseau had always liked. 'Idleness is enough for me, and provided I do nothing, I much prefer to dream awake than asleep . . . The idleness I like is that of a child . . . letting the whole day wander by without order or intention, following nothing but the whim of the moment.'[6] Before the *Reveries* he had never achieved this in writing, because he had always written for some purpose, for the sake of some audience. 'While men were my brothers I concerned myself with projects for earthly happiness. These projects were always relative to the whole; I could only be happy in public happiness.'[7] Only now, in his isolation, feeling that he was 'on earth as if on a strange planet',[8] does he write down his reveries.

In the *Dialogues* he had said that this 'taste for reverie . . . is what very often happen to Orientals . . . whom Jean-Jacques resembles in many ways'.[9] Elsewhere he had elaborated this idea:

among us it is the body which moves, among the Orientals it is the imagination. Our walks come from the need to stimulate our [otherwise] too inflexible muscles and go off in search of new objects. Among them the movement of the brain makes up for that of the person; they remain motionless and the universe walks past in front of them.[10]

What passes through Rousseau's mind is not always pleasant. He still turns over his quarrel with the *philosophes*, he still worries about lies he has told in the past, he is still tormented by guilt over his treatment of his children. But there are also remarkable passages in the *Reveries* where we feel an ebb and flow between his isolation in himself and an identification with the world, between expansion and withdrawal, between acquiescence and ecstasy. There is a continual movement from the past to the present, from the world outside to the world within. Here Rousseau realizes most vividly that transparency of the soul that he set out to achieve in the *Confessions*.*

The Reveries of the Solitary Walker

Here I am, then, alone on the earth; having now no brother, neighbour, friend or society but myself. The most sociable and loving of human beings has been rejected by unanimous agreement. They have sought in the subtleties of their hatred whatever torment could be most cruel to my sensitive soul, and they have violently broken all the bonds which held me to them. I would have loved men in spite of themselves; they have been able to escape from my affection only by ceasing to be men. They are, then, strangers, unknown, in the end nothing to me, because they have wished it. But I, detached from them and from everything, what am I myself? That is what remains to be discovered . . .   995

Alone for the rest of my life, because I can only find consolation, hope and peace in myself, I ought not, nor do I want, to occupy myself with anything except myself . . .   999

I am undertaking the same task ås Montaigne, but with a completely opposite intention. For he only wrote his *Essays* for other people, while I am writing my reveries only for myself . . .   1001

These hours of meditation and solitude are the only hours of the day when I am fully myself and my own, without distraction or obstacle, when I can really be said to be what nature has wanted . . .

Finding no more nourishment for my heart on earth I gradually grew accustomed to feeding it on its own substance and to finding all its pasturage within me . . .   1002

[Rousseau describes his feelings after an accident when he had been knocked down one evening by a large dog.]

Night was coming on. I saw the sky, some stars, some grass. This first sensation was a delicious moment. I felt nothing except through [what I saw]. In that moment I was born to life, and I seemed to fill all the objects I saw with my own light existence. I remembered nothing, I was completely contained in the present. I had no distinct

* Both works need much longer extracts than those given here to do justice to their remarkable qualities.

notion of my individuality, nor the least idea of what was happening to me. I knew neither who I was nor where I was. I felt neither evil, nor fear, nor anxiety. I looked at my blood flowing as I might have watched the water in a stream, not even thinking that the blood belonged to me in any way. In my whole being I felt an overwhelming calm, which, whenever I recall it, I cannot compare to any other

1005 known pleasure . . .

Vain arguments will never destroy the agreement that I see between my immortal nature and the constitution of the world, and the

1018 physical order I see prevailing . . .

Among the small number of books that I still sometimes read, Plutarch is the one I most enjoy, and the one from which I benefit most. It was the first reading of my childhood, it will be the last of my old age . . .

The maxim of the Temple of Delphi — Know Yourself — is not

1024 so easy to follow as I believed in my *Confessions* . . .

[In the Fifth Walk Rousseau describes his happiness on the island of Saint-Pierre (see Chapter 17) and reflects on the nature of that experience:]

Everything on earth is in a continual [state of] flux. Nothing keeps a fixed and constant form, and those affections which attach us to external things inevitably pass away and change like them. Always in front of us or behind us, they recall the past which has gone or anticipate the future which is often not to be . . . In our most vivid enjoyment there is scarcely one moment when our heart could truly say: I would like this moment to last for ever. And how can one call happiness that fleeting state which still leaves our heart restless and empty, which makes us regret something beforehand, or still desire something afterwards?

But if there is a state where the soul finds a position stable enough to rest in altogether complete, and gather there its whole being . . . where time is nothing for it, where the present lasts for ever without marking its duration or any trace of succession; with no other feeling — either of deprivation or enjoyment, of pleasure or pain, of desire or fear — except that of our existence, and that feeling alone being able to fill it entirely; while such a state lasts he who finds it could call himself happy. Not with an imperfect, poor or relative happiness, such as one finds in the pleasures of life, but with a full, perfect, and sufficient happiness, which leaves no emptiness in the soul that it feels the need to fill.

Such is the state in which I often found myself on the island of

Saint-Pierre, in my solitary reveries, either lying in my boat, letting it drift at the will of the water, or seated on the shore of the agitated lake, or elsewhere, beside a beautiful stream or a brook murmuring over the pebbles.

What is the nature of the enjoyment of such a situation? Nothing external to yourself, nothing except yourself and your own existence; while such a state lasts you are self-sufficient, like God. The feeling of existence, deprived of all other affection, is by itself a precious feeling of contentment and peace; it is in itself enough to make this existence sweet and dear to anyone who can separate himself from all the sensual and terrestrial impressions which incessantly distract us from it, and trouble our sweetness here below . . .

An unhappy man, who has been excluded from human society, and can no longer do anything useful or good either for others or himself, can find in this state compensation for all the human happiness that fortune and men have taken from him . . .   1046–7

I love myself too much to be able to hate anyone, whoever he may be. That would be to enclose or contract my existence, and I want rather to extend it over the whole universe . . .   1056

I have never believed that man's liberty consisted in doing what he wanted, but rather in never doing what he did not want to do . . .   1059

[In the Seventh Walk Rousseau gives a long account of his interest in botany.]
I never meditate or dream with greater pleasure than when I forget myself. I feel ecstasy, an inexpressible rapture, in as it were dissolving myself in the system of beings, in identifying myself with the whole of nature . . .

Taking refuge in the arms of our common mother I have tried to withdraw from the attacks of her children. I have become solitary or, as they say, misanthropic and unsociable, because the wildest solitude seemed to me preferable to a society of wicked men . . .   1065–6

[Botany] has become a kind of passion for me which fills the emptiness of the passions I no longer have. I clamber up rocks and mountains, I bury myself in valleys and woods, to rid myself as much as possible of the memory of men . . .   1070

The *Reveries* complete a process of withdrawal from society that had begun in the *Dialogues:* 'I have retired into myself and [am] living between myself and nature.'[11] Rousseau wanted to find and assemble in himself the attributes of man in a state of nature, to be like primi-

tive man 'wholly wrapped up in the feeling of his present existence'
(see p. 56). Jean-Jacques, he wrote in the *Dialogues*, 'is what nature
has made him; education has modified him only very little'.[12]
'This man will not be virtuous . . . Goodness, compassion and
generosity — those first inclinations of nature which are no more
than emanations of self-love — will not be erected in his head into
austere duties.'[13] At the end of the Sixth Walk in the *Reveries* he
wrote: 'I was never truly fitted for civil society.'[14]

This final work exalts solitude and a condition of being self-
sufficient. Because of their almost hypnotically self-contained quality,
and the calm and beautiful assurance with which they are written, they
are sometimes seen as a distinct and separate solution[15] to the problem
of society — the fall from innocence — which Rousseau had outlined
in his *Discourse on Inequality*. To my mind, however, the *Reveries*
are less a new kind of solution than a more acute statement of the
problem. They may indeed have acted as a solution to Rousseau; for
the person who writes, the act of writing can often be therapeutic.
But for us who read them today it is impossible not to be aware of
the extent to which these last autobiographical works were com-
pensations for the ill-treatment he had received from his own society.

In fact, Rousseau said as much himself. In the *Confessions* he
wrote: 'My imagination which in my youth was always going ahead
of me, now looks back. With these sweet memories it compensates
for the hope that I have lost for ever. I no longer see anything in the
future that appeals to me; only going back to the past can give me
pleasure.'[16] In the *Dialogues* he wrote:

> In the contemplation of nature . . . [Jean-Jacques] found a sub-
> stitute for the attachments he needed. But he would have left
> the substitute for the thing [itself] if he had had the choice; he
> was only reduced to communing with plants after vain efforts
> at communion with humans. I will gladly leave the society of
> plants, he has said to me, at the first hope of finding again the
> society of men.[17]

He wrote the *Reveries*, he said, because 'the leisure of my daily
walks has often been filled with delightful thoughts that I am sorry
to have lost by not remembering them. By writing down those which
may still occur to me I will keep hold of them; each time I re-read
them I will enjoy them once more.'[18] The act of writing was like the act
of making the herbaria which he filled with the plants he had gathered;
it was a way of making 'me forget the persecutions of men, their

hate, their scorn, their outrages, and all the evils with which they have repaid my tender and sincere attachment to them'.[19] He needed to forget other men because he was irresistibly drawn to them: 'Here I am, alone on earth . . . the most sociable . . . of human beings.' Even in his most intimate and withdrawn moments he reminds us of the society to which he would like to belong.

Rousseau had both an inclination and a need for solitude — it is one of the recurring themes in his writing — but he never chose for himself the extreme isolation of his final years. The tragedy of his life was that he was opposed not only to the political *status quo* of his time, the *ancien régime*, but also to the very opposition to that *status quo*, the *philosophes*. 'At the head of each of these two parties', he wrote in a footnote to the *Dialogues*, 'are my most implacable enemies.'[20] In the face of their hostility he would like to have been self-sufficient, complete in himself and in the natural world, regaining the goodness that primitive man possessed, with the present moment lasting for ever. But nothing stands still and we are not alone. Time and society are inescapable facts of our existence. Solitude can provide no solution.

That should not be a matter of regret. Rousseau himself has made us aware of that enlarged and enriched sense of ourselves that comes from participation and belonging. It is partly because that sense in him was so acute that his experience of solitude was so vivid. In all his work there is a continual oscillation, tension and dialectic, between what is most personal and what is most social. His very greatness is to have comprehended both aspects of our lives, both the need to be at one with ourselves, and the need to relate to our fellow-men. He was 'the historian of the human heart'[21] who 'taught [men] to enter into their own hearts to find there the seeds of social virtues'.[22]

Rousseau was an extraordinary person, and he had lived an extraordinary life. But in his writing he reaches out to us and conveys what is most ordinary — the needs of the heart, our common humanity.

23 EPIGRAMS

How blind we are in the midst of so much enlightenment.[1]

Whoever wants to deprive others of their liberty almost always ends up losing his own.[2]

The demon of property infects everything he touches.[3]

The money you possess is the instrument of freedom; the money you pursue is the instrument of slavery.[4]

Luxury corrupts everyone; both the rich who enjoy it and the poor who envy it.[5]

You will be poor as long as you want more.[6]

Exclusive pleasures are the death of pleasure; true pleasure is what we share with the people.[7]

Such are men; they change their language like their clothes and only speak the truth in their night-gowns.[8]

The darkness of ignorance is worth more than the false light of error.[9]

The heart is a law unto itself; try to bind it and you lose it; give it liberty and you make it your own.[10]

Everything that destroys social unity is worthless.[11]

It is strength and liberty that make excellent men.[12]

The rich keep the law in their pocket and the poor prefer bread to liberty.[13]

The pleasure of having is not worth the pain of acquiring.[14]

It is easier to conquer than to rule. With a big enough lever you could shake the world with a finger; to sustain it needs the shoulders of Hercules.[15]

Everything conspires to deprive a man who is set in authority over others of his sense of justice and reason.[16]

Distrust those cosmopolitans who look in their books for the duties they disdain to fulfil at home. Intellectuals like that love the Tatars, to be exempt from loving their neighbours.[17]

Possession is nothing if it is not reciprocal.[18]

Once we leave our nature there are no limits that restrain us.[19]

Society must be studied in the individual and the individual in society. Those who want to treat politics and morals apart from one another will never understand either.[20]

NOTES

References, except where otherwise stated, are to the relevant volume (in roman numerals) and page (in arabic numerals) of the Pléiade edition of the *Œuvres Complètes*.

The following abbreviations are used for the individual works:

Inégal. = *Discours sur l'origine d'inégalité*
Econ. = *Discours sur l'économie politique*
Héloïse = *La Nouvelle Héloïse*
Contrat = *Du Contrat Social*
C. de B. = *Lettre à Christophe de Beaumont*
Montagne = *Lettres écrites de la Montagne*
Corse = *Projet de Constitution pour la Corse*
Conf. = *Confessions*
Pologne = *Considérations sur le Gouvernement de Pologne*
Dial. = *Dialogues: Rousseau Juge de Jean-Jacques*
D'Alem. = *Lettre à D'Alembert* (Garnier Flammarion Edition, Paris, 1967)
Leigh = *Correspondance Complète*, ed. R. A. Leigh (Geneva and Oxford, 1965–)
Studies = *Studies on Voltaire and the Eighteenth Century*

Details of translations used, where applicable, are given in the Preface.

The articles mentioned below should be consulted in conjunction with the books referred to in Further Reading.

The anonymous poem, before the Introduction, is quoted in Jean Guéhenno, *Jean-Jacques* (Paris, 1962), vol. II, p. 214.

1 INTRODUCTION

1. *Conf.*, i. 113–14
2. *Persiffleur*, i. 1108
3. Rousseau, *Le Persiffleur*, i. 1108: 'Rien n'est si dissemblable à moi que moi-même' (see also *Conf.*, i. 128). Diderot, *Le Neveu de Rameau* (ed. J. Fabre, Geneva, 1950), p. 4: 'Rien ne dissemble plus de lui que lui-même.'
4. *Persiffleur*, i. 1109
5. See, for example, *Conf.*, i. 12, i. 640; *Dial.*, i. 811, i. 817
6. Hume, *Letters* (ed. J. Greig, Oxford, 1932), ii. 26/7, ii. 29, i. 530
7. Letter to Malesherbes, 4 Jan 1762, Pléiade, i. 1131
8. Quoted by Leigh: XI: 276

9. *Héloïse*, ii. 27
10. *Dial.*, i. 697
11. *Fragment*, i. 1115
12. Letter to Rousseau, 30 Aug 1755. Leigh, III. 156–7
13. *Inégal.*, iii. 138
14. *Dial.*, i. 935. See on this subject, A. O. Lovejoy, 'The Supposed Primitivism of Rousseau's *Discourse on Inequality*' in his *Essays in the History of Ideas* (Baltimore, Md, 1948)
15. *Emile*, iv. 322
16. *Fragment*, iii. 533
17. Letter to Duchesne, 23 May 1762. Leigh, X. 281
18. *D'Alem.*, p. 210. See on this subject, R. A. Leigh, 'Liberté et Autorité dans le *Contrat Social*' in *Jean-Jacques Rousseau et son Œuvre* (Paris, 1964)
19. *Fragment*, iii. 555
20. *Observations* (to the King of Poland), iii. 56; *Emile*, iv. 468; *Jugement sur le Projet de Paix*, iii. 599–600. For other remarks on revolution, see, *Inégal.*, iii. 113; *Contrat*, iii. 385; *Montagne*, iii. 836; *Dial.*, i. 935. Also the Letter to Comtesse de Wartensleben, cited in Chapter 16, note 12; *Emile et Sophie*, iv. 919
21. *Montagne*, iii. 881
22. *Inégal.*, iii. 183
23. *Contrat*, iii. 425
24. *Dial.*, i. 728
25. *Dial.*, i. 887–8
26. *Emile*, iv. 844
27. *Econ.*, iii. 253; *Fragment*, iii. 493; *Pologne*, iii. 975
28. *Contrat*, iii. 428
29. *Emile*, iv. 858
30. *Pologne*, iii. 955
31. Cecil Rhodes, quoted by H. Arendt, *Origins of Totalitarianism* (New York, N.Y., 1968), vol. II, p. 4
32. *Contrat*, iii. 420 n
33. *Contrat*, iii. 381
34. *Emile*, iv. 493
35. *Dial.*, i. 813
36. *Fragment*, iii. 554
37. See *Dernière Réponse* (to M. Bordes), iii. 72; *Dial.* i. 864; *Essai sur l'Origine des Langues* (ed. C. Porset, Bordeaux, 1968), p. 121
38. *Inégal.*, iii. 202
39. *Lettres Morales*, iv. 1100

2 LIFE

1. *Conf.*, i. 12
2. *Conf.*, i. 31
3. *Conf.*, i. 237
4. *Conf.*, i. 225–6
5. *Education de Sainte-Marie*, iv. 41, 44
6. *Conf.*, i. 272
7. *Conf.*, i. 327
8. *Conf.*, i. 404
9. *Conf.*, i. 314
10. *Boswell on the Grand Tour* (ed. F. A. Pottle, London, 1953), p. 258
11. *Persiffleur*, i. 1111

12. *Conf.*, i. 347
13. Letter to Malesherbes, 12 Jan. 1762. Pléiade, i. 1135–6
14. *Conf.*, i. 356
15. *Conf.*, i. 363
16. *Rêveries*, i. 1014
17. Letter to Romilly, 6 Feb. 1759. Leigh, VI. 22
18. *Conf.*, i. 388–9
19. *Conf.*, i. 393
20. *Conf.*, i. 401
21. *Conf.*, i. 416
22. Quoted in Leigh, XI. 262
23. Quoted in Leigh, XI. 301
24. *Conf.*, i. 590
25. *Conf.*, i. 216
26. *Sentiment des Citoyens* (1764), pp. 1 and 6. Leigh, XXIII. 378, 380–1
27. Juvenal, *Satires*, iv. 91
28. Hume, *Letters* (ed. J. Greig, Oxford, 1932), ii. 13
29. Bernardin de St-Pierre, *La Vie de J-J. Rousseau*, in Rousseau, *Œuvres Complètes* (Seuil edition, Paris, 1967), pp. 37, 29, 32, 35, 28, 38

3 WORDS

1. *Emile*, iv. 345 n
2. *C. de B.*, iv. 957
3. Letter to Mme d'Epinay, March 1756. Leigh, III. 296
4. *Dial.*, i. 669
5. Letter to Pictet, 1 March 1764. Leigh, XIX. 190

4 MORALS

All page numbers in the text refer to Pléiade, iii, except for the *Preface to Narcissus*, which will be found in Pléiade, ii.

1. *Conf.*, i. 351
2. *Conf.*, i. 352
3. *Discours sur les Sciences et les Arts*, iii. 3
4. *Tristia*, Bk V. X. 37
5. Quoted in Leigh, II. 342
6. Quoted in the Introduction to *Discours sur les Sciences et les Arts* (ed. G. R. Havens, New York, 1946), p. 31
7. *Conf.*, i. 56
8. *Contrat*, iii. 351

For this chapter see the excellent introduction and notes to the edition by G. R. Havens, cited above; also Leo Strauss, 'On the Intention of Rousseau' in *Hobbes and Rousseau* (ed. M. Cranston and R. Peters, New York, 1972).

5 INEQUALITY

All page numbers refer to Pléiade, iii.

1. *Inégal.*, iii. 213
2. *Inégal.*, iii. 125
3. *Inégal.*, iii. 212
4. *Inégal.*, iii. 116
5. *Politics*, 1. 1254 a 36–38

6. See on this subject, R. Wokler, 'Perfectible Apes and Decadent Cultures', *Daedalus* (Summer 1978)
7. Leigh, III. 156–8. Also Pléiade, iii. 1379–81
8. Leigh, III. 153. Also Pléiade, iii. 1384
9. *Emile*, iv. 676

For this chapter see the essay by A. O. Lovejoy, cited in Chapter 1, note 14; also U. S. Allers, 'Rousseau's *Second Discourse*' in *The Review of Politics*, vol. XX (1958).

6 GOVERNMENT

All page numbers refer to Pléiade, iii.

1. *Econ.*, iii. 245
2. See on this subject and this chapter generally: R. Wokler, 'The Influence of Diderot on Rousseau', *Studies*, CXXXII (1975)
3. Pléiade, iii. 1392 (e)
4. *Fragment*, iii. 492
5. *Inégal.*, iii. 184
6. *Contrat*, iii. 365
7. *Econ.*, iii. 263
8. *Econ.*, iii. 269–70

7 MUSIC

The page numbers in sections I and III refer to *Œuvres Complètes* (Paris, 1837) vol. III. The page numbers in section II refer to the *Essai sur l'origine des langues* (ed. C. Porset, Bordeaux, 1968).

1. *Dial.*, i. 872
2. *Conf.*, i. 181
3. Gluck's comment on the opera being a model of 'the accent of nature' is quoted in Pléiade, i. 1626
4. Burney, *General History of Music* (London, 1935), vol. II, pp. 971, 1000
5. *Conf.*, i. 384
6. *Conf.*, i. 384
7. Noel Boyer, *La Guerre des Bouffons et la Musique Française* (Paris, 1945), quoted by Charles B. Paul, 'Music and Ideology', *Journal of the History of Ideas*, vol. 32 (1971), p. 406
8. Burney, op. cit., II. 970
9. Rameau, *Erreurs sur la Musique de l'Encyclopédie* (1755), *Complete Theoretical Works* (ed. E. R. Jacobi, New York, 1969), V. 220
10. *Héloïse*, ii. 133
11. Burney, op. cit., I. 706
12. Quoted by C. Girdlestone, *Jean-Philippe Rameau* (New York, 1969), p. 527
13. Quoted by R. Wokler, 'Rousseau, Rameau and the *Essai sur l'Origine des Langues*', *Studies*, CXVII (1974), p. 191, n. 31
14. Quoted by C. Girdlestone, op. cit., p. 526
15. Letter to D'Alembert, 26 June 1751. Leigh, II. 160
16. Letter to Le Sage, 1 July 1754. Leigh, III. 1
17. *Inégal.*, iii. 210
18. *Inégal.*, iii. 147
19. I owe this fact to Dr Robert Wokler. See his 'Rousseau on Rameau and Revolution' in *Studies in the Eighteenth Century*, IV (ed. R. Brissenden and J. C. Eade, Canberra, 1978)

20. *Dial.*, i. 681
21. *Contrat*, iii. 386

8 WAR

All page numbers refer to Pléiade, iii.

1. *Conf.*, i. 408
2. *Conf.*, i. 422
3. *Conf.*, i. 422
4. *Conf.*, i. 423
5. *Projet de Paix Perpetuelle*, iii. 572
6. *Projet de Paix Perpetuelle*, iii. 584
7. See the article by G. Davy in *Etudes sur le Contrat Social*, (Publications de l'Université de Dijon, 1964). This collection also contains an article by S. Sterling-Michaud on Rousseau's debt to the Abbé de St-Pierre

9 OPTIMISM

All page numbers refer to Pléiade, iv.

1. This sentence occurs in Leibniz's Correspondence with Samuel Clarke. Quoted by Peter Gay, *The Enlightenment* (London, 1970), vol. II, p. 143
2. Preface to Poem. Quoted by Leigh, IV. 64
3. *Conf.*, i. 429
4. *D'Alem.*, 206 n. See also *Emile*, iv. 588
5. Letter to Voltaire, iv. 1066
6. For a discussion about this supposition and this letter generally, see R. A. Leigh 'From *Inégalité* to *Candide*' in *The Age of Enlightenment. Studies presented to Theodore Bestermann* (Edinburgh, 1967)

10 THEATRE

All page numbers refer to the Garnier Flammarion edition (Paris, 1967).

1. *D'Alem.*, 44–5
2. *D'Alem.*, 47–8
3. *Georgics*, III. 513
4. *Héloïse*, ii. 5
5. *Héloïse*, ii. 26
6. *Conf.*, i. 495
7. Letter to Mme d'Houdetot, 23 March 1758. Leigh, V. 60
8. *Conf.*, i. 385
9. *D'Alem.*, 242
10. Letter to Le Sage, 1 July 1754. Leigh, III. 2
11. *Héloïse*, ii. 59
12. *Emile*, iv. 677
13. *Héloïse*, ii. 59
14. *Emile*, iv. 718
15. *Emile*, iv. 340

11 'THE NEW HELOÏSE'

All page numbers refer to Pléiade, ii.

1. *Conf.*, i. 421–2
2. *Conf.*, i. 425–6
3. *Conf.*, i. 427–8

4. *Conf.*, i. 430–1
5. *Héloïse*, ii. 47
6. *Héloïse*, ii. 89
7. *Héloïse*, ii. 73
8. *Héloïse*, ii. 101
9. *Héloïse*, ii. 138
10. *Héloïse*, ii. 148–9
11. *Héloïse*, ii. 231, ii. 236
12. *Conf.*, i. 435
13. *Héloïse*, ii. 479
14. *Héloïse*, ii. 476
15. *Héloïse*, ii. 20–21
16. *Héloïse*, ii. 470
17. *Héloïse*, ii. 609
18. Lionel Gossman, 'The Worlds of *La Nouvelle Héloïse*', *Studies*, XLI (1966), p. 262. His criticisms are developed in 'Rousseau's Idealism', *Romantic Review*, vol. 52 (1961)
19. Pléiade, ii. 1657 (p. 536 (b))
20. *Conf.*, i. 436
21. Letter to Vernes, 24 June 1761. Leigh, IX. 27
22. Petrarch, Sonnet No. 338, *Canzoniere, Trionfi, Rime Varie* (Milan, 1958), p. 422
23. *Héloïse*, ii. 689
24. *Héloïse*, ii. 697
25. See S. S. B. Taylor, 'Rousseau's Contemporary Reputation', *Studies*, XXVII (1963), p. 1557
26. Hume, *Letters* (ed. J. Greig, Oxford, 1932), vol. II. 28. For a recent review see J. Rousset, 'Rousseau romancier' in *Jean-Jacques Rousseau* (Neuchâtel, 1962)

12 'THE SOCIAL CONTRACT'

All page numbers refer to Pléiade, iii.

1. *Conf.*, i. 404–5
2. *Conf.*, i. 405 and note
3. *Conf.*, i. 516
4. *Geneva MS*, iii. 284
5. *Contrat*, iii. 351
6. *Æneid*, XI. 321–2
7. *Emile*, iv. 836
8. *Fragment*, iii. 477
9. *Dial.*, i. 965 n. See also *Geneva MS*, iii. 283
10. *Dial.*, i. 813
11. *Emile*, iv. 334. See also *Héloïse*, ii. 359
12. See on this subject, J. Plamenatz's essay in *Hobbes and Rousseau* (ed. M. Cranston and R. S. Peters, New York, 1972). Also Chapter 3 in B. Barber, *Superman and Common Men* (London, 1972)
13. *Héloïse*, ii. 589 n
14. Alfred Cobban, *Rousseau and the Modern State* (2nd ed., London, 1964), p. 56
15. Letter to Rey, 7 Nov 1761. Leigh, IX. 221
16. Letter to Rey, 4 April 1762. Leigh, X. 180
17. Sebastian Mercier, *De J-J. Rousseau* (Paris, 1791), vol. ii. 99. Quoted by C. E. Vaughan, *Rousseau's Political Writings* (Cambridge, 1915), vol. II, p. 17

18. *Letter to a Member of the National Assembly* (1791), pp. 30–1

For this chapter see the essay by R. A. Leigh, cited in Chapter 1 note 18; also, in the same collection, R. Polin, 'La fonction du Législateur chez J-J. Rousseau'; also I. Fetscher, 'Rousseau's concepts of liberty', *Nomos IV* (New York, 1962)

13 'EMILE'

All page numbers refer to Pléiade, iv.

1. *Dial.*, i. 687
2. *Conf.*, i. 386
3. *Emile*, iv. 241
4. *Conf.*, i. 521
5. *Emile*, iv. 241
6. *Emile*, iv. 250
7. *Emile*, iv. 857
8. Letter to Tronchin, 26 Nov. 1758. Leigh, V. 242
9. Letter to Deluc, 24 Feb. 1765. Leigh, XXIV. 87
10. *Emile*, iv. 262
11. *Héloïse*, ii. 24
12. *Dial.*, i. 668
13. *Emile*, iv. 321
14. *Emile*, iv. 370, iv. 417
15. *Emile*, iv. 600. See also *Lettres Morales*, iv. 1109
16. *Emile* (MS Favre), iv. 60
17. Leigh, II. 277
18. Leigh, XI. 288
19. E. H. Wright, *The Meaning of Rousseau* (Oxford, 1929), p. 64
20. *De Ira*, XI. 13
21. *Emile*, iv. 700
22. *Emile*, iv. 736–7
23. See *Contrat*, iii. 372. Also *Geneva MS*, iii. 295
24. *Emile*, iv. 720
25. *Emile*, iv. 837
26. *Emile*, iv. 837
27. Letter to Duchesne, 23 May 1762. Leigh, X. 281
28. Quoted by P. D. Jimack, Introduction to *Emile* (Everyman's Library, London, 1974), p. xxv, a useful essay; see also A. Bloom, 'The Education of Democratic Man', Daedalus (Summer 1978)

14 PROFESSION

All page numbers refer to Pléiade, iv.

1. Letter to Franquières. Pléiade, iv. 1134
2. *Rêveries*, i. 1016–18
3. *Dial.*, i. 879
4. *Conf.*, i. 642
5. Letter to Deschamps, 25 June 1761. Leigh, IX. 28
6. *Emile*, iv. 591

15 TO THE ARCHBISHOP

All page numbers refer to Pléiade, iv.

1. *Conf.*, i. 407

16 GENEVA

All page numbers refer to Pléiade, iii.

1. Letter from Moultou to Rousseau, 16 June 1762. Leigh, XI. 90
2. *Montagne*, iii. 685
3. *Montagne*, iii. 702–3
4. *Montagne*, iii. 716
5. *Montagne*, iii. 715
6. *Montagne*, iii. 781, 778
7. *Contrat*, iii. 424.
8. Quoted in G. Vallette, *J-J. Rousseau, Genevois* (Geneva, 1911), p. 329
9. Letter to Deluc, 24 Feb. 1765. Leigh, XXIV. 87
10. Bernardin de St-Pierre (op. cit.), p. 33
11. *Conf.*, i. 650
12. Letter to Comtesse de Wartensleben, 27 Sept. 1766. Leigh, XXX. 384–6

For this chapter see the chapter on Geneva in R. R. Palmer, *The Age of Democratic Revolutions*, Vol. I (Princeton, 1959).

17. NATURE

All page numbers refer to Pléiade, i.

1. P. Burgelin, Pléiade, iv. lxxxix
2. *Héloïse*, ii. 456
3. *Conf.*, i. 409
4. *Conf.*, i. 162
5. Letter to Malesherbes, 26 Jan. 1762. Pléiade, i. 1140
6. *Conf.*, i. 180
7. *Conf.*, i. 641
8. *Conf.*, i. 641
9. *Conf.*, i. 180
10. *Rêveries*, i. 1063
11. *Rêveries*, i. 1065
12. *Rêveries*, i. 1067
13. *Rêveries*, i. 1068
14. *Rêveries*, i. 1062
15. *Conf.*, i. 642
16. *Conf.*, i. 643–4

18 CORSICA

All page numbers refer to Pléiade, iii.

1. *Contrat*, iii. 391
2. *Corse*, iii. 905
3. *Corse*, iii. 911
4. *Corse*, iii. 927
5. *Corse*, iii. 924
6. *Corse*, iii. 919
7. *Corse*, iii. 943

19 PESSIMISM

The page numbers refer to C. E. Vaughan, *Rousseau's Political Writings*, (Cambridge, 1915), Vol. II.

1. *Emile*, iv. 340 n
2. *Emile*, iv. 524 n
3. *Emile*, iv. 633 n
4. Letter to Deschamps, 8 May 1761. Leigh, VIII. 320–1. See also the first two footnotes to the *Letter to D'Alembert*.
5. *Emile*, iv. 530
6. *Fragment*, i. 1115; *Dial.*, i. 1636 (697 a)
7. *Emile*, iv. 350–1 n
8. *Emile*, iv. 522–3
9. *Héloïse*, ii. 13
10. Letter to Franquières, Pléiade, iv. 1136
11. *Emile*, iv. 633 n
12. Mercier de la Rivière, *L'ordre naturel et essentiel des sociétés politiques* (Paris, 1767), p. 185
13. *Contrat*, iii. 398
14. *Emile*, iv. 676. See also *Inégal.*, iii. 199
15. *Metamorphoses*, VII. 20

20 CONFESSION

All page numbers refer to Pléiade, i.
1. Letter to Malesherbes, 12 Jan. 1762. Pléiade, i. 1134–5
2. *Conf.*, i. 402–3. See also *Dial.*, i. 840
3. *Emile*, iv. 451
4. *Essai sur l'origine des langues*, ed. cit., p. 31
5. *Dial.*, i. 936
6. *Lettres Morales*, iv. 1112
7. Letter to Henriette, 4 Nov. 1764. Leigh, XXII. 9
8. *Conf.*, i. 516
9. *Ebauches*, i. 1149
10. *Satires*, III. 30
11. *Conf.*, i. 516–17
12. *Conf.*, i. 59
13. *Conf.*, i. 278
14. *Conf.*, i. 1370 (p. 278 b)
15. *Conf.*, i. 3
16. *Ebauches*, i. 1149. See also Hume, *Letters* (Oxford, 1932), vol. II. 2
17. *Conf.*, i. 279
18. *Conf.*, i. 589
19. A. MacIntyre, *A Short History of Ethics* (London, 1967), p. 185
20. *Dial.*, i. 664–5
21. *Dial.*, i. 664
22. *Dial.*, i. 972
23. *Dial.*, i. 935
24. *Dial.*, i. 972

For this chapter see J. H. Broome, *Rousseau: a study of his thought* (London, 1963)

21 POLAND

All page numbers refer to Pléiade, iii.
1. *Pologne*, iii. 954
2. *Montagne*, iii. 836
3. *Pologne*, iii. 1040

4. *Pologne*, iii. 962
5. *Pologne*, iii. 954–5

22 REVERIES

All page numbers refer to Pléiade, i.

1. Letter to Dusaulx, 16 Feb. 1771. *Correspondance Générale* (ed. Dufour-Plan), XX. 46
2. *Fragment*, i. 1120
3. *Rêveries*, i. 1000–1
4. *Rêveries*, i. 1061–2
5. *Ebauches*, i. 1170
6. *Conf.*, i. 640–1
7. *Rêveries*, i. 1066
8. *Rêveries*, i. 999
9. *Dial.*, i. 816
10. *Fragment*, ii. 1324
11. *Dial.*, i. 727
12. *Dial.*, i. 799
13. *Dial.*, i. 864
14. *Rêveries*, i. 999
15. See for example J. Starobinski's 1976 Lecture in *Proceedings of the British Academy*, Vol. LXII (1976)
16. *Conf.*, i. 226
17. *Dial.*, i. 794
18. *Rêveries*, i. 1059
19. *Rêveries*, i. 1073
20. *Dial.*, i. 965 n
21. *Dial.*, i. 728
22. *Dial.*, i. 687

For this chapter see Georges Poulet, *Studies in Human Time* (Baltimore, Md, 1959)

23 EPIGRAMS

1. *D'Alem.*, 85
2. *Pologne*, iii. 1793 (p. 1017 a)
3. *Emile*, iv. 690
4. *Conf.*, i. 38
5. *Observations*, iii. 51
6. *Pologne*, iii. 1008
7. *Emile*, iv. 690
8. *C. de B.*, iv. 966
9. *C. de B.*, iv. 1004
10. *Emile*, iv. 521
11. *Contrat*, iii. 464
12. *Rêveries*, i. 1057
13. *Montagne*, iii. 890
14. *Conf.*, i. 38
15. *Contrat*, iii. 410
16. *Contrat*, iii. 411
17. *Emile*, iv. 249
18. *Emile*, iv. 684
19. *Rêveries*, i. 1056
20. *Emile*, iv. 524

DATES

1712	28 June, birth of Jean-Jacques Rousseau in Geneva. 7 July, death of his mother.
1722	His father leaves Geneva; he is boarded with pastor Lambercier at Bossey.
1724	He returns to Geneva and is apprenticed to an engraver.
1728	March, he runs away. Meets Mme de Warens at Annecy. Is sent to Turin and becomes a Catholic.
1729	He returns to Savoy. Years of wandering, learning and desultory employment.
1735–6	Summers at Les Charmettes.
1740–1	He teaches in Lyons.
1742	He goes to Paris and presents his system of musical notation to the Academy of Sciences.
1743–4	He spends a year in Venice as Secretary to the French Ambassador; then returns to Paris.
1745	He meets Thérèse. Friendship with Diderot and Condillac.
1746	Birth of his first child, who is put in the Foundlings' Hospital. He becomes secretary to the Dupin family.
1749	He writes articles on music for the *Encyclopedia*. October, his 'illumination' on the road to Vincennes.
1750	His *First Discourse* wins the prize from the Dijon Academy. It is published the following year.
1751	His 'reform'; he gives up his job as secretary and starts copying music. *Observations* (to the King of Poland) published.
1752	*Last Reply* (to M. Bordes) published. He writes *The Village Sorcerer*; October, it is performed at Fontainebleau. December, performance of *Narcissus* at the Comédie-Française; the play is published with a *Preface*.
1753	Visit to Saint-Germain, first thoughts on *Discourse on Inequality*. Publication of the *Letter on French Music*.
1754	Completion of *Discourse on Inequality*. Visit to Geneva, he is received back into the Protestant Church and takes up his rights as a citizen.
1755	Publication of *Discourse on Inequality* and Vol. V of the *Encyclopedia* with his article on 'Political Economy'. Writes *Letter to M. Philopolis*.

1756   April, he moves to the Hermitage. Finishes work on the papers of the Abbé de St-Pierre; writes *Letter to Voltaire on Optimism*; first thoughts of *The New Heloïse*.

1757   He falls in love with Mme d'Houdetot; quarrels with Mme d'Epinay and moves to Montlouis.

1758   He writes the *Letter to D'Alembert* and completes *The New Heloïse*. Final break with Diderot.

1759–60   He works on *Emile* and *The Social Contract*.

1761   Publication of *The New Heloïse*. He completes work on *Emile, The Social Contract* and the *Essay on the Origin of Languages*.

1762   He writes the *Letters to Malesherbes*. Publication of *Emile* in Paris and *The Social Contract* in Amsterdam. 9 June, *Emile* is condemned and burnt in Paris and Rousseau's arrest ordered by the Parlement. He leaves France. 19 June, *Emile* and *The Social Contract* are condemned and burnt in Geneva. Rousseau settles in Môtiers.

1763   Publication of the *Letter to Christophe de Beaumont*. He renounces his citizenship of Geneva.

1764   Publication of *Letters from the Mountain*.

1765   He completes his *Dictionary of Music*, and works on the *Confessions* and the *Project for Corsica*. 6 September, the 'stoning' at Môtiers. He goes to the island of Saint-Pierre, then, after six weeks, to Strasbourg and Paris.

1766   January, he arrives in England. Quarrel with Hume. He works on the *Confessions*.

1767   May, he returns to France. Publication of the *Dictionary of Music*.

1768   He marries Thérèse.

1769   He works on the Second Part of the *Confessions*.

1770   He returns to Paris, resumes work copying music.

1771   His readings from the *Confessions* are stopped.

1772   He completes work on the *Government of Poland* and begins the *Dialogues: Rousseau Judge of Jean-Jacques*.

1776   He completes the *Dialogues* and attempts to place them on the High Altar of Notre-Dame. He begins the *Reveries of the Solitary Walker*.

1778   2 July, Rousseau dies at Ermenonville, outside Paris.

FURTHER READING

IN ENGLISH

Titles marked with an asterisk (*) are, or have been, available in paperback.

By Rousseau

*First and Second Discourses** (New York, 1964). Introduction by R. G. Masters. Only English version with all Rousseau's Notes to the *Second Discourse*. Helpful edition.

*The Social Contract and Discourses** (Everyman's Library, London, 1973). Introduction by G. D. H. Cole. Contains all three *Discourses*, and also sections of *The Geneva MS* and Book V of *Emile*. Good introduction, very useful volume.

*The Social Contract** (New York, 1974). Introduction by C. M. Sherover. Also contains *Discourse on Political Economy* and the Dedication to the *Second Discourse*. Helpful notes.

*The Social Contract** (Harmondsworth, 1968). Introduction by M. Cranston. Best modern translation.

Political Writings (London, 1953). Introduction by F. Watkins. Contains *The Social Contract* and writings on Corsica and Poland.

*The Government of Poland** (New York, 1972). Introduction by W. Kendall.

*The Creed of a Priest of Savoy** (New York, 1956). Translated by A. H. Beattie.

*Emile** (Everyman's Library, London, 1974). Introduction by P. D. Jimack. Good introduction, variable translation.

*Emile for Today** (London, 1975). Introduction by W. Boyd. Extracts only, selected for educational interest.

*Politics and the Arts** (Ithaca, 1960). Introduction by A. Bloom. Helpful edition of the *Letter to D'Alembert*.

*On the Origin of Language** (New York, 1966). Translated by J. H. Moran.

The New Heloïse (Philadelphia, 1968). Translated by J. McDowell. Abridged version, serious omissions.

*Confessions** (Harmondsworth, 1953). Translated by J. M. Cohen.

Confessions (Everyman's Library, London, 1931).

The Reveries of the Solitary Walker (Harmondsworth, forthcoming). Translated by P. France.

Citizen of Geneva (London, 1937). Selections from the *Letters* by C. W. Hendel.

About Rousseau

The best general introductions are: E. Cassirer, *The Question of Rousseau**
(New York, 1954); R. Grimsley, *The Philosophy of Rousseau** (Oxford, 1973);
E. H. Wright, *The Meaning of Rousseau* (Oxford, 1929).

There are interesting chapters in K. Barth, *From Rousseau to Ritschl* (London,
1959); L. Colletti, *From Rousseau to Lenin** (London, 1972); P. Gay, *The Party
of Humanity* (London, 1964); C. Lévi-Strauss, *Structural Anthropology*, Vol. II
(London, 1976); M. Berman, *The Politics of Authenticity* (London, 1971).

J. Guéhenno's biography, *Jean-Jacques Rousseau* (London, 1966) provides a
sympathetic account of his life. R. Grimsley, *Jean-Jacques Rousseau: A Study
in Self-awareness* (Cardiff, 1961) is a psychological study. The biographies by
F. C. Green (Cambridge, 1956) and L. G. Crocker (New York, N.Y., 1968–73)
are informative but display a regrettable hostility to their subject.

The best two approaches to Rousseau's political thought are: A. Cobban,
Rousseau and the Modern State (2nd edn, London, 1964); M. Einaudi, *The Early
Rousseau* (Ithaca, 1967). C. W. Hendel, *Jean-Jacques Rousseau: Moralist**
(London, 1934) makes a detailed intellectual reconstruction and provides
summaries of many lesser-known works. J. C. Hall, *Rousseau: an introduction
to his political philosophy* (London, 1973) is concise and to the point, if a bit
uninspired. R. G. Masters, *The Political Philosophy of Rousseau* (Princeton, N.J.,
1968) is wide ranging and informative, if a bit idiosyncratic. There is an incisive
chapter in J. Plamenatz, *Man and Society** Vol. I (London, 1963), and some
interesting essays in *Hobbes and Rousseau** edited by M. Cranston and R. S.
Peters (New York, N.Y., 1972). *Du Contrat Social*, edited by R. Grimsley
(Oxford, 1972) has a helpful long introduction and useful notes; the actual text
is in French. The pioneering edition by C. E. Vaughan of *The Political Writings
of Rousseau* (Cambridge, 1915) has been superseded in many ways but is still
worth consulting. So too is Durkheim's essay on *The Social Contract*, published
in E. Durkheim, *Montesquieu and Rousseau** (Ann Arbor, 1960).

R. Grimsley, *Rousseau and the Religious Quest* (Oxford, 1968) provides a
clear account of the religious writings. M. B. Ellis, *Julie or La Nouvelle Héloïse*
(Toronto, 1949) is a full-length study of the novel as a synthesis of Rousseau's
thought. For his writing on music and language see the articles by R. Wokler,
cited in the Notes to Chapter 7; J. Derrida, *of Grammatology** (Baltimore, Johns
Hopkins, 1974) is also interesting, and fitfully illuminating, on this subject.

For indications of Rousseau's influence see J. Macdonald, *Rousseau and the
French Revolution* (London, 1965); M. J. Temmer, *Time in Kant and Rousseau*
(Geneva, 1958) and *The Art and Influence of Rousseau* (N. Carolina, 1973).

There are many informative articles in *Studies on Voltaire and the Eighteenth
Century*.

IN FRENCH

By Rousseau

Modern readers of Rousseau are fortunate in having magnificent editions of
both Works and Letters available to them. The Pléiade Edition of the *Œuvres
Complètes* (Paris, 1959–   ), edited under the direction of B. Gagnebin and
M. Raymond, contains authoritative texts, helpful introductions and excellent
notes by leading Rousseau scholars. Vol. i. contains the autobiographical works,
Vol. ii. *La Nouvelle Héloïse* and fictional works, Vol. iii. the political works,
Vol. iv. *Emile*, and moral, educational, religious and botanical writings. Vol. v.
will contain the writings on aesthetics, language, music and theatre. (There is a

good modern edition of the *Essai sur l'origine des langues*, edited by C. Porset (Bordeaux, 1968).)

Equally helpful is the *Correspondance Complète* (Geneva & Oxford, 1965–), edited by R. A. Leigh, an outstanding work of scholarship. Thirty volumes have so far appeared, out of a projected total of forty.

About Rousseau

Two interesting general studies are P. Burgelin, *La philosophie de l'existence de J-J. Rousseau* (Paris, 1950) and B. Groethuysen, *J-J. Rousseau* (Paris, 1949). J. Starobinski, *J-J. Rousseau: la transparence et l'obstacle* (2nd edn, Paris, 1970) is a brilliant account of his longing for unity. R. Derathé, *Rousseau et la science politique de son temps* (Paris, 1950) is an important work on the relation of his political thought to that of his predecessors. M. Raymond, *Rousseau: La Rêverie et la quête de soi* (Paris, 1962) contains perceptive essays on some of the autobiographical writings. Two impressive recent studies are B. Baczko, *Rousseau: solitude et communauté* (Paris, 1974) and M. Launay, *J-J. Rousseau: écrivain politique* (Grenoble, 1971). A short up-to-date account is J-L. Lecercle, *Rousseau: modernité d'un classique* (Paris, 1973).

The *Annales de la Société Jean-Jacques Rousseau* (Geneva, 1905–) contain many important articles and provide references to the extensive literature covering all aspects of Rousseau's life and work.

INDEX

References to page numbers of footnotes are in italics,
as are titles of written works.